Europe
in
Flames

EUROPE IN FLAMES

THE CRISIS OF THE THIRTY YEARS WAR

JOHN MATUSIAK

To all my special friends across the years.

First published 2018

The History Press
The Mill, Brimscombe Port
Stroud, Gloucestershire, GL5 2QG
www.thehistorypress.co.uk

British Library Cataloguing in Publication Data.
A catalogue record for this book is available from the British Library.

ISBN 978 0 7509 8551 2

Typesetting and origination by The History Press
Printed and bound by CPI Group (UK) Ltd

Eilt, dass ihr den Verstand zum Nutzen noch gebrauchet,
Eh dann Europa ganz, das golden Land, verrauchet!
Ach, glaubt mir, einmal sich erreten von den Kriegen
Ist mehr, als tausendmal unüberwindlich siegen.

Hasten, use your common sense,
Before the whole of Europe, that golden Land, goes up in smoke!
Believe me, avoiding war
Is more than a thousand victories.

Andreas Scultetus, *Friedens Lob- und Krieges Leid-Gesang* (1641)

CONTENTS

1	The Crucible	11
2	Crisis of Emperors	38
3	'The Start of Our Destruction'	63
4	'Fatal Conflagration'	86
5	Crisis of Empires	110
6	'Soldier under Saturn'	136
7	Crisis of a Continent	159
8	'Lion of the North'	184
9	Magdeburg and Breitenfeld	210
10	The Plenitude of Power	235
11	War without Limit, War without End	264
12	The Crisis of the Peace	289
	Acknowledgements	316
	Index	317

SWEDEN

Baltic Sea

MARK

Hamburg
Stralsund
Lübeck

Lutter
Magdeburg
Breitenfeld
Leipzig
Lützen
Dresden

Prague

Heidelberg
Nördlingen
Regensburg
Donauwörth
Vienna
Augsburg
Linz
Munich
Graz

Casale
Valtelline

1

THE CRUCIBLE

[Germany] is now become a Golgotha, a place of dead mens skuls; and an Acaldama, a field of blood. Some nations are chastised with the sword, others with famine, others with the man-destroying plague. But poor Germany hath been sorely whipped with all these three iron whips at the same time and that for above twenty yeers space.

Edmund Calamy, *England's Looking Glass* (1641)

In the spring of 1648, the Augustinian abbess Clara Staiger surveyed the devastation at her convent of Marienstein just outside the Bavarian city of Eichstätt, and lamented the loss with a deep sense of gloom and foreboding that mirrored the sentiments of so many survivors of the shipwreck of the previous thirty years. 'May God come to our aid like a father,' she wrote, 'and send us some means so we can build again.' In this particular case, the perpetrators had been the Swedish-French armies of Generals Wrangel and Turenne, but before them countless other soldiers had been visited upon the abbess's homeland from the four corners of the Continent – Spanish, French, Swedish, Danish, Italian, Croat, Scottish; Catholic, Lutheran, Calvinist; conscripts, mercenaries and freebooters alike – all bringing plague, poverty and destruction in their wake and spawning a death toll that the most reliable estimates now set at some 8 million souls. One soldier alone, Peter Hagendorf, had marched more than 15,000 miles over the course of his service, travelling with his family in tow and enduring not only robbers, foul weather, gunshot wounds, scant food and scarcer pay for his trouble, but also the deaths of his first spouse and children. 'At this time my wife went into labour,' he wrote after he had been ordered to Stade, downriver of Hamburg, early in 1628, 'but the child was not yet ready to be born and so shortly died. God grant him a joyous resurrection.' Three daughters – Anna Maria, Elisabeth and Barbara – would also be entrusted to the consolations of a merciful Creator over the next five years before their mother, Anna Stadlerin of Traunstein, herself succumbed in Munich, some days after the birth of Barbara.

Clara Staiger's own hopes for divine deliverance, meanwhile, were hardly gratified promptly, if an account produced two decades later by the Lutheran theologian Joachim Betke is any guide:

> How miserable is now the state of the large cities! Where in former times there were a thousand lanes, today there are no more than a hundred. How wretched is the state of the small and open market towns! There they lie, burnt, decayed, destroyed, so that you see neither roofs nor rafters, doors or windows. Think of how they treated nunneries, churches, priories and temples: They have burnt them, carried the bells away, turned them into cesspits, stables, sutlerships and brothels … Oh God, how pitiable is the state of the villages …! You travel ten, twenty or forty miles without seeing a single human being, no livestock, not one sparrow, if there are not some few places where you find one or two old men or women or a child.

Not all areas, it is true, had been continuously occupied or callously ravaged and destroyed like tragic Magdeburg, for example, where the population had fallen from 25,000 in 1618 to only 2,464 a quarter of a century later, and where one resident, Otto von Guericke, spoke of the packed corpses floating horribly at the city's Water Gate long after its sack in 1631 – 'some with their heads out of the water, others reaching out their hands towards heaven, giving onlookers a quite horrible spectacle'. Certain places, indeed, which lay outside the most intense killing fields stretching from Pomerania in the Baltic to the Black Forest, had remained untouched by the conflict. Ulm, for instance, where the shoemaker Hans Heberle had kept his *Zeytregister*, or chronicle, of events, was spared serious inconvenience during the early years at least, while Staiger's Marienstein actually appears to have fallen into what may best be considered the middle category of privation. But even Ulm at its most peaceful did not escape the resulting economic upheaval, for on 15 March 1623, as Heberle recorded, 'no more than four sacks of grain entered the granary' and 'spelt went for forty-two and rye as much as forty gulden', as a result of 'bad money'. Two years later, moreover, the nearby towns of Langenau, Öllingen, Setzingen, Nerenstetten and Wettingen had suffered 'great plagues' and 'all kinds of maliciousness' at the hands of enemy troops. 'The men,' wrote Heberle, 'were badly beaten, and many women were raped' – all of which, the shoemaker tells us, 'continued for nine days'.

Yet at the dawn of the same century, the Holy Roman Empire of the German Nation, as it was formally known, had betrayed few outward signs of the looming crisis that was already threatening to consume both it and the continent to which it belonged. A multi-ethnic, multilingual and multi-confessional state, governed since 1438 by an elected Habsburg emperor in conjunction with a motley assortment of dukes, counts, margraves, lords, archbishops, 'prince-bishops', 'Imperial Knights' and urban oligarchs representing some eighty or so 'Imperial Free Cities', it was as vast in extent as it was variable in complexion, stretching from the Alps in the south to the Baltic in the north, and from the more prosperous southern and western territories of Bavaria, Alsace and the Palatinate to the fertile agricultural plains of the east, and the starkly contrasting regions of the north-west, whose barren heaths and wastelands had become prey to ravaging armies operating in the war-torn Netherlands where Spanish troops were embroiled in a bloody struggle against Dutch independence. In its full compass, the Empire comprised, indeed, not only modern Germany and Austria, but Slovenia, Hungary, Luxembourg and the Czech Republic, as well as parts of eastern France, southern Denmark, northern Italy, western Poland and – technically at least – the modern Netherlands, Belgium and Switzerland, though the latter had long since functioned separately.

There could be no doubt, of course, that the task of administering this vast mosaic was made all the more formidable by the existence of some 1,000 separate autonomous units within its jurisdiction – all varying considerably in size and stature and all jealously protective of their 'liberties'. Organised since the early sixteenth century into ten regional bodies known as *Kreise* or 'Circles', responsible for local defence, public peace and monetary and economic matters, the Empire included not only territories like Saxony, Brandenburg and Bavaria – all with a population of over a million and worthy of consideration as unified and discreet 'states' in their own right – but also micro-princedoms like Anhalt, only a little larger than Essex, and divided between no less than four rulers. Hesse, Trier and Württemberg, meanwhile – each with populations of 400,000 – had undergone similar fragmentation as a result of ingrained antipathy to the principle of primogeniture, and even the Palatinate – another of the major Imperial princedoms with a population of perhaps 600,000 – was itself divided into two major components: the 'Lower' Palatinate, a rich wine-growing district between the rivers Mosel, Saar and the Rhine, which had previously belonged to Bavaria and in which Calvinism had more recently gained control, and its so-called 'Upper' counterpart, a formerly Lutheran and relatively poor agricultural area between the Danube and Bohemia.

Bohemia itself, moreover, had been held by the Habsburg dynasty only since 1526 – along with its dependencies of Moravia, Lusatia and Silesia – and remained an autonomous kingdom within the Empire, with a population of some 1.4 million, no less distinctively proud of their traditions, idiosyncracies and 'liberties' than their German counterparts whose passion for independent action seemed, at every turn, to stifle the ongoing Habsburg quest for more effective central control or, as many feared, absolute hegemony. When Protestant authors even balked at the Empire's official designation, rejecting the term 'Holy' and questioning the expression 'of the German nation', there seemed hardly more scope for unity of purpose than that unity of faith which had been so decisively shattered by Martin Luther a hundred years earlier. And while jurists quibbled over endless other technicalities, the more practical problems generated in particular by the nature of the Imperial Circles continued to hamstring the day-to-day processes of government. Swabia, for example, covered an area more or less equal in size to modern Switzerland, but included no less than sixty-eight secular and forty spiritual lords, as well as thirty-two Imperial Free Cities. All were represented in the *Kreistag* or Circle Assembly, which met sixty-four times between 1555 and 1599, and each was a direct vassal of the emperor. But they ranged in importance from the compact duchy of Württemberg, covering 9,200 square kilometres, down to the paltry lands of individual Imperial Knights, some of whom owned only one part of one village. More significantly still, over half of the members of the Swabian Circle, and almost half its population were Catholic, while the rest were either Lutheran or Calvinist, providing a perfect formula for paralysis, or much worse still bloody conflict, which was equally the case in most of the Circles of south and west Germany.

Under such circumstances, it was hardly surprising that the potential for successful co-operation both between and within the Circles should have proven so limited. Their inability, on the one hand, to maintain local defence had been conclusively demonstrated by the invasion of Westphalia in 1599 when the entire Spanish field army of the Netherlands had gone in search of winter quarters, only to be met by mutinous troops from the Rhenish and Westphalian Circle who had been vainly raised to resist them. And attempts at inter-Circle co-operation on the economic front had been no more fruitful either. For just as the weaving regulations, common currencies and grain controls agreed during 1564–72 between the Swabian, Bavarian and Franconian Circles proved exceptional and impermanent, so attempts even at establishing a coherent system of boundary markers between territories had proved all but impossible in places other than the Palatinate where a network of specially-erected columns provided welcome guidance to otherwise bemused visitors. Elsewhere, travellers frequently experienced difficulty in establishing where they were, notwithstanding the existence of numerous customs posts on both land and water, which were, of course, no less niggling a symptom of localism in their own right. On the Elbe between Hamburg and Prague, indeed, there were as many as thirty toll stations, and between Mainz and Cologne on the Rhine no less than eleven, each equipped with a small cannon to sink ships attempting to avoid payment.

To the Hessian, it has been said, 'fatherland' was Hesse and 'abroad' was Bavaria, and as the ultimate testament to its disunity, the Empire likewise employed two principal coins whose precious metal content, and therefore value, varied in accordance with where and when they had been minted. The south, west and hereditary Habsburg lands, on the one hand, used the florin, which was divided into 60 *Kreuzer* – each worth 4 pfennigs (pennies) – while the subdivision of the thaler used in the north and east varied from 24 to 36 smaller coins of different names, depending upon the territory concerned. Where attempts at rationalisation occurred, as in 1551 and 1559, they had encountered a variety pitfalls, so that by 1571 responsibility for currency matters had been passed to three associations of Circles who were requested to 'correspond' on the matter. And if the Emperor's subjects had difficulty in deciphering the contents of their purses, their lot was no more enviable, it seems, when it came to determining the date, since the Gregorian calendar used by Catholic Europe had not been welcomed by Protestants who retained the Julian Old Style, which lagged behind by all of ten days.

For some foreign observers, naturally enough, it was a source of no inconsiderable relief that the Holy Roman Empire remained a confusion within a complexity, a name rather than a nation. 'If it were entirely subject to one monarchy,' wrote Sir Thomas Overbury in 1609, 'it would be terrible to all the rest.' Yet for all its diversity and divisions, its anomalies, complexities, quirks and contrasts, this self-same sprawling entity, governed traditionally from its Habsburg nerve centre in Vienna, had not only extricated itself from the protracted civil wars of religion that had bedevilled a kingdom like France, and avoided the bitter fighting engendered by the Dutch War of Independence, but achieved a degree of comparative economic prosperity – particularly in the area formally designated its 'German section' and known more popularly as 'the Germanies' – that made it the envy of many. In the preface to the *Topographia Germaniae*, the Frankfurt publisher Mathäus Merian lauded the numerous cities, castles, fortresses, villages and hamlets of his native land, which were, he claimed, as favourably situated as almost any in Europe. And if Merian's musings may well have been gilded by an understandable hankering for the happier days of peace that had by the 1640s become such a distant memory, they were more than amply matched by many other commentators of his day, both German and foreign alike. For Martin Zeiller, author of the *Topographia*, Lower Austria was home to a sociable, hospitable people, lushly served with everything to equip them for long and happy lives, while visitors, likewise, were equally impressed by the fertile coastal districts of the North, the 'Börder' areas of Central Germany, large areas of Lower Bavaria, the densely populated Vogtland, and above all, the beauty and harmony of the Rhenish Palatinate and Alsace. When the Englishman Thomas Coryat journeyed from Basel to Mainz on his way back from a visit to Venice in 1608, he was able to do so alone, on foot and unimpeded, encountering soldiers only once along the way. And though he found it prudent to sail down the Rhine below Mainz on a passenger barge, since the roads in that area were reputed to be infested with outlaws, Coryat nevertheless commented altogether favourably upon the orderliness, peace and prosperity of the Upper Rhine Valley, where bread and vegetables were so cheap that one could have a nourishing meal for a farthing and buy a year's supply of grain for £2.

Nor was this last claim an exaggeration, for by 1600 both Prussia and Pomerania, soon to be decimated by marauding armies, had become major suppliers of grain to the whole of western Europe, generating vast trade with the great markets of Amsterdam, Hamburg and London via the ports of Danzig, Königsberg, Riga and Stettin. And though the condition of the peasantry, which made up some 85 per cent of the Empire's population, varied markedly with location, for many their lot was more than tolerable. Both Upper and Lower Austria had been shaken by a violent rural uprising from 1594 to 1597, caused by heavy financial burdens and services resulting from war with the Turks, and such outbursts were not untypical of episodes elsewhere: in the ecclesiastical principality of Augsburg; in the Bavarian county of Haag; in the small territory of Rettenberg to the south of Kempten; and among the Sorb population of Upper Lusatia and Silesia. In the eastern lands of Brandenburg, Mecklenburg, Pomerania, Silesia and Prussia, furthermore, the east German 'Junker' nobility, prompted by the prospect of rich profits from the export of grain, had deliberately set out to annex the peasants' holdings and raise their labour services accordingly – in Mecklenburg from three-and-a-half days a year in 1500 to three days a week in 1600.

In what German land [asked a writer in 1598] does the German peasant enjoy his old rights? Where does he have any use or profit of the common fields, meadows or forests? Where is there any limit to the number of feudal services or dues? Where has the peasant his own tribunal? God have pity on him.

Yet in south-west Germany where small farms predominated and were usually leased on a lifetime basis, services and dues remained both fixed and generally reasonable, while west of the Elbe the circumstances of the peasantry had shown no appreciable deterioration at all during the 1500s. Indeed, north-west Germany was largely a land of free, small-scale peasant-holders who had progressively acquired full rights of inheritance, and even in those places where serfdom still existed, it was rarely deemed an unnatural or insufferable burden.

While peace obtained, therefore, the doughty German peasant had no more cause for complaint than his counterparts elsewhere. And for much of the Empire, too, the buoyancy of handicrafts and industrial production in the half century or so up to 1618 likewise gave no appreciable hint of crisis or approaching catastrophe. Silesia, Westphalia, the Lower Rhine and Swabia were known for their knitting and weaving, north-west Germany for its copper and brassware, central Germany for pottery and glass, and south Germany for products of wood and precious metals. The merchants of southern Westphalia, in their turn, had ignored the opposition of urban guilds to develop large-scale manufacture of scythes, sickles and ploughshares, while their counterparts to the north established a flourishing linen industry, with Osnabrück as its centre. It was Westphalian merchants too, who, along with their Saxon counterparts, exploited the expanding market for coarse cloths, resulting from the large labour force of Negro slaves in the Spanish colonies, and Nuremberg merchants who extended the production of cheap linen for this purpose to Bohemia, which by the beginning of the seventeenth century had become one of central Europe's foremost producers of textiles. Even more profitable were the mining centres located in the Harz mountains, Tyrol and Styria, the Siegerland and Lahn-Dill areas and the Upper Palatinate, along with Bohemia and Moravia's tin-producing zones, which alone accounted for as much as two-thirds of the continent's entire supply.

Saxony, moreover, was not only the greatest mining area of all, but the richest place in Germany, abounding in natural resources and boasting a flourishing agriculture and textile industry, which had helped gain international recognition for the twice-yearly fairs held every March and September at Leipzig. 'The riches I observed at this Mart were infinite,' wrote Thomas Coryat, who reserved a particular note of admiration for the 'incredible' wealth of the goldsmiths in attendance. And although the notoriously bibulous Duke John George I, ruler of Saxony from 1611 to 1656, would spend much of his time immersed in an alcoholic haze, he was neither typical of his more industrious subjects nor representative, for that matter, of at least a few of his more enterprising peers and predecessors. Indeed, his grandfather, Augustus I, had been shrewd enough to acquire shares in a mining company that allowed him to grow rich by means of influencing the price movements of iron and copper ore, as well as vitriol, alum, cobalt and coal. And just as Augustus went on to encourage new mining techniques and improve the stamping and iron mills of his duchy, so his contemporary, Duke Julius of Brunswick, another princely entrepreneur of some considerable stature, had not only employed his factories and workshops to produce everything from brass boxes to garden ornaments and chess sets, but gone on to renew the decaying iron pits and forges at the northern and eastern slopes of the Harz mountains, which turned out excellent thin steel for the export of culverin and arquebuses, as well as cannonballs, produced from the sullage, that would soon be shattering city walls and soldiers' bones alike.

For even in times of peace and comparative prosperity, it seems, the instruments of death and destruction could still be used to turn a tidy profit, notwithstanding nobler princely enthusiasms, extending well beyond the needs of war, that had made many Imperial cities among the most delightful centres of their kind in all Europe – adorned with extravagant buildings and boasting some of the Continent's foremost artists and musicians like Dresden's Heinrich Schulz, and the renowned Orlando di Lasso, who, before his death in 1594, had been awarded the Order of the Golden Spur by Pope Gregory XIII. Munich's renowned 'Antiquarium', which was begun in 1570 to house the art collection of Duke Albrecht V, was said, with its Italianate and neo-Roman frescoes, to rival even the Vatican, while Ferdinand II of Tyrol was prepared to lavish similarly vast sums on ambitious building projects like Ambras near Innsbruck, where he housed his magnificent art collection, and the Star Castle not far from Prague in which he salted away his secret wife Philippine in pampered splendour. Comparable edifices arose, in fact, all over the Empire – at Dresden, Wismar, Heidelberg, Salzburg, Prague and other places – so that even the Margrave of Ansbach-Bayreuth, one of the poorest principalities in the Empire, was nevertheless prepared to lavish 237,000 florins on his Plassenburg Palace, while the imperial residence in Vienna – the Amalienburg, built by Rudolf II in 1575 – came to excel anything else of its kind in other contemporary capitals, making it small wonder, perhaps, that this particular emperor was no less ready than other princes of his territories to employ alchemists in the hope of meeting his immense expenses.

The artefacts in such majestic dwellings – like the exquisite *kunstschrank* or art cupboard delivered to Duke Philip II of Pomerania in 1617, which had been ordered from Philipp Hainhofer of Augsburg five years earlier, with the intention that it should contain a complete survey of art and science to that date – were also altogether more suggestive of high culture and fine living than the horrors of impending war, as indeed were the splendid gardens in which the palaces themselves were set. For, to the everyday observer, it still seemed almost inconceivable as the seventeenth century dawned that anything other than gracious pleasure and wellbeing might lie in store for the Empire's elites. In 1559 the first orange, lemon and citron trees were planted at Stuttgart, while in 1562 the Imperial Ambassador at Constantinople brought lilac and gillyflower to Vienna. And when lesser German noblemen and their families were not strolling and picnicking amid the kind of pre-war harmony depicted so evocatively by the Flemish artist Lucas van Valkenborch, they too were equally inclined to indulge their fancies, albeit with a less self-conscious eye upon posterity. For amid the background tremors of religious friction and baleful rumblings of political dissent, they still found time on festive occasions for tournaments, animal-baiting and shootings, ring-runnings, sleigh rides, masquerades, ballets, dances and plays – often performed by travelling English troupes – as well as dazzling firework displays at which likenesses of the Sultan of Turkey or the Tsar of Russia or, in the predominantly Protestant north, the 'Bishop of Rome' were gleefully incinerated.

Eating and drinking too, it seems, were major sources of recreation among the Empire's well-to-do in the heady days of peace when such indulgence was still an option. At a nobleman's wedding at Liegnitz in 1587, 54 Polish oxen, 6 cows, 97 goats, 267 sheep, 55 calves, 16 pigs and 46 suckling pigs were all consumed with carefree abandon, and it was characteristic of the times that one waggish German prince should sign his letters *Valete et inebriamini* (Be well and get drunk). Christian II of Saxony, indeed, drank himself to death at the age of 27, and when Germany's first temperance society was established to do battle against the evils of alcohol, it was a fitting comment on the times that its first president should later die of liver damage. 'Owing to immoderate eating and drinking,' wrote Erasmus Winter in 1599, 'there are now few old people, and we seldom see a man of thirty or forty who is not affected by some sort of disease, either stone, gout, cough, consumption, or what not.' Wealthy burghers, too, were equally proud of their appetites, which, like the dress of their womenfolk, served as brazen tokens of their prosperity. Dinners lasting seven hours, with fourteen toasts, were not, it seems, unusual as Germans drifted heedlessly to the brink, while one particular gourmand, who had made his fortune as a circus performer, earned national fame by eating at one meal a pound of cheese, thirty eggs, and a large loaf of bread – after which he promptly fell dead.

For the omnipresent poor in town and countryside alike, of course – and above all for the so-called *gutsherrschaft* or class of landless labourers – the simple task of everyday survival was an altogether grittier priority. The protective wing of the craft guild had already been broken irreparably by the progressive exploitation of day labourers, and in some industries the working day began at 4 a.m. and ended at 7 p.m., punctuated only by 'breaks for beer'. In 1573, as their employers reaped record profits, braziers worked a ninety-two-hour week, and six years later there were widespread strikes throughout Germany against the introduction of textile machinery – merely increasing the already crippling pressure among the growing numbers of urban poor. At Augsburg, largest of all the Imperial Free Cities with 50,000 inhabitants, almost half of taxpayers owned no property whatsoever, while another quarter had not more than 300 florins to their name, so that in times of a bad harvest when grain prices soared, the most vulnerable came close to starvation. During the Great Famine of 1570, in fact, only the subsidised sale of lard and bread by the city's authorities – 23,000 loaves in all – had saved the populace from catastrophe. And even in the smaller towns and villages of comparatively prosperous areas, let alone those other great cities of the Empire whose fortunes remained precarious, a similar pattern of deprivation seems to have repeated itself, especially between 1596 and 1600 when harvest failure facilitated severe outbreaks of plague in Hessen, Nassau, Lower Saxony, Thuringia, Silesia, Pomerania and East Prussia.

Nor, of course, was the incidence of such poverty in the Empire's 2,200 towns and 150,000 villages unconnected to the precipitous rise in population that would soon be reversed so drastically by the harrowing toll of war. At Augsburg, once again, the number of tax payers increased by 14 per cent between 1558 and 1604, and though towns remained small on the whole, the same demographic expansion and related rise in prices was nevertheless evident throughout Germany where the population appears to have increased from around 14 million in 1560 to some 16 or 17 million in 1618. In Saxony, the most urbanised area of all, where no more than 70 per cent of the population was involved in agriculture, only fourteen urban centres had more than 2,000 inhabitants, the largest being Leipzig with 7,500 and Dresden, the capital, with 6,450. Other capitals were not much larger either, so that by 1600 Heidelberg had merely 6,300 people, Stuttgart 9,000 and Munich 10,000. Instead, the largest cities were the commercial centres like Stettin with 12,000, Frankfurt with 18,000, Hamburg with 22,500, Breslau and Magdeburg, both with 30,000, and Cologne with around 40,000. But large and small alike were all expanding, and the same scourge of inflation invariably followed in tow, with the result that at Augsburg, which was typical of the times, the price of rye, barley and oats rose by 69 per cent from 1550 to 1618 while the wages of unskilled building workers increased by only 47 per cent. In the Mansfeld copper belt too, to take but one example, wages in 1600 were no longer sufficient to buy bread for the families of miners.

But even where such challenges existed, there remained once again signs of growth and regeneration uncharacteristic of a land facing calamity. How far shifts in international trade away from northern Italy, the south Netherlands and Upper Germany toward France, Britain and Holland may have affected regional trade within the Empire, especially in the German hinterland beyond the Rhine and North Sea coast, remains uncertain. But while the merchants of the Hanseatic League faltered in Lübeck and along the south-west Baltic coast, they nevertheless regrouped successfully around Hamburg, Bremen and German North Sea outlets to boast by 1600 a fleet still larger than those of England, France and Spain, and second only to that of the Dutch. When, moreover, Augsburg lost no less than seventy of its internationally-known trading houses between 1556 and 1584, as a result of the bankruptcies of the Spanish and French crowns, Nuremberg merchants opened others in Leipzig and at Breslau, Posen, Danzig and Krakow. Equally significantly, as German territories adjusted to harsher terms of trade, higher inflation and greater underemployment, so internal trade was nevertheless consolidated and greater exploitation undertaken of the immediate hinterlands between Hamburg and Prague along the Elbe and Vlatva, and Silesia and West Prussia along the Oder and Vistula, as well as further territory across the Carpathians stretching into industrial north Bohemia and Slovakia, and onwards to the pasturelands of Hungary. Controlled by urban centres like Leipzig and Nuremberg on its western periphery, this east-central European economy was still being consolidated, in fact, on the very eve of the Thirty Years War which would soon lay waste to everything.

And in the meantime, as the Empire's economy adapted and evolved, so the merchants and burghers who had come to take their quiet lives for granted, continued in the main to flourish, luxuriating for the present in their privileged lot while snugly immuring themselves as far as they might from the creeping peril all around. The façade of Bremen's town hall, built in 1609, just like the splendid merchants' houses of Hamburg, left little doubt about the residing wealth of north German towns and the prosperous citizens that had benefited so markedly from membership of the Hanseatic League, which had until recently dominated trade in the Baltic. Many cities too, like Nuremberg, which had become burgeoning business centres in an increasingly aggressive capitalistic world, now boasted an expanding middle class that imitated the great courts of their betters in culture and manners, mimicking Spanish fashions in particular and indulging their fetish for newfangled playthings like those mechanical toys serving as table ornaments which gave fresh scope not only for the ingenuity of the Empire's numerous goldsmiths, but for the poe-faced rancour of disapproving moralists like the preacher of 1581 who noted how 'an unchristian love of gold has seized upon everybody and all classes'. 'Whoever has anything to stake,' he complained, 'instead of engaging in honest and strenuous work … thinks to grow rich … by all sorts of speculation, money dealing and usurious contracts.' For conservative patrician families of long-standing like the famous Welsers and Imhofs were now increasingly rivalled by a newer more thrusting type of entrepreneur, many of whom were foreign, like the Venetian-born Bartholomäus Viatis, or Johann von Bodeck, son of an Antwerp merchant, and Lazarus Henckel from Upper Hungary.

Among such men, not unnaturally, the primary business of life was business itself. But, as their rulers contested the Empire's destiny with increasing vigour, even they, like many of humbler status too, could not entirely ignore the broader tide of events. And by 1600 a widening window on the lofty world of political affairs was readily at hand, both to feed the curiosity and stoke the misgivings of one and all. For the self-same literary revolution that had led the Parisian scholar Henri Estienne to declare Frankfurt the 'Athens of Europe' four decades earlier had, in the meantime, generated its own 'newspaper believing public', which the poet Johann Fischart was already ridiculing for its gullibility, but which demonstrated nonetheless the growing consciousness that, in spite of so many appearances to the contrary, all was not entirely well, both within and without Germany. Since the early 1500s, in fact, numerous reports on political events, or *Zeitungen* as they were called, had enjoyed considerable appeal, so that by 1599 at least 877 are known to have existed – one of the more successful being a journal produced by Michaël Eytzinger between 1580 and 1583 to report on the troubling conflict between Protestants and Spaniards at Aachen in the prince-bishopric of Cologne. Shortly before 1609, moreover, Johann Carolus had begun publishing weekly reports at Strasbourg in quarto format, containing news from no less than seventeen European cities. Vienna had such a newspaper in 1610, Frankfurt in 1615, Berlin in 1617, with other Protestant cities quickly following suit – to such a degree, indeed, that even schoolmasters saw fit to fulminate against parents who neglected the education of their children by running to bookshops and drinking places in order to read of current events. 'This they consider *summum necessarium*, the most needful thing,' wrote one bristling critic, who, in venting his indignation, nevertheless ignored the more troubling implications arising from the great mass of slanderous lampoons, libellous pamphlets, satirical poems and squibs which were printed clandestinely and sold by hawkers in market places and taverns and, above all, at the gates of German colleges.

For new universities had also proliferated during the previous century, acting not only as seats of learning but, much more significantly still, hothouses for the religious divisions that were soon to send the superficial harmony of the previous decades crashing down. Between 1517 and 1618, the number rose from fourteen to twenty-five, and while some contained no more than 400 students, the largest, Lutheran Wittenberg, boasted between 1,800 and 2,000, all suitably imbued with the reforming zeal of their teachers and numbering in their midst those self-same ministers of 'the Word' who were firmly set upon stirring the coals of conflict when the time came for their return to an outside world that had known only peace in their lifetime. The other leading university, Rostock, was Lutheran too, as were Tübingen, Leipzig, Greifswald, Heidelberg, Königsberg, and Marburg, which followed close behind. Nuremburg, in its turn, had established the beginnings of a university at Altdorf in 1573, as had the Duke of Brunswick, at Helmstädt, one year later, further confirming, it seemed, a Protestant assault on the moral and intellectual high ground and a proselytising intent that led one Venetian diplomat to claim in 1577 – albeit with no little exaggeration – that nine-tenths of Germany was by then Protestant.

It was no coincidence either that the smaller Catholic universities which had hitherto largely stagnated were also undergoing renewal – most notably at Cologne, Vienna and Ingolstadt – or, more ominously still, that control of their philosophy and theology faculties should have steadily fallen to members of Ignatius Loyola's Society of Jesus, who had initially arrived in the Empire in the 1540s with little more than a simple reputation for rigour that had before long degenerated into widespread loathing and paranoid distrust. 'The young women,' wrote Hermann Weinsberg of Cologne shortly after the Society's appearance in his city in 1544, 'are good Jesuits; they go to church first thing in the morning, and fast a great deal.' And the Jesuit priests themselves had at first been keen, wherever possible, to avoid all hint of controversy. One of their leading figures in Germany, Peter Canisius of Nijmegen, had indeed explicitly endeavoured to keep them away from princely courts and palaces, and they had been issued, too, with specific instructions not to meddle in Imperial affairs of state. But, as the vanguard of the Counter-Reformation, they were nevertheless progressively associated with ultra-orthodoxy and a sinister commitment to secret sabotage and ruthlessness – extending even to tyrannicide – that was only exacerbated by their predominantly Spanish and Italian membership and their unwavering emphasis on the veneration of the Virgin Mary and the cult of relics, as well as pilgrimages and gorgeous ceremony.

By 1600, in fact, there were no fewer than 1,111 Jesuit fathers operating in Germany, spread over twenty-five colleges, nine residences and three noviciates, propagating their lay fraternities among students, burghers and noblemen alike, and helping in the process to initiate that great blossoming of the Catholic Baroque which left such an inimitable architectural mark upon posterity. But with every new convert and each new edifice, suspicion at their success and the means by which they achieved it intensified. To frenzied contemporary critics like Elias Hasenmüller, whose *History of the Jesuits* appeared in 1594, and the anonymous author of the *Monita Secreta Societatis*, which claimed in 1612 to reveal the order's secret agenda for restoring Roman despotism, the Society's priests were comparable to Janissaries, Templars, Assassins, Pharisees, the Plagues of Egypt, the Flood, and Balaam's ass, while in Germany more generally, they were widely decried as the 'black horsemen of the pope', accused, among many other things, of impregnating salt cellars and saucepans with poisons, and generating in the process a bitter antipathy that infected both Protestants and indeed Catholics alike. Even for a Franciscan writing at Ingolstadt in 1583, they were nothing less than 'the scourge of monks', while a Dominican had openly confessed six years earlier how he felt compelled to cross himself whenever he met one. Later they would be accused of accumulating a fabulous fortune from the gold of Paraguay and trade with Japan, and of holding even the Roman Curia in thrall after the near-election of one their number, Cardinal Roberto Bellarmine, to the papacy in 1605. Later too, in 1645, student priests of the Jesuit order would stun contemporaries by fighting alongside 1,500 Imperial dragoons in defence of the Moravian fortress of Brno (Brünn). And all the while, those self-same prejudices that had prompted a gang of small boys to pursue a group of them through the streets of Augsburg in 1582 with cries of '*Jesuswider*' (Antijesus) continued to be fuelled remorselessly by a propaganda onslaught, in which no accusation seemed too outlandish.

One German woodcut of 1569, for instance, depicted the Pope in the form of a sow, giving birth to members of the Society as piglets, while in 1593 the Lutheran theologian Polycarp Leiser published the notorious *Historia Jesuitici ordinis*, which condemned them for practising pederasty and bestiality with full licence and pardon from the Vatican. *Eine wahrhaftige neue Zeitung* (*A Truthful New Journal*, 1614) informed its readers that Cardinal Bellarmine himself had committed adultery no less than 2,236 times with 1,642 women, before detailing the agonising demise of the culprit, irrespective of the fact that he was still a full seven years short of death at that time. And as Protestants wove their webs of misinformation and calumny, so the Jesuits themselves frequently responded in kind. For while Peter Canisius, on the one hand, advised his subordinates to use temperate language in response to even the more outlandish charges levelled against them, not all complied. Conrad Vetter, for example, would publish ten pamphlets between 1594 and 1599 in which he used the grossest terms of abuse, excusing himself on the grounds that he was simply following the lead of his Lutheran opponents. And the Jesuits of Cologne were hardly less outspoken in declaring that 'the stubborn heretics who spread dissension everywhere' in Catholic territory,

> ought to be punished as thieves, robbers and murderers are punished; indeed more severely than such criminals, for the latter only injure the body, while the former plunge souls into everlasting perdition ... If forty years ago Luther had been executed or burned at the stake, or if certain persons had been put out of the world, we should not have been subjected to such abominable dissensions, or to those multitudes of sects who upset the whole world.

Yet if Jesuits were the object of universal fear and loathing among the townspeople of Germany's Protestant heartlands, so too, it seemed, in Lutheran communities far and wide across the Empire, was another infection, widely considered no less diabolical in origin or corrosive in effect – as even an unwitting innocent like Johannes Kepler would discover to his cost in 1611 when, in spite of his ground-breaking scientific discoveries, he found himself refused a chair at the Lutheran university of Tübingen, on grounds of apparent sympathy for the Calvinist Doctrine of the Communion. Almost three decades earlier, the hysteria generated by Jean Calvin's advocacy of predestination and radical presbyterianism had already been expressed by one commentator in a way amply reflecting what Philip Melanchthon chose to term the *rabies theologorum* of the day:

> If anybody wishes to be told in a few words concerning which articles of faith we are fighting with the diabolical brood of Calvinist vipers, the answer is, all and every one of them ... for they are no Christians, but only baptised Jews and Mohammedans.

And by 1582, as the surge of anti-Calvinist literature attained new heights, a Lutheran pastor named Nivander was going further still, listing forty characteristics of wolves before demonstrating that these were precisely the distinctive marks of the Calvinist foe.

Nor, it seems, had the flood much abated ten years later, as Stanislaus Rescius brooded on the fact that, at the Frankfurt fair, 'we have noticed for several years past that the books written by Protestants against Protestants are three times as numerous as those of Protestants against Catholics.' For while most of the forty-six published sermons celebrating the Lutheran jubilee of 1617 still vilified first and foremost the Catholic enemy, calling for an immediate crusade against Rome – centre of idolatry and sodomy and seat of 'the Beast of the Apocalypse' – many commentators like the Lutheran court preacher Matthias

Hoë von Hoënegg, who became chaplain-in-chief to Duke John George of Saxony in 1613, saw little to choose between either of his avowed religious foes, as the titles of his works amply confirmed. Written in 1601, *A solid, just and orthodox detestation of Papists and Calvinists* was followed ultimately by *A weighty (and in these dangerous times very necessary) discussion of whether and why it is better to have conformity with Catholics ... than with the Calvinists.* And as the ever-pugnacious Hoënegg duly aligned himself with the long list of militants comparing Calvinism unfavourably with Islam, he left no doubt either about his solution to the threat posed by his Protestant rivals: 'I remain determined to make war for the Lord,' he declared prophetically, 'and I thank my God that he has taught my hands to fight.'

As the 'theological rabies' escalated, moreover, so too had the casualties on both sides. Johann Funck, accused of Calvinist leanings, had been put to death in Königsberg's market place in 1566 amid general rejoicing, while in 1601, it was the turn of Chancellor Nicholas Krell to be beheaded in Dresden for altering Lutheran ritual along Calvinist lines and for supporting France's Huguenots. Likewise, when Landgrave Maurice of Hesse-Kassel saw fit to impose Calvinism upon his reluctant subjects in 1605, his troops were ordered to beat back a resisting crowd of Lutherans before tearing down the images in their churches. In Brandenburg, similar disorder accompanied debates concerning the nature of the consecrated Host, and when David Pareus, Professor of Theology at the Calvinist University of Heidelberg, issued his *Irenicum sive de unione et synodo evangelicorum liber votivus* in 1614, the results were equally predictable. Calling for the convention of a general Evangelical synod to heal the schism between Lutheranism and Calvinism from which Catholicism was deriving such tremendous advantage, the response was a furious rebuttal from the Lutheran theologians Hutter and Siegwart. On only one point of principle, Pareus had argued – and one not affecting the foundation of belief – was there significant divergence between the two faiths. But Hutter in particular was resolute on the errors of 'damnable Calvinism', and by the time of his death in 1622 Pareus had witnessed the full consequences of such intransigence.

'These raging theologians,' mourned one Protestant writer in 1610, 'have so greatly aggravated and augmented the disastrous strife among the Christians who have seceded from the papacy, that there seems no hope of all this screaming, slandering, abusing, anathematising, etc., coming to an end before the advent of the Last Day.' And in the meantime, hardly surprisingly, the Jesuit Professor of Holy Scripture at the University of Mainz, Adam Contzen, had drawn his own conclusions about the rift between Lutherans and Calvinists in two swiftly penned manifestoes: *De Unione et Synodo Evangelicorum* and *De Pace Germaniae.*

Deeply alarmed at the prospect of a reconciliation between the sworn enemies of his religion, he roundly condemned Pareus's 'syncretism' but took consolation nevertheless from what he considered the imminent and definitive triumph of the old religion. If so many had already defected from Lutheranism to Calvinism, Contzen reasoned, what was to prevent them from completing the circle and returning to the Catholic fold? 'It is easy,' he concluded, with an ominous naivety that explains much of the disaster that followed, 'to restore the faith of Europe.' For, in addition to his gifts as a biblical exegete, the Jesuit was also confessor to Duke Maximilian of Bavaria, crusader-in-chief of the Catholic cause within the Empire and spearhead of the Counter-Reformation surge that would soon be heralding war.

In the event, of course, Contzen's – and indeed Maximilian's – hopes for reunification were to prove no less vain than Pareus's solitary plea for unity among Protestants. Indeed, as some rulers and contemporary artists were already reflecting, such giddy aspirations were not only baseless but consigned to imminent destruction amid a disaster that, as Landgrave Maurice of Hesse-Kassel made clear to Louis XIII of France on 23 March, 1615, was unlikely to suffer containment once unleashed:

> I am very much afraid that the states of the Empire, quarrelling fiercely among themselves, may start a fatal conflagration embracing not only themselves … but also all those countries that are in one way or another connected with Germany. All this will undoubtedly produce the most dangerous consequences, bringing about the total collapse and unavoidable alteration in the present state of Germany.

'And it may also perhaps,' he added, with what proved to be stunning understatement, 'affect some other states.' For one year earlier, in a crowded canvas painted by Adriaen van de Venne, taking as its theme Christ's promise to make his disciples 'fishers of men', massed ranks of Protestants and Catholics had already been depicted facing each other across an unbridgeable river as priests and pastors feverishly compete to drag naked men and women into their own boats. On one bank of de Venne's painting stand the Protestant champions of Europe – the Dutch general Maurice of Nassau, James I of England, Christian IV of Denmark – and their councillors and theologians; on the other, Philip III of Spain, his sister Isabella, regent of the southern Netherlands, and her husband, Albert, along with members of their respective courts; while to the rear hovers the Pope amid a vermillion throng of cardinals. Over one and all, stretching from one side to the other but universally ignored, shines the rainbow of God. And though the painting was intended as an ironic commentary upon the Twelve Years Truce of 1609 between Catholic Spain and her rebellious Dutch subjects in the War of Independence that was continuing to divide de Venne's own homeland along the River Scheldt, it remained a powerful and poignant image applying with no less force to the current predicament of the Holy Roman Empire and the territories surrounding it.

For no amount of cultural refinement or underlying economic vitality in the Empire at large could mask indefinitely, let alone resolve, the critical religious tensions that were soon to dash the fragile constitutional balance established more than half a century earlier by the compromise Religious Peace of Augsburg. Framed over six months in 1555 'to protect the German nation, our beloved fatherland, against ultimate division and collapse', the settlement had remained at bottom a reluctant exercise in transitory and tentative toleration, born, like the temporary lull in the Netherlands, more from the mutual exhaustion of the contending parties involved than from any genuine desire for reconciliation. Though rather more, perhaps, than the simple breathing space as which it is frequently dismissed, it nevertheless amounted, as its progenitors fully appreciated, to little more than a provisional 'public peace' which still assumed the validity of the time-honoured medieval vision of a *corpus Christianum*, entailing one Church and one Empire, single and indivisible. And at a time when the proponents of religious reform were as confident of their ultimate victory as Catholics were resentful of their losses and determined to win back lost ground, the eventual renewal of hostilities was always in prospect. To the extent that it replaced eight years of armed conflict with a state of comparatively tepid cold war lasting almost eight times as long, the Augsburg Settlement was not, of course, without credit of kind. But it was fraught throughout with hidden contradictions and long-term pitfalls, leaving little doubt that within its pages lay all the hallmarks of future war.

Certainly, if the intensity of the ongoing invective among priests and preachers is any guide, the prospects for peaceful coexistence had never been encouraging. In 1565, the Catholic writer Johann Nas accused his Lutheran enemies of practising 'murder, robbery, lying, deceit, gluttony, drunkenness, incest and villainy without fear, for faith alone, they say, justifies everything'. Nor did he hesitate to add how every Lutheran woman was a prostitute. And while Catholics took the damnation of Protestants as an axiom of theology, so reformers like the preacher Andreas Lang could declare with equal certainty in 1576 how:

Papists, like other Turks, Jews and heathens, are outside the pale of God's grace, of forgiveness of sins, and of salvation; they are destined to howl, lament and

gnash their teeth everlastingly in the burning fire and brimstone of the flames
of hell.

Scandalous stories of the most provocative kind, like the outrageously tall tale
of the fictitious 'Popess Joanna' – a favourite myth within Protestant literature
– obtained widespread credence, prompting one particular Lutheran clergyman
to declare to his horrified congregation in 1589 not only that an English whore
named Agnes had indeed been installed as pontiff, but that she had 'given birth
to a boy during a public procession'. The Popes themselves on the other hand,
according to a further sermon of the same year, had always been and still were,
without a single exception, sodomites, necromancers and magicians – many of
them able to spit hellfire out of their mouths. Satan, claimed one account, 'often
appeared visibly' to them 'and joined with them in cursing and trampling the
cross of Christ underfoot', as naked dances, 'which they called divine service',
were conducted over the Saviour's image. And while ranting bigots declaimed
from their pulpits, so congregations drank in their words with an unquestioning
eagerness that allowed one Protestant clergyman to confirm with no little satisfaction in 1584 how 'children in the streets have learned to curse and mark the
Roman antichrist and his damned crew' – none of which, it must be said, would
have overly surprised the dead emperor most responsible for the Religious
Peace of Augsburg in the first place.

In 1553, an English envoy had already written of Charles V that 'he is so weak
and pale as to seem a very unlike man to continue'. 'He covets to sit up and
walk,' the same account went on, 'and is sometimes led between two, with a
staff also in his hand, but like as he desires to be thus afoot, so immediately after
he has been a little up, he must be laid down again, and feels himself so cold, as
by no means he can attain any heat,' Racked by gout and ruined by galloping
consumption of pickled eels, live oysters, Spanish sausages and huge tankards
of iced German ale taken at whim both day and night, Charles had for decades
carried his huge Habsburg empire on his back like a geriatric tortoise until he
could do so no more, finally abdicating in 1558 but choosing beforehand to split
his dominions along the very lines which, some forty years earlier, he had found
wholly unacceptable. Ferdinand, his brother, was to retain the Imperial crown
and the Habsburg lands in eastern and central Europe, while Philip, his son, was
to inherit Spain, Italy, the Netherlands and the riches of the New World. As a
result, Holy Roman Emperors would henceforth be left with the trappings of
power but little of the financial backbone needed to make those trappings good.
Nor could they sustain their pretended status as 'universal' rulers. And in the
interim, with the Peace of Passau of 1552, Charles had not only acknowledged

that his own attempts to impose religious unity upon his German subjects had failed beyond recall, but seen fit to laden his successor with the unenviable task of plucking a semblance of hope from the smouldering coals of an armed religious conflict that had persisted within the Empire since 1547.

For a settlement based upon the principle of parity between faiths, which the new emperor subsequently attempted to contrive, was an effective impossibility when the parties involved were neither in balance nor, for that matter, even remotely intent upon mutual toleration in the longer term. In 1545, faced with a mounting Protestant tide, the Catholic Church had finally convened the Council of Trent, and in doing so committed itself irrevocably to the task of Counter-Reformation. Purged of those very flaws that had spawned Protestantism in the first place and armed with a new zeal, embodied in a phalanx of new religious orders, it hoped to overturn the initiative which its enemies currently enjoyed, rolling back their previous successes and reasserting its own unquestioned supremacy. Plainly, it was not an agenda for reconciliation and nor, arguably, could it have been otherwise when the 'universal' Church was confronted with such a confident foe in its precious Imperial heartlands. For by 1555 all the duchies in central and northern Germany were solidly Lutheran and even the formerly dependable prince-bishoprics of the northeast seemed on the verge of succumbing. In south Germany too, the Palatinate, Baden, Württemberg and Ansbach had turned Protestant, and while Bavaria and the south German prince-bishoprics remained nominally Catholic, large numbers of their inhabitants had likewise been fired with the new faith. Apart from Cologne and Aachen, indeed, all important Imperial cities were either predominantly or wholly Protestant. And more alarmingly still, that most feared of all Protestant creeds, Calvinism, was also on the offensive, soon gaining its most significant success to date with its adoption as the official religion of the Palatinate by Frederick III in 1562 and subsequent acceptance by several less senior rulers in the years that followed.

Even in Austria, home of the emperors and bulwark of the West against the onslaught of the Turks, who currently occupied two thirds of Hungary and had established a frontier less than 100 miles from Vienna, Protestantism posed a threat no less potent and every bit as direct. For during the reign of Ferdinand I, which ended in 1564, the Lutheran catechism had been adopted in most parishes, and Lutheranism had come to prevail, too, not only in the University of Vienna, but within the Austrian legislature itself which had sanctioned clerical marriage as well as communion in both kinds. 'It was considered a sign of an enlightened mind,' declared one contemporary observer, 'to despise Christian interment, and to be buried without the assistance of a priest.' And as the contagion spread, only the Tyrol, out of all the hereditary Habsburg homelands, remained essentially untouched, rendering the emperor, his relatives and his supporters, to all intents and purposes a religious minority among their own people, compelled by their Protestant-dominated Estates to grant varying degrees of toleration on all fronts and at all levels: everywhere, in fact, except the Tyrol itself and Croatia. In some quarters, indeed, there were even reports of outright atheism. 'Thousands and tens of thousands in the towns – yea, even in the villages,' reckoned one commentator in 1567, 'no longer believe in God.'

As the old religion came under such sustained attack across the Empire, therefore, truces rather than treaties were always the only feasible option and it was a truce, in essence, that had finally emerged at Augsburg in September 1555. Faced with an urgent need for a makeshift solution to a conflict that had become temporarily unsustainable for both sides, Charles V himself had not attended, preferring instead to delegate authority to his brother, Ferdinand, to 'act and settle' disputes of territory, religion and local power. And in consequence the future Emperor Ferdinand I had been left with little choice beyond the hapless task of legalising a muddled and inherently unstable status quo by means of the Imperial legislature or 'Diet'. In doing so, moreover, he would seal the triumph of separatism at the expense of religious unity, and mark the victory of the Empire's princes at the expense of the emperor's own. For the rulers of Imperial territories – armed with the advice of doctors learned in Roman law, from whom their councillors were increasingly drawn – had already been fortifying their own administrative systems in defence of their 'German liberties' by establishing Courts of Appeal to circumscribe their creaking Imperial counterparts whose jurisdiction had never been clearly designated beyond the fact that one, the *Reichskammergericht* or 'Imperial Supreme Court', was mainly under the influence of the Empire's representative institutions, and the other, the *Reichshofrat* or 'Aulic Council', was exclusively accountable to the emperor in Vienna. Intent, too, upon consolidating their authority in relation to their own representative institutions, the same rulers were therefore firmly placed to withstand Habsburg 'absolutism' if ever and whenever the need arose. And this was not all. For should any future emperor attempt to redress the prevailing constitutional balance, he would henceforth face a stubbornly self-confident opposition, fully prepared to outface him on the grounds that, having blinked once, he might surely do so again.

But if the Peace of Augsburg came ultimately to encapsulate a critical eclipse of Imperial authority as the price for a fragile *modus vivendi*, which was likely to dissolve irrevocably in the event of a decisive switch in the religious or political balance of power, it was also part of a protracted process whereby successive

Holy Roman Emperors had in any case come to lack both the means and, indeed, the will, to impose order upon their independently-minded subjects. Attempts around 1500 to create effective central institutions and a 'national' system of taxation had languished as soon as they were made, and although the cohesion of the Empire as a united polity remained the heartfelt preference of most German princes a century later, the time for stern reckonings was increasingly close at hand. As late as 1625 the Lutheran Landgrave Ludwig of Hesse Darmstadt admonished his sons in his will to respect the occupant of the Imperial throne as their 'natural ruler and highest lord' and never to take up arms against either the emperor or the House of Habsburg. Yet for the Protestant Erasmus von Tschernembl, addressing the Estates of Upper Austria a decade and a half earlier, it was the right of the nobility 'to choose their prince' just as 'the territory decides for itself whether its ruler shall be hereditary', while for others of similar outlook, the proudest feature of the Empire's constitution, like that of the *aurea libertas* or 'golden liberty' of the Polish-Lithuanian aristocracy, was its resistance to tyranny from the centre.

What some contemporaries like Henning Arnisaeus and Theodor Reinking therefore fondly considered a blueprint for rational government, based upon an organic system of checks and balances, was for others not only a masterpiece of dysfunction, but in a context of religious ferment, nothing less than a potential powder keg, held together by little more than the ailing authority of its Habsburg rulers. For the great French jurist Jean Bodin, indeed, the Empire could not be considered a monarchy at all, and it was this, according to one English observer who had visited its territories five times, that explained why 'the Empire at this day languisheth like a sparke lapped in ashes'. As storm clouds gathered, it is true, the most pressing priority for all concerned was never innovation or reform. On the contrary, it was the proper interpretation of tradition and protection of principles laid down at the time of the Empire's very inception. And this same spirit of constitutional conservatism was reinforced, paradoxically enough, by the very complexity which was also the system's greatest potential weakness in times of crisis. For the high degree of local autonomy, which facilitated a century of private wars and pandemic local struggles, nevertheless offered a degree of flexibility that had so far prevented the Empire from tearing itself apart. Likewise, the strength of local authorities in their own territories, the regional structure provided by Imperial Circles, and the accessibility of justice from the Imperial Supreme Court and Aulic Council, could also partially serve, under the right conditions, to compensate for other imperfections at the Empire's centre.

But by the 1590s these same courts had lost their reputation for neutral justice among the emperor's Protestant subjects, and when the Catholic majority in the Imperial Diet attempted to transfer more authority to the so-called *Deputationstag*, a subordinate body dominated by them, Protestants had not only refused to comply but dissolved the Diet itself. In both 1608 and 1613, indeed, the Imperial Diet would become paralysed by religious disputes, and though the Empire, even by this point, was not actually threatened imminently with the kind of material destruction that all parties were beginning to fear, the new impasse betokened a situation where both emperor and princes might well be more inclined than ever to solve disputes by taking matters into their own hands. A creaking constitution, in spite of its dogged resilience against the odds, could not, after all, indefinitely withstand those forces of religious disarray which were never remotely envisaged by its creators. Nor might it, for that matter, endure the vagaries of an international crisis, as a result of which Catholic and Protestant foes alike felt compelled to intervene in Imperial affairs in furtherance of their own self-interest. An ambitious prince, an error of judgement or, worst of all, an incompetent emperor might well, therefore, represent a potential breaking point for both constitution and Empire, especially when the most fundamental of that constitution's principles – the election of the emperor himself – had the potential to prove so explosive.

For even in times of comparative harmony, a strenuous contest of push and shove had invariably developed between emperors and princes, princes and their own Estates, and also for that matter between princes and princes, resulting not only from the Empire's territorial fragmentation and religious differences but, more fundamentally still, from the general operation of the Imperial Diet and, more specifically, the elevation of an elite minority within it who had been empowered by the so-called 'Golden Bull' of 1356 to choose the emperor. These 'electors' – comprising the King of Bohemia, the Duke of Saxony, the Margrave of Brandenburg, and the so-called Count Palatine of the Rhine, along with the archbishops of Cologne, Mainz and Trier – all constituted the first 'curia' or chamber of the Diet, though the crown of Bohemia had become in effect the emperor's exclusive property since its assimilation by the Habsburgs in 1526. And while this had not detracted from the considerable status of the other electors in either the Empire at large or within the Diet itself, it had predictably raised the political significance of Bohemia enormously – particularly when the Bohemian monarch was himself elected – and added further complexity to a situation in which there were already those of equivalent or arguably even greater power in the Diet's second chamber, where a further fifty secular rulers, including the most powerful of all, the Duke of Bavaria, were represented. Most, at the time of the Peace of Augsburg, were in fact Protestant and each had a single vote, along with another thirty archbishops or bishops, while some fifty abbots and other prelates were represented as an entire group with one vote only, and another hundred counts and lords – likewise represented as an entire group but entitled to a total of two votes – made up the rest of the second chamber.

It was an intricate, at times mind-boggling, arrangement devised with the best of intentions to ensure a subtle balance between Imperial authority and the manifold voices of the Empire's other power centres. Yet in reality there were only two forces which counted at the Diet, the Emperor himself and the electors. For the third chamber, consisting of the Imperial Free Cities (some sixty-six in 1555, later rising to eighty or so), enjoyed only the right to consultation without the potential to vote, and the second chamber was not only religiously suspect but too disunited to be capable of exerting the kind of influence that should otherwise have been its due. Nor could a common resolution of the second and third chambers be passed against the will of the electors or their director, the Archbishop of Mainz, who also doubled as the Empire's Arch-Chancellor. Functioning slowly and with difficulty, the Imperial Diet, or 'Reichstag', was therefore a place in which much talking was done, and even more writing – since the various chambers communicated among themselves exclusively by written communiqués – but little was achieved, as questions of precedence and legal quibbles gave rise to infinitely prolonged debates which often never concluded. In the words of Samuel von Pufendorf, the seventeenth-century constitutional lawyer, the Empire's institutions were in fact *irregulare aliquod corpus et monstro simile* – 'a sort of unco-ordinated body resembling a monster'. And the Imperial Diet, more notoriously than any other body perhaps, could not have been worthier of such a description.

Even so, it was this rambling hotchpotch entity, so aptly reflecting the conflicting forces constantly at play within the Empire as a whole, that had bravely if vainly engineered the Augsburg 'peace' of 1555. By the settlement's terms, the so-called *Reichsstände* or 'Imperial Estates', i.e. those rulers and cities represented at the Diet, were to be free to choose either Catholicism or Lutheranism as their proposed faith, though Calvinists, along with Zwinglians and Anabaptists, were not only to be 'totally excluded' from negotiations but refused official recognition of any kind and henceforth formally banned. At the same time, the agreement that each secular ruler should dictate the religious complexion of their own territory – eventually dubbed the principle of *cuius regio, eius religio* ('whose domain, their religion') by Joachim Stephani of the University of Greifswald in 1582 – was also extended to the 1,500 or so Imperial Knights, who had no representation in the Diet, while the Imperial Free Cities and the Catholic ecclesiastical states, each of which was ruled by a so-called 'prince-bishop', were to be treated as exceptions. In the first case, where both Lutheran and Catholic groups existed side-by-side, each group was to enjoy freedom of worship – an eminently pragmatic solution which applied, however, to only eight of the cities concerned, since the rest were effectively homogeneous. And it was the second exception in any case, concerning the ecclesiastical states, that would prove of altogether greater long-term consequence. For the Catholics also succeeded in ensuring that any secularisation of ecclesiastical property, such as monastic land, that had occurred after 1552 was to be considered illegal, thereby raising the imminent prospect of a stream of bitterly resented re-appropriations.

Even more provocative, meanwhile, was the clause known as the *Reservatum Ecclesiasticum*, which ordained that 'where an Archbishop, Bishop, or other priest of our old religion shall abandon the same, his archbishopric, etc., and other benefices shall be abandoned by him', allowing 'a person espousing the old religion' to both replace him and 'enter on the possession of all the rights and incomes of the land'. Intended above all to prevent the catastrophic possibility that one of the three electoral archbishoprics of Mainz, Cologne and Trier might fall into Protestant hands as the result of an incumbent's conversion, and thereby facilitate the election of a Protestant emperor, this ruling was naturally hotly contested and never, indeed, formally included in the final peace terms of 1555. Yet such was its personal significance for the emperor that its imposition was ultimately secured by means of a supplementary edict, which led in due course to the outbreak of war in 1583 when Gebhardt Truchsess, Archbishop of Cologne, did indeed turn Protestant after seeking to marry a nun, and in doing so threatened not only to overturn the religious status quo within the Empire, but provide a new source of support for Dutch rebels against their Spanish overlords.

Fought between the archbishop's advocates, which included the Dutch Republic and the Palatinate, and the Spanish and Bavarian supporters of his Catholic replacement, Ernest of Bavaria – who was himself a drunken pluralist complete with concubine – the conflict would last five rancorous years before a Catholic victory was finally achieved, and demonstrated all too plainly that the Peace of Augsburg was, at most, a worthy attempt at reconciling the ultimately irreconcilable. After his formal accession to the Imperial throne in 1558, Ferdinand I had, it is true, exercised a distinctly – in some respects remarkably – tolerant spirit towards his religious opponents, extracting concessions from the Council of Trent on points of practice during its closing years in the early 1560s and even admitting Lutherans to his household. But his introduction of the Jesuits to his lands left little doubt of his underlying objectives, and convinced his enemies that, like other Habsburg emperors before and after, he remained a man of weasel words and ways. Protestant rulers had, it is true, been partially compensated for the *Reservatum Ecclesiasticum* by the so-called *Declaratio*

Ferdinandea, which embodied the principle that both the nobility and towns in ecclesiastical territories should be allowed to practise Lutheranism if they had done so 'for a long time and for years'. Yet even this ill-defined sop to Protestant sensibilities was not included in the formal settlement and remained secret, indeed, for almost two decades, after which many prelates provoked untold tension by simply ignoring it. And it was this selfsame tendency to hedge key principles with restrictions and exceptions, however understandable in the contemporary context, that so materially impaired the settlement's effectiveness in other respects, too.

'Would God we might establish genuine peace in Germany! We fear that a great storm is gathering in the heavens: may God almighty graciously deign to disperse it,' declared one of the Frankfurt delegates at the Imperial Diet of 1566, where the continued exclusion of Calvinists from the Augsburg agreement eleven years earlier had proven more contentious than ever. For by then the Palatinate had become the driving force behind Calvinism's forward thrust, and Heidelberg, in particular, its hub and citadel after Frederick III had openly declared himself a Calvinist the very day following the peace, and opened his capital to emigré theologians from France, the Netherlands and Italy, all bent, amongst other things, upon the abolition of the *Reservatum Ecclesiasticum*. Ignored initially by all of the bishoprics east of the River Weser, the *Reservatum* had subsequently come under persistent, if unavailing, assault at the Diets of 1556, 1559 and 1576, prior to the outbreak of war over the archbishopric of Cologne. But the wound was not lanced and the resulting conflict proved a critical turning point in the struggle between Protestantism and Catholicism in Germany as a whole. For it not only signified the first successful attempt to halt the forward march of Protestantism since the Peace of Augsburg, but engendered a seminal treatise – the anonymous *De Autonomia*, published at the Duke of Bavaria's expense in 1586 – which argued that the Catholic cause must be saved in Germany before it was too late, and, in doing so, encapsulated the heart and soul of Counter-Reformation Catholicism, which had already been stirring in the previous decade and would now assume a new and fateful momentum.

For the Church itself, while not condemning the Peace of Augsburg dogmatically, had nevertheless refused to recognise it formally. Indeed, the Pope had only complied at all – 'although sorrowfully' – upon the advice of a commission of Jesuit fathers who cynically recommended that Catholics should suspend hostilities only 'until that day should come when Christ would give them sufficient strength to triumph'. As such, the warning signs were apparent from the outset, since regionalism and even separatism were now effectively embedded in the cumbrous mechanism of the Imperial constitution, and the Empire remained continually susceptible to the tides of broader European conflict. Plainly, the Emperor's Spanish Habsburg cousins were too powerful to ignore, and the Empire, in its turn, henceforth too vulnerable to be ignored by them – especially when rebellious Dutch Protestants were more inclined than ever to probe for allies in its midst, as the Protestant advance turned to retreat. And in the meantime, perhaps most fatefully of all, the classes that marched in the van of economic progress and had most to gain from peace – the merchants of the northern ports, the landowners of the north-eastern territories, the entrepreneurs of Nuremberg and Frankfurt – had no effective voice in the government of their country to reverse the drift to war. Like the humbler townsfolk of the cities and peasants of the German countryside, who would pay the heaviest price of all when conflict finally came, they lived indeed in an entirely different world from the magnates who dominated the Imperial Diet and the princely strife that came increasingly to dog that institution.

All would hinge ultimately, therefore, upon men and events, and in particular the whims and resolve, recklessness or rectitude of a governing class tragically remote from the aspirations and interests of its people. War, it is true, was not wanted, since its more obvious consequences were hardly in doubt. Indeed, when the new century dawned, the shadow of conflict seemed almost in retreat. Since 1598, in fact, when Spain made terms with France, the great European wars had actually been halting, one after another: between Spain and England in 1604; between the Empire and the Sultan in 1606; between Denmark and Sweden in 1613; and between Sweden and Russia in 1617. Even those die-hard adversaries, Spain and the Netherlands, had, of course, agreed their twelve-year truce in 1609, while by 1618 Swedes and Poles would be on the verge of arranging a truce of their own, as would Poles and Russians. But all were aware that their treaties did not settle the disputes that had led them to bloodshed in the first place. And neither had they forgotten the need to keep their swords honed, their cavalry saddled and their cannon primed. So when Germany produced no prince capable of seeing beyond the prejudices of his religion – let alone the dynastic rivalries of his forefathers or his constitutional right to plough an independent furrow – and a succession of emperors proved men of crippling limitations, unequal to the task of transcending local or sectarian ambitions, there could be little prospect of escape from the Empire's predicament, save ultimately, perhaps, in the universally dreaded release of wholesale war.

2

CRISIS OF EMPERORS

A good reputation is especially necessary to a prince, for if we hold him in high regard he can accomplish more with his name alone than a less well esteemed ruler can with great armies at his command. It is imperative that he guard it above life itself, and it is better to risk fortune and grandeur than to allow the slightest blemish to fall upon it, since it is certain that the first lessening of his reputation, no matter how slight, is a step in the most dangerous of directions.

Testament Politique du Cardinal Duc de Richelieu (1680)

When Rudolf II, ruler of the Holy Roman Empire, head of the Austrian branch of the House of Habsburg, and King of Bohemia and Hungary, gazed down in 1605 from the lofty window of his precious Imperial bolthole at the Palace of Hradčany, overlooking the city of Prague, he could not do so without feelings of both pride and grave unease. Cradled in the undulating folds of the surrounding countryside, Prague was Bohemia's capital, *Regni Bohemiae Metropolis*: a place of both charm and tradition, where the River Vlatva timelessly caressed the ancient arches of the Charles Bridge and divided the Old and New Towns on its right bank from the Malá Strana on the other, where Italian, German and Dutch merchants – especially those *mercatores aulici* who supplied the Imperial court – lived lives of affluence, not too far distant from the medieval 'Hunger Wall', built by Emperor Charles IV to relieve indigence and famine in the 1360s. On the one hand, it was a city of high culture, intellectual ferment and political intrigue: one that had drawn the Shah of Persia to it at the dawn of the new century, and a place, too, where secret agents from as far afield as England rubbed shoulders with artists, men of letters, pioneers of science, Jesuits like Edmund Campion, heretics like Giordano Bruno, alchemists like John Dee, and ambassadors from Muscovy seeking aid against the Turk. Equally, it was a thriving economic hub which had taken full advantage of its strategic location to become a major transit point for the export to Germany of locally produced textiles and minerals, as well as livestock from Austria, Hungary and Poland, and iron from Styria.

Yet it was not Vienna, birthplace of the emperor and traditional nerve centre of both the Holy Roman Empire and the Habsburg lands that had for at least two centuries constituted the empire's heart. On the contrary, Bohemia itself had only fallen into Imperial hands after the Battle of Mohács just under eighty years earlier when Louis II, its Jagiellon king, was defeated and slain by Suleiman the Magnificent's Turkish army. And thereafter Habsburg emperors had continued to reside in close proximity to the courts of their relatives at Innsbruck and Graz, maintaining a watchful presence and consciously equating the interests of their own ancestral lands with those of the Empire at large. But it was to Prague that the present incumbent of the Imperial throne had nevertheless chosen to make his way in 1583, acknowledging the city's virtues as a point of more general access to his domains, though sheltering too, even more importantly, from the troubled politics of his German and Austrian heartlands and seeking solace in his darkening later years among the astrolabes and celestial diagrams of his laboratories, and the concubines he these days seldom saw and never touched. After the Imperial Diet of 1598, in fact, he would fail to attend another, preferring instead to fill his stables with horses he never rode, and to toy with the curiosities of his private zoo which boasted, all too aptly perhaps, a dodo from Mauritius. Such, indeed, was his isolation that he had taken to showing himself periodically at the windows of the Hradčany to scotch recurring rumours that he was already dead.

Fifty-three years earlier, he had been born the eldest son of Emperor Maximilian II, and had gone on to spend eight of the most formative years of his youth, from the age of 11 onwards, at the court of his maternal uncle King Philip II of Spain. There, as his Spanish mother, Maria, was quick to emphasise, Rudolf had acquired all the refinements and princely accomplishments expected of a Habsburg ruler-to-be. But upon his return, the young man's father had become concerned about his distant and stiffly self-conscious manner, which, though typical of his Spanish upbringing, was soon translating into altogether more unsettling behaviour, characterised by periodic bouts of lethargy and depression. His 'melancholy', moreover, while not uncommon in the Habsburg line, led him to shun the publicity of court life and withdraw into a private world of artistic and esoteric interests – as well as sexual impropriety – which not only marred his reputation but continued to dull his application to state business after his own succession to the Imperial throne in 1576.

Though dangled as a prize in a string of diplomatic negotiations for marriages, Rudolf would never in fact wed, and during his periods of self-imposed
isolation, which frequently coincided with the need for an unwelcome decision,
there were reports of homosexual affairs with his court chamberlain, Wolfgang
von Rumpf, and a series of valets, one of whom, Philip Lang, appears to have
controlled him for many years, attracting widespread hatred in the process. Yet
Rudolf's alleged homosexuality had not prevented him, it seems, from indulging in a succession of affairs with women, some of whom claimed to have been
impregnated in the process. Indeed, he is known to have sired several illegitimate
children with his mistress Catherine Strada, including an eldest, Don Julius
Caesar d'Austria, born sometime between 1584 and 1586, who would go on
to achieve a notoriety all of his own after moving to Český Krumlov at his
father's behest and reportedly murdering and disfiguring the daughter of a local
barber who had been living in the castle. 'On the 18th of February,' wrote Václav
Březan, 'Julius, that awful tyrant and devil, bastard of the Emperor, did an incredibly terrible thing to his bed partner, the daughter of a barber, when he cut off
her head and other parts of her body, and people had to put her into her coffin
in single pieces.' And while Rudolf condemned the act and declared that his son
be imprisoned for the rest of his life, neither the stigma nor the disappointment
would be entirely eased by Julius's death in 1609 from what was described as a
ruptured ulcer. For rumours continued to circulate that he had been strangled
at his father's instruction after refusing to bathe, living in squalor, and exhibiting
all the telltale signs of acute schizophrenia.

By then, in any case, the father was already firmly locked in the seclusion of
the Hradčany, held fast by his obsessions and seen by few people other than his
domestic servants – creatures, it was rumoured, who might be bribed to encourage him to grant unwelcome favours, sign suspicious documents, or worst of
all, tailor his will and testament to their whim. The time-honoured Habsburg
imperative to create a unified Christian empire had not, it is true, altogether
vanished from his thinking, but it was largely superseded by more personal
priorities: the patronage of artists and natural philosophers; an overwhelming
passion for alchemy and astrology; and above all a compulsive need to collect,
whether it be minerals or gemstones, past masterworks by Dürer and Brueghel,
or wild animals like the lion and tiger that were allowed to roam free about the
palace – as documented all too vividly by account books recording compensation payments to survivors of attacks, or to family members of dead victims.
Among those welcomed to his court were Elizabeth Jane Weston, a writer of
Renaissance Latin poetry, who composed numerous odes to him, the renowned
botanist Charles d'Ecluse, and a string of contemporary artists of the Northern

Mannerist style, many of whose works were unusually erotic in nature. Above all, however, there were especially honoured places for the astronomers Johannes Kepler and Tycho Brahe, whose 'Rudolfine tables' (which were eventually finished by Kepler) became the first comprehensive table of data of the movements of the planets.

For the emperor's quest for the 'Philosopher's Stone' and preoccupation with the occult – which resulted in a specially commissioned horoscope from Nostradamus, dedicated to him as 'Prince and King' – proceeded side-by-side with the encouragement of more recognisably scientific modes of inquiry. Indeed, his renowned *Kunstkammer* – incorporating 'the three kingdoms of nature and the works of man' – not only became Europe's most extensive 'cabinet of curiosities' but a valuable research tool for scholars, which played no small part in assisting the development of modern science. Housed in the Hradčany's northern wing, which was specifically built for the purpose between 1587 and 1605, its collection of minerals and gemstones alone occupied thirty-seven cabinets in three vaulted chambers, each of which was 60 metres long. And at the centre of all – cataloguing, augmenting and administering – stood the emperor's polyglot court physician, Anselmus Boetius de Boodt, whose own *Gemmarum et Lapidum*, published in 1609, would prove one of the finest mineralogical treatises of the century.

It was no small irony, therefore, that many of Rudolf's beloved collections would eventually be looted during the sack of the Hradčany by Swedish troops on 26 July 1648 – the very last year of the conflict he had inadvertently helped to spawn – and no small surprise either that the emperor's endless quest for peace of mind amid them had never proven wholly successful. For at a time when the Imperial constitution was undergoing steady examination, and political and religious antagonisms within the German portions of his Empire – as well as Bohemia itself – were continuing to mount, he was also borne down by the chronic threat of Turkish invasion and the ongoing inefficiencies of a central government machine, if such it can be called, that was not only rendering the frontier regions of his lands a prey to foreign armies but seriously hampering their further development. Notwithstanding the comparative economic health of the Empire overall, the rapid population growth in evidence across Europe was continuing to place pressure on scarce resources, and to trouble, in particular, those Imperial princes of more limited means. For while agricultural production had grown, most available land had now been cleared for arable farming, leaving less for pastoral use or industrial crops, and leading to a run of exceptionally high food prices during the 1590s which was also the cause of a partial contraction of the market for manufactured goods. As a result, many towns, particularly in the south-west, were experiencing a downturn in industrial output at precisely the

point that their rulers were already running up heavy debts from the construction of civic amenities or, more ominously, the creation of new defences.

Certainly, not all the Empire's rulers could boast the financial resources of the
dukes of Saxony and Bavaria. On the contrary, the Elector of Brandenburg, for
example, owed 18 million thalers and the Elector Palatine almost 2 million, making
it hardly surprising that this period saw a spate of 'household economy' books,
advising princes on how best to cut their coats according to their cloth. And neither was the subsequent tension between rulers and their Estates, whose consent
was required for taxation in almost all territories excepting Bavaria, any less predictable. Even Rudolf's eventual successor for that matter – his brother Matthias
– owed almost 30 million thalers at the time of his accession in 1612, though this
was comparatively small beer when weighed against his other problems, since the
Imperial crown had by that time not only been critically compromised by the
deficiencies of his predecessor, but further weakened by the original decision of
Ferdinand I in 1564 to divide the territories that the Habsburgs had been steadily
developing since the thirteenth century between three of his five sons.

Originating from the Danubian *Ostereich*, this patchwork of inherited lands
or *Erblande*, encompassing a population of some two million souls, included by
the seventeenth century: Lower Austria, centred upon Vienna; Upper Austria,
administered from Linz; Inner Austria, comprising Styria, Carinthia, Carniola,
Istria and Trieste, and controlled from Graz; and another agglomeration of territories known as Further Austria or *Vorlande*, made up of Vorarlberg and the
scatter of lands across to Alsace. The Tyrol, too, was a key possession, along with
those territories beyond the *Erblande*, which, since 1526, had encompassed sec-
tions of Hungary and the lands of the crown of St Wenceslas – Moravia, Silesia
and Lusatia, and, of course, Bohemia – with an overall total of some four million
subjects, which made them not only the Empire's most populous component,
but one of Europe's most densely peopled areas. All, like the broader empire of
which they were part, had their own distinctive characters and histories, and all
had been assimilated largely piecemeal. And it was this tangled patrimony that
Ferdinand had duly decided to subdivide and devolve upon his death, granting
the Imperial title and the crowns of Hungary and Bohemia, as well as Upper and
Lower Austria, to his successor, Maximilian II, while leaving the Tyrol to the son
that was his namesake, and Inner Austria to his son Charles – though even this
was not the limit of the resulting knotted nexus. For by 1590 Charles himself
had been succeeded in Inner Austria by his eldest son, Ferdinand of Styria – who
would become the future Emperor Ferdinand II – while the Tyrol had passed
to another of his children, Leopold, leaving the Imperial crown in the hands
Maximilian II's own son, who had become Rudolf II in October 1576.

Plainly, where Habsburg family politics were involved, the road to rationalisation was far from straightforward. Nor was it always paved with either goodwill or fair play or, in this case especially, patience. For there followed a prolonged 'brothers' quarrel', as Rudolf's reign swiftly faltered and the new emperor's gnawing distrust of his family grew in direct proportion to his own incompetence and his eldest sibling's consequent determination to challenge him. Already envying the wealth and power of his Habsburg cousin the King of Spain, Rudolf not only distrusted his brother Matthias – who represented him in Vienna – as an obvious, though unrecognised, claimant to the succession, but viewed him, with good reason, as a possible supplanter. And this was not the limit of Rudolf's inter-sibling troubles, since he harboured equal resentment for the second of his three surviving brothers, Albrecht, whom he never forgave for marrying the Spanish Infanta, Isabella Clara Eugenia, whose hand he had himself so diligently pursued some twenty years earlier. Since none of the brothers – including another named Maximilian – were to produce any children, moreover, there was the added problem that the succession was likely to pass eventually to their nephew, Archduke Ferdinand of Styria – son of the deceased Charles, and widely dismissed as 'a silly Jesuited soul', whose own capabilities hardly recommended him for leadership at a time of such formidable challenges.

It was clearly a budding crisis for the emperor and his prospective successors, and equally palpably an incipient crisis of much broader and more serious dimensions for the Empire itself, as the ruling incumbent became increasingly embroiled in confounding the ambitions of those not competent to replace him in any case. For while Ferdinand I had been able to salvage a sinking ship at Augsburg in 1555 and his successor, Maximilian II, had kept the listing vessel afloat by a judicious combination of muted tolerance and watchful inaction, the future was now altogether less certain, as the Empire became mired in both Habsburg family rivalry and Habsburg family ineptitude. That it might withstand the rule of an increasingly pathetic recluse, locked in self-imposed exile at its edges, was still likely, but the strain upon its resilience could only be magnified when the individual concerned devoted so much of his dwindling energy to confounding interlopers intent upon his throne. And it would be multiplied still further in the longer run – perhaps to the point of fracture – when the two most likely successors to that throne were, on the one hand, a colourless lightweight, whose watchword – 'unity is greater than light' – was as insubstantial as the vanity that underlay it, and, on the other, a personable, music-loving and indigent mediocrity, who in spite of his more amiable features was nevertheless implacably resolved, regardless of care or cost, to fulfil his duty to God as a true Catholic prince, and sweep the Protestant plague from his lands.

Appointed Governor of Austria by his brother Rudolf in 1593, the future Emperor Matthias had emerged as the leading contender for the throne after the death of his elder brother Ernst two years later. But, in spite of an easy charm and comparative moderation in religion – which may well be explained by the fact that he escaped the Spanish education imposed upon his brothers – he was nevertheless self-indulgent and lazy, and possessed, above all, by a recklessness that matched his craven ambition. In 1578, despite the express prohibition of his family, he had journeyed secretly from Vienna to Brussels to become titular head of the defiant Dutch provinces currently resisting his uncle, Philip II. But his hopes of achieving a reconciliation with Spain by bringing 'light' to the Protestant rebels resulted only in frustration and the predictable disapproval of the Spanish king, who refused either to recognise him or assist his efforts. Before long, as one close adviser put it, Matthias's new role, had become 'a labyrinth from which he expects his deeds to earn little thanks', and by 1581 he had indeed been forced to resign by his own Dutch 'subjects', who seized the opportunity to declare full independence from Spain in the same year.

It was hardly the most promising political debut. But his growing reputation as a religious dilettante caused further dismay as he visited Protestant Denmark in a tour of northern Europe during 1586–87 and subsequently enlisted several Calvinist advisers prior to his return to Vienna in 1590, where his suspect sympathies gradually declined under the influence of the city's bishop, Melchior Klesl, who would become his chief counsellor. Even now, though, Matthias did not hesitate to play off Protestants against the emperor, as his brother's difficulties increased and his own ambition took wing accordingly. For by 1605 he had already forced the ailing emperor to allow him to deal with Protestant rebels in Hungary and single-handedly engineered the resulting Peace of Vienna, which secured the right of Transylvanians to elect their own independent princes in future and guaranteed religious freedom in Hungary: a measure that not only sent signals of encouragement to Protestant radicals elsewhere in the Empire but encouraged Emperor Rudolf to consider other concessions of his own in an effort to outbid and face down a competitor, who was by then openly angling to replace him. 'All Catholics very much lament it, but the Protestants are delighted,' wrote Archduke Ferdinand of Styria, as he reflected upon Matthias's role in assisting one more palpable decline in the dignity of the Imperial crown.

And as someone who rightly regarded himself as next in line of succession to Matthias both for the Imperial crown itself and the thrones of Austria, Bohemia and Hungary, Styria's archduke had good reason for concern – not least because his own deficiencies were also so apparent. Educated at his Bavarian mother's behest by the Jesuits of Ingolstadt's university, he had accepted his indoctrination with an ardour and naivety that left his tutors aglow with satisfaction. 'Nothing sown in this fertile soil,' remarked the university's rector, 'seems to perish,' so that even Ferdinand's staunchest supporters would eventually squirm at his dependence. 'The court of Graz,' complained Melchior Klesl, 'is ruled as much by the counsel of the Jesuits as by that of his advisers; they are with, around, and about the archduke day and night.' And their impact was palpable. For Ferdinand had taken his coronation oath to observe the liberties of his subjects, on the perverse assumption that these liberties had nothing to do with religion. 'Better a desert than a country full of heretics!' he had subsequently declared upon banishing the Protestant leaders of the Styrian Estates and replacing them with his own officials on the assumption that the Counter-Reformation and political absolutism could be made to work hand-in-hand, regardless of popular disapproval. For at the feast of Easter in 1596, it was claimed that Ferdinand had been the only citizen of Graz to receive the sacrament in accordance with the Catholic faith, though by 1598 he had nevertheless forcibly expelled all Protestant pastors and schoolmasters from the city, and only one year later seen fit to close all Protestant churches and chapels.

And in the meantime, as Habsburg family bickerings continued to fester and the longer term outlook for the future rule of the Empire seemed hardly more encouraging than at present, his Imperial uncle's troubles were being compounded by Ferdinand's own undoubted success in championing orthodoxy. For while the Archduke of Styria served the needs of his Church with unswerving diligence, Rudolf appeared altogether less energetic in abandoning the policy of peaceful coexistence grudgingly pursued by his predecessor over half a century. Indeed, although he too had been raised by Jesuits in his uncle's Catholic court in Spain, and his overall commitment to Rome was not in question, Rudolf was still considered altogether too tolerant, not only of Protestantism itself, which he seems to have considered a useful counter-weight to the most repressive aspects of papal policies, but even of other religions including Judaism. Weighed down by the burden of his illness, moreover, he no longer cared for the Jesuits and largely withdrew from Catholic observances, attending confession – in great trepidation – only at Easter, and ultimately denying himself the last sacramental rites upon his death. Instead, he put his primary support behind conciliarists, irenicists, and humanists. And when the papacy sent agents to his court to press the need for firmer action, he often backed those whom he considered most inclined to compromise.

Yet in spite of appearances to the contrary, Rudolf's reign would nonetheless witness the first great wave of Counter-Reformation 'roll-back' in Germany and signal, in the process, that the Peace of Augsburg, and any tattered pretense at compromise, balance and toleration that went with it, was effectively over. If, moreover, he had not gone far enough or moved with sufficient alacrity to satisfy his more earnest Catholic critics, for Protestants his reign would provide crushing confirmation of what they had fearfully anticipated all along: that the Habsburgs' universalist pretensions made an onslaught inevitable, and that this onslaught would be pressed home with particular vigour in their traditional strongholds, where Lutheranism had not only established itself among a large section of the nobility but in numerous towns and villages. As early as the 1560s, in fact, many Austrian clergy were already freely altering the liturgy and treating their concubines as legal wives at a time when probably two thirds of the population were Protestant in sympathy, and the declining recruitment of priests meant that one priest was frequently having to serve up to four parishes. Such, indeed, was the scale of the crisis that Albrecht V, Duke of Bavaria – that staunchest of defenders of Roman piety – had himself informed the Council of Trent that he could hardly keep his lands in allegiance to the Holy See unless the gift of the chalice to the laity and clerical marriage were allowed, as indeed they were after a Bavarian Diet held at Ingolstadt in 1563 had sanctioned them both, along with the use of the German language at baptism.

Only eight years later, however, Protestantism had been eradicated in Bavaria, and the same process of Counter-Reformation that had been conducted with such vigour in the southern territories of the Empire more generally, was soon being duly pressed home in other areas as the sixteenth century entered its final decade. By 1590, Lutheranism had been suppressed in Lower Austria, by 1596 in Upper Austria, and by 1603 in Styria and Carinthia. The nobility alone, indeed, preserved their freedom of worship, and this was by no means the limit of the Catholic offensive. For during the early 1570s the Archbishop of Mainz and the Abbot of Fulda, dismissing the *Declaratio Ferdinandea*, had already carried out their own anti-Lutheran purges, and in the following decade the reformed religion was also eradicated in the prince-bishopric of Würzburg. By 1600, Bamberg, Hildesheim, Osnabrück, Münster, Paderborn, Cologne and Trier were following suit, along with Aachen, which had been finally restored to the Catholic fold by force in 1598 after turning Protestant seventeen years earlier under the influence of a surge of refugees from the Netherlands. And in all cases, the seemingly irresistible tide had been assisted by the creation in 1568 of the *Congregatio Germanica* (Council of German Affairs) in Rome, and by the upsurge in diocesan seminaries, synods and schools which were springing up all over Catholic Europe under the influence of the Council of Trent. Thanks to the presence of papal nuncios at Vienna, Graz, Munich and Cologne, Tridentine orthodoxy was defined with enhanced clarity and imposed with increased rigour. And such was the emphasis upon Germany as the central battlefield in the thrust for hearts and souls that a specific training centre for German clergy, the *Collegium Germanicum*, had been founded in Rome in 1552, though most of the young Germans sent there proved so obdurate in their aversion to foreigners that the majority had to be sent home only two years afterwards.

'The enemy,' wrote the Heidelberg pastor Boquin in 1576, 'seemed at last disposed of, when lo, he raised a new army and entrenched himself in his stronghold.' And in such circumstances, it was little surprise, perhaps, that the exodus of Lutherans from the *Pfafengasse*, or 'Priests' Alley', as the ecclesiastical territories along the Rhine and Main became known, had swiftly swollen to a flood. Most sought sanctuary as close to their former homes as possible, where they invariably formed militant and restless communities of exiles, while some, like those driven from Würzburg to nearby Ansbach in 1588, made their journey in a single body, singing the biblical song of bitterness – 'By the waters we sat down and wept' – along the way. But all hopes among the displaced for divine deliverance, let alone a joyous return to their homes, seemed, at very best, a distant prospect – and nowhere more so, indeed, than in Würzburg itself where Julius Echter von Mespelbrunn, bishop from 1573 to 1617, turned his territory into a brashly self-confident showpiece of Counter-Reformation achievement, beautifying and refurbishing churches, building a new university, lavishly restoring the episcopal palace, and also, it must be said, drastically improving clerical standards. For while an individual like Wolf Dietrich von Raitenau, Archbishop of Salzburg from 1587 to 1612, might remain notorious elsewhere for his expensive concubine, three sons and seven daughters, priests in Würzburg were nevertheless earnestly exhorted to abandon their mistresses and restore their neglected churches from a property tax imposed upon those Protestants forced to migrate.

Many small towns, in fact, suffered irreparable economic damage as a result of the re-imposition of Catholicism. Karlstadt in Franconia, for example, lost the immense sum of 72,233 florins after the expulsion of eighty burghers in 1586, though where political resistance to the Catholic offensive occurred, it was often vigorous, if vain. In 1594, just as they had done eighteen years earlier, the Palatinate and its sympathisers proposed that taxes for the war against the Turks should be withheld unless Protestant demands were met, with the result that Catholics threatened to withdraw from the Imperial Diet if the emperor submitted. Earlier, moreover, in both 1562 and 1575, the Palatinate had endeavoured to use the Imperial elections, first of Maximilian II and then of Rudolf II to push its demands, though failure was effectively inevitable here too, since Saxony, in particular, and most other Lutheran territories were opposed to such radical aims and methods, which only served to reinforce their ingrained hatred of Calvinism, as they themselves descended into dissent and defection within their own ranks. For between 1537 and 1577, there had been no less than ten major doctrinal clashes involving so-called 'Gnesio Lutherans' who wished to maintain Martin Luther's teachings unchanged in all aspects and the followers of Philip Melanchthon who, before his death in 1560, had become more receptive to an altered stance on the issues of the eucharist and predestination. Ultimately, even the so-called Formula of Concord, drawn up by a committee of Lutheran court chaplains, had managed to reunite no more than two thirds or so of the Lutheran world, leaving the 'Melanchthonians' with little option other than to merge with the Calvinists.

More significant still, however, was the defection of leading Protestant rulers, creating division within the reformers' leadership just when unity was most needed. For not only did Frederick III of the Palatinate adopt Calvinism in 1559–60, but Count John of Nassau followed in 1578, along with Landgrave Maurice of Hesse-Kassel in 1603. This last conversion, indeed, gave rise to a bloody student rebellion when Marburg's famous university, an important seminary for Lutheran pastors, was occupied by the landgrave's troops, though the impact even of this development paled into insignificance by compari-son to other events that had already occurred elsewhere. For Saxony itself, Lutheranism's hitherto unwavering bastion, had also appeared in danger for a brief while of succumbing to the Calvinist scourge during the stewardship of Duke Christian I between 1586 and 1591. Appointing Calvinists to senior posi-tions in both schools and universities, as well as his court, he also introduced changes to the Saxon Church, which brought it closer to Calvinism, and offered military assistance to Henri IV, the Calvinist King of France, before signing a military alliance with the Palatinate the following year. Only his premature death at the age of 31, in fact, saved the Lutheran cause at all in his homeland, and even this was scant consolation after the new ruler of Brandenburg openly embraced Calvinism in 1613 and imposed it upon his subjects. Riots followed in the streets of Berlin, along with brawling in Brandenburg's Estates, until a fragile compromise, tolerating both forms of Protestant worship, was eventually cobbled together.

Nor, indeed, was intolerance and disorder of this kind the only darker mani-festation of the contemporary preoccupation with spiritual matters, or, for that matter, the only baleful symptom of a growing crisis of central authority within the Empire. For hand-in-hand with the manic repression of religious rivals went an equally avid wave of persecution over which the faltering machinery of the Imperial courts exerted little control at all. As early as 1484, with Innocent VIII's bull, *Summis desiderantes*, and the publication of the infamous *Malleus Maleficarum*

('Hammer of Witches') three years later, the ground had arguably been laid for the extraordinary proliferation of witch trials that assumed unheard-of proportions in both Catholic and Protestant areas from the second half of the sixteenth century onwards. And though the regulations for the trials of sorcerers, established in the penal statutes of Emperor Charles V in 1532, had remained comparatively mild at first, such restraints would be steadily discarded as wholesale persecution gathered momentum amid the frenzied religious ethos of the day. Whether Luther's own obsession with Satan may have played some part or whether his own fixation was merely one more symptom of the general tenor of the time remains uncertain, but there was no doubting the increased incidence of execution, and not only in areas like Saxony where the death penalty was pronounced irrespective of whether or not a witch was thought to have inflicted actual harm. In the ecclesiastical territories of Trier, Mainz, Würzburg, Bamberg, Fulda, Ellwangen, and Salzburg, as well as in the duchy of Brunswick-Wolfenbüttel, and in the Austrian possessions on the Upper Rhine, persecution raged particularly intensely. And while several enlightened men, such as the Calvinist physician Johann Weyer and later the Jesuit Friedrich Spee, sought to arrest this 'witch craze', they could do little to staunch the flow of victims, which included children, peasants, burghers, burgomasters, lawyers, physicians, priests, ministers and, of course, women, as special witch courts sprang up outside the existing judiciary – circumventing, among other things, the normal controls on the use of torture – as the *Reichskammergericht* and other central organs found themselves powerless to intervene.

For Imperial princes, it is true, the intensity and intolerance of the times mainly tended to manifest itself in rather less hysterical forms. But they too were no less inclined to independent action, even in those cases where their underlying loyalty to the emperor was not in doubt. Impatient with the laxity of bishops, the dukes of Bavaria, for example, had not hesitated to take the task of reforming the Church into their own hands – and with a fervour brooking no compromise. In 1570, for example, Duke Albrecht of Bavaria established the *Geistliche Rat*, a council which effectively usurped episcopal functions as it imposed reforms backed by the full power of government. And under the duke's Jesuit-educated grandson – the diminutive and shrill-voiced Maximilian, who replaced him in 1597 – the day-to-day intrusions became even more apparent. Ultimately, he would dedicate both himself and his lands to the Virgin Mary in a vow written in his own blood and deposited in a silver tabernacle at her Altötting shrine. But even as his reign opened, the young duke's most powerful councillors became compelled to attend Mass daily, while his subjects, high and low alike, were made to kneel at the spot where they found themselves upon the ringing of the Angelus bell and the recitation of the so-called 'Turk's prayer', forcing even the high and mighty to dismount from their horses and climb down from their carriages in solemn subjection. For those inclined to balk at such conformity, moreover, Maximilian had also initiated a system of spies and informers, which extended in scope not only to witches but adulterers too.

Yet Duke Maximilian's activities within his principality of Bavaria were still only one aspect of a broader policy to expand his influence throughout the Empire of which he was such a key member. Upon his succession at the age of 24, the tireless newcomer had swiftly demonstrated a passion for administration that enabled him to establish not only a stable and solvent government but a justified reputation as one of Germany's ablest princes. In a letter of 1598 written to his father, who had just abdicated in his favour, Maximilian was already in no doubt whatsoever that 'respect goes only to those who have a lot of land or a lot of money.' And, as Duke of Bavaria, he would come to enjoy both. For, like other German princedoms, Bavaria had its own Estates, and by 1612, 'the representatives of the people' within the Bavarian *Landschaft* had not only voted him a handsome annual subsidy for seven years – equal by itself to double the revenues of the Duke of Saxony – but agreed to invest him with the power to make peace and war as he chose, and, in the event of the latter, to raise all necessary taxes at his own discretion.

Equipped with such freedom of action, Maximilian enjoyed a relationship with his subjects quite unlike anything prevailing in any other territory of the Holy Roman Empire, or indeed Western Europe as a whole. In consequence, while the *Landschaft* had met thirty-three times between 1514 and 1579 and six more times before 1612, it would never assemble thereafter until 1669. And as further confirmation of his supremacy, Maximilian had gone on to issue a complex legal code just prior to 1612, which underwent no discussion at the session for that year – a wholly unprecedented breach of established convention, which he was able to flout for two simple reasons, the first resulting from his proven financial expertise, the second from the successful eradication of Protestantism by both himself and his predecessors. By 1612, indeed, he had halved the debts inherited from his father, and was subsequently able to establish a surplus, so that even in wartime he could finance his army without recourse to his Estates. No less impressively, he had also been able to create a special fund, the *aerarium*, for the active defence of Catholicism within the Empire whenever the need arose, though traces of Protestantism within Bavaria itself were already, to all intents and purposes, a distant memory following the clash of 1563 when attempts to withhold taxes until toleration was granted were finally crushed and mass expulsions began.

Under Maximilian's stewardship, therefore, the Wittelsbach dukes of Bavaria had fast become not only the guardians of the newly-strident Church of Rome within the Holy Roman Empire but also the most powerful German rulers next to the Habsburgs, notwithstanding the fact that they were not among the electors of the emperor himself – something which Maximilian, in particular, would prove especially keen to rectify. For while cautious, he was also ambitious, possessing not only the strategic initiative to direct events but also the means to make waves at a time of his choosing. At the beginning of the Lutheran Reformation the court of Munich had coolly weighed the arguments for and against joining the Protestant cause, and it was only reasons of state that had ultimately persuaded Bavaria's rulers to side with Rome. But as a result of their decision, they would come to enjoy an influence that makes the usual maps of the Holy Roman Empire at this time wholly deceptive. For the comparatively small duchy between the Danube and the Alps had progressivly emerged as the political fulcrum of the entire Empire over the century that ensued. Alarmed by the possibility of Bavarian defection, the frightened curia in Rome conceded to the Wittelsbachs all the rights over the Church which the Protestant rulers had previously usurped in their own domains. But more significantly still, the Wittelsbachs also prevailed upon the curia to gift them a series of key bishoprics, regardless of the prescripts of canon law. On the one hand, the neighbouring sees of Freising and Regensburg conveniently rounded off the duchy, while the Freising manors themselves extended deeply into Austrian lands. At the same time, the further acquisition of the prince-bishopric of Liége in the far north-west actually split the Spanish-controlled southern Netherlands in half and made its new Wittelsbach ruler the neighbour of the United Provinces of the rebel-lious Dutch Republic as well as France. Likewise, the bishopric of Hildesheim established the Wittelsbachs in the centre of Lower Saxony, though even this paled by comparison with the greatest coup of all when a Bavarian prince was elevated to the archbishopric of Cologne in 1583, at the point when the city was on the verge of adopting Lutheranism. Two years later the suffragan bishopric of Münster was added, and from about 1580 onwards Paderborn and Hildesheim also fell into constant occupation by Wittelsbach bishops.

By the time the wealthy and strategically important north-western dukedom of Jülich-Berg allied itself with Maximilian in 1613, therefore, he was already pre-eminent among his counterparts, dominant not only in south-east Germany but in the north-west too, where he enviously eyed both the Palatinate and its ruler's status as an elector of the Holy Roman Emperor. For the Elector Palatine, as he was known, was still, in terms of political leverage at least, arguably the premier secular prince in Germany, outside the Imperial family, notwithstanding

the inconvenience that his territories were divided in two. And to add to
Maximilian's concerns, both Elector Frederick IV and his successor, Frederick
V, were not only defectors to Calvinism but committed to arresting the progress
of the Counter-Reformation more generally, with the able assistance of their
premier adviser, Prince Christian of Anhalt. Though the Palatinate's rulers had
proved unable as yet to gain the complete trust of their fellow German princes
or to secure any more than words of sympathy at the courts of England, France
and elsewhere, they remained undaunted in fact, and nothing, it seemed, would
prevent them from courting fire at every turn and on every front.

As such, the leading role of Bavaria and the Palatinate in any future struggle
was already guaranteed. For while Saxony remained wealthier than both, its
Lutheran Wettiner dukes were cautiously conservative in politics, and Saxony's
current ruler, the beer-swilling John George, who was 30 years old in 1618,
had no real mission beyond a comparatively tepid defence of Lutheranism,
the maintenance of peace and commercial prosperity, and a largely rhetori-
cal commitment to the preservation of the 'German liberties' in the face of
Habsburg absolutism. Nor was another elector of the emperor, the Margrave
of Brandenburg, any more consequential in practice. Ruler of the largest but
poorest possessions in the north-eastern plain of Germany, John Sigismund
inherited Prussia in 1618 and thereby gained – in Königsberg – an outlet to the
sea. But while most of his subjects were Lutheran, he himself was Calvinist and
did little to annoy his Habsburg overlords for fear of Polish intervention in his
newly acquired fief. Continually harassed by court intrigues, John Sigismund
was more content, in fact, to follow the lead of Saxony than press home the
interests of his own Hohenzollern house, though both he and the Duke of
Saxony alike exhibited a special gift for alienating honest advisers while tamely
submitting to the evil counsels of men who were open to shameless bribery by
foreign potentates.

Only a Holy Roman Emperor of sufficient will, authority and ability was
therefore truly in a position to outface and overawe the Duke of Bavaria. But
while Maximilian's loyalty to the Imperial throne was never in serious doubt, the
danger that he might act independently in what he considered the emperor's,
the Empire's, the Church's or, of course, his own best interests, was ever-present.
For although the Empire, with its vast population and territorial extent, might
on the one hand still rank, ostensibly, as the greatest state in western Europe,
it was now, quite plainly, a mere shadow of the original *Imperium Christianum*
that had taken shape under Charlemagne after his coronation on Christmas
Day 800. And while Rudolf, its current emperor, might still dream of a 'third
way' between religious extremes and plan crusades against the Turk to seal the

unity of his subjects, he was also more than intelligent enough to appreciate the yawning gap between his own residual sense of majesty and the stark realities of limited practical power. One of his earliest public acts, indeed, had been to head a procession of the Corpus Christi brotherhood in Vienna in May 1578, but when Lutheran stallholders refused to make way for his passage and a jug of milk was knocked over in the ensuing melée with guards, the result had been a 'Milk War' riot, which not only demonstrated all too painfully the woeful limitations of Imperial mystique but precipitated a serious illness that left him permanently altered.

Deprived of his main emotional prop and confidante after the departure of his mother for Spain in 1581, it was at this point indeed that Rudolf II had finally headed for his collections and laboratories, and when one of his chemical experiments went disastrously awry in September 1591, burning his cheek and beard and killing his master of horse, he descended further into bouts of fury at his courtiers and the crippling lassitude that left him happier in the company of his pet lion, Ottakar, than in the council chambers of his palace, where even his more capable advisers grew increasingly frustrated by his fitful attendance. By the turn of the century, in fact, as his family whispered of change and the first stirrings of subterfuge gathered pace in Vienna, Linz, Graz and elsewhere, he was beset by fears for his life, interpreting Tycho Brahe's astrological prediction for September 1600 as clear proof of an imminent assassination attempt, and seeking counsel from that self-same throng of parasites and voracious parvenus – popularly dubbed the 'regiment of valets' – who made just such an eventuality conceivable.

For by now the emperor was not only an innocent victim of mental illness, but directly responsible for a prolonged and ultimately futile struggle against the Ottoman Turks that had been steadily sapping the Empire's resources since 1593 and creating new and onerous demands for taxation. Known as the Long Turkish War, it consisted largely of sieges and small scale skirmishes, but while substantial sums amounting to as much as 20 million florins were generously granted in 1594 and 1603, the eventual Treaty of Zsitva-Török in 1606 brought no significant gains over and beyond the fact that the sultan and emperor became obliged to recognise each other as equals. Seven years into the conflict, the Empire's border troops had already been owed 1 million florins in back pay, while the field army was well on its way to arrears that would amount to double that figure by the end of the war. Yet the cost was merely exacerbated by the final settlement, as a result of which the humiliating annual tribute of 30,000 florins paid by the Habsburgs since 1547 was replaced by a final 'free gift' of 200,000. And this once again was not the sum of Rudolf's misfortunes, since the Turks were allowed to retain the important strategic centres of Kanizsa and Erlau, while even peace itself, in any strict sense of the term, was far from guaranteed. For the treaty was to last only twenty years, during which time cross-border raiding would be tolerated, so long as no regular troops were involved. Ultimately, indeed, it was only good fortune for the emperor that the Turks found themselves unable to resume the war after 1606, as a result of revolts within their own territories and the distraction of their war with Persia, which did not finally end until twelve years later.

Wholly predictably, therefore, the Treaty of Zsitva-Török had served as a final straw, and at a Habsburg family council, organised by Bishop Klesl in Vienna in the same year, the decision to act was finally taken. Three years earlier, even the Spanish ambassador had raised the possibility of deposing Rudolf, though the Pope had been reluctant to condone such a step. But Prince Stefan Bocskai's great Hungarian-Transylvanian uprising of 1605 — which had itself been triggered by Rudolf's persecution of Protestantism and attacks upon the Hungarian Estates — had already been managed successfully by Matthias, and the pressure now to invest him with further authority became overwhelming, notwithstanding the fact that he was, arguably, little more than one degree more competent than his brother. Faced with growing evidence, too, that the hostile and energetic court of the Palatinate in Heidelberg was already toying with plans to challenge the Habsburg monopoly of the throne, the decision was therefore taken to recognise Matthias as both head of the House of Habsburg and future Holy Roman Emperor. And when Rudolf subsequently stubbornly refused to delegate authority to his sibling in the manner required, he found himself thwarted once more, as Matthias duly allied himself with the Estates of Hungary, Austria, and Moravia, and forced his brother to yield the rule of these lands to him in 1608.

In effect, the emperor was left with only one bastion for what would prove a humiliatingly vain last stand: Bohemia itself, which was prepared to remain loyal for the time being, but only at the highest and most fateful of prices. For at least two thirds of Bohemians were Protestant and at most one tenth Catholic, and in July 1609, against the express advice of his ministers Lobkowitz, Martinitz and Slavata, Rudolf made the fateful decision to sign the *Majestätsbrief* or so-called 'Letter of Majesty', granting freedom of conscience to all his Bohemian subjects, irrespective of their social standing, and delegating ecclesiastical control within the kingdom to the Bohemian Estates. Catholicism, it is true, would remain considerably more evident among the nobility than other ranks, but the nobles' commitment was limited and their own popularity minimal, as even Count Vilém Slavata, who was hardly likely to be prejudiced against his own caste, readily admitted. Rarely convicted of capital crimes, paying no taxes and regarding the peasantry as their natural enemies, they were by no means the most worthy guardians of their own professed faith, though the entire religious complexion of the Imperial crown itself might henceforth depend upon their good offices when the King of Bohemia – himself an elector of the Holy Roman Emperor – was in turn elected by them.

Within two years, therefore, Rudolf's attempt to reassert his control by means of the Letter of Majesty merely succeeded in prompting an appeal from the Bohemian Estates to his brother Matthias, which would prove the final gambit of the contest. Enlisting the support of his nephew Leopold, the 30-year-old Bishop of Passau and Strasbourg, whose reputation for ambition and adventurism was wholly deserved, the emperor duly opted for a show of strength involving Leopold's 12,000-strong mercenary force known as the *Passauer Kriegsvolk*. But although the Passau mercenaries did indeed capture Prague's Malá Strana and prepared to attack the New and the Old City, they were eventually thwarted by troops of the Bohemian Estates and Matthias himself, who, after appropriate guarantees of religious toleration, was duly offered Bohemia's crown. The Letter of Majesty, with its formalisation of the role of so-called *Defensores* elected by the Estates to ensure its observance, was solemnly reaffirmed, and while Rudolf was left to nurse his fury after acceding to the advice of the Spanish envoy and papal nuncio, his successor duly settled down to a reign of leisurely inconsequence and prevarication. For the next five years, while Matthias ruled, Bohemians would indeed remain secure in the enjoyment of their religious and constitutional liberties, though they lived their lives at the heart of a political fault line of truly seismic proportions. And within months of his ouster, the emperor and king who had held their allegiance formerly, was dead – cursing, it is said, both Bohemia and its capital from a window of his once beloved Hradčany Palace. By then little more than a private person, the privacy that he had sought so earnestly for so much of his life had ultimately proved the bitterest pill of all, and his release from his torments on 20 January 1612 was no doubt a blessed one.

But, in spite of his curses, the ramifications of the prolonged struggle between the former emperor and his successor extended much further than Bohemia – as critical as the fortunes of that kingdom would eventually prove to be. For the 'brothers' quarrel' not only strained relations between the main courts of the Habsburg lands to breaking point but, arguably, undermined the previously unassailable authority of the Imperial title itself by emboldening radicals within the various Estates to believe that violent confrontation could advance their political and religious goals. The rulers of the Palatinate were not alone in thinking that attack might now prove the best form of defence, since the emperor's own intrinsic weakness had nevertheless been marked by a renewed intent to assert his authority both politically and religiously. Nor had such a lesson been lost on those humbler subjects, who sought to bolster their religious security with cudgels, fists and worse. For some twenty Imperial cities experienced rebellions or rioting between 1595 and 1618, and it was hardly coincidental, perhaps, that the most serious and significant of these incidents had occurred during 1606–07, at the very height of the contest for control of the Empire itself.

Neither was it any accident that the resulting storm centre should have been the thriving community of Donauwörth. Situated on the junction of the Danube and Wörnitz rivers some 25 miles north of Augsburg, it was one of the eight Imperial Free Cities where both Lutherans and Catholics were officially tolerated. But until 1605 Catholic clergy had scarcely dared to hold open processions within its confines, carrying no insignia when they paraded on Holy Days and keeping to the backstreets at all times for fear of reprisals. By the start of the century, in fact, the city's Catholic population had already shrunk to no more than sixteen households, though their situation in this respect, at least, was by no means unique. At Dortmund, for example, by 1602 there were said to be only thirty Catholics left, while in Kaufsbergen some eighty cowed adherents to the old religion faced around 700 warmly committed Protestants, and in almost all such cases, the minority wisely opted for discretion. Yet in Donauwörth, with its population of some 4,000, the situation was to prove explosively different. For the spiritual welfare of the tiniest Catholic community of its kind was jealousy upheld by the nearby Benedictine monastery of the Holy Cross, where a strident core of passionate young monks, fired with religious zeal from their education at the Jesuit college of Dillingen, was proudly asserting the monastery's exemption from the jurisdiction of the local city authorities. And under the wing of the Bishop of Augsburg, who was equally determined to press home the right of Catholics to advertise their customs and beliefs in the time-honoured fashion, these self-same monks were bent on showdown and defiance – with utterly predictable consequences.

For when, on St Mark's Day at the end of April 1606, a Catholic procession boldly wound its way, in full challenging pomp, across the city market to a local village and back again, the participants were rudely subjected to beatings, ridicule and the destruction of their banners. Worse still, in the aftermath of the furore, the ringleader of the assault – a goldsmith by the name of Schenk – is said to have declared that the entire matter was no business of either the Duke of Bavaria or, for that matter, the emperor himself. Rather than discuss the issue with them, indeed, the townsfolk should throw the pair into the Danube. And with the rubicon thus crossed, further provocation was swift to follow. For in spite of the city council's attempts to mollify its citizens, a so-called 'Council of the Twenty', comprising townsfolk and guild representatives, promptly took possession of Donauwörth's key which signified, in effect, the handing over of civic authority to the rebels, and a defiance of any Imperial ban that was likely to follow, irrespective of the fact that such a ban would entail the loss of all legal protection for both the city's leaders and their property.

Yet it would take one further incident, and the entrance of another player into the drama, to bring down the full weight of the emperor's displeasure upon the perpetrators. For only two months after the initial disorder, a leading Capuchin, Father Laurence of Brindisi, was mobbed en route to the Imperial court by a rowdy Lutheran crowd chanting 'Capuchin scum', after which, upon hearing the plight of the local clergy and heeding their calls for action, he decided to present their case to the emperor himself, who, by the time of the friar's arrival, had in fact been forced to abandon Prague as a result of an outbreak of plague. Undaunted, the single-minded Capuchin nevertheless chose to preach an impassioned sermon blaming the contagion itself upon the sinful concessions made to Protestants at Donauwörth and elsewhere, adopting so inflammatory a tone, indeed, that only an urgent request from Maximilian of Bavaria for him to leave at once, in order to exorcise his wife, prevented a potential breakdown in order, though even this was not the end of the matter. For the exorcism, which required several gruelling sessions over several days, still furnished ample opportunity, ironically enough, for the tireless Capuchin to enlist Maximilian himself for the Catholic cause in Donauwörth. Indeed, by the time that Laurence returned to Prague the following February, he was able to assure the emperor that Bavaria was ready to enforce the Augsburg Settlement and thereby guarantee the city's Catholics their freedom of worship, notwithstanding the ongoing outrage of their opponents, which was soon being vented as violently as ever. For when an Imperial commissioner, along with two Bavarian agents arrived in the city, to ensure the smooth execution of a full St Mark's Day procession in April 1607, the results were once again predictable, as priests, monks, commissioner and agents alike found themselves virtually besieged by a rowdy Lutheran mob, and unable to leave the monastery where they had assembled. As the protest ran its course, furthermore, Donauwörth's magistrates, Protestants to a man, had not raised a finger.

The entire episode had represented, in fact, yet another flagrant challenge to Imperial authority, and left the emperor with little choice other than to reassert central control or risk confirmation of his irrelevance. Accordingly, the city was ordered in August to allow its Catholics freedom of worship or incur an Imperial ban on its city council, making them 'open outlaws' and liable to the ban's enforcement by none other than Maximilian of Bavaria – a threat which, however politically necessary under the circumstances, merely cast further shadows on the functioning and impartiality of the Empire's two premier courts. For the *Reichskammergericht*, in particular, had already delivered a number of highly controversial judgements before 1600, restoring secularised estates to the Catholic Church, and had become effectively paralysed in the same year after the Elector Palatine and a number of other Protestant princes, seeing no chance of gaining a majority for their own views, refused to co-operate with it. Worse still, the Aulic Council in Prague, accountable to the emperor in person, had in the meantime firmly established its own reputation for favouring the Catholic cause even more strongly than its counterpart in Vienna, and it was this judicial tool that Emperor Rudolf now saw fit to employ in an effort to resolve his current predicament.

Most provocative of all, however, were two further considerations, since the court's ruling was not only open to the charge of partiality but also constituted a clear breach of normal legal rules, according to which Donauwörth belonged to the Imperial Circle of Swabia and the jurisdiction of its director, the Lutheran Duke of Württemberg, rather than Duke Maximilian's Bavarian Circle, which was now, seemingly, being called upon to implement the ban. When the emperor saw fit in June 1609, moreover, to grant Maximilian the city as a pledge for the expenses he had occurred in imposing it, and the duke then opted to occupy the town permanently as a prelude to systematically suppressing the Protestant majority, the entire fabric of the Peace of Augsburg appeared fatally compromised. Propped up by Bavarian arms and a Bavarian ruler of seemingly dubious intentions, a weak and ineffective emperor had therefore opted to flex his muscles at what was arguably the worst possible moment in the worst possible place in the worst possible manner, and in doing so, brought his territories to the brink of widespread war.

Upon news of the occupation, Duke Philip Ludwig of Neuburg had at once appreciated the implications. 'Maximilian, Maximilian,' he lamented, 'you do not realise the consequences of what you are doing.' And even before the subsequent decision to lay waste to Protestantism within the city, the wider backlash had already become clear at the Imperial Diet summoned to appear at Augsburg in January 1608. In truth, a confrontation between militants led by the Elector Palatine and the emperor was already a foregone conclusion, since the former was bent upon changes beneficial to Protestantism in general and Calvinism in particular, while Rudolf was merely hoping for money to pay off debts incurred by the Turkish War. But events in Donauwörth, scarcely 100 km from Regensburg where the Diet was held, had driven even normally moderate

Lutheran rulers, such as the dukes of Neuburg and Saxony into the Palatinate's camp. In consequence, they demanded at least an increase in Protestant representation in the *Reichskammergericht*, though the emperor's representative – the notoriously intransigent Archduke Ferdinand of Styria – felt no need to compromise, since Catholics still possessed a majority in two of the three chambers of the Diet: four to three among the electors, and thirty-three to fifteen among the princes, with only the towns, which lacked a binding vote in any case, remaining predominantly Protestant. Indeed, there was even talk of a jointly orchestrated armed coup against the Diet by Ferdinand and Maximilian, if the archduke did not prevail by peaceful means.

In the event, such an expedient did not materialise, but in February the Catholic princes in the Diet's second chamber nevertheless introduced a motion demanding once more that all ecclesiastical lands secularised since 1552, such as the bishoprics of Magdeburg and Halberstadt, should be duly restored. Essentially a strategic ploy, the proposal was actually intended to encourage the Protestants to give way on other issues, in order to encourage its withdrawal. Yet the result was merely to make the Protestants' position untenable, so that in April the Palatine delegation simply walked out of the Diet after submitting a formal protest. They were followed, moreover, by the representatives of Brandenburg, Ansbach, Kulmbach, Baden-Durlach, Hesse-Kassel and Württemberg, and though the Saxon contingent, along with some others, remained, there was little doubt that what had transpired marked a qualitatively new phase of the struggle, as Ferdinand reluctantly dissolved proceedings on 3 May, with the emperor absent, as he had been throughout, and seemingly indifferent to the momentous consequences of what had come to pass.

For nine days later – in the chapterhouse of the secularised monastery of Auhausen, appropriately enough – the so-called 'Protestant Union' came into existence at the instigation of the Elector Palatine, the Dukes of Neuburg and Württemberg, and the rulers of Ansbach, Kulmbach and Baden-Durlach. Known also as the Evangelical Union, it was founded upon a ten-year pledge of mutual defence against attack, and came ultimately to involve nine princes in all, including the Margrave of Brandenburg, the landgrave of Hesse-Kassel and the Count Palatine of Zweibrücken, as well as some seventeen cities, the most powerful of which were Strasbourg, Nuremberg and Ulm. With the Palatinate as its leader, Henri IV of France as its main external supporter, and Christian of Anhalt, the Elector Palatine's adviser-in-chief, as its 'general', the alliance was seen by its opponents as a dangerous move towards anarchy – and not merely by supporters of the emperor but by many Lutherans too, since the Union was predominantly Calvinist in orientation, and more conservative Protestants, such as the Elector of Saxony, remained deeply distrustful of its purportedly defensive nature, preferring to hold aloof in the interest of maintaining Imperial unity against the more worrying prospect of foreign intervention in any future war.

Nor, it must be said, were the prospects for international escalation any mere chimera. For on 10 July 1609, Maximilian of Bavaria had duly formed a corresponding Catholic League, consisting of fifteen archbishops and bishops, five abbots and the city of Aachen, all bolstered by promises of subsidies from Philip III of Spain. And while the emperor's stature had declined so precipitously that the Austrian Habsburgs themselves were expressly excluded from the alliance, the potential for wider conflict was no less prominent on the Protestant side too, since the Palatine activists in particular shared not only a starkly ideological approach to European politics as a whole, but had also forged close links with the most prominent standard bearer of all those involved in their anti-Catholic crusade: the proudly defiant 'heroes' of the anti-Spanish Dutch Republic. Since the late 1560s, indeed, following the conversion of Elector Frederick III to Calvinism in the first place and the continuation of his policies by his successor, the court of Heidelberg had been convinced of the existence of an international Catholic alliance, headed by the Habsburgs and the papacy, which made religious war inevitable and the forging of links with England, the Huguenots of France and the Dutch rebels a matter of the utmost priority. Indeed, for Prince Christian of Anhalt-Bernburg, who had gained unchecked control of the Palatinate's foreign relations as a result of the alcoholism and infirmity of the Elector Frederick IV (1592–1610), the support of these allies represented, quite literally, a matter of life and death – for the Palatinate, for its princes, and for the entire spiritual salvation of Europe as a whole.

Born in Bernburg in 1568 and baptised a Lutheran, Christian of Anhalt had, in fact, developed into a child prodigy who had been tutored by Caspar Gottschalk in Latin, Italian and French from the age of 2, and gone on to participate in a series of diplomatic missions – to Constantinople and elsewhere – while still in his youth. As a member of the royal House of Ascania, moreover, he was from 1603 a ruling prince of the revived principality of Anhalt-Bernburg, by which time he had become an ambitious, urbane diplomat and an experienced soldier and administrator, who had led the Palatinate's army in aid of the French king Henri IV in 1591, and been appointed Governor of the Upper Palatinate by Frederick IV four years later, after which he settled in Amberg. Attracted to Calvinism during a stay at the court of Saxony in the company of Elector Christian, beginning around 1586 and lasting several years, he took up his new post in the Palatinate with all the passion of a religious convert who had arrived in his natural spiritual home. And he had done so at a time when the Palatinate in general and its court in particular were ripe for further radicalisation, as Calvinist immigrants like Ludwig Camerarius, Hippolytus von Colli and the brothers Christoph and Achatius von Dohna became his protégés, and Frederick IV sank into dotage and the customary beery oblivion of so many German princes.

Neither would the succession of Frederick's son in 1610 – after the father's death from 'extravagant living' – do anything to inhibit the minister's primacy. For Frederick V was only 14 years of age upon ascending the throne and already thoroughly immersed in the kind of Calvinist thinking that closely matched Christian's own. In 1604, indeed, he had been sent to Sedan at his mother's urging, to live in the court of his uncle, the Duke of Bouillon – an old friend of Anhalt's – and there he had been tutored by the Calvinist theologian Daniel Tilenus, a professor of theology at the Academy of Sedan, who, as a result of the French Wars of Religion and the Dutch revolt against Spain, advocated not only unity among Protestant rulers but their need to intervene physically in protection of their brethren. Thus indoctrinated and subsequently subjected to what had proved to be a rancorous succession process, the new Elector Palatine was therefore almost ideally equipped from the outset to nestle cosily under the protective wing of his chief mentor – a process that appears to have been enhanced after a close scrape with death when he was struck by fever during a meeting of the Protestant Union. Described by contemporaries as thereafter subject to 'melancholy', he seems to have transferred further responsibility to the ever-willing and ever-zealous mentor and minister, who now found himself firmly ensconced at the helm of European Calvinism's concerted drive to prominence.

Even more crucial to this process than ever, moreover, was the Palatinate's relationship with the Dutch Republic, which had been formed not only by their close confessional bond, but by personal and domestic connections on a number of levels and by a shared strategic interest in the Rhineland. In 1593, on the one hand, Frederick IV had married Louisa-Juliana, half-sister of Maurice of Nassau, leader of the Dutch Republic. And from the other direction, her uncle, Count John VI of Nassau-Dillenberg, was a leading member of the Palatine Council until his death in 1606, while John's brother-in-law, John Albert, Count of Solms-Braunfels, had become Palatine court chamberlain in 1602. At a time when personal links and, above all, family loyalties underpinned so much of the political process and heavily influenced its direction, such connections were, of course, of no little significance. But numerous Palatine officers had also carried out worthy service in the Dutch army, and the shared interest in the Rhineland had been heavily reinforced by both the Spanish invasion of Westphalia in 1599 and the five-year war for the religious leadership of Cologne, begun in 1583, in which, as we have seen, both the young Dutch Republic and the Palatinate as well as Spain became closely involved.

Yet Christian of Anhalt's diplomatic endeavours had by no means been confined to the Netherlands. An invitation to James I of England, on his accession in 1603, to become head of an international Protestant alliance had been politely refused, but there had also been further overtures to Henri IV of France, notwithstanding the latter's conversion to Catholicism in 1593. Anhalt had, after all, led a military expedition to Henri's assistance in 1591 and was, indeed, owed 1.3 million thaler for his troubles – a debt that his descendants were still claiming from France in 1818 – though this, too, would not coax the French king to the kind of adventurism that might undermine his much more important quest for civil peace at home. Instead, the Palatinate's chief minister was left to fish in troubled waters within the Empire itself – and with considerably more success. For, from 1607, he corresponded enthusiastically with Protestant leaders in Bohemia, and in the same year concluded a treaty with his nephews, the margraves of Ansbach and Kulmbach, and the city of Nuremberg – ostensibly for the protection of the Upper Palatinate against an attack from Bavaria. Much more importantly still, he had subsequently masterminded the expansion of this alliance into the altogether more significant Protestant Union.

Believing unequivocally in the existence of a Papal-Habsburg conspiracy to eradicate Protestantism, and convinced beyond any doubt of the consequent need for the Empire's non-Catholics to forge both internal and external alliances to counter the threat, Anhalt had been deeply influenced, it seems, by undercurrents at Calvinism's more eclectic edges, which postulated a magical system of universal knowledge making it possible to comprehend the divinely predestined course of history by means of biblical exegesis. It was a militant recipe of the most potent kind and flavoured by the kind of millenarian expectations that characterised so much thinking of the day. With a 14-year-old boy as Anhalt's only potential foil after 1610, it was hard to see how the Palatinate could draw back from confrontation any more than the forces pitched against it. And though young Frederick V was no mere cipher, diligently consulting with his advisers on almost every important issue of state and inspecting every document issuing from Anhalt's hand, he too was prey to the same misgivings and ambitions. Convinced that 'German liberties' were under mortal threat, secure in a divinely-inspired appreciation of history's future course, and knowing full well that if theologians could not agree the sword must ultimately decide, the sole remaining questions were merely when and where.

3

'THE START OF OUR DESTRUCTION'

I see blood and dust before me,
And a thousand armed men.
I see how so many gilded banners fly for victory and robbery:
Yet I am burning.
Let those who cannot burn begin an illustrious existence.

Caspar Stieler, *Die Geharnischte Venus* (1660)

Like most other places in most other times, the Holy Roman Empire of the early seventeenth century had more than its fair share of sages, seers and prophets. In 1614, the Thuringian preacher Ezechiel Meth had greatly perturbed the authorities of Saxony by asserting not only that he was the divinely-ordained 'great prince Michael' but that Lutheran forms of baptism and communion were nothing more than sorcery, and that there were neither eternal souls nor any prospect of resurrection from the dead. In the same year, an anonymous book published in Kassel with the title of *Fama Fraternatis* – one of a large number of Rosicrucian treatises – expatiated upon the doctrine of the sequence of the ages, first put forth by the medieval mystic Joachim von Fiore, suggesting that the last age of the earth and a new prophet, Elijah, were to be expected. But similar apocalyptic notions were also disseminated in more exalted quarters, and not least of all by that illustrious Moravian scholar and 'great teacher of nations', Jan Amos Komenský – better known as Comenius – who likewise predicted the imminence of a final catastrophe, presaged by the arrival of a new saviour who would destroy both the 'evil eagle' (the Habsburgs) and the 'wicked dragon of the west' (the papacy, the Holy Roman Empire and Spain). Profoundly convinced of the limitless possibilities of the educated mind,

Comenius had already begun work on a mighty 'pansophy' or treasury of all knowledge, but was plainly no less inclined than any of his contemporaries to pedal in portents.

The illustrious Johannes Kepler, it is true, looked upon his own astrological work rather more sceptically, treating it primarily as a means of gaining much-needed income to subsidise his more serious astronomical studies. 'This Astrologia is certainly a crazy daughter,' he wrote in 1618, 'but, dear God, what would her mother, the highly rational Astronomia, do if she did not have this crazy daughter?' For the 'Mathematicorum Salaria [earnings of scholars],' he continued, 'are so slight that the mother would certainly starve if the daughter did not earn anything.' Yet even Kepler's misgivings did not prevent him, just like David Herlitzius, the 'Physikus' (municipal physician) of Stargard and court astrologer of Pomerania, from treating the great comet of November 1618 as a highly significant *prodigium*, or warning, of divine anger. In his '*prodromus*', or 'introduction', about the 'tailed star', Herlitzius noted its appearance at a time when Jupiter, the Sun, Venus, Mercury and the Moon were 'beneath the Earth', i.e. below the horizon, while the 'evil and mischievous planets', Saturn and Mars were above. 'Mars peregrinus,' it seemed, had left the 'eleventh house' of the heavens at this time and was four degrees in front of the tail of the Lion, foreshadowing many murderous attacks, false alliances and betrayals. And since the comet had flared in the constellation of the Scorpion, 'the first heavenly house', it followed that pestilence, monstrous births, rain and floods, widespread death and, above all, hate among kings would surely follow – along, it seems, with a rise in the price of fish.

Not long before, in his *Prognosticum Astrologicum* of 1617, an almanac for the following year, Kepler too had predicted – though with a glibness not untypical of the astrologer's art – how trouble was in store. 'Then May will not pass,' his forecast ran, 'without difficulty in places and affairs, especially where the commons otherwise have great freedom, because everything is really shattered.' But with the actual appearance of a 'terrible torch' in the night skies of 1618, what was no doubt originally intended as little more than a throwaway comment in a piece of purse-filling hackwork soon assumed altogether more momentous proportions, as chroniclers far and wide reported terrifying earthquakes, poisonous rivers of blood and hideous sulphurous rains, and local magistrates exhorted their citizens to frequent prayer for deliverance. A nova of 1604 had already caused widespread unease, prompting the Englishman Robert Fludd to foretell the coming of a mighty potentate who would transform the world by '*clementia et potentia, arte et marte*' (clemency and power, art and war), but the response to the celestial warning of 1618 attained altogether unprecedented dimensions. Even princes, like the Duke of Pomerania, specifically ordered the clergy to preach repentance from their pulpits, while the *Theatrum Europaem* contained the most memorable prophecy of all, describing a 'dreadful comet' that appeared 'around the start of our destruction'. 'God almighty,' the prediction continued, had not only 'signalled his place as a preacher of atonement at the high altar of heaven, so that people could see how he would punish them for their sins' but decided 'to bring his punishment rod over them', thereby giving 'ample warning of damage' and admonishing them 'in times of grace to abstain from sin and plead for divine mercy'.

Though there was no mention, it must be said, of the price of fish, it made grim reading and amply reflected the general tenor of the times. Yet long before then, the signs of impending war had been plain enough to discern, not by means of 'ancient wisdom' or divination, but through the medium of impenetrable stone and tempered steel, hewn and forged in ever greater profusion, as fortresses rose and arsenals expanded across the Empire in grim anticipation of the coming fray. All over Germany, indeed, governments had been spending heavily on defence, so that foreign visitors coming even from the war-torn United Provinces of the Dutch Republic noted the contrast between their own land, where soldiers were in most cases surprisingly rarely seen, and the Empire, where every potentate, great or small, seemed to boast a private army, flamboyant in dress and strident in presence. Even a self-proclaimed lover of peace like Landgrave Maurice of Hesse-Kassel, notwithstanding his further reputation as a humanist patron of the arts and intellectuals, had finally succumbed to the mania, creating a new militia of some 9,000 men in 1600, to be followed the year after by a 288-page directive on how this force should be deployed in an emergency – an emergency that was not long in coming, incidentally, after the peace-seeking prince duly saw fit to stage the invasion and annexation of neighbouring Hesse-Marburg, which he celebrated in 1618 with the creation of a special 'military academy' to train his regimental officers.

In ducal Prussia, meanwhile, where the government was unable to persuade the local Estates to fund the creation of a new militia, taxes were nevertheless voted in 1601 for new fortifications at Pillau and Memel, as well as for two warships to patrol the Baltic approaches. Dresden, likewise, made a particularly warlike impression with its moats and ramparts, its thick ashlar walls and its extended bastions peppered with the menacing mouths of some 500 great cannon, which included a deadly 'organ gun' whose 24 barrels were capable of being fired simultaneously. Specifically redesigned according to the most modern Dutch principles by Wilhelm Dilich of Hesse, author of the definitive contemporary work on the subject, the *Peribologia*, Dresden also boasted its

famous armouries, consisting of five separate floors, and weapons and equipment for up to 10,000 men in time of war. According to an inventory dated
1606, and running to 1,500 manuscript pages, the Duke of Saxony's own personal collection of more precious items comprised some 1,400 pistols, 1,600
long arms and 2,200 swords and daggers, as well as miscellaneous horse and body
armour with all necessary accoutrements. Even in peace, moreover, some 300
mercenaries kept watch along the battlements of the duke's capital, guarding its
gates and patrolling its streets.

Nor, of course, was it any surprise that the crusader-in-chief of Calvinist
resistance to the Counter-Reformation, the Elector Palatine, should have taken
such pains to gird his own cities for the divinely-sanctioned conflict to come.
New walls, bastions and moats were initially built around Frankenthal and
Heidelberg, and in 1606 an entire fortress-city was created at Mannheim, with
a citadel and vast star-shaped chain of walls, which were widely reputed to be
impregnable. At Hanau, meanwhile, which was allied to the Palatinate by its
Calvinist count, an entirely new defensive outwork was created between 1603
and 1618, swiftly prompting the Catholic powers of the Rhineland to step up
their own planning. For at Ehrenstein, overlooking Coblenz at the junction of
the Rhine and Moselle, the Archbishop of Trier spent lavishly on his electorate's safety, while from 1615 onwards the Bishop of Speier set about fashioning
the great fortress of Philippsburg at Udenheim, to the south of the Palatinate.
The lords of Alsace, too, built new walls at Benfeld, Breisach and Hagenau at the
same time that the Duke of Bavaria was refortifying Munich, Ingolstadt, Rain
and some other frontier towns, at a cost of almost 1 million thalers.

Nothing, then, could speak more eloquently – or ominously – of the perva-
sive readiness for war infecting the Empire's rulers for at least a decade and more
before the 'fatal conflagration' of 1618 than the towering dark ramparts that
had by then become such an overwhelming feature of so many German cities.
Fashioned from millions of bricks and often as much as 40 feet deep, 30 feet high
and several miles long, they dominated skylines, dwarfed and oppressed their
inhabitants and cast a gloomy pall over newcomers who witnessed them for the
first time. Visiting Hamburg in 1617, the English poet, humourist and traveller,
John Taylor, was particularly astonished by the size of the army of artisans at
work upon the city's walls. 'And when I perceived these fortifications,' Taylor
recorded in his *Three weekes, three daies and three houres observations and travel from
London to Hamburgh*, 'I was amazed, for it is almost incredible for the number of
men and horses that are daily set on work about it.' 'The work itself,' he concluded, 'is so great that it is past the credit of report.' And though Taylor made no
direct reference to the likelihood of war, the implication was clear enough, for

by the time that he wrote the political signs, too, had been no less baleful for the best part of a decade, as the Imperial centre in Vienna faltered and contending rulers shaped to exploit the various pressure points that were steadily emerging both within and without the Empire – especially in a small but strategically crucial principality abutting the nascent Dutch Republic.

Certainly, it was not without good reason that, until his death in 1592, Duke William of Jülich-Cleves-Mark-Berg-Ravensberg had been known to his contemporaries as William the Rich, and it was no surprise either that the affairs of his five separate territories were a matter of such intense interest to his neighbours, both near and more remote. For they extended from the River Weser in the east to the River Meuse in the west, and bordered not only the United Provinces and the Spanish Netherlands, but completely surrounded the archbishopric of Cologne. Nor was this all, since they included, at the same time, the prosperous textile industries of Bielefeld, Hagen, Herford, Elberfeld and Barmen, the powder and paper mills of Pfaffrath and Gladbach, the ceramic industry of Siegburg and, above all, the world famous centre for sword and knife production located in Solingen. Some of the busiest overland trade routes to central Germany and thence eastern Europe also started in the duke's Rhine ports of Wesel, Duisburg and Düsseldorf, which handled goods to and from the Netherlands and England, where the highly prized Solingen wares went by the name of Cologne blades.

Yet the chequered history of Duke William's multiple territories had made it impossible for him to establish a worthwhile central administration, and enabled his nobles, in effect, to become independent rulers within their own indidual domains. To compound matters, the various sub-duchies were themselves rent by religious cleavages, since Jülich and Berg had remained faithful to Rome, while Mark and Ravensberg opted for Lutheranism, and Cleves for Calvinism – the result of which was a further incentive for the nobility to sell its affiliations to whichever power seemed to offer the better security for the maintenance of their authority. Under such circumstances, only the most skilful ruler could prevail, and William, to his considerable merit, had coped with admirable finesse. But the wolves were invariably circling and the death of the duke's imbecile successor, John William, on 25 March 1609, after seventeen years of inept rule, stirred into action not merely a gaggle of presumptive heirs and doubtful claimants, but, much worse still, the contending foreign powers, all of whom were intent upon either maintaining or upsetting the political equilibrium in this part of central Europe. For as early as the 1580s the Catholic-dominated Estates of Jülich had been given assurances of support from both the Archbishop of Cologne and Spain in the event of a Protestant succession attempt, engineered on behalf of the Dutch or their Palatine allies.

With both the Protestant Union and Catholic League duly poised for a test of arms, the situation was therefore delicately poised, to say the least. And though the Union was weakened by divisions between Lutherans and Calvinists, and invitations to both James I of England and Christian IV of Denmark had been deferred by its members at Rothenburg in August 1608, Christian of Anhalt had nevertheless decided to press matters independently, seeking a marriage between his own Prince Frederick and James I's daughter Elizabeth in the autumn of 1608, while encouraging his personal friend Erasmus von Tschernembl, leader of the Protestant Estates of Upper Austria, to look to the Union for support against the mounting threat from the emperor. For Rudolf II's ongoing resentment at his brother's rise was still mounting steadily at this time, and in such circumstances, the thorny problem of the Jülich-Cleves succession was far too tempting an opportunity for the benighted incumbent of the Imperial throne to ignore, as he sought, in one fell swoop, to assert his Imperial rights, to bolster the prestige of the House of Austria, to strengthen the Catholic cause, and to oblige his high and mighty Spanish cousins to a long overdue debt of gratitude.

In fact, the legal position of the prospective claimants to Jülich-Cleves was far from clear, and this in itself not only heightened the political danger, but increased, in Rudolf's mind at least, both the scope and need for Imperial intervention. On the strength of compacts reaching back a century, Christian II, Elector of Saxony until 1611, was himself a potential contender, but he had pursued his options so feebly that he was soon pushed aside by two relatives of the sisters of the late John William: one of whom was John Sigismund, Elector of Brandenburg, son-in-law of the eldest sister; and the other of whom was Wolfgang William, son of the Count Palatine of Neuburg and a second sister. Each, in fact, was Lutheran, but owing to strained relations between Neuburg and the Palatinate, the candidate favoured by both the latter and the Dutch was Brandenburg, notwithstanding the additional complication that Brandenburg himself was prevented from cementing a formal alliance with his supporters by a long-standing agreement with the ruling families of Saxony and Hesse, which precluded his involvement in external treaties. As such, the best that could be brokered had been a private arrangement of April 1605, by which the Dutch, in return for loans of 100,000 thalers from Brandenburg and the Palatinate, duly promised to occupy Jülich-Cleves on John Sigismund's behalf when its current duke finally died.

And it was into this wholly impenetrable minefield that Emperor Rudolf II duly blundered on 2 April 1609 – little more than a week, ironically enough, before the Twelve Years Truce between Spain and the Dutch Republic finally brought their own hostilities to a temporary end. As representatives from the rival claimants made their way to Düsseldorf to lay claim to John William's duchies, his widow, supported by the Jülich Estates, was already resolved to resist both of the interloping 'princes pretendant' with the aid, as it now so happened, of an emperor whose impartiality had already been shattered beyond retrieval by the Donauwörth episode. Rejecting an offer by Neuburg and Brandenburg to rule jointly pending independent arbitration – an eminently sensible proposal that had been mediated by the landgrave of Hesse-Kassel and guaranteed by members the Protestant Union – Rudolf accordingly commissioned his favourite nephew Leopold, Bishop of Passau and Strasbourg, to discard his crook for a sword and take possession of the disputed territories on the widowed duchess's behalf, calling, in the meantime, upon military assistance from the Spanish Netherlands, should such prove necessary. In the process, Bishop Leopold was to assume command of the Catholic garrison of the fortress of Jülich in a supposedly impressive show of the emperor's authority that would prove, or so his Imperial uncle hoped, as welcome to the Spanish government in Brussels as it was intolerable to both France and the Netherlands.

The result, however, was a tense and protracted stand-off, as Leopold found himself blockaded in his fortress stronghold by troops of both claimants, and the emperor witnessed his position in Prague steadily crumbling around him. Writing to Robert Cecil, Earl of Salisbury, on 17 October 1609, the English agent in The Hague, Ralph Winwood, left little doubt of the stakes involved:

> The issue of this whole business, if slightly considered, may seem trivial and ordinary, but duly examined with all the consequences necessarily ensuing (if freely I may deliver my poor judgement) doth, as it shall be carried, uphold or cast down the greatness of the house of Austria and the church of Rome in these quarters.

And though neither side wished to initiate hostilities, Leopold's mobilisation of reinforcements in the diocese of Passau, not to mention his visit to the Spanish in Brussels in October and the formation of the Catholic League that July, did indeed convince the princes of the Protestant Union that their fears of a repetition of the Donauwörth affair were wholly justified, and committed them to counter-measures. For in May 1609 they had already agreed that although their alliance was not committed to support the claimants, members should nevertheless provide assistance individually if requested, and by November they were posturing much more menacingly still, proposing at a meeting of the leading princes that the Union should, as a body, reinforce the armies of the two claimants with a force of 5,000 men, on the grounds, as the Palatinate's representative

Michael Loefenius put it, that 'all the Protestant estates are limbs of one holy body and that the illness of one will affect all the others'.

In the meantime, moreover, Christian of Anhalt was continuing his efforts to broaden the international base of support for his crusade against Catholic and Habsburg tyranny, visiting Paris in December to discuss French intervention with Henri IV, while simultaneously encouraging approaches to James I and the Dutch States-General. By early 1610, indeed, he had succeeded in securing a decision from an assembly of the Protestant Union held at Schwäbisch Hall over January and February that its members commit themselves publicly to support for the thwarted claimants in Jülich-Cleves. And as a further coup, he was also able to deliver extraordinary news of an offer from Henri IV to send troops to the siege of Jülich and to mount major diversionary campaigns in the Netherlands and northern Italy to prevent Spanish intervention. For a French king, whose greatest fear was supposedly a major European war, such an extraordinary commitment was, perhaps, little more than proof of his desire to gain control of the Union's activities before Anhalt pushed events any further. Certainly Sir Ralph Winwood, like other contemporaries, considered the king's decision, as things appeared, 'a deeper mystery than every man's capacity can conceive and a project more strange than any man (I think) will easily believe'. But, in the short-term, Henri had nevertheless served Anhalt's purposes admirably, allaying – at least partially – the chancellor's fears of the inevitable consequences of an unsupported confrontation with Spain, while maintaining the momentum of a build-up to a military reckoning that the Palatinate's leaders continued to consider both necessary and unavoidable.

Yet the war that Anhalt sought so keenly was nevertheless checked by a combination of circumstances beyond his control, not the least of which was Henri IV's assassination on 14 May 1610, followed by Emperor Rudolf's effective overthrow in 1611 and subsequent death on 20 January 1612. Thereafter, Leopold's occupying force was indeed expelled from Jülich by its besiegers who were subsequently reinforced by Dutch and English contingents commanded by Maurice of Nassau, before being replaced by a Dutch garrison. Worse still from Anhalt's perspective, as both the French regent and new emperor counselled prudence, the prospect of a more general pacification seemed increasingly plausible, as the Imperial cities of the Union pressed for the disarmament of both the Union's and the League's forces. For, contrary to expectation, Anhalt's brinkmanship and tendency to conduct the Union's diplomacy secretly and informally had in fact increased the cities' fears and sown fundamental divisions within the Union, leaving Saxony an outright opponent and forcing the resignation of Neuburg after his offer to direct the regency of the Palatinate upon the death of Frederick IV on 8 September 1610 was rejected. With the Dutch unwilling to disrupt the Twelve Years Truce with Spain so soon after its inception and with James I reluctant to commit himself to anything more than a six-year defensive alliance and the marriage of his daughter to the new Elector Palatine, Anhalt's plans would therefore have to be put on temporary hold.

Yet while Anhalt bit his lip and bided his time, the underlying problem had not receded. 'I only wish,' King James of England had confided at the time, 'that I may handsomely wind myself out of this quarrel wherein the principal parties do so little for themelves.' And his scepticism was more than justified by the emergence of what amounted to a second Jülich-Cleves crisis in 1614 when the two 'pretendant princes' fell out among themselves, and the commander of the joint Neuburg-Brandenburg garrision – the German Colonel Frederick Pithan, who was in Dutch service – subsequently decided to summon reinforcements. Suspecting a Dutch-Brandenburg conspiracy, Wolfgang William therefore seized control of Düsseldorf, causing Pithan to dismiss the Neuburgers from Jülich and, in doing so, confirm Wolfgang William's residing fears. To cap all, the Neuburg candidate then saw fit to convert to Catholicism and marry the daughter of Maximilian of Bavaria in an effort to win support from the Catholic League after John Sigismund's own conversion to Calvinism in 1613 with a view to enlisting the aid of the Netherlands and England. In consequence, by August 1614, 15,000 Spanish troops had arrived in the duchies at Wolfgang William's request, and after their capture of the important Rhine crossing at Wesen, the Dutch too mobilised.

On this occasion, however, the posturing of the two external parties amounted to no more than that. Exhausted by the war that had made them temporarily halt hostilities in 1609, neither had the stomach or means to renew hostilities for the time being, and another truce was quickly sealed at Xanten, which by 12 November, after English and French intervention, had become a full-blown treaty. To Brandenburg were allotted the predominantly Protestant duchies of Cleves, Mark and Ravensburg, and to Neuburg the mainly Catholic Jülich and Berg. But the Estates of each remained anxious to achieve overall unity and, to further blight the treaty's future prospects, both heirs retained their over-all claims. Nor were the two princes successful in securing the evacuation of Spanish and Dutch armies – notwithstanding the best efforts of James I during 1615 and 1616 – leaving the towns of Wesel and Jülich under foreign occupa-tion. As such, the Treaty of Xanten was never more than an act of expediency, and although a solution of a sorts had once again been cobbled together in the familiar fashion, the undeniable fact remained that the entire Jülich-Cleves dis-pute had not only revealed the hardening of the frontiers between the Protestant and Catholic camps, but, perhaps more worryingly still, their inextricable and potentially explosive connection to broader international tensions, which might, at the wrong moment, rock not only the Holy Roman Empire but all Europe.

For the moment, however, the cause of peace did at least appear to have received a filip of sorts from a rather more unexpected quarter in the shape of Melchior Klesl, Bishop of Vienna, who had become Imperial Chancellor after Emperor Matthias's election. Converting to Catholicism while a student at Vienna University, he had risen, as a result of Jesuit and Habsburg patronage and a silken tongue that was every bit as capable as his mind, to become Matthias's counsellor-in chief. And in doing so, he had established an equally firm reputation as a clerical wheeler-dealer no less familiar with the teachings of Machiavelli than the precepts of the four evangelists. Yet in spite of his reputation as a man of few fixed principles and even fewer friends, it was Klesl's pragmatism that now made him, arguably, the last best hope for peace, as he sought to arrest the drift towards confrontation by achieving a 'composition' of the contending religious factions, premised upon the dilution and transformation of both the Protestant Union and the Catholic League. For each alliance, as the bishop wisely appreciated, contained not only centrifugal forces, which might well be subtly exploited by skilful management, but also more moderate members who might easily be encouraged to co-operate with the right inducements. The first priorities were to revive the traditional Imperial alliance with Catholic Mainz and Lutheran Saxony, thus restoring an important bridge across the religious divide, and then to convert the League into a wider non-confessional body under Imperial presidency which would include the Lutherans and thereby isolate the Palatinate.

But even Klesl's best efforts were only partially successful, for in August 1613 representatives of the Union had walked out of the Diet at Regensburg immediately after it opened when it became clear that, while some judicial reforms might be granted, their main demands regarding the abolition of the *Reservatum Ecclesiasticum*, the restoration of independence to Donauwörth, and the recognition of the religious liberty of Aachen – where in 1612, after several years of agitation supported by the Union, a Catholic magistracy installed by Spanish troops in 1598 had been overthrown – would not be met. By 1614, to Klesl's satisfaction, the Duke of Neuburg had withdrawn from the Union, to be followed three years later by the Margrave of Brandenburg. And the bishop's initial impact on the League became more pronounced still, after he had secured Austria's admittance in 1613 and thereby prompted the withdrawal of Maximilian of Bavaria, who feared that this was indeed a prelude to the admittance of Lutherans. Yet even the dissolution of the League itself in 1617 was only accompanied by the formation of a new version in the same year, led once more by Maximilian of Bavaria at the head of the original members of 1609.

And in other areas, too, Klesl's early successes proved hollow. For if the Union had lost Neuburg and Brandenburg and been weakened by the comparative moderation of the cities that had come to dominate the Protestant agenda within the Empire, Christian of Anhalt had already strengthened it elsewhere, or so he believed, by alliances with England, the Netherlands and Sweden in 1613, and further understandings with Savoy and Venice – all the while expanding his grander strategy and, in the process, internationalising the scope of any future conflagration. Equally ominously, the Jülich-Cleves succession crisis had convinced him that no Habsburg emperor would hesitate to use the troops of his Spanish cousins within the Empire itself – a fact, he believed, that had been confirmed by General Ambrogio Spinola's Imperial commission to restore the Catholic magistracy to Aachen. As such, the election of a non-Habsburg emperor was essential, as Matthias's advanced years made his replacement imminent, and a Habsburg family compact to replace him with Archduke Ferdinand of Styria was duly discovered in 1617. Later commenting that he would rather countenance the election of a Turk or the Devil, Anhalt would have hoped ideally for the coronation of the Palatinate's own Frederick V – though the preponderance of Catholics within the electoral college made this impossible – and he was even prepared to offer support for the candidacy of Maximilian of Bavaria, who could not, however, be persuaded to consort with the Protestant enemy.

Yet with vexations came opportunity, too, and as Anhalt's options foundered on the one hand, so new openings appeared on the other – and not always in the most obvious of places. For where empires were concerned, and especially the Holy Roman with its familial links to Spain, the nexus of inter-connections and potential pressure points was virtually infinite. At a time of unprecedented discord and disarray, indeed, Habsburg pretensions to 'universality' made Habsburg rulers, in effect, universally vulnerable, and while Holy Roman Emperors remained, quite literally, the poor relations of their Spanish cousins, family feeling and political interest could not only be relied upon to align the policies of Madrid and Vienna in most, if not all, questions touching European affairs, but just as easily guarantee that any conflict within the Empire could swiftly become a major European convulsion. It was no coincidence, after all, that Anhalt's agents had been active in Venice since her great quarrel with the papacy in 1605-8 or that Savoy's war with Spain between 1613 and 1617 had prompted overtures for a broader anti-Habsburg alliance. And if recent events had exposed the weaknesses of the Protestant Union, its architect could at least take serious consolation from the collapse of its Catholic equivalent from similar internal discord, particularly when the forthcoming expiration of the Twelve Years Truce between Spain and the Dutch Republic in 1621 made a major European war effectively inevitable. As such, with the death of the aged, ailing and childless Emperor Matthias unlikely to be far off, Prince Christian of Anhalt could make hay whenever, however and wherever he chose, in places near or far, and in circumstances likely or largely unpredictable.

Certainly, the so-called 'Uzkok War', which began in 1615 when a Venetian army with substantial Dutch and English reinforcements laid siege to Archduke Ferdinand of Styria's city of Gradisca, was one of the more unforeseeable, indeed bizarre, episodes of the early seventeenth century. Yet since Ferdinand of Styria found himself in desperate need of Spanish assistance at the very time that his own designs upon the Imperial throne were reaching fruition, and at a point where Spain's ruler, Philip III, was preparing to waive his own claims in return for the cession of Alsace, Tyrol and certain Imperial territories, the war's ramifications were considerable – not only for Spain and the Empire, but for Europe in general, as it became clear that a conflict of the most unlikely kind had the potential to escalate into a pan-continental crisis. The 'Uzkoks', after all, were merely – as their Serbian name confirmed – 'refugees' from the Balkans who had been offered asylum in Habsburg lands in return for naval service against the Turks in the Adriatic. But when they turned their attention on Christian shipping too, and the Dutch agreed in September 1616 to raise 3,000 men from the Dutch Republic in support of Venice, the fragile balance of forces in Europe was once more threatened.

As a flotilla of ten English and twelve Dutch warships set sail for the trouble spot, the possibilities for escalation were once again considerable. But this was not the limit of the resulting imbroglio, since no aid could now reach Ferdinand from Spanish Naples and no assistance was available from Spanish Milan either, as a result of the outbreak of another conflict: the so-called 'War of the Mantuan Succession', into which France now duly slithered by encouraging Savoy to renew hostilities with Spain, thus tying down Spanish forces. In consequence, a force of some 4,000 German Protestants, raised with the consent of the Protestant Union's leaders by Count Ernst von Mansfeld – a former officer in the Army of Flanders who had been taken prisoner at Jülich and subsequently offered himself to the Protestant Union when no one chose to ransom him – found itself fighting in association with some 10,000 French volunteers, with the result that only Spain could produce the necessary subsidies to prevent Ferdinand's surrender, albeit at a price. For a cash provision of some 1 million thalers also proved more than enough to secure the cession of Alsace and the Imperial enclaves of Finale Liguria and Piombino in Italy that Ferdinand had hitherto resisted, in return for Philip III's acceptance of his eventual succession as Holy Roman Emperor. Accordingly, in March 1617, Ferdinand and the Spanish ambassador to the Imperial court, Don Iñigo Vélez de Guevara, Count of Oñate, sealed the agreement, and indeed settled the 'Uzkok War', since the Venetians were now unwilling to continue a struggle of what was bound to be a long duration.

But if another crisis had been circumvented, it had not only served as a warning of far more dire things to come, but actually created further conditions to make the impending conflict all the more likely and all the more catastrophic when it finally arrived. For on the one hand, alliances favoring aggression had been either generated or reinforced, while the confidence of militant Protestants everywhere had been bolstered by the apparent willingness of both England and the Dutch Republic, and even Savoy and Venice, to co-operate so readily with their Protestant German allies. Equally, the decisive intervention of Spain on Ferdinand's behalf had eased the decades of mistrust and misunderstanding that had weakened relations between the two main houses of Habsburg. Henceforth, although Alsace was never eventually ceded as planned, the so-called 'Oñate Agreement' established a framework within which Vienna and Madrid could work in unison to secure their mutual interests both north and south of the Alps – and, in so doing, created further dangers of its own, of course. For not only did it appear to confirm the Palatinate's darkest fears, it also made events within the Holy Roman Empire all the more significant for Spain's rebellious Dutch enemies who were seeing themselves more and more clearly as champions not only of their own religious and nationalist cause but of representative, non-aristocratic government in general, in the face of an absolutist onslaught waged by outmoded imperial oppressors. With Spain and the Empire newly in harmony, therefore, the air was now loaded with talk of Catholic conspiracy on an international scale, and wars of liberation duly became something far more potent still: nothing less, in effect, than life-or-death struggles to determine the entire direction of Europe's political future.

Nor was this all. For Spain's new alignment with its Habsburg cousin entailed a geostrategic dimension that now made the unimpeded passage of Spanish troops across mainland Europe to the Empire and on to the Netherlands all the more critical, since the Twelve Years Truce had not ended Dutch attacks on Spain's overseas possessions. On the contrary, in 1615–16 a fleet of six large warships had sailed westabout to the Moluccas, raiding several Spanish colonies in America and destroying whatever Spanish and Portuguese vessels crossed their path. Hardly less provocatively, the Dutch East India Company had also established forts as far afield as the coast of Guyana, the Hudson river and the

Gold Coast, leaving their enemies convinced that a renewal of war at the earliest possible opportunity was the only possible solution. As early as December 1616, therefore, the Spanish Council of State duly resolved that if Dutch troops were sent to assist the Duke of Savoy, the resumption of war would be unavoidable. And although this eventuality had not materialised, by March 1618 the same internal debate was still raging over whether or not to renew the truce when it expired three years later. Neither was the dialogue encouraging, for, as Don Carlos Coloma, a senior commander of the Army of Flanders, was to declare: 'If the truce is continued, we shall condemn ourselves to suffer at once all the evils of peace and all the dangers of war.'

More than ever, then, the crucial question for Spain was how to deliver troops across land – where they would be unimpeded by Dutch naval might – from Spanish Lombardy to both the Low Countries and, if needed, to Alsace and the Tyrol. The western mountain passes, on the one hand, were controlled by the hostile Duke of Savoy, the central ones by the neutral but powerful Swiss cantons, while the most convenient Alpine crossings of all for Spanish access to Austria and northern Europe were actually controlled by the Protestant Grisons or 'Grey Leagues' – apart, that is, from the Catholic corridor of the Valtelline which had revolted against its Protestant masters in both 1572 and 1607, and stood ready to raise the rebel standard once again at the slightest prompting. Stretching east and west, northwards from Lake Como, and running directly to the Inn river, the Valtelline – or Adda Valley – was therefore an area of critical logistical importance to Spain and of critical strategic significance, too, to both France and Venice, who, in accordance with the power-political realities of the day had no hesitation in supporting the dominance there of the Grey Leagues – with the result that the valley became one more likely flashpoint in a potential wildfire that had been smouldering menacingly since 1603, after the Spanish constructed a major redoubt, the so-called 'Fuentes Fort', at the valley's entrance. When further demonstrations by the Valtelliners resulted in savage repression on behalf of their Protestant rulers in 1618, moreover, refugees fleeing to Innsbruck and Milan were quick to appeal to both branches of the Habsburg family for intervention.

Already, then, the Holy Roman Empire's many structural deficiencies had become tightly enmeshed with developments and processes far beyond the unravelling of any single power, as a crisis of Imperial leadership coincided fatefully with a crisis of empires and what would ultimately prove to be the defining crisis of a continent. As Rudolf II dabbled in his laboratories, indeed, an altogether more powerful alchemy had been unfolding around him, and as his nondescript successor subsequently sat feckless and uncomprehending upon the

Imperial throne, unable to see beyond the self-gratification that had carried him there, the forces of dissolution had continued to gather pace. Like the collapse of any rotting structure, the process was a gradual one. And for a while, arguably, as the Empire's tottering edifice continued to creek and groan, the inactivity of its rulers had actually assisted its temporary survival. But if the absence of sudden movements or external shocks might, for a fleeting period, sustain the whole decrepit framework against the odds, the arrival of an impetuous new occupant intent upon sweeping alteration was certain to prove fatal, as events would now prove.

For in the wake of the Oñate Agreement, the Imperial heir apparent, Ferdinand of Styria, had joined Emperor Matthias in Vienna and travelled to Dresden to see John George of Saxony 'to discuss something of importance concerning the empire'. Matthias, in fact, had only recently recovered from an illness that had placed him in fear of his life, and it was this, coupled to Spanish support for Ferdinand, and Klesl's desire to withdraw from the political fray, that probably prepared him for passive acceptance of what now followed, as a Habsburg cavalcade including both himself and Ferdinand duly proceeded to Prague and a fateful meeting with the Bohemian Estates that had been carefully orchestrated by Zdenko Adalbert Popel von Lobkowitz, the Bohemian chancellor and leader of the aptly nicknamed *facción española*. Beforehand, at a private meeting of the nobility, the chancellor had not only pretended that Ferdinand's nomination as Matthias's successor to the Bohemian crown was a matter of course, but persuaded his audience that opposition to the hereditary candidate would, on the one hand, be offensive, and, more importantly still, counter-productive, since the Letter of Majesty, so highly prized by all, was to be otherwise unconditionally guaranteed. And while Count Heinrich Schlick, the most exalted Protestant in the company, put no faith in Lobkowitz's assurances, he too had little choice but to fall in with the plan, since there was such confusion in any case about the procedure for choosing a new monarch that no agreed rival emerged to challenge him.

In the event, only Count Jindřich Matyáš Thurn demurred, contending that it was the Estates' prerogative to elect the king and not merely to ratify him. But he too was cannily outmanouevred by Lobkowitz's ploy of arranging the vote on 5 June 1617 to take place in order of seniority, thus ensuring that those whose support he had already elicited would be first to voice their decision. In consequence, Thurn and his colleagues, who had been anticipating a lively debate, were left to sit in horrified silence as the greatest Bohemian nobles, including Schlick, declared their support for Ferdinand, forcing the rest to follow suit tamely and accept the appointment of Ferdinand as 'king designate'. Schlick, in fact, nursed his misgivings silently, while Thurn duly opted to bide his time, knowing full well that the real reckoning was still at hand. For within a fortnight, the coronation had been accomplished and Bohemia's new king duly installed – complete with an ostensible guarantee of the religious rights enshrined in Rudolf II's original Letter of Majesty that he had no intention of maintaining.

Under the circumstances, it represented the smoothest possible passage to what would prove to be the long overdue trigger for war without limit. Even before Lobkowitz had effectively railroaded them into acceptance, the Bohemian Estates had in fact feared that a Catholic king of Ferdinand's inclination would be likely to attempt the imposition of absolutism at the expense of their political and religious liberties. But while Lutherans favoured the candidacy of the Duke of Saxony, and Calvinists the nomination of the Elector Palatine, they were unable to offer an effective alternative, and in the period that followed, their worst misgivings were rapidly realised. For of the ten Deputies now appointed to oversee the kingdom on Ferdinand's behalf, seven were staunchly Catholic, and an unabashed programme of religious repression was soon underway, involving, first of all, a far-ranging inquiry into the origins of the foundations upon which church livings depended, with a view to returning them to Catholic clergy under the pretext of respecting the initial donor's wishes. At the same time, all Protestant literature was swiftly subjected to the censorship of the royal chancellery, whereas previously it had been authorised solely by the so-called *Defensores* placed in post by the Letter of Majesty. And for Count Thurn, in particular, there was a further personal sting in the tail, as a result of his initial objection to Ferdinand's election. For, as Bargrave of Kárluv-Týn, he had enjoyed the most lucrative administrative post in the kingdom, but now found himself appointed to the far less profitable role of Chief Justice.

Yet Bohemia was not Bavaria, and neither was Ferdinand endowed with the skills or resources that had enabled Bavaria's duke to renege on similar promises earlier. Prior to the arrival of Ferdinand's heavy hand, indeed, Bohemia had been that rarest of all things in Europe, a religiously tolerant society. More significantly still, it was also an old state, proud of its distinctive language and traditions, and one that had long been a haven for political troublemakers and religious nonconformists of various hues – a tendency that had famously exploded in the early fifteenth century when supporters of the religious reformer Jan Hus engaged in a series of wars for religious liberty after his execution. Rejecting Church authority, 'Hussites' also believed that the laity should receive the Eucharist *sub utraque specie* – that is 'in both kinds', involving not only the bread but the wine, too. And 'Utraquists' of the more moderate Hussite variety had indeed been granted this concession eventually by a Catholic Church and emperor incapable of imposing uniformity by force. But the resulting accommodation had never been accepted by radicals, who remained resolutely opposed to any compromise with Catholicism and eventually fell under the influence of either Martin Luther or, more usually, Jean Calvin, whose ideas resembled Hus's on many points.

As a result, by 1618 the majority of Bohemians had embraced Protestantism or Protestant-like ideas, and doctrinaire Catholicism of the kind advocated so fervently by the incoming King Ferdinand had become a distinctly minority preference both in Bohemia and in the surrounding territories of Silesia, Lusatia and Moravia, which were subsumed under the Bohemian crown. Worse still, the task facing the new ruler was not only religious but political too, since Bohemia's Estates exhibited a long-standing independence of spirit, which had constantly sought to strengthen local autonomy and weaken the influence of the elected monarch. Since their incorporation into the Empire in 1526, Bohemia, Moravia, Silesia and Lusatia had all been governed from Prague by a group of Catholic magnates – the so-called *facción española* – whose administration was in permanent conflict with the interests of the resolutely independent but impoverished lesser nobility who remained jealous of their ancient rights of electing the king and dominating their peasants. And nor had the court party in Prague attempted to arrest a discernible economic slowdown in the kingdom's towns, or alleviate the resulting disillusionment of urban workers and agricultural tenants, with the result that all classes had, in effect, become united in the cherished memory of their Hussite past and the lost glory once enjoyed during their independence under the native king George Podiebrad who had died in 1471.

In the meantime, moreover, the power struggle within the Habsburg family from around 1605 onwards had also been exploited by the Bohemian nobles, who set out to form 'confederations' of the Estates of Austria, Bohemia, Moravia, Hungary and Silesia, and succeeded in extracting important concessions from Matthias in return for his coronation, which for a short period had virtually transformed these territories into aristocratic republics under his nominal presidency. In June 1615, indeed, there had been an unsuccessful attempt by the Bohemian Estates to use a general Diet in Prague, encompassing the fellow Estates of all the Habsburg dominions, to establish an independent organisation – with a common army – which, although unsuccessful, had further confirmed Bohemia's resistance to centralised control and the uniformity that went with it. In the event, the Hungarian Estates had not sent representatives, and the Austrian representatives, who were also concerned about the dangers of Habsburg absolutism, had been offended by Bohemian and Moravian demands that the German language be completely excluded from use in Diets, courts and schools. Indeed, to Bohemia's great indignation, the Prague meeting had actually resulted in two remarkable financial concessions to the emperor after his flat refusal to compromise: the Estates' agreement to waive their right of taxation for five years and their consent to take over a considerable proportion of royal debt.

But the defeat of Bohemian radicalism on this particular occasion was less significant than what it promised to represent, if fanned by the kind of political insensitivity now exhibited by the kingdom's new ruler. For Bohemia, too, was exhibiting clear signs of a clash of political cultures, not dissimilar to that involving Spain and the United Provinces, and it was no mere coincidence when Klesl, who had become a cardinal in 1615, warned that Bohemia 'may become a Dutch government'. For while, in Bohemia's case, the primary agents of change were the feudal nobility rather than the gentry and middle classes intent upon commercial expansion, the priority for Bohemians and Dutch alike was the protection and indeed development of their constitutional prerogatives against the forces of centralisation and uniformity. In both cases, too, as contemporaries were making clear, constitutionalism was fuelled not only by religion and a keen consciousness of the wider European struggle, but by nationalism of the most virulent kind. 'Like a caterpillar in a cabbage, a serpent in the breast, a rat in the granary, a goat in the garden, so in Bohemia the German steals, cheats and deceives,' one Bohemian patriot defiantly declared at this time. And in the meantime, while all Bohemia simmered, Christian of Anhalt continued to strike at the root of Habsburg power by strengthening contacts between Heidelberg and the Bohemian Estates and sending two of his most trusted lieutenants – Ludwig Camerarius and Christoph von Dohna – to Prague during the winter of 1616–17.

As such, the passive acceptance of Ferdinand's election – achieved as it was by nothing more substantial than an ingenious act of political sleight-of-hand on Chancellor Lobkowitz's part – had fooled no one but him, it seems. For as early as 1611, the moderate Moravian leader Karl Žerotin was convinced that there were 'more malcontents in Prague now than years ago', and even Lobkowitz had achieved only Ferdinand's 'acceptance' as opposed to his election. In reality, the overall consensus continued to lie with Schlick and Thurn, making subtlety and moderation crucial, and careful management of Bohemia's traditions and aspirations more important than ever for any prospective ruler, since counter-reformation zeal and all the provocation it entailed was sure to be doubly provocative in Bohemia's case, given its religious history. Moreover, for the best part of twenty years, since Rudolf's decision to relocate to Prague, Bohemia had seen itself as an indispensable component of the Empire, so that Matthias's decision to quit the capital on Christmas Day 1617 – following an astrological forecast of misfortune were he to remain – had already assumed a symbolic significance no less important than its practical ramifications, since it not only entailed a loss of honour for the city, but dangerous isolation, as news of the outside world became rarer after the departure of the emperor's councillors and the foreign ambassadors that attended him, and outsiders found themselves increasingly cut off from a kingdom whose new monarch had left so quickly, entrusting the execution of its affairs largely to the ten regents he had appointed in his place.

Although these representatives were committed to acting under close instructions from Ferdinand, furthermore, their actions still showed no signs of moderation. On the contrary, they continued their attack upon the use of Catholic endowments for the payment of Protestant ministers, and were soon prohibiting the admission of non-Catholics to civil office. Even more provocatively, they ordered Protestant worship to stop entirely in two towns – Broumov (Braunau) and Hroby (Klostergrab) – and when the leaders of the latter were imprisoned in one of the towers of the Hradčany for daring to dispute the destruction of their little town's Lutheran church, which had been in the middle of construction, the outrage reached boiling point. 'Things were now swiftly coming to the pass,' wrote Polyxena Lobkowitz, the Chancellor's wife, 'where either the Papists would settle their score with the Lutherans, or the Protestants with the Papists.' And surely enough the latter outcome became inevitable when the *Defensores* appointed by the Letter of Majesty duly decided to convoke a meeting of the Bohemian Estates on 5 March 1618 to request a change of policy from the emperor, who flatly refused and vainly commanded the delegates to disperse. For by 21 May they were in session once again, and ordered as before to abandon their discussions – this time after only two days, and, more fatefully still, on the order of what was suspected to be the council of regents, who had thereby acted wholly unconstitutionally.

One day earlier, the narrow twisting streets of Prague's centre had begun to mill with angry people, and in a secret meeting at the house of Jan Smiřický, one of the *Defensores*, the decision was finally taken to bring the Estates into open revolt and make the breach irreparable by the judicial murder of the most hated regents. Accordingly, at around 8.30 a.m. on 23 May a procession of 100 or so delegates, some armed and some mounted, marched upon the Hradčany, cheered on by a noisy crowd, to deliver a letter containing their grievances. Received at first in the Castle Chancery, they then processed to the upper floor and barged into the council chamber itself – 'unannounced, quite cheekily and causing great importunity' – where four of the regents were present, along with Philipp Fabricius, a secretary. Two in particular, moreover, became the object of especially intense hostility: Vilém Slavata, a 46-year-old aristocrat who now headed the Bohemian treasury and had become one of the richest men in the kingdom as a result of his marriage to the heiress Lucia Ottilia; and Jaroslav Borita von Martinitz, his no less distinguished and equally loathed colleague. Both had opposed the Letter of Majesty from its inception and both now attempted a faltering defence of their recent decisions as rebukes and accusations rang out from beyond the doors of the room, which had been deliberately left open for the overflowing delegates.

Thurn, it seems, was orchestrator of the episode, though the deputation's spokesman was Defensor Rischany, who finally asked those present whether Slavata and Martinitz should be found guilty of high treason. And when the cry went up that they should not only be condemned but thrown at once from the very window before which they sat, the fate of the two regents was sealed. Martinitz first and Slavata swiftly afterwards were both hurled forth, the latter having added to the outrage of his executioners by first requesting a confessor and then proceeding to cry out 'Jesu Maria!' as he fell. 'We'll see if his Mary can help him,' cried one perpetrator, sparing no sentiment – only to exclaim upon leaning from the window, 'By God, she really has,' as Martinitz hobbled away intact from the bottom of the empty moat below. Whether his descent of some 45 feet or so had indeed been eased by angels as Catholic propagandists would claim remains doubtful. More likely, perhaps, is the explanation of the rebels who suggested that he, like the other victims who followed, had been saved by a soft landing in a heap of dung. But, whatever the cause, Martinitz was indeed spared, as was Slavata, who had clung on tenaciously to the window ledge until dislodged by a blow across his fingers from the hilt of a sword. And the same was true even for secretary Fabricius, who had also found himself rudely ejected, notwithstanding the fact that no grievance had been raised against him.

Martinitz's only significant injury, indeed, was caused by his own sword – which his attackers had neglected to unbuckle – and not in the fall itself but as he slithered down the slope to help Slavata who had fallen at the very bottom. Shots rang out from the window above, yet in spite of all, the pair were eventually successful in reaching the nearby home of Chancellor Lobkowitz, whose wife bolted the door after them and persuaded two pursuers to go away. Nor, it seems, did Polyxena Lobkowitz's charity end there, for the next day Martinitz was duly spirited away to Bavaria, while Slavata was kept in hiding and his injuries tended. Fabricius, too, was safely dispatched to Vienna – to be ennobled in 1623 as *Freiherr von Hohenfall*, Lord of the High Jump, since he alone of the three had remained on his feet upon landing. Rushing forth to the waiting emperor and his would-be successor Ferdinand, Fabricius knew, no doubt, the ramifications of the news he bore. For the 'Defenestration of Prague' represented not only the final act of defiance to the House of Habsburg in Austria, but a direct opportunity, too, for those more adventurous elements in Spain wishing to hijack the initiative and launch a reckoning of their own.

Chief among these was Count Oñate himself. For, with Matthias too old and ill to act and Ferdinand without authority to respond independently, the ambassador embarked upon a series of remarkably high-handed and fateful acts, which not only strengthened the will of the Habsburgs to fight, but also made that will effective, by providing the money, men and arms necessary for the task. Ordering the Spanish troops still stationed on the Isonzo river after the conflict with Venice to proceed to Vienna, Oñate likewise cajoled Matthias into persuading Archduke Albert, Governor of the Netherlands, to release one of the best commanders in the Army of Flanders, Count Charles Bucquoy, who had made his name at the Battle of Nieuport and Siege of Ostend. But this was not all, as further troops were raised by appeals to the viceroys in Milan and Naples, and a fortune was raised on Oñate's own account – to such good effect, indeed, that by the end of August 1618, when Bucquoy arrived to take up command, almost 12,000 men had been mustered, leaving the ambassador himself in debt to the tune of some 130,000 florins.

Yet while Oñate rubbed his hands and emptied his pockets, news of the defenestration and the ambassador's vigorous responses had been met with consternation by others in his homeland. 'The stirs in Bohemia were speedily advertised hither,' reported Sir Francis Cottington from Madrid to his government in London, 'and with it they are not a little troubled, as they already groan under the excessive charges and expense which they are daily at for the subsistence of those princes of Austria and especially this king of Bohemia.' The Duke of Lerma, moreover, whose haughtiness as the king's *privado* or favourite had led enemies to claim that he wished to eclipse his own master, wanted, in fact, to countermand Oñate's arrangements altogether, until Balthasar de Zuñiga's experience of Imperial affairs persuaded him both of the importance of denying Bohemia to the potential enemies of Spain, and of the advantages to be derived from the recent agreement with Ferdinand. For the Holy Roman Emperor was not only lord of numerous fiefs in Italy, but had rights throughout the Rhineland and still currently controlled Alsace and the Tyrolean passes – all of which were so crucial for Spanish access to the Netherlands and security against French interference. Nor, indeed, were Zuñiga's fears about the impact of the Bohemian coup upon Spain's other enemies to prove any less compelling ultimately. For within two months the Protestant party in the Valtelline had murdered their Catholic enemies, whom they accused of 'Hispanismus', and seized control of the pass, cutting off Milan from the Tyrol at the same time that Savoy and Venice concluded a formal alliance against future aggression.

But the debate in Madrid remained strenuous, since the Spanish empire, like its Holy Roman equivalent, was also in a state of looming crisis, particularly regarding money, after the extravagant enterprises of Philip II's later years, leading to the notorious bankruptcy of 1596, had involved the crown in such heavy debts that the government's regular income was currently not even sufficient to meet the interest. According to an inquiry of October 1598, indeed, the annual deficit had then stood at 1,600,000 ducats, and the situation had not changed appreciably in the interim. On the contrary, the collapse of urban industries in Castile had actually left her markets wide open to foreign manufactures, and since 1597 Spanish merchants had begun to appreciate for the first time that the American market was overstocked. Although the record year for Seville's trade with America was 1608, and the trade figures fluctuated around a high level until 1620, the whole pattern of Spain's commerce was in fact changing in the reign of Philip III to the serious detriment of the national economy, as Mexico developed its own products, and Peru its agriculture. As a result, there would henceforth be less demand not only for Spanish cloth, but for the wine, oil and flour which had bulked so large in the trans-Atlantic shipments of the previous century. More worryingly still, the ships now setting out from Seville were in any case carrying an increasingly large proportion of foreign products – so large, in fact, that Sancho de Montada, writing in 1619, was convinced that nine-tenths of the American trade was by this point in foreign hands.

With a declining population and diminished supplies of American silver into the bargain, it was little surprise, therefore, that some councillors of a more prudent disposition, like Count Salazar, should have balked at any prospect of further military involvements and warned that 'the royal finances cannot provide such sums at the present time'. In direct contrast to the Dutch Republic which opposed it, moreover, Spain had become socially moribund – a society in stasis, ruled by a Church and nobility that were, if anything, more powerful at the start of the seventeenth century than they had been in the fifteenth. Already in possession of some 95 per cent of the soil of Castile at the start of the sixteenth century, they had continued to accumulate lands: the Church by acquisition of lands in mortmain, the great nobles by establishing *mayorzagos* (entails) and building up vast entailed states. And, in the meantime, the remnants of a vigorous urban class that had once existed in towns like Burgos and Medina del Campo had finally disappeared, to be replaced by well-established communities of foreign merchants who dominated the commercial life that serviced, for the time being at least, the needs of a complacent and stultifying élite. In the words of González de Cellerigo, writing in 1600:

Our condition is one in which there are the rich who loll at ease or poor who beg, and we lack people of the middle sort, whom neither wealth nor poverty prevents from pursuing the rightful kind of business enjoined by Natural Law.

But while Cellerigo called for lower taxation, reforms of the court and swollen bureaucracy, and special privileges and tax concessions for labourers and married men, so that the countryside could be repopulated and the fields brought back to cultivation, both Church and aristocracy remained tied to the continued propagation of their traditional ideals, martial and crusading. 'The natives of these kingdoms, each in his own sphere and station, desire honour and estimation above everything else,' a minister of the crown would write in 1641, and it was these same two intoxicants that had finally won the day in Madrid's corridors of power twenty-three years earlier. The king, as his father had realised, was a nonentity incapable of government in his own right, devoid of natural talent and energy, and, like his imperial cousin in Prague, more cause than cure of the crisis evolving around him. 'God, who has given me so many kingdoms to govern,' reflected Philip II, 'has not given me a son fit to govern them.' And as Spain thereby slithered into its own 'crisis of emperors', so all-important affairs of state had become entrusted by turns to an indolent Valencian aristocrat, the Marqués de Denia, later created Duke of Lerma, who, throughout his twenty years of personal rule, remained a prisoner in a gilded cage, the pawn of a small group of Castlian and Andalusian magnates.

Most tragically of all, however, it was this same clique, tied to the traditional ideals of their class, that in controlling Lerma, also assisted the king on his course to one of the most critical wagers in the history of European conflict. In a society where fiscal oppression, poor harvests or bad trade could turn the artisan or peasant of today into the pauper of tomorrow, it was only fitting perhaps that gambling had become an incorrigible Spanish addiction. The so-called *picaro*, living on his wits, constantly on the move, defeated one day, triumphant the next – always looking for the miracle to be had from the single spin of a dice – was, in fact, already a national stereotype. But now, with supreme irony, he was about to become a fitting symbol of Philip III's own government, as the king prepared to risk all in the old familiar way. For while those like Don Fernando Carillo deemed peace an 'indispensable measure because of the shortage of money', their monarch considered the situation 'so urgent that the council must find a way', regardless of the peril, to risk the abyss. 'Germany,' declared Philip, 'simply cannot be lost!'

4

'FATAL CONFLAGRATION'

The people have to abandon their own goods along with many supplies. Some simply run away, forced to abandon wife and child. The troops seize children from the breast, murdering them unjustly, and their parents likewise. They murder them terrifyingly, causing great misery and lamentations. Some hope to hide themselves under the hay or straw, in sheds and in barns, and they stay lying there and starving and finally even being burned.

A resident of western Bohemia, *Erschreckliche und erbärmliche Zeitung aus Böhmen* (1621)

'If it be true that the Bohemians intend to depose Ferdinand and choose another king,' commented the Archbishop of Cologne, 'we may expect a war of twenty, thirty or forty years; for Spain and the House of Austria will stake all they hold in this world sooner than relinquish that kingdom.' But as summer made way for autumn in 1618 and the initial shock of events in Prague turned into a grim appreciation of all that lay in store, the situation still gave hope of a kind, or so some believed, for a less protracted conflict. In the wake of the defenestration, the Bohemian Estates had elected thirty-six Directors to replace Ferdinand's hated regents, and appointed Count Thurn commander-in-chief of a new citizen militia that easily defeated the few surrounding towns remaining loyal to the old order. Born in 1567 to the Count of Linz and his second wife Barbara Schlick, daughter of the Count of Bassano, Thurn had travelled widely – to Istanbul, Syria, Egypt and Jerusalem – during service in the Imperial Habsburg embassy as a young man, and from 1592 had served in the Imperial army against the Turks, rising to the rank of colonel before eventually attaining the rank of War Councillor. By marriage, he had also acquired considerable estates in Croatian Krajina among other places and purchased the lordship of Veliš manor in 1605, which brought him membership of the Bohemian Estates and subsequent promotion to the rank of Marshal of the Nobility. As such, he was a figure of considerable substance and his stalwart defence of Protestantism and Bohemian rights had won him the residing confidence of the supporters he now led.

But like the enemies he confronted, Thurn was faced with empty coffers, and further troubled by the knowledge that his own citizen army was largely untried for the daunting task ahead. Comprised of every fifth townsman and every tenth peasant, it would be pitched against battle-hardened but well-rested veterans from wars with Savoy and the Netherlands, and while several of Thurn's fellow Directors had pledged their estates to pay for their own detachments, there was not enough money available to pay for the remainder. In consequence, heavy taxes and high loans were unavoidable, and as the first spoliations of Church property began, so numerous Catholics fled for refuge – though not to Austria, which they considered to be in as dangerous a state as Bohemia, but to Bavaria. Jesuits were expelled, previous attempts at re-Catholicisation abandoned and a justification of Bohemia's actions duly published in the form of an *Apology* intended to gain the sympathy of Protestant princes in Europe at large. Emphasising the misdeeds of 'evil and turbulent people' around the king – and especially the influence of the Jesuits 'whose impetuses, writings and endeavours have always been aimed primarily toward fraudulently subjugating not only His Majesty, but also all Protestant residents and estates of this entire kingdom under the lordship of the Roman See' – the document made explicit reference to the papacy as 'a foreign authority', while carefully avoiding all mention of Ferdinand himself, in an effort to present its authors' actions as defensive rather than rebellious. Yet many Bohemians were still inclined initially to hold aloof or favour some form of accommodation with Matthias, while the important cities of Budweiss and Pilsen declared outright against the Directors, and Moravia, though claiming to remain neutral, allowed free passage to Bucquoy's invading army.

Even so, the summer had brought its share of consolation, too, for Bohemia's defenders. For while Spain's decisive stance had encouraged Germany's Catholic princes to sink their differences and reactivate their League under the sole direction of Maximilian of Bavaria, the wars over the Uzkoks and Mantua, which were drawing to a close at the time of the defenestration, had already created important links between the anti-Habsburg powers, which were now swiftly reinforced. And although Christian of Anhalt and Frederick V had been as surprised as any by events in Bohemia, they too were suitably buoyed by new developments. For in August, Frederick gratefully accepted the services of a regiment raised initially for the Duke of Savoy by Ernst von Mansfeld, and as Mansfeld's 2,000-strong force made its way to Bohemia – largely paid for by Savoy's ruler who also allowed credit for the operation to go to the Palatinate – there had been further good news when, in June, the Bohemian Estates wrote to the Protestant Union, requesting full membership and hinting that the reward for military assistance might possibly be the election of Frederick as their king in place of Ferdinand.

The Bohemians, it is true, had also made similar hints to Charles Emmanuel of Savoy, Bethlen Gábor of Transylvania and the Duke of Saxony, and the Bohemians' duplicity had been gleefully exposed by the Habsburgs who seem to have intercepted virtually every letter leaving Prague for a foreign destination. But for a time, even gross indiscretion and deceitfulness could not temper either the energies or, indeed, the overall optimism of Habsburg absolutism's enemies, as the Estates of Lusatia, Silesia and even Upper Austria expressed support for the rebels, and in September, with the approach of winter, Bucquoy's forces withdrew to quarters in eastern Bohemia after penetrating as far as Čáslav. Only Hungary, in fact, stood aloof, though the forces of Bethlen Gábor could be relied upon to overcome loyalist elements there, and in September 1618, too, there was further encouragement from Mansfeld who succeeded in capturing the stronghold of Pilsen. With the Spanish invader temporarily neutralised, and with offers of military and financial assistance growing, there was consequently good reason for both Thurn and his cohort of Protestant allies to feel at least cautiously optimistic for the year ahead.

And 1619 did, indeed, initially bring its share of good tidings. For on 20 March, Emperor Matthias died and his successor was not only rejected by Bohemia, but by the Estates of both Upper and Lower Austria and Moravia, too. 'Now,' proclaimed Christian of Anhalt, 'we have in our hands the means of overturning the world,' and it was easy enough to see why the euphoria in Prague was, if anything, exceeded by the jubilation in Heidelberg. For by May, Thurn had exploited Bucquoy's temporary withdrawal to advance for a short time as far as Vienna itself, even bombarding the emperor's very own residence, before a cavalry regiment from Flanders under Henri Duval Dampierre charged through Thurn's camp, entered the city and burst into the Hofburg. Anhalt, moreover, had not only persuaded the Duke of Savoy to increase his financial support after a visit to Turin, but was further encouraged by talk between the Dutch and Venetian republics of a mutual defence pact against Spain. From now on, in Anhalt's fevered imagination, all was possible: the Dutch, the English and the Protestant Huguenots of France were to supply men and money for the cause; Savoy and Venice would block the Alpine routes; Žerotin in Moravia and Tschernembl in Austria would lead their Estates to unite with Bohemia in rebellion against the Habsburgs; and Frederick V, Elector Palatine, would not only become King of Bohemia but, in this capacity, ensure the election of a Protestant emperor.

It was a heady mix of fantasies, fuelled in part by a stream of Rosicrucian pamphlets prophesying the downfall of Antichrist in 1620. But, like most delusions of the kind, Anhalt's hopes were soon foundering on a reef of hard political realities. He had encouraged his king to win the support of James I, to whose daughter Elizabeth he had been married in 1616, but the father-in-law was still no more inclined to commit to hard military action than he had been then. On the contrary, little courage, less money, a genuine attachment to Spain and a deep-seated horror of rebellion in any shape or form made him absolutely proof against Frederick's artful appeal that 'these Bohemian Estates should not be oppressed nor despoiled of their liberty and the exercise of their religion'. 'There are some of the princes in Germany,' James told his son-in-law's ambassador, 'who wish for war in order that they may aggrandise themselves. Your master is young and I am old. Let him follow my example.'

And as the King of England simultaneously pontificated and prevaricated, the Dutch response to the news of Matthias's death was hardly less guarded. The implications of an increase in Habsburg power in Europe were palpable enough, but their reaction was altogether less impassioned and clear-cut than Philip III's. The Dutch States-General declared to the Protestant Union that 'the Bohemian war will decide the fate of all of us, especially yours since you are the neighbours of the Bohemians.' But it was the subsequent half of the message that served as the most telling indication of the limits of Dutch commitment at this stage. 'For the present,' the message continued, 'we shall seek out all ways of bringing you help ... though we have many difficulties to face.' Those difficulties included, amongst other things, the King of England who, instead of providing a lead to the Protestant cause, was continuing to force a serious quarrel upon the Dutch over the North Sea herring fisheries. But most important of all was the clear and present danger of an overwhelming assault on Bohemia that neither Thurn's will, Anhalt's bravado nor the Protestant Union's flimsy show of arms could do anything to resist.

Anxiously holding the front line in Flanders as the Twelve Years Truce began to near its end, Ambrogio Spinola, commander-in-chief of the Spanish forces, had encapsulated his own predicament perfectly before daring to reduce his own garrisons in the Netherlands for even more urgent service, as he deemed it, against the Bohemian rebels:

If we do not do so [he advised his king], it is quite possible that the House of
Austria may be turned out of Germany bag and baggage. If the Protestants
succeed in doing this they will then join the Dutch in an attack upon these
provinces, not only as a return for the help which they are getting from them,
but because they will imagine that whilst your Majesty's forces are here, they
will not be left undisturbed in the enjoyment of their possessions. If all the
German and Dutch Protestants were to unite in attacking us after a victory in
Germany it would be hopeless for us to attempt to resist them.

And those very successes that had initially stirred Christian of Anhalt's optimism to such dizzy heights were also at long last bringing the 'House of
Austria' itself to the brink of action. For with Lusatia and Silesia, led by the
Margrave of Jägerndorf, now, like Moravia, declaring for the rebels, and with
the Hungarian nobility, under Bethlen Gábor, finally in open revolt, Ferdinand
had been able to muster enough support by June 1619 for a military campaign that was no longer avoidable. On 10 June, after appeals for men from
the Spanish Netherlands, Lorraine, Italy and Croatia, and with the aid of
further subsidies from Spain and the papacy, Bucquoy had routed Mansfeld
and his regiment at Záblatí in southern Bohemia, cutting off communications
between Prague and Thurn's army around Vienna, and bringing the siege
to an end almost immediately. Now at the head of an Imperial army numbering some 30,000 men after further reinforcements from Tuscany, Spanish
Lombardy and the Spanish Netherlands, he therefore eagerly awaited further
orders, which were not long in coming.

  For just one month later, Ferdinand was not only treated by the Archbishop of
Salzburg to a spectacular military display and waterfolly, as well as a performance
of Peri's *Orfeo*, but most important of all, a loan of 40,000 thalers. And on 31 July,
by a triumph of common interests over local differences, representatives from
Bohemia and its associated kingdoms of Lusatia, Silesia and Moravia duly met
to inaugurate a new constitution, a *Confederatio Bohemica*, inspired in part by that
of the Dutch, which, while preserving the monarchy in elective form, subjected
the monarch to closer supervision and enshrined the privileges of Protestants as
fundamental laws of the kingdom. Shortly afterwards, they signed a special treaty
of alliance with the Estates of Upper and Lower Austria, and since all thoughts
of negotiation with Ferdinand had now been utterly abandoned, both crown
lands and those belonging to the Roman Catholic Church were also duly confiscated to pay for the Confederation's defence in what was now the impending
conflict. All that remained, indeed, was Ferdinand's formal deposition, which
duly occurred on 22 August.

Four days later, a successor was duly nominated by an overwhelming majority, though the choice in many respects was an odd one. There had been some support, in fact, for the rulers of Transylvania and Saxony, with Schlick in particular favouring the latter, who swiftly declined out of reluctance to be associated with rebellion. But the offer of the crown to Frederick V of the Palatinate was nevertheless made enthusiastically enough – albeit on the partial misapprehension that he was responsible for Mansfeld's dispatch to Pilsen and the greater error that he could bring with him not only the support of the Protestant Union, of which he was head, but also assistance from England and the Dutch Republic. Certainly, he was one of the best-connected princes in Protestant Europe, with links not only to England by his marriage, but also to the Netherlands through his mother, and to Sweden via his aunt Anna Maria, the first wife of Charles IX. Likewise, his religious credentials were impeccable, as his motto, 'Rule me, Lord, according to your word', clearly implied, though he was no fanatic. For while he avidly attended the Calvinist sermons that were such a feature of his court, his sympathies were admirably ecumenical in nature. Almost never referring to himself in his correspondence as 'Calvinist', he had indeed even taken the sacrament of the last supper with his future wife in England during Easter 1613, so that if any prince could now mobilise the kind of broad-based support presently required, it was almost certainly he.

Yet the belief that Frederick could successfully enlist widespread international support for his new Bohemian venture was largely without substance. At his eventual coronation, a Rosicrucian print boldly depicted him in the company of the four lions on whom he could supposedly rely: the two-tailed lion of Bohemia, the Palatinate lion, the lion of the Netherlands and the lion with drawn sword of Great Britain. But each in turn proved neither willing nor able to bear their teeth or flex their claws. The Dutch, it is true, showed greater enthusiasm than their English counterparts, knowing full well the ramifications of Frederick's likely defeat by Spain, for as Dudley Carleton, the English ambassador in The Hague put it: 'If the Spaniard should dispossess the new king and make a prey of that kingdom ... they expect here no greater courtesy than Polyphemus promised Ulysses – that he should be the last eaten of his companions.' Yet in England the appeals of the Archbishop of Canterbury that Parliament should be called upon to support Frederick continued to fall upon deaf ears, while those same problems that had made the Dutch more hesitant initially were still in evidence. More importantly still, there remained nagging questions about Frederick's own competence. For although part of his inheritance, the Upper Palatinate, bordered Bohemia, it was a part he had rarely visited, and he was neither wealthy nor experienced – so that there was an uncomfortable resonance in the comment of a Protestant observer, who later bemoaned the decision to elect 'a man who had never seen either a battle or a corpse … a prince who knew more about gardening than fighting.'

During August and September 1619, moreover, the young nominee found himself in a quandary, as his counsellors offered conflicting advice. For most of Frederick's native Palatine advisers, as well as his mother, the wisest course of action was rejection of Bohemia's offer – not least because 'acceptance would begin a general religious war'. But others, like Anhalt and Ludwig Camerarius, continued to maintain that since war remained inevitable upon the termination of the Twelve Years Truce between Spain and the Dutch Republic, and since there seemed clear-cut evidence on every front of a militant Catholic alliance to destroy Protestantism throughout Europe, it was better to act now – a conclusion being drawn increasingly in the Netherlands too, it seems, if the observations of Dudley Carleton are any guide. 'This business of Bohemia is like to put all Christendom in combustion,' commented the ambassador in September 1619, before noting the Dutch leaders' growing belief that 'since the revolution of the world is like to carry us out of this peaceable time, it is better to begin the change with advantage than with disadvantage.' For, if Bohemia were to be 'neglected and by consequence suppressed,' as the ambassador put it, 'the princes of the religion adjoining are like to bear the burden of a victorious army.' 'Where it will stay,' he added gloomily, 'God knows, being pushed on by the Jesuits and commanded by a new emperor, who flatters himself with prophecies of extirpating the reformed religion and restoring the Roman Church to the ancient greatness.'

By then, moreover, while Frederick V hesitated upon his own acceptance of the Bohemian throne, a new emperor had indeed been installed: on 28 August – only two days after Bohemia's Estates, unknown to the imperial electors, had made their own decision to opt for Frederick in place of Ferdinand. To say that the situation in Frankfurt, where the imperial election took place, was confused is something of an understatement. For although the Bohemian Estates intended that Frederick should be their king, thus providing him with a second and potentially crucial vote in the imperial election, in addition to the one he merited as Elector Palatine, he had still not accepted, and Bohemia's right to repudiate Ferdinand was not in any case generally recognised. Nor was there universal agreement among the rest of the seven electors concerning Ferdinand's suitability for the Imperial crown. The candidate most likely to succeed against him was, in fact, Maximilian of Bavaria, who, extraordinarily enough, was at one point the favoured candidate of the Palatinate in their desperation to block Ferdinand. But the duke refused to stand, and the Elector Palatine, who was

himself a potential candidate, could not expect the support of his fellow electors. Certainly, the archbishops of Cologne, Mainz and Trier were all likely to
support Ferdinand, while John George of Saxony, like his father before him,
disliked both Calvinism and rebellion, and John Sigismund of Brandenburg,
who had recently acquired East Prussia as a fief of the Polish crown, remained
all too aware that any hostile act against the Habsburgs would result in reprisals
from Sigismund of Poland.

Although the odds continued, therefore, to favour the Habsburg contender,
the Spanish and Austrian governments had continued to fret throughout the
summer, reading volumes into any hint of correspondence between the electors,
while Archduke Albert in the Netherlands, for fear that a Protestant might be
chosen, urged Philip III to increase the subsidies for Flanders to their wartime
footing of 300,000 ducats a month. Nor was the complexity of the situation
alleviated when John George, as a device to strengthen his bargaining power
with Ferdinand, proposed that no vote at all be taken until the Bohemian crisis
had been resolved. With deadlock looming and general consternation prevailing, it was no small irony therefore that a resolution was finally provided by the
ineptitude of the Palatinate itself. For when a further desperate proposal for the
candidacy of Maximilian of Bavaria was issued, despite his unyielding refusal to
stand, the Duke of Saxony finally lost patience and ordered his representative to
vote immediately for Ferdinand – as did the representatives of Brandenburg and
the three archbishops. Ferdinand, in his turn, voted for himself, while, with the
most supreme irony of all, the Palatinate's representative – having curiously failed
to challenge the emperor's right to vote as King of Bohemia – actually ended up
confounding his superiors in Heidelberg by voting for the Habsburg too.

By then, however, there was at least the consolation of knowing that Bethlen
Gábor, overcoming his chagrin at not being elected himself, had begun the conquest of Habsburg Hungary, capturing Kosiče on 5 September. And it was news,
perhaps, of Bethlen's installation as 'protector of Hungary' that finally swung the
balance in Frederick's own mind. For although he remained, as he confessed
to his wife, 'in agony about what to do', on 28 September he finally accepted
the Bohemian crown. The Palatinate had, after all, been for over sixty years a
declared enemy of the Habsburgs and of the Roman Catholic Church, and with
Anhalt at his shoulder Frederick was unlikely to forgo the blow against both that
was now on offer. To avert a major conflict and perhaps in some recognition of
the support that the Palatinate had lent to his nomination as candidate for the
Imperial crown, Maximilian of Bavaria had written to him in urgent but conciliatory tones, assuring him that there was no international Catholic conspiracy of
the kind imagined by Anhalt, and pointing out that his powers as king under the

new Bohemian constitution were hardly worth fighting for. Yet Frederick had been presented, as he saw it, with an opportunity that 'is a divine calling which I must not disobey' and on the last day of October he duly reached Prague.

Making a splendid entrance in the company of many Bohemian and German nobles, and cheered by the exuberant throngs that lined his way through the city and up to the Hradčany, there was little hint of what lay in store. Before his arrival, the Palatine coat of arms had replaced the Austrian two-headed eagle in every feature of the palace's heraldry, though the new king's coronation on 4 November deliberately adhered to all the traditional forms aside from a change in the entrance professional and the absence of a Catholic eucharistic service. As a bold affirmation of the new order, thirty-eight Bohemian clergymen presided, while Abraham Scultetus preached in High Dutch and Corvinus in Czech as a symbol of Bohemia's altered allegiances. But when Frederick received the traditional coronation blessing and accepted the holy unction upon his forehead, he did so without the slightest display of Calvinist demur. For while some of the ladies of Prague had already found Queen Elizabeth's *décolletage* mildly shocking, both she and her husband had nevertheless been able to win over a portion of Prague's Catholics by their 'amiable grace', and such goodwill could not be lightly compromised. Accordingly, upon leaving the cathedral, the royal couple threw coins to cheering crowds, as wine flowed in the streets, just as custom demanded. And even beforehand, all had been sanctified by good omens, for from the day of Frederick's arrival, or so it was said, no one in the entire capital had died.

'My only end is to serve God and His church,' Frederick had declared upon deciding to accept the throne. And for a time, it did indeed seem as though the Lord had blessed his servant. For on 13 October Bethlen defeated the last Habsburg army in Hungary and soon entered Bratislava (Pressburg), after which the Transylvanians moved up the Danube to join forces with Thurn's army in November for a second siege of Vienna, involving a force numbering more than 25,000 men. Bucquoy, meanwhile, who had done little more than hold Budweiss in eastern Bohemia, now withdrew to strengthen the beleaguered capital, which convinced Dudley Carleton in turn that Bethlen would take the city by storm 'if he be not diverted by the Polac' – notwithstanding the fact that the King of Poland was, in any case, under threat from Gustavus Adolphus of Sweden who had been approached to keep him in check 'by threatening an invasion of his country in case he molests Transylvania'. And even this was not the limit of the swelling anti-Habsburg tide. For in December a representative of the new Turkish sultan, Osman II, would arrive in Bratislava offering military aid, while the Venetian and Dutch republics also agreed a fifteen-year alliance during which each side promised to pay the other 30,000 thalers a month in case of attack.

In fact, then, there was nothing inevitable about Frederick's eventual defeat, and up to this point, too, it is altogether more convincing to attribute his behaviour less to personal ambition than to deep-seated religious faith and genuine concens for an Imperial consitution in imminent danger from Habsburg ambitions. He had accepted the Bohemian crown, on the one hand, because it offered a potentially dazzling future for his dynasty, but he had done so also to protect the rights of all Protestants and not merely Calvinists, both within Bohemia and more generally. As such, his priorities were still essentially defensive, in the face of an allegedly aggressive, unscrupulous, intolerant emperor, who, along with his Jesuit flatterers, was attempting to destroy the Empire's elective foundations. By no means an extremist, his conviction that he had been divinely appointed for his task was commonplace among Catholics, Lutherans and Calvinists of all complexions, and in accepting the Bohemian crown, he had, to his credit, weighed the legality and military practicability of his options carefully, concluding that the prize and the circumstances made the risks worth taking. True, he was in little doubt that by accepting the crown of Bohemia, he was assuming the leadership of a rebellion and at the same time turning it into not only an Imperial affair against the mighty Habsburg dynasty, but a conflict of European dimensions. Yet he harboured few doubts either about the possibility of his success at a time when the military advantage usually lay with the defenders of strongholds rather than attackers in the field.

From the outset, indeed, Frederick proved himself not only comparatively competent in his new role but in some respects remarkably tolerant of religious diversity. He did not, on the one hand, attempt to replace existing councillors or officials with new ones, and the decision to place Anhalt in command of the military leadership was actually favoured by the Bohemian Directors who had offered the role to him the previous August. Nor, as one contemporary caricature suggested, did he attempt to 'teach the world, reform all schools, churches and law courts, and bring everything to the state in which Adam found it.' For after the conversion of St Veit's Cathedral to a Calvinist place of worship duly began on 21 December 1619 and Count Thurn warned of a potentially hostile reaction, Frederick denied direct responsibility for the measure, answering that 'I myself neither did it nor bid it.' 'Your people,' he continued, 'have done it themselves, I merely let it happen.' And while he was prepared to grant the Jesuit church in Brno to the Calvinist *Brüderunität*, he was generally true to a guarantee he had made to his people shortly after his coronation in which he had pledged his commitment to the Letter of Majesty, and pointed out that 'he had been strongly moved to molest and oppress no one on account of their religion … or also to have no one prevented in their customary religious practice.'

These same principles even applied, indeed, to one of the most reviled of all Christian sects who were hated equally by Protestants and Roman Catholics alike. For while visiting Brno in Moravia on a royal progress in February 1620, Frederick came into contact with a small group of Anabaptists who seem likely to have been barred from residence within the town and had set up a community not far from the palace where he was staying. But his encounter was anything but hostile. On the contrary, he was presented with gifts of an iron bedstead, a few knives and fur gloves, along with a vase for the queen. And when the king wrote of the meeting to his wife, he made no mention of the Anabaptists' religion, commenting instead upon the fine quality of their wares and noting that if they were ever to be in the vicinity of Prague, he 'would visit them quite often'. Plainly, their company had been tolerable at the very least, and it was an episode which says much about both the man and his kingship: gentle and accommodating where possible, wholly sincere in terms of Christian values and equally sincere in the political conviction that absolute intolerance went hand-in-hand with the kind of absolutism now threatening all Europe from Vienna and Madrid.

Yet Frederick's decision to brave the vicissitudes of a winter journey through Moravia, Silesia and Lusatia in early 1620 had been prompted by much more than any wish simply to socialise with his new subjects, Anabaptist or otherwise. On the one hand, his resplendent retinue of 300 attendants was intended to impress the populace that the majesty of Bohemia's first Protestant king was equal or superior to that of the Habsburgs. But his journey was also aimed at winning the homage of the nobility and, more importantly still, guaranteeing their support for the approaching conflict. In particular, Frederick was hoping that the Moravian Estates would be prepared to double the size of their troop contribution and mobilise every twentieth man in only two weeks – under the circumstances, still a comparatively modest appeal that nevertheless demonstrated the limits of his hosts' devotion to their new ruler. For while Frederick was awarded some 15,000 Moravian gulden in addition to a number of confiscated properties, he was refused his troop allocation, and offered instead no more than 1,500 infantry and 500 cavalry, with the specific proviso that they be used to defend Moravia only, and for no more than six months.

That war was by no means a distant danger for the Moravians made their half-hearted response all the more alarming. For even as Frederick was meeting his Anabaptist subjects at Brno, news arrived of an invasion of 8,000 Cossacks from Poland into Upper Silesia and the principality of Teschen, organised by Archduke Karl, Bishop of Breslau and Neisse, and brother to the freshly crowned Emperor Ferdinand II. Making for Vienna in order to join Ferdinand's forces there, they had actually passed within a few miles of where Frederick was staying, and during the night of 7 February, it was possible to see from Brno the glow of the villages burnt by what would prove to be the very first flames of the Thirty Years War. In the event, Frederick was forced to prolong his stay while he attempted to co-ordinate a counter-attack, calling upon the Duke of Brieg in Breslau to cut the aggressors off. But the plan was unsuccessful and the only response was an indignant message to the King of Poland demanding the Cossacks' withdrawal, as Frederick once again took up his journey, leaving Brno for northern Moravia on 14 February before reaching the episcopal town of Neisse, which had gone on to rid itself of its hated bishop, Archduke Karl, who had been forced to flee to Poland. Duly guaranteed their freedom of worship and allowed by Frederick to reform the Catholic Church of Maria in Rosis, Neisse's Lutherans also welcomed Frederick warmly.

And the same atmosphere of goodwill was generally maintained throughout the remainder of Frederick's progress, notwithstanding the fact that at Breslau on Palm Sunday, 12 April – not long after the king's departure for home – some Lutherans insulted the Calvinist minister and disrupted his service at the castle, where some twenty-six people were assembled. One month earlier, Frederick had granted this small Calvinist community freedom of worship, offering them use of the great hall in the royal castle for their services, and the incident demonstrated clearly enough that not all his subjects shared his tolerance. But elsewhere the king's affability had generally won him the affection of the people he encountered. According to one observer, indeed, he had behaved so graciously that 'the common man gained a particular affection to his Majesty, and wished him luck and victory against the enemy, that they might be for a long time with this lord in peace and tranquillity.' Those who had hosted and served him had received gilded drinking vessels and money, and even some of those who had merely congratulated him had enjoyed similar generosity.

Despite the rigours of the journey, the periods of terrible cold, the political and military disappointments and the intervention of Cossacks, Bohemia's new king had nevertheless remained in good spirits throughout, buoyed by that same unwavering faith in his divine mission that would fill even his closest advisers with misgivings. Irritated by some minor aspect of Frederick's conduct of the royal progress, even Camerarius complained how he 'takes the matter lightly and leaves everything to God and good hope', and soon after his journey had begun, Frederick had indeed written to his wife to tell her how 'it is necessary to entrust oneself in everything to the will of God.' 'That,' he continued, 'is my entire consolation amid the many setbacks one encounters.' Likewise, one month later he was again confirming how 'I must follow whither my calling brings me.' Indeed, his use of the French term *vocation* gave his message added emphasis, though his correspondence with his wife was conducted in this language throughout. 'I beg you not to let go of yourself,' he told her on 16 February, 'because you do yourself harm and offend God to grieve without reason. In the end one must resolve to want what God wants, and each must follow what he is called to do.'

Not altogether surprisingly, perhaps, one of the most trying aspects of Frederick's journey had been his separation from the queen, and the constant exchange of letters and gifts between the couple leaves little doubt of the intensity of the emotional bond between them. Many of the king's letters contain apologies for having been too preoccupied to write even more often, but they ended almost invariably with protestations of eternal love, declarations that she was never out of his thoughts, expressions of his annoyance at sleeping alone, promises to be true unto the grave, or hopes that God would grant them the grace to be together for many years to come. In his first letter from Brno, he promised that he would return as soon as possible, and asked her to keep her own promise not to be too melancholy during his absence. She was, after all, nursing their fourth child, a boy who would become famous as Prince Rupert of the Rhine, and whose birth on 17 December 1619 was joyfully construed as yet another sign of God's blessing on her husband's reign – a fact not lost amid the flood of propaganda accompanying the child's baptism on the last day of March 1620.

Earlier that very same month, however, the most powerful princes of the Empire had exhorted Frederick to abdicate, at a meeting of Catholic and Protestant Imperial princes in Mühlhausen, which had included the electors of Mainz, Trier, Cologne and Saxony, and the Duke of Bavaria. All condemned the Bohemian election and resolved to back Emperor Ferdinand II's determination to undo it. Ferdinand, moreover, openly threatened Frederick, warning him that if he did not relinquish the Bohemian crown by 1 June 1620, he would be declared a rebel against the Empire and subjected to the severest punishment laid down by the Imperial constitution – an Imperial ban. Rendered thereby an outlaw and accordingly deprived of any legal protection, Frederick would also be forbidden to hold titles or property of any kind, and refused access to all assistance, making him in effect the victim of a demand for unconditional surrender before even a shot had been fired. And though no price was actually placed upon his head, there was no doubt either that he would make a tempting target for predatory, vengeful neighbours and rivals – not the least of whom was Maximilian of Bavaria, who, unbeknown to all but the emperor himself, had already been promised the electoral dignity that the ruler of the Palatinate continued, in theory, to carry.

In the meantime, moreover, Frederick's almost casual dismissal of the looming ban as yet another corruption of Imperial law wholly belied the true scale of his predicament. For in January an invasion of Transylvania by Polish 'Lisowczycy' mercenaries had not only compelled Bethlen Gábor to abandon the siege of Vienna and return home in haste, but encouraged him to make a separate nine-month truce with Ferdinand, even though the Hungarian Diet still remained officially in a state of rebellion. Born in 1580, the son of a Hungarian nobleman who had lost his ancestral estate at Iktár, as a result of the Ottoman occupation of the central territories of the Kingdom of Hungary, Gábor had been raised by Stefan Bocskai, leader of the great Hungarian-Transylvanian uprising of 1605, and played a key role in encouraging that rebellion in the first place, firmly opposing Habsburg autocracy and the persecution of Protestants, which his own Calvinism made it impossible for him to accept. Nor had his installation as Prince of Transylvania in 1613, with Ottoman support and the reluctant accept-ance of Emperor Matthias two years later, served to curb his restless spirit, even though his limited financial resources had always made his subsequent victories seem to many 'a torrent without a source'. But the news from his homeland of the Lisowczycy victory at the Battle of Humenné – not to mention the emperor's sweetener of thirteen counties in the east of Royal Hungary – was enough for him to seek a breathing space and, more importantly still, leave his Bohemian allies to their own, increasingly vulnerable, devices.

For largely as a result of Oñate's ongoing efforts, Philip III's commitment to the Imperial cause was becoming greater with every passing month. More cautious voices like those of the king's chief minister, Don Balthasar de Zúñiga, were, it is true, expressing increasing concern about Spain's predicament. 'To convince ourselves that we can conquer the Dutch,' the minister had written in April 1619, 'is to seek the impossible, to delude ourselves.' And Zúñiga's outlook was scarcely more sanguine when he considered the situation within the Holy Roman Empire, which required 'all those supreme efforts that are normally made when one is confronted by a total disaster.' Spain, in his view, was effec-tively presented with the ultimate dilemma as a result of what amounted to the perfect strategic storm: a crisis for both her own empire and the sister empire to whose fortunes she was inextricably linked. For unless she intervened mas-sively on behalf of Ferdinand, Bohemia's rebels would surely prevail, giving the

Protestants control of Ferdinand's empire and fatally compromising the Spanish position in both Italy and the Low Countries. But if massive military assistance was indeed forthcoming, the result was likely to be another conflict of equal or even longer duration than that involving the Netherlands. The greater an empire's sway, the greater the chances of its dissolution and the greater its need, therefore, to hold the line at any and every point of weakness. It was the classic Imperial conundrum and now it applied to a crisis of two empires simultaneously, both bound together, it seemed, on a rapidly crumbling mountain peak.

Within the Spanish Council of State, in fact, there was talk of the possibility of 'eternal war'. But while Zúñiga and others foresaw tragedy on a continental scale, Oñate and his king still planned busily for what they mistakenly considered a winnable conflict. The ambassador had arranged for 300,000 ducats to be credited to him from Madrid in February 1619 and a further 300,000 in May, though the latter had to be delivered in cash, since the bankers of Nuremberg and Frankurt supported the Elector Palatine and would not accept Oñate's bills. In November, he received 150,000 ducats and in January 1620 another 100,000, and as the Spanish viceroys in Italy recruited troops for Flanders and Bohemia, sending 8,000 through the Valtelline in June and 7,000 more in November, Oñate duly intervened to commandeer them all. For Ferdinand, not surprisingly, Oñate was 'the man with whose friendly help the affairs of the Habsburg family are being arranged'. From a less partisan perspective, however, he was arguably nothing less than warmonger-in-chief of the coming conflict – the individual, indeed, who greased the political engine and oiled the military wheels, and without whose machinations even Emperor Ferdinand and Philip III themselves might yet have drawn back from the brink, at least temporarily.

By the early spring of 1620, therefore, Bucquoy in Bohemia and Dampierre in Lower Austria, at the head of over 12,000 troops, stood fully poised to do the emperor's bidding, as part of what was rapidly becoming an extraordinarily wide-ranging continental strategy, since Spain now urged Sigismund III of Poland to stand firm against Gustavus Adolphus of Sweden while monitoring the movements of Bethlen Gábor in Transylvania, and agents were also sent to the Hanseatic towns to see whether they too would stand by the emperor. At the same time that a fleet was dispatched to Flanders in readiness for the expiry of the truce, moreover, Archduke Leopold in Alsace was supplied with 500 men to reinforce the vital Rhine bridgehead at Breisach, in preparation for the invasion of the Palatinate, which was now the subject of intense discussion in Brussels. For when Maximilian of Bavaria's plea to Frederick had been roundly rejected, he had been visited in Munich in October 1619 by both Ferdinand and Oñate, and persuaded to declare his willingness to use the army of the Catholic League in Bohemia, with the proviso of substantial Spanish support in the Rhineland, and upon the further crucial understanding that he should be assured eventual possession of at least the Upper Palatinate and, more importantly still, the electoral title that went with it. Since both Maximilian and Frederick belonged to the Wittelsbach family, and since Bavaria had some claim in law to both the land and the title, the transfer, Oñate argued, could be effected relatively easily. And this, it seems, was enough for the Catholic League to commit a force of 25,000 troops to be used as the Duke of Bavaria saw fit.

In Madrid, meanwhile, the prospect of a Spanish occupation of the Lower Palatinate under Spinola was ever more enticing to Philip III, since by making himself master of Heidelberg, the Spanish general could guarantee at last the crucial lines of communication from Genoa and Spanish Lombardy, through the Valtelline and thereafter through the Tyrol and on through the Rhineland to Brussels. The original route of the so-called 'Spanish Road' through Franche-Comté and Lorraine had been dogged by the threat from the French garrisons at Metz, Toul and Verdun, and, above all, by the hostility of the Duke of Savoy. But its replacement, which had been opened in 1593 through the Valtelline after nearly thirteen years of hard negotiation, and which ran along the northern shore of Lake Constance to follow the north bank of the Rhine as it flowed eastwards to Basel, still faced one major threat of its own: the implacable hostility of the Elector Palatine, whose presence made it necessary for Spanish recruits and supplies to cross the Rhine at Breisach on their tortuous route to the Netherlands. Though any one of a number of good Atlantic and Biscayan ports offered many advantages over the Rhineland route and the Spanish Road in general, privateers from England and La Rochelle, not to mention Dutch warships and the line of sandbanks stretching from Dunkirk to the Scheldt, which made it necessary for vessels to sail in dangerously close to the guns of Calais, rendered naval transport all but impossible for Spain in time of conflict. As such, all hinged on the Palatinate, and the pretext and circumstances were now at hand for its subjection.

Nor, of course, was any of this lost upon the princes of the Protestant Union who increased the urgency of their appeals to England and their Dutch allies, whose combined support was still a prospect of much concern to Philip III in Madrid:

> The invasion of the Palatinate [he informed Archduke Albert in March 1620] will give the English a fair pretext for openly interfering in Germany and for sending all their forces to the assistance of the Dutch ... You will thus be attacked by the combined forces of England and Holland, and then, if we are

to take part in the Bohemian war, we shall be at the expense of maintaining
two armies, and we shall have to fight a war with England, though a war with
that power has always been held by us to be most impolitic. Its inconvenience
at this time will be especially great on account of our poverty.

Yet to Spain's good fortune, England's king was still happier in the posture
of mediator than the role of warrior, and the Spanish ambassador in London,
Don Diego Sarmiento de Acuña, Count of Gondomar, had already inveigled
him with a potent mix of flattery, deception and outright bribery, as the prospect of a Spanish marriage for his son was dangled before him. In response,
James was content to inform the Protestant Union's members how he had it,
on Gondomar's own authority, that they had nothing to fear from Spain and
therefore no need of the loan of £100,000 that they were seeking from the
City of London. Aggrieved beyond measure that the English king should fail so
miserably to assist his son-in-law, the Dutch, too, held back, offering no more
than 5,000 troops, along with a subsidy of 50,000 florins a month, so that the
Union might recruit more troops of its own.

But for all their own undoubted desperation, the Protestant princes of
Germany were already, it seems, less than wholehearted themselves in support of their Bohemian counterparts. At a meeting in June 1619, for example,
the Union had resolved to raise an army of 11,000 men, but only for defence
against the Catholic League – 'to protect liberty and law' and 'to maintain our
religion like true patriots', since 'one should not oppose the House of Austria
lightly', especially 'without either troops or money from England'. And at a
further meeting in November, only the margraves of Ansbach and Baden had
actually supported Frederick's decision to accept the Bohemian crown. Beyond
this, the Calvinist Elector of Brandenburg alone offered encouragement, and
when he died at Christmas, his young successor George William – even though
married to Frederick's sister – was unable to persuade the Lutheran Estates of his
principality to continue his father's defiant policy. Since Brandenburg's public
debt was among the largest in Germany, the refusal was indeed unequivocal,
and since the Duke of Saxony's own finances were under increasing pressure,
he too was more than ready for deal-making. Accordingly, at a meeting of electors held at Mühlhausen on 20 March 1620, which had been called to prevent
the 'Bohemian fire' from spreading into Germany, John George had accepted a
promise from his Catholic counterparts, including Ferdinand, that there would
be no attempt to regain by force the secularised church lands in the Upper or
Lower Saxon Circles until the princes in possession had received a legal hearing. More significantly still, however, the 'Mühlhausen guarantee' was swiftly

followed by a further offer from Ferdinand that Lusatia be offered as a pledge in return for a commitment on John George's behalf to capture it from the rebels.

It was bait, of course, that the Duke of Saxony could not resist, and a ploy which not only compounded the foundering King of Bohemia's predicament, but brought his situation to the verge of crisis – a line that was duly crossed in July 1620 by an unwelcome intervention from France. For Louis XIII, all too well aware of his own difficulties with recalcitrant Protestant subjects, had exhibited much initial sympathy with the beleaguered Holy Roman Emperor, even offering at one point to lead an army on his behalf. And although that particular option had not actually materialised, he now chose nonetheless to dispatch a diplomatic mission to Germany, under the Duke of Angoulême, in the hope of mediating between Maximilian of Bavaria and the Margrave of Ansbach whose armies were jockeying cagily for advantage. The hard-pressed Protestant Union, however, had already been further weakened by the withdrawal of Strasbourg in return for guarantees that its territory be unmolested by Spinola, and Maximilian too was wholly amenable to a truce allowing the release of his army for service in Bohemia, making the resulting Treaty of Ulm almost a formality for Angoulême to arrange. By its terms both the Catholic League and Protestant Union agreed to respect the other's neutrality in Germany without prejudice to whatever action either side might choose to take in Bohemia. And though Spinola complained that this still left the Union free to oppose the Spanish invasion of the Palatinate, the overall result of the treaty was undeniable: an immeasurable strengthening of Habsburg power in relation to Bohemia.

In the meantime, moreover, even before the campaigns in both Bohemia and the Rhineland were underway, the Habsburgs were further cheered by encouraging news concerning Spanish lines of communication with northern Italy, after the Valtelline had witnessed what amounted to a reign of terror orchestrated between August 1618 and January 1619 by the Calvinist pastor Jörg Jenatsch on behalf of the Protestant 'Grey Lords'. The Roman Catholic Bishop of Chur had been deposed, and over 150 victims executed, tortured or exiled by self-styled 'peoples' courts' on charges of conspiring with Spain, before Jenatsch's men finally swept down across the floor of the Valtelline, torturing to death in the process an old Catholic priest in Sondrio and opening a new Protestant church. But what had finally made a counter-stroke inevitable was a subsequent declaration of support for the Bohemian rebels, which resulted in a Spanish-backed rising by the Italian-speaking Catholic population, headed by the Planta family. With all the violence that would become such a feature of the coming thirty years, the priest's murder in Sondrio was avenged by the death of 140 of Jenatsch's congregation, while elsewhere the *sacro macello*, or 'holy butchery', accounted for another 600 Protestant lives. France in the meantime refused appeals for help, as did Venice, and when the Grey Lords counter-attacked at Bornio at the head of the valley, they were soundly defeated by the Duke of Feria, who proceeded to construct a chain of forts to hold the Valtelline for the future.

Thereafter, even the Duke of Savoy dared not impede the passage of the 8,000 troops who now made their way along the Spanish Road to join Spinola, so that by August 1620, the general could not have been better placed to complete his task, armed with the emperor's commission to act within the Holy Roman Empire, and at the head of a force altogether better equipped and organised than its opponents. From Dudley Carleton's perspective in The Hague, the contrast with the German Protestant forces – 'which begin commonly to consult, when the Spaniards have resolved; to levy, when they march; to move when they are in possession' – could not have been more stark. Nor was the bitter harvest resulting from these discrepancies long in arriving, since Spinola was soon en route to Coblenz, where his army was reinforced from Franche-Comté and northern Italy to make it 16,000 strong with 3,000 cavalry. And this was not all. For the campaign that ensued was both brilliantly conceived and executed, as the Spanish army crossed the Rhine on a bridge of boats to Ehrenbreitstein, advanced on Frankfurt and caused consternation among its enemies, who were at a loss to determine its ultimate destination, since Spinola was in a position either to wheel back upon the Palatinate, go on to Bohemia, or turn north and force a crossing of the Ijssel into the Netherlands from the right bank of the Rhine.

In response, Maurice of Nassau hastily moved men forward to stand guard near the Spanish garrison at Wesel, while the Protestant Union put some of its men in the Rhineland near Mainz and the remainder in the Hunsrück, a line of hills on the right bank of the Moselle between Trier and Coblenz. But the hard-pressed defenders were unable to anticipate their opponent's eventual decision to turn back to Wiesbaden, cross over to Mainz and take possession of Kreuznach and Oppenheim. Had Spinola opted for the obvious and made directly for the Palatinate in the manner anticipated, he would have been faced with a dogged fight through the defiles of the Hunsrück, giving time for the Dutch to send reinforcements up the Rhine and into the Palatinate. By following a more circumspect route, however, Spain's premier general had demonstrated the crucial military principle not only that less is sometimes more, but that patience is sometimes bolder than boldness itself. For by the end of September, he was master of the Rhine from Coblenz to Mainz, the Dutch had been kept at bay downstream, and the forces of the Protestant Union, having failed to hold Oppenheim against him, had retired up river to Wörms.

In the meantime, on 17 July, just a fortnight after the Treaty of Ulm, Jean Tserclaes, Count of Tilly, who had been appointed by Maximilian of Bavaria to command the Catholic League's forces, had set out with an army of 30,000 troops – which included the philosopher Descartes – into Upper Austria. By then, indeed, the agreement reached at Ulm was already in ashes, since the emperor was now convinced, as Chancellor Lobkowitz told the Duke of Angoulême, that there was 'nothing more to be gained from treaties'. Instead, 'he was resolved to secure complete obedience from his subjects,' which, Lobkowitz added, he believed 'could only be assured by the sword.' And the sword was indeed in capable hands. For while the Duke of Bavaria was not a professional soldier, his keen political sense gave him a good grasp of the strategic fundamentals of the coming campaign and a shrewd appreciation of the type of general needed to complete the task on his behalf, so that Upper Austria not only swiftly submitted, but accepted, without resistance, the removal of Protestants from office and the closure of churches that followed.

Count Tilly himself, in fact, was the scion of a family of Liége and, at the age of 61, arguably one of the more noble representatives of the Counter-Reformation. A pupil of the Jesuits, he had originally wished to enter the order in his own right, before deciding to serve its ideals as a Christian warrior in a range of campaigns: with the Spanish army against the Dutch; under Henry of Guise against the Huguenots; and in the emperor's service in Hungary from 1600 to 1612, when Maximilian had made him commander of the Bavarian troops. At all times, moreover, he had proved true to his reputation as a 'monk in armour', despising the low pleasures of most contemporary officers and advancing his faith by an unswerving dedication to the arts of war rather than the wiles of politics, while maintaining, wherever possible, a strict regard for the interests of innocent civilians. For while, like all generals of his day, he considered terror a permissible tool of warfare, he nevertheless endeavoured to restrict its cruelty to permissible limits – to the extent, indeed, that both he and Maximilian now became deeply shocked by the ferocity of the Imperial troops in Upper Austria, lodging heated complaints with Ferdinand and employing Bavaria's more substantial financial resources to good effect in ensuring much better discipline among the troops of the Catholic League that he and Maximilian led. Consisting of Walloons, Flemings, Italians and a handful of Spaniards, the League's army possessed, in fact, what amounted to nothing less than a crusading spirit, fuelled in part by the Carmelites who attended it, of whom one, Padre Domenico à Jesu Maria, was the Pope's special representative.

By the time that Tilly's men had moved into Bohemia to join forces with Bucquoy at the end of September, moreover, their morale had been further boosted by news that John George of Saxony had indeed made himself master of Lusatia. The objective thereafter was a decisive engagement with the enemy's main army, jointly commanded by Anhalt, Thurn and Mansfeld, and with that army's resources of men and money rapidly dwindling, the outcome seemed increasingly assured. Mansfeld, indeed, disgruntled and unpaid, was refusing to leave his headquarters, as landowners and cities defaulted on their contributions, and the Bohemian queen's secretary noted how 'our friends have no minds to dig wells until they grow athirst'. The confiscations had not saved Frederick's government from bankruptcy, and it was not only lack of finance and foresight that had brought his regime to such a state of disarray. For the inexperience and tactlessness of both the king and his young wife had been compounded by a failure to win the common people to their cause. Frederick's disavowal of responsibility for the attack on the magnificent medieval art of St Veit's Cathedral had in fact convinced no one, and only popular opposition thereafter had in any case prevented a foolhardy decision to topple the famous statues on Charles Bridge into the Vlatva river below.

Such actions had alienated not only Catholic Bohemians, but Protestants too, who bitterly resented so needless an assault on their cultural heritage, while Queen Elizabeth's penchant for French fashions also continued to cause no little stir among the coyly conservative ladies of the Bohemian nobility. Much more important still, however, was Frederick's failure to overcome the tensions among the lands of the Bohemian crown in his attempts to raise an army – which mutinied twice when the government was unable to pay them – and his flat, if understandable, refusal to adopt the more radical social programme that his increasingly dire circumstances actually necessitated. At the time of the confederation between Bohemia and Austria, Tschernembl had demanded precisely such an option. 'Let the freedom of subjects be proclaimed in the land and villeinage abolished,' he had proclaimed, in the hope of unleashing those self-same energies that had driven the earlier Hussite war, and against which Ferdinand and his allies might yet have struggled in vain. But as those allies now closed in on Prague, the rebel leaders, backed by their knights and burghers rather than their people, had no effective policy to offer the man for whom time appeared to be running out and who was already being dubbed the 'Winter King' on the assumption that he was unlikely to reign till spring.

Nor, in truth, did Frederick actually possess the means to carry out effective policies of any kind, though the invading armies, by contrast, were now both poised and united, notwithstanding a brief difference of opinion involving Bucquoy, who had temporarily hesitated to submit to Maximilian's authority. The general had in fact advocated a move northeastwards into Moravia, unlike

Maximilian himself and Tilly, both of whom wanted to defeat the rebels at a single stroke before the Turks could intervene, and in order to avoid a long period in winter quarters which would weaken their troops. But ultimately it was the emperor himself who ordered Bucquoy to comply, declaring that the Blessed Virgin was his very own *Generalissima*, and by 7 November the combined Catholic armies had indeed reached the outskirts of Prague to face a force of some 21,000 defenders, led by Christian of Anhalt, who had raced back to defend the city. Outnumbered by roughly three to two, exhausted by forced marches and disgruntled by lack of pay, Anhalt's troops hardly represented, in any case, a Bohemian army, comprised as they were of German mercenaries, men from Moravia and Silesia, and Hungarian Protestants. But it was this motley assemblage that nevertheless now took up position at the summit of the steep White Mountain rising up to the west of Prague, and these weary fighters who consequently held Bohemia's fate in their hands, ahead of the brief encounter that would, arguably, prove the most decisive battle of the coming thirty years.

Early on the morning of 8 November, Polish and Walloon horsemen had seized a village at the base of the mountain and slaughtered the unsuspecting Hungarian soldiers without quarter, a harbinger of the violence to come and the passion that had been studiously stirred by Pope Paul V's Carmelite representative, whose presence had been specifically requested by Maximilian and who had assumed a role that was to give the battle itself an intensely religious character. On their march through Bohemia, the Bavarians had found in an abandoned farmhouse a desecrated image of the Nativity, in which the eyes of all of the figures, with the exception of the Holy Infant himself, had been torn out. Thereafter, Padre Domenico had specifically chosen to turn the campaign into one of vengeance fought with the help of the Virgin Mary and the saints, in order to defend their honour against heretics and iconoclasts. Scapulars with Our Lady's image were distributed to the troops, and as Maximilian, Tilly and Bucquoy sat in council after the initial skirmish, debating the virtues of a direct assault on the mountain, which was Maximilian's preferred strategy, they were interrupted by the monk himself, who burst in uninvited, bearing the defaced image of the Virgin and declaiming frantically about visions that had guaranteed victory with the help of God's angels.

It was an intervention that proved decisive. For the troops received the order to attack with enthusiasm, and, as Bucquoy's Irish Jesuit confessor, Thomas Fitzsimmons, prayed aloud the *Salve Regina*, they duly began their push up the mountain to stage a rout of the enemy that required less than two hours to complete. As the assault began, the left flank of the defenders rapidly disintegrated, although a counter-attack seemed to repulse the Catholic advance until Tilly

committed his Italian cavalry and Polish Cossacks, headed by Padre Domenico
on horseback, holding up his crucifix and desecrated image of Our Lady, while
leading the battle cry, 'Maria'. The result was panic and disarray, as Anhalt's troops
broke ranks for the first and indeed last time, fleeing in droves to Prague where
they crossed into the Lower Town which was already packed with the peasants
who had taken shelter there with their carts and livestock – convincing King
Frederick, who had found out too late that the battle had been started, that his
capital could not be saved. Ultimately, in fact, he had emerged to join his troops
just at the moment of the victorious Catholic charge, and by the early hours
of next morning he was gone for good, together with his wife and entourage
– not long before Padre Domenico, at the behest of Maximilian and Bucquoy,
celebrated a triumphant *Te Deum* in Prague's Capuchin church. Though subsequently urged to make a stand in Moravia, which was as yet untouched by the
war, and to join forces with Bethlen Gábor, Frederick had been so dispirited
by his defeat – and, arguably perhaps, the whole experience of his short reign
– that he chose instead to seek safety in the Dutch Republic, albeit still talking
boldly of holding the Protestant line in Europe as a whole, while Anhalt made
for Scandinavia and Thurn for Constantinople to persuade the sultan to help
the exiles continue the fight.

Not knowing the Czech language and surrounded by Germans, Frederick
had soon been cruelly exposed as the foreigner king he undoubtedly was – a
victim, as Pope Paul had predicted, of the 'filthy labyrinth' that awaited him
upon his acceptance of the Bohemian crown. And though in Silesia at least, his
former general, the Margrave of Jägerndorf, had been joined by several leaders
of the Bohemian Estates and established himself with 12,000 men at Neisse near
the Moravian frontier, this too brought only embarrasment. For Jägerndorf,
much like Mansfeld in Pilsen, was prepared to live off the land and sell himself
to the highest bidder, as his former paymaster became not only a hostage to
fortune but the hapless victim of remorseless ridicule. One illustrated leaflet was
soon depicting Frederick toppling from a wheel of fortune into the water below,
from which he is pulled by Dutch fishermen with their nets. In falling, he had
lost not only his crown and sceptre but the English Order of the Garter. Other
engravings, in their turn, depicted the exiled king as a beggar with his wife and
three children, or toiling for his Dutch hosts, who had permitted him, in fact,
to keep a miniature court at The Hague. Elsewhere he is to be seen building a
house on sand, weighing and selling cheese, or forlornly digging his own grave.
The variations are almost as endless as the torrent they comprised. 'Oh! Poor
winter king, what have you done?' ran one song current in Germany at the end
of 1620, which did at least temper irony with a little pity:

How could you steal the emperor's crown
By pursuing your rebellion?
Now you do well to flee
Your electoral lands and Bohemia.
You will pay with your grief
And suffer mockery and shame.
Oh! Pious Emperor Ferdinand, grant him pardon!
Do not hold his folly against him.
He's a very young man,
Who did not realise beforehand
How much a crown weighs.
Now it is weighing very heavy on his head.
If he had known, he would not have done what he did.

But whether 'pious Emperor Ferdinand' would indeed forgive Frederick 'his folly', let alone ignore his attempt to 'steal the emperor's crown' was never at issue. For as the Imperial ban of January 1621 made clear, the pretender to the Bohemian throne had 'by putting himself at the head of rebels, disobedient and untrue, shown himself both traitorous and injurious to his Imperial Highness and Majesty, and committed an offence against the peace of the Empire and other wholesome Imperial statutes'. Nor, of course, would Bohemia herself escape the price for her disloyalty: a price so high, moreover, that it would become the stuff of bitter folksong for decades to come. 'The iron is hot,' Maximilian informed Ferdinand in the wake of his victory, and the emperor, surely enough, would now apply it with his own distinctive brand of condign retribution.

5

CRISIS OF EMPIRES

The trees stand no more, the gardens are desolate;
The sickle and the plough are now a cold sharp blade.
Martin Oplitz, *Trostgedichte In Widerwertigkeit Dess Krieges* (1621)

'The news of the overthrow in Bohemia is confirmed, but is too bad to repeat,' wrote a certain Mr Aylesbury to Sir Henry Martin on 28 November, 1620. And as news of the Battle of White Mountain filtered back to London and across the rest of Europe, the same sense of desolation was matched in equal measure both by shock at what had come to pass and foreboding at what was yet to come. 'The loss of soldiers was not much unequal,' observed the English soldier-diplomat Sir Edward Conway, 'but the loss of cannon, the baggage, reputation, is the Imperials' victory who, as it seems, hold Bohemia by conquest.' From this point forth, moreover, Bohemians, like their Protestant counterparts elsewhere, could expect only what Conway aptly termed 'the Law of the Conqueror', since the campaign of 1620 had delivered more than hapless Bohemia into enemy hands. Lusatia, Silesia, Moravia and pockets of resistance in the Habsburgs' Austrian homelands were, on the one hand, all overrun, along with the Rhine Palatinate, while the Upper Palatinate lay defenceless. Yet far from concluding the war, the Imperial victory on the outskirts of Prague had merely expanded it. For in light of the scale of his defeat and in view of the implacable nature of Habsburg hostility, Bohemia's defeated king had little to lose by talk of continued resistance. 'I recommend everything to God and am resolved to take everything in patience from His paternal hand,' Frederick had confided characteristically to his wife on the eve of battle. 'He has given it, he has deprived me of it, he can reward me, his name be glorified.' And on the morning after defeat, as the Bohemian army melted away and Frederick himself fled with his family – leaving behind the crown, sceptre and royal orb of Bohemia, the jewel-encrusted collar of his Order of the Garter and, worse still, the chancery documents that included his secret correspondence with the Habsburgs' various enemies – he remained no less intent upon stirring the Protestant cause in Europe, sending Volrad von Plessen and the unstintingly pugnacious Camerarius to various princes in northern Germany in search of help, and another emissary, Paul Jesin, to Moravia and Hungary.

From The Hague, indeed, Frederick's government-in-exile would ceaselessly strive for an anti-Habsburg coalition, the need for which, naturally enough, had increased drastically in the wake of Bohemia's subjection. In 1621, an Imperial courier named Father Hyacinth was intercepted carrying a secret package of letters from the emperor and the papal nuncio in Vienna, which fell into Mansfeld's hands and revealed in embarrassing detail the plans of the Habsburgs and the papacy for reorganising the Empire after Frederick's defeat. And one year later Camerarius duly published them, along with a witty yet damning commentary entitled *Cancellaria Hispanica* ('The Spanish Chancery'). Its content revealed the full extent of papal chicanery in Spain, Italy and Germany to secure both the Palatine Electorate for Maximilian of Bavaria and the re-Catholicisation of Protestant areas of the Empire, and, in doing so, provided further fuel for Frederick's continued efforts not only to fight *pro rege bohemiae*, i.e. for the kingdom of Bohemia on his own account, but *pro causa communi*, or in other words 'for the common cause', entailing the restoration of a religious and political status quo favourable to the Protestant states. Two years after his defeat at White Mountain, Frederick was still repeating the familiar theme – significantly enough from the military headquarters that he had gone on to establish at Gemmersheim: 'I will have nothing to do with a suspension of arms, for that will be my ruin. I must have either a good peace or a good war.'

And while most Protestant leaders felt little true sympathy with Frederick's quest for the Bohemian crown or, indeed, his fate thereafter, their own security needs now not only coincided with his appeals for joint action, but even made his elevation to the status of a *cause célèbre* something of a necessity. When Frederick met Christian IV of Denmark, his wife's maternal uncle, at a conference of Protestant princes at Holstein in March 1621, the Danish king angrily inquired who had advised him 'to drive out kings and to seize kingdoms'. 'If your councillors did so,' Christian continued, 'they were scoundrels.' Yet the conference, convened by the Danes and attended by Dutch and English as well as German Protestant representatives, would nevertheless demand that the emperor dissolve the Imperial and League armies, restore Frederick to his ancestral lands and electoral title, and grant religious liberty throughout the territories of the Empire, including Bohemia. Otherwise they threatened to raise an army of their own, which Christian would command, to clear the Palatinate of Spanish troops. And though the threat proved empty on this occasion, the day of the peacemaker had clearly passed for the foreseeable future, as Christian of Brunswick, Frederick's new principal general, made palpably clear in his typically colourful judgement on that arch-peacemaker of all peacemakers, James I of England, which he delivered in an after-dinner diatribe before a Scottish officer:

> Just as Alexander, Julius Caesar and Henry IV [of France] are reputed and celebrated as the most outstanding heroes of the world, so that old pant-shitter, that old English bed-shitter is rated, on account of cowardice, the biggest prick of all.

For James, though not alone in his inaction, did indeed sit idly by as Bohemia felt the full force of Imperial wrath in the aftermath of White Mountain. On 21 June 1621, the most notorious execution in Czech history had taken place in the packed Old Town Square of Prague. Seven hundred Saxon soldiers had been brought in to secure the site – thus involving Saxony in the executions – and at five in the morning, twenty-eight prisoners were duly led under heavy guard to the platform, draped in black, upon which the scaffold stood. They included some of the most prominent members of Czech society, many in their 60s and 70s, though the emperor had at least accorded them the consolation of a Protestant preacher, and one, Jan Theodor Sixt of Ottersdorf, was pardoned at the last moment. For the others, however, no agony was spared. Johannes Jessenius, rector of Prague's university, who had long polemicised and machinated against Ferdinand – even advocating an alliance with the Turks – was beheaded and quartered after his tongue had been cut out, while the rest were dispatched in a protracted ritual, which lasted around four hours and necessitated the use of four separate swords for Jan Mydllar the executioner to accomplish his grisly task. For the next ten years, moreover, twelve of the severed skulls would continue to grin ghoulishly from the tower of the Charles Bridge overlooking the Vlatva.

That morning, meanwhile, Emperor Ferdinand had prayed for the condemned before the image of the Blessed Mother at Mariazell in Styria. He had acted, as he remarked to the abbot of the monastery, because he had no choice. And under the advice of Prince Gundakar of Liechtenstein, whom he appointed Bohemia's Imperial governor, he would subsequently issue a general pardon precluding further executions, bodily punishments, or deprivations of status, except for those already condemned *in absentia* and those persisting in rebellion. But fines and loss of property were still to be imposed, and though the so-called 'Blood Court', established in February 1621, would sometimes find its sentences commuted at the emperor's personal order, Ferdinand made little attempt to moderate the corruption accompanying the sequestration of rebel lands – much of which was granted to Liechtenstein, Martinitz, Slavata, Bucquoy, and the emperor's closest confidant and adviser, Ulrich von Eggenberg. To name but one other example, Baron Maximilian von Trauttmansdorff, an Imperial Counsellor of State, bought an estate valued at 300,000 florins for only two thirds of that sum and, with gifts and loans from the emperor of 165,000 florins, eventually paid little more than a tenth of the going price. No special body, beyond Liechtenstein's own Imperial court, had been set up to oversee the entire process, and when the operation was finally halted in 1628, it became clear that no proper accounts had been kept.

In all, 486 of the 911 noble estates in Bohemia were either given away or sold, often to foreigners, including the invading army's officers, many of whom were Belgian and Italian, and who rapidly became part of what amounted to a new Bohemian ruling class, established, to all intents and purposes, on the basis of a new and deeply resented serfdom. In consequence, Bohemia's lesser nobles in particular, who were mainly Protestant and had performed an important role in maintaining links with the peasantry, found their share of the land reduced from around a third of the total to no more than a tenth. And the offense to national honour was matched, if not exceeded, by the subsequent economic impact of the conquest, since the plunder exacted by the army of occupation, followed by the punitive contributions levied by Liechtenstein on town and countryside alike, led to a general collapse, in which most prices rose, while the value of land plummeted, largely as a result of increased sales. Since the beneficiaries of the new regime did not therefore derive quite the rewards they had anticipated, the situation was compounded, moreover, by currency operations that allowed a group of manipulators, including some Imperial councillors, to act in effect as countefeiters. Running a profitable swindle by producing 19 florins, then 27 and subsequently 39 and even 47, from one 8oz mark of silver, Liechtenstein and his associates – including a Dutch Calvinist financier by the name of Hans de Witte who had been long established in Bohemia – were actually in a position to lend the emperor some 6 million florins in February 1622, in return for one year's profits from the mint. And as a result, they were not only allowed to purchase all the silver available in the kingdom, but to prohibit the import and circulation of foreign currencies, and issue florins at the rate of 79 to the mark.

In his *Republic of Bohemia*, published in 1633, Pavel Stránský reflected upon the disruption of the times, which broke the power not only of the nobility, but the towns, too, as those dependent on money wages became destitute, craftsmen and tradesmen resorted to barter, and students were forced to abandon their schools and universities for lack of a reliable currency:

> It was then, for the first time, that we learned from experience … that neither plague, nor war, nor hostile foreign incursions into our land, neither pillage nor fire, could do so much harm to good people as frequent changes to the value of money.

Yet general economic chaos was not the limit of what Ferdinand saw fit to term his 'mercy and goodness' towards Bohemia. For while some 160,000 inhabitants went into exile and the middle and commercial classes virtually disappeared, the Czech language also found itself under systematic challenge, particularly at court. And with a civil service no longer staffed by members of families traditionally represented in the Estates, but by new men whose self-interest lay in loyalty to Vienna – now bearing the title 'royal officers in the kingdom of Bohemia' – Ferdinand also gave free rein to a more familiar, and even more hated group. On 10 May 1621, just before the executions in Prague, he had written his last will and testament, and in entrusting his ancestral lands to his 'beloved son' Ferdinand Ernst, he also made clear the ongoing need, as he saw it, to extirpate all sects and heresies 'to the extent that this was humanly possible'. Nor was it any coincidence that in commending his soul to his Redeemer and the intercession of the Blessed Mother and his favourite saints, he should also have included the as yet uncanonised Blessed Ignatius Loyola, founder of the Society of Jesus. For the Jesuits had swiftly returned in the wake of Ferdinand's victorious army, and, in association with the papal legate Cardinal Carafa, lost no time in guaranteeing a sweeping programme of re-Catholicisation, which included the abolition of the Letter of Majesty, the proscription of Calvinism and the expulsion of the Bohemian Brethren. Though Lutheran pastors were initially spared the same treatment, as a sop to John George of Saxony, this favour was duly rescinded in October 1622, with the added consequence that by the following year, no Protestants of any type had the right to hold funerals or baptisms in accordance with their beliefs. Only Judaism, in fact, was granted official toleration outside the Catholic faith.

In the meantime, however, the ramifications of Frederick V's initial defiance had spread beyond Bohemia to the fate of the Palatinate itself. For the Imperial ban of January 1621, which had been imposed by Ferdinand without reference to the Empire's electoral college, entailed not only Frederick's banishment and the confiscation of his possessions – or, in other words, the loss of the Upper and Lower Palatinates – but, equally importantly, his deposition as an Imperial elector. Such was the gravity of the punishment, indeed, that Ferdinand had hesitated before imposing it, knowing full well the broader implications of what would follow. But he was bound by the talks he had held with Maximilian of Bavaria in Munich on the eve of the Imperial election of 1619, and too beholden to renege on his promise of granting the duke both the right to occupy the Upper Palatinate and the privilege of obtaining Frederick's electoral status. This had been the secret price of the Catholic League's intervention in Bohemia in the first place, and while Ferdinand appreciated the increase in power and prestige that electoral rights were sure to bring the Wittelsbach family, the fact remained that Bavarian troops were still in occupation of Upper Austria as a decisive surety. With the Jesuits and Capuchins of Vienna adding constant pressure, along with the Pope's special envoy, Father Hyacinth, Ferdinand's hands were therefore effectively tied.

And as the noose tightened on the Palatinate, the most natural source of support for its banished ruler, his father-in-law, James I, remained content with hollow talk of mediation, notwithstanding the fact that in June 1621 the English Parliament, 'being touched with a true sense and fellow feeling' of Bohemia's distress, had published a declaration supporting whatever military action would be necessary to defend 'the true professors of the same Christian religion professed by the Church of England in foreign parts'. In the summer of 1620, Spinola had made a leisurely progress through the Rhineland, but just as James stood by passively then, he was still no more inclined to raise his sword one year on, and while the Dutch tried to shame Frederick's father-in-law into action, their efforts were met with the customary stone wall barrier of vanity and obfuscation. A formal embassy sent to demonstrate how 50,000 florins had been paid to Bohemia by the United Provinces for nineteen months and to the Protestant Union for eleven, in addition to the cost of sending contingents of troops to Wesel, the Rhineland and to Bohemia, met only with delaying tactics and tedious queries concerning Anglo-Dutch fisheries. Ultimately, indeed, the discussions lasted 454 days, and achieved nothing, though James's Council of War did at least discuss the Dutch proposal that England should distract Spinola from the Palatinate by landing troops at Sluys, and submitted a request for £500,000 to MPs, who promptly demonstrated the shallowness of their own

convictions by rejecting it, and opting for the more modest – and cheaper –
option of naval action.

Such was the king's resulting predicament, in fact, that he dared not allow
Frederick and Elizabeth to come to London at this time for fear of inciting
popular demonstrations against his government. But for an inveterate dreamer
of James's nature, of course, there were always grounds enough for believing that peace might yet be plucked from the ashes. Certainly, the Protestant
Union showed little stomach for a fight at a gathering held in Heilbronn in
January 1621 to debate the Imperial ban on Frederick and its concerns about
Spinola's recent occupation of Mainz, Kreuznach and Oppenheim. 'Those who
were wont to be on horseback in other men's quarrels do now so easily give
way to this inundation of strangers,' wrote Carleton scornfully, as the meeting
threatened to abandon Frederick unless he renounced his right to the Bohemian
throne. And when several of the princes of the Lower Saxon Circle failed to
arrange joint military action with Christian of Denmark during discussions at
Segenberg in March, the Union itself was on the brink of collapse – a process
finally completed by Spinola with the pretence of a spring offensive in the
Rhineland, in the full knowledge that if the truce with the Dutch expired as
expected, he would not be able to sustain it. Just as he had planned, an accord
was duly drawn up with the princes of Ansbach and Württemberg by which
they agreed to disband their forces if Spain guaranteed their rights as neutrals.
And in May the Protestant Union duly met to confirm this arrangement for all
its members – never meeting again thereafter.

Yet this was not the only encouragement of its kind for the King of England's
peacemaking aspirations. For in Madrid, Philip III had also hesitated at his
Habsburg cousin's decision to award the Upper Palatinate to the Duke of Bavaria,
fearing the provocation it would cause to Protestant states. He had initially
proposed, indeed, that if Frederick were to present himself suitably chastened
before the emperor and undertake not only to renounce Bohemia, but abandon
the Protestant Union and reimburse Spain the cost of the campaign, he might
then be allowed to return to the Palatinate. At the same time, the Spanish king
was also prepared to suggest that Frederick, or his infant son, might at least be
restored to the Lower Palatinate and share the electoral title in rotation with
Maximilian. And when it is remembered, too, that northern Italy had been
settled and that Louis XIII, plagued by Huguenot conspiracies and the rivalry
of great nobles, was equally anxious to support an international settlement, there
were even more grounds for optimism, it seemed. If Frederick was sensible,
Ferdinand and Maximilian pliable, and the truce between Spain and the
Dutch renewable, perhaps the King of England and those of a similarly pacific

disposition might yet have their way. But Frederick was not, Ferdinand and Maximilian anything but, and the truce already beyond all hope of recall. And it was the last consideration, above all, that rendered not only the renewal, but indeed both the duration and very nature of the Thirty Years War unavoidable.

The Twelve Years Truce had never, in fact, been popular in Spain. Attributed, albeit unfairly, to the deficiencies of the Brussels administration, it was bitterly criticised at regular intervals in the so-called *consulta* prepared for the king, and not, it must be said without good reason, since evidence of Dutch encroachment in Mediterranean, West Indian and Far Eastern waters had continued to mount steadily, intensifying the widespread mood of hawkish dissatisfaction that was summarised by the President of Spain's Council of Finance in 1616. 'The peace,' he declared bitterly, 'is worse than if we had continued the war.' But like other Spanish grandees of his kind, swollen with honour and lean on memory, he was prepared to overlook the circumstances of military stalemate and financial insolvency that had made peace necessary in the first place. Zuñiga and Oñate within the Holy Roman Empire, Fuentes, Villafranca and Feria in Milan, Osuna in Naples, Bedimar in Venice, Gondomar in London and Cardenas in Paris were all indeed of similar mind – blaming the truce, rather than the circumstances which caused it, for Spain's decline in power, and resolving to safeguard the lines of communication to Flanders by strengthening Habsburg influence on every front, whether in Bohemia, the Palatinate, Austria, or any other component of an endless nexus. Above all, they contended, the precious Valtelline, so crucial for the operation of the Spanish Road, must be safeguarded by the benevolent neutrality of France and England.

But if war might be necessary to restore Spanish interests, not to mention Spanish pride, its success would have to be premised upon a purge of the corruption and incompetence at the very heart of government. The swamp in Madrid would indeed need to be drained and, above all, the man at its centre sucked out of power. For when popular protests at the unbridled corruption of the administration had first begun to create tremors at court, the notorious Don Francisco Gómez de Sandoval y Rojas, Duke of Lerma, had saved his own position as royal favourite merely by jettisoning some of his creatures. Several councillors of finance were arrested in 1609 and the house of one was so full of bullion that it had taken three days to transfer it all back to the treasury. Yet the problems continued, as Lerma not only failed to further the unity and co-operation of the various states within the Spanish peninsula, but came perilously close to abandoning all responsibility towards them. 'Here,' complained one angry Catalan sent by the city of Barcelona on an important mission to Madrid, 'it's all a matter of gaming, hunting and comedies, and no one will be bothered with anything.' And as the gap between court and country widened, and the need for action mounted, so the appetite for subterfuge and secret manipulation finally turned on Lerma himself, who in October 1618 became the victim of a palace intrigue centred upon his own son, the Duke of Uceda.

Ultimately, in fact, the royal favourite would be spared the full indignity that his incompetence had merited, and allowed not only to retire from court with a cardinal's hat, but with a rumoured fortune of no less than 44 million ducats. Yet he was gone for good and had been replaced by 1622 by Zuñiga's nephew Gaspar de Guzman Olivares, Count of San Lúcar, who had won the goodwill both of Lerma's son and the future Philip IV, whose household he had entered seven years earlier. Usually known as the count-duke after his elevation to a dukedom in 1625, he came from a junior branch of the great aristocratic family headed by the Duke of Medina Sidonia and was the antithesis of his predecessor: hard, dynamic, puritanical; a man with the personality of a battering ram whose dark complexion and heavy build added to his charisma; and one who would prove himself, over the next twenty years, to be the outstanding politician of seventeenth-century Spain. He was the personification, in fact, of the restless bureaucrat, always in a rush about the court – his voice booming down the corridors and his hatband and pockets stuffed with papers, which made some compare him to a scarecrow. But he possessed a mind no less active than his lifestyle, which led him to rise at five, before spending the rest of the day, after confessing and taking communion, in a blur of activity. Always he accompanied the king, whether hunting or on his travels – working along the way, giving audiences from the saddle or dictating letters to the coachful of secretaries who followed in his wake until he finally retired at around eleven. 'From his bedroom to his study, in his coach, in corners, and pausing on the staircase,' wrote one eye-witness, 'he heard and dispatched the business of an infinite number of people.'

Such, indeed, was Olivares' frenetic energy that four of his secretaries were killed, it is said, by the rigours of his routine. And he too suffered alternately from acute lack of sleep when he needed it and an inability to rest when opportunity offered. But there was more to the count-duke than the ox-like constitution which Velázquez captured so eminently in his portrait. Not least, he possessed an eye for fine detail, amassing maps and reference works to enable him to assess the progress of his policies abroad, and an ear for sound advice, drawing upon the counsel of a wide range of advisers to supplement his own knowledge. As a member of the Andalusian aristocracy, moreover, he had no need, unlike Lerma, to ingratiate himself with the great families of Castile. No personal considerations would therefore be allowed to stand in the way of that restoration of Spain which he considered himself called upon to accomplish. And in his intense nationalism, desire for root and branch reform, and disgust with the old ministers and their policies, he represented, at the age of only 34, the hopes and ideals of a whole new generation in Castile itself.

Ebullient though easily dejected, shrewd yet on occasion gullible, Olivares was not without faults. Certainly he was stubborn, proud and boastful, and he was also prone to tantrums. On one occasion, during an audience with the ambassador of the friendly state of Genoa, he banged in fury on a window frame, though the same remarkable tenacity that he revealed so strikingly in a letter to a critic in 1625, was plainly a double-edged sword when applied to the ailing condition of Spain:

> I do not consider it useful to indulge in a constant, despairing recital of the state of affairs … I know it, and lament it, without letting it weaken my determination or diminish my concern; for the extent of my obligation is such as to make me resolve to die clinging to my oar till not a splinter is left.

From some perspectives, indeed, he seemed to embody, perhaps in heightened degree, those very failings that were already undermining Spain's 'Golden Age' – above all, its expectation of the miracle and its willingness to embark upon great enterprises without fully calculating the possibilities of success. As one Venetian ambassador wrote of him:

> He loves novelties, allowing his lively mind to pursue chimeras, and to hit upon impossible designs as easy of achievement. For this reason he is desolated by misfortunes; the difficulties proposed to him at the beginning he brushes aside, and all his resolutions rush him towards the precipice.

And in no respect more, perhaps, than in his perception of the map of Europe in relation to the war with the Netherlands was this more amply demonstrated. For just as sixteenth-century Castile had remained 'a republic of the bewitched, living outside the natural order of things', relying upon miraculous benefits from El Dorado, so seventeenth-century Spain – and the man at its heart – now demanded an even greater act of faith.

In 1619, Philip III had been taken aback by the complaints of the Council of Portugal that its Far Eastern empire could not survive a further decade of Dutch encroachment under the terms of the truce. 'If the republic of these rebels goes on as it is,' urged his adviser Zuñiga, 'we shall succeed in losing first the two Indies, then the rest of Flanders, then the states of Italy and finally Spain itself.' And this, indeed, was precisely the kind of compelling logic that so closely matched Olivares's own – just like Don Carlos Coloma in Flanders, who reasoned in June 1620 that, unless the Dutch agreed to abandon the Indies and open the Scheldt, the war would have to be resumed:

> One cannot but note [Coloma observed] that it looks as if God had permitted the troubles in Germany so that when in His Divine Mercy He uses the victorious arms of Your Majesty to bring them to an end, you may retain the prestige which is your due, whilst the Dutch rebels may be filled with a livelier apprehension of their own approaching doom, and His Imperial Majesty may be led to repay Your Majesty in the same coin with his armies and with his authority in the task of rooting out this new and pestilential republic.

There remained, of course, voices of caution, not least in Brussels, where the regent of the 'Spanish' southern Netherlands, Archduke Albert, saw all too plainly the pitfalls as well as the opportunities offered by abandonment of the truce:

> I see Your Majesty [he had written in December 1620] entangled in Bohemia, in the Palatinate and, through the Valtelline, in Italy, and were you to take on your shoulders a war in these provinces with Holland this next summer you would find it a heavy piece of work.

One year later, moreover, he had not changed his mind, urging in February 1621 that the truce be prolonged, 'whilst we see how things turn out in Germany and the Palatinate, for it would be a bad business for us to have so many wars on our hands at once.'

But that July the archduke was dead, along with the truce he had made, uttering a last feeble protest on his deathbed that 'even if all Europe is to be subject to one monarch, that time is not yet.' In the event, the decision to opt for war had been prompted as much by Dutch belligerence as by the wishes of Zuñiga or the new force in Madrid, Olivares, for whom Zuñiga would soon be making way. For Olivares, in fact, the war in the Netherlands was essentially defensive, as he made clear to Philip IV who succeeded his father in March 1621. 'Almost all the kings and princes of Europe are jealous of your greatness,' he told the new monarch. 'You are the main support and defence of the Catholic religion,' and for this reason, he continued, 'your principal obligation is to defend yourself and to attack them.' And it was a message to which the 16-year-old Philip was more than prepared to listen, if not to execute personally. For although he was lively, quick-witted and intelligent, with well-developed aesthetic interests, he was also lazy and self-indulgent – a patron of Velázquez, who in the sphere of government became almost literally a rubber-stamp, using a die which read '*Yo el Rey*' to sign state documents prepared for him by Olivares. The father of at least thirty-two illegitimate children, notwithstanding his oppressive religiosity, his behaviour would pendulate between degraded dissipation and hardly less degrading acts of contrition for his many misdemeanours.

Certainly, the situation facing Spain's new king and his young chief minister was more than daunting. For by 1621 both Holland and Zeeland were indeed displaying considerable enthusiasm for renewing the conflict, on the simple grounds that war meant profit. When the nobility of the southern provinces of the Netherlands had declared their loyalty to Spain in 1579 in an effort to preserve their political authority and their Catholic faith against the social revolution being enacted by William of Orange's Calvinist supporters, Holland and Zeeland had prospered greatly, as Antwerp floundered under blockade, Amsterdam flourished in its place, and the sea captains of the rebellious United Provinces proceeded to gorge upon Spain's overseas empire. Moreover, while the Dutch East India Company, which had been founded in 1602, was sufficiently well established to prosper in time of peace, it was only in wartime that a West India Company, funded in large part by Calvinist immigrants from the provinces of the south, could be established to plunder the rich shipping lanes of the Caribbean and the South Atlantic. Under such circumstances, to prolong the truce was to delay the windfall of rich dividends, while a permanent peace settlement would at best merely offer access to the Indies under licence, requiring the payment of dues to both the Spanish and Portuguese governments. Though the inland Dutch provinces, and especially Gelderland and Overijssel, might therefore be swayed towards peace by fear of invasion from the Spanish base of Wesel, the commercial imperatives for war remained overwhelming.

And for the Dutch leader Maurice of Nassau, meanwhile, there was also the potent drive of personal ambition. For it was only by warfare that the princely splendour and authority of the House of Orange could be preserved within a republican polity, though this was not Maurice's only concern. The dream of leading one great campaign to bring about unification with the southern provinces was by 1621 more powerful than ever – irrespective of how unity might disrupt the expanding economy of the north, or the possible effect upon the Calvinist minority in Holland and Zeeland of integration with the wholly Catholic population of the south. Lured by the prospect of profit and driven by the passions of a religious crusade, both ministers and merchants saw little need for caution when the ships of Holland outnumbered the combined mercantile marines of England, Spain and France, and the Bank of Amsterdam controlled the flow of capital not only in the northern provinces but throughout northern Europe as a whole. No one, therefore, with an eye to the balance sheet wished to endanger this prosperous state of affairs by peace. And in Maurice of Nassau, the financiers and merchants of Amsterdam – whose *handel op dem vijand*, or trade with the enemy, still horrified devotees of mercantilist economics – had a general who could fill their coffers even further.

Upon William of Orange's murder in 1584, the fate of the United Provinces had hung in the balance, as a Spanish army crossed the Rhine and the Maas with the intention of isolating Calvinist Holland and Zeeland from the north-eastern Catholic provinces of Groningen, Friesland, Gelderland and Overijssel, which had uneasily agreed to carry on the fight for independence. But in Jan van Oldenbarnevelt, the Dutch discovered a skilled administrator, capable of manipulating the urban patriciate to which he belonged and of persuading the delegates of the other provinces to follow Holland's lead in the republic's States-General. And in Maurice of Nassau, whom Oldenbarnevelt brought forward to strengthen the common cause, the Dutch had a man who, at the age of only 20, had begun to demonstrate the skills which were to make him one of the finest soldiers of his age. Born in 1567 and elected stadholder of Holland in succession to his father eighteen years later, Nassau's leadership as captain-general of the Dutch forces had resulted in the seizure of Breda in 1590 and a spectacular offensive through Zutphen, Deventer and Nymwegen in 1591 to restore communication with the north-eastern provinces. By the following year, moreover, Gelderland had been cleared of Spanish troops, leaving the Dutch well placed to make further incursions into Groningen and Geetruidenberg thereafter.

Gifted, tenacious and ruthless, a strategist of genuine genius, albeit one of infinite care rather than panache, Maurice appeared an unstoppable force. And as he appeared to carry all before him, so he had also transformed the art of war, adopting and adapting the new ideas on mobility, and on the proper relation between musketeers, cavalry and pikemen. Instead of using his men in clumsy uneconomic columns, for example, he arranged them in shallower, linear formations about five ranks deep. The musketeers were organised in separate groups, detached from the pikemen, and the army itself was divided into units of about 500 men, an altogether more flexible arrangement than the Spanish unit of 3,000. New methods of fighting were accompanied, at the same time, by regular pay, training and drill, the establishment of a first-class commisariat and the adoption of new techniques of gunnery and fortification, derived in no small measure from the Leiden lectures of Simon Stevin under whom Maurice studied mathematics, and whose teachings he skilfully applied to the theory of ballistics, military engineering and in particular siege warfare. Nor, in his mastery of land warfare, had the Netherlands' captain-general failed to grasp the crucial importance of sea power either. For the entire territory of Holland and Zeeland was a patchwork of polders, lakes, meres, dykes, rivers and canals, rendering all warfare in such an area, as the Spaniards were repeatedly made to learn, amphibious to a greater or lesser degree.

If ever a people required a man of the moment, therefore, it was the Dutch in their struggle for independence, and if ever a leader appeared to answer the needs of his people in their hour of crisis, it was Maurice of Nassau – so much so, in fact, that his brilliant cavalry victory at Turnhout in 1597 had not only compounded Spain's bankruptcy the year earlier, but reduced her Army of Flanders to little more than a dogged defence of the so-called 'Obedient Provinces' of the south. Thereafter, Philip II's successors in the Netherlands, his daughter Isabella and the Austrian Habsburg Archduke Albert, were left little opportunity for headway, even after the arrival in 1604 of an opponent worthy of Maurice's strength, Ambrogio Spinola, Marquis of Los Balbases. For while the governorship of Albert and Isabella proved less odious than earlier regimes, their subjects in the south were still contemptuously terrorised by the Spanish army, and the social stagnation, which had accompanied the migration to the north of their richest, most powerful and enterprising people, continued to sap their resources. It was no coincidence that of the 300 largest clients of the newly-founded Bank of Amsterdam, more than half were former southerners – and no coincidence either that among them were two of the largest stockholders of the Dutch East India Company, Dirk van Os and Isaac le Maire. The Trips – who patronised Rembrandt – and the de Geers who jointly dominated the thriving trade with Sweden were both from Liège, and the influx of creative talent to the burgeoning cities of the north also extended to skilled tradesmen of all descriptions, but especially silk and cloth workers. Under such circumstances, even if Spinola might succeed in reducing Ostend to smoking ruins and grind his enemies to a truce three years later, the longer-term balance of forces seemed undeniable.

The Twelve Years Truce of 1609, however, had also brought to the surface political tensions within the Dutch Republic itself, which, as they evolved over the next nine years or so, would represent a crisis in their own right, for, contrary to appearances, the Dutch regime was anything but democratic. Nominally at least, in his role as Stadholder, Maurice was nothing more than the first magistrate of the confederated republics. Indeed, the constitution of the United Provinces was deliberately designed to thwart not only monarchical but centralising tendencies of any kind, so that even the States-General was entirely dependent upon the decisions and instructions which their members were given by the Estates of each province. But by sheer force of personality Maurice had come to occupy, like his father before him, a quasi-regal position, while Holland, with its thriving capital of Amsterdam, outdid all other provinces in terms of wealth, power, energy, and indeed radical republican sentiment. All economic and political power, at the same time, was concentrated in the hands of the small oligarchy of 'regents' whose administrative head or 'advocate' – later called 'grand-pensionary' – equalled in reality the influence of the stadholder. And the result had been a delicate balance, maintained originally by the fact that the crucial figure of the 'advocate', in the form of Jan van Oldenbarnevelt, had been a staunch supporter of Maurice.

But the image of the United Provinces as the fulfilment of Aristotle's ideal of a well-ordered state – a happy mixture of monarchy, aristocracy and democracy – was already breaking down by the time that Hugo Grotius, one of the 'regents', had depicted it as such in 1610. The conclusion of the truce with Spain, which was Oldenbarnevelt's work, had been bitterly opposed in fact by Maurice. And in the burning question of Church government and the relationship between State and Church – both closely connected with the problems of peace or war – the regents also favoured a less rigid and more conciliatory course, whereas the stadholder, fully supported by the religiously strict and politically bellicose middle and lower middle classes, championed more radical measures. Inflamed by obscure theological controversies over the issue of predestination, generated by the teachings of Jacobus Arminius, who not only offended Calvinists by his advocacy of free will in determining the salvation of the soul, but broadened the political scope of the rift by proclaiming the right of all public authorities to arbitrate in church affairs, these differences festered dangerously, and culminated ultimately in a head-on clash, which Maurice openly entered in 1617 by declaring himself opposed to Arminius and, by implication, the regents who supported his position. Supported by the common people, who continued to regard the Prince of Orange as their natural *Hooge Overheid* or Supreme Authority, the scene was set for Maurice to stage a final showdown with the regents in general and Oldenbarnevelt in particular, which would determine not only the stadholder's own status but the future of the truce and, more importantly still, the broader prospects for peace in Europe as a whole.

In effect, the assault on Maurice's position had taken place on two fronts. Ideologically, it fell to Grotius to argue from his position as a lawyer, philosopher and historian of international reputation that the stadholder's role should be limited. The ancient Batavian ancestors of the Dutch were, he argued, ruled traditionally by their patricians, while the powers accorded to the current leader of the republic were limited and purely a matter of convenience. But it was

Oldenbarnevelt who had struck at Maurice's power more practically by encouraging the recruitment in Holland of special professional levies, or *waargelders*, to preserve order and check mob violence. Realising that war threatened Holland's predominance in the republic and the power of the regents, since war was bound to exhaust the province's financial resources and damage the republican institutions favoured by the burgher oligarchy, Oldenbarnevelt had therefore deliberately set out to create a force independent of the stadholder's command. And in doing so, predictably enough, he had sealed his own fate. For in a secret session of the States-General, convened without the representatives of Holland, Maurice secured full powers, and by 1617 had replaced all the regents in Holland favourable to Oldenbarnevelt with supporters of his own. Grotius was imprisoned and later exiled after a dramatic escape, but Oldenbarnevelt was condemned and executed on 13 May 1619 on the basis of allegations which included the promotion of heresies and acceptance of bribes from foreign powers.

'Is this the wages of the three and thirty years' service that I have given to the country?' declared the defendant upon hearing his sentence. But Oldenbarnevelt's indignation was more than exceeded by both the scale of his defeat and the wave of popular antipathy towards the truce that had underpinned so much of what he had stood for. Certainly, the conviction that it had enabled Spain to steal a march on the United Provinces was widespread, for not only had the Spaniards taken Wesel and achieved military and diplomatic successes throughout Europe, culminating in the invasion of the Palatinate, it was also firmly believed that they had been enabled by the pause in hostilities to amass vast stores of bullion. And such was the gravity of the choice now facing the States-General that the available options were debated on no fewer than six separate occasions between November 1620 and January 1621, before the arrival in March of the deposed King of Bohemia himself. The Dutch Republic had, of course, been the only state to provide substantial aid for the Bohemians, not only out of sympathy for their cause, but also to engage as many Spanish troops as possible far from the Dutch frontier. And when the exiled ruler and his attractive English wife finally set foot in The Hague – hailed as heroes and innocent victims of a Catholic and Habsburg conspiracy that could no longer go unavenged – they were welcomed by their hosts with an enthusiasm that both reflected and amplified the prevalent war fever of the day.

For Maurice in particular, of course, the visit was to become the perfect vehicle for a masterpiece of carefully crafted propaganda that required only one more brush stroke to complete. For just one month later, a certain Madame de'Tserclaes, the Catholic widow of a Brabanter exiled in Holland, staged an unexpected intervention that would serve the war party's purposes almost perfectly. A regular visitor to her daughter in Brussels and known personally to both Archduke Albert and Maurice himself, de'Tserclaes had occasionally acted as their go-between, with the result that in February 1621 she conveyed proposals which may or may not have represented an attempt to suborn the stadholder from his loyalty to the States-General, but actually provided him with precisely the opportunity he required to stoke the growing war fever. For when Albert's proposals were followed one month later by an open request that the States-General should receive a mission led by Petrus Pecquius, his chancellor, Maurice not only welcomed the visit publicly, but encouraged such exaggerated expectations of its outcome that when Pecquius indelicately demanded as his initial bargaining point the nominal return of the Dutch to their former allegiance, the popular outrage was such that only Maurice's personal intervention spared his hapless guest from lynching. Whereupon the unfortunate emissary, who had already been mobbed by angry crowds in Delft, was brusquely sent home carrying a provocative message from his saviour, which confirmed in no uncertain terms that Archduke Albert was wholly 'misinformed' if either he or indeed the King of Spain himself were hoping for any recognition, however minimal, of Spanish authority.

Whether Maurice had ever intended to do anything other than exploit the mission from Brussels for his own political purposes is, of course, extremely doubtful. But if his plan throughout had been to convince his countrymen that war was the only alternative to abject submission, he could not in fact have succeeded more admirably – both at home and indeed in Spain itself, where his action seems to have served as a final tipping-point. For on 30 March Philip III died, leaving both his successor and his councillors firmly intent upon a renewal of conflict. 'I can assure you that the truce with Holland will not be reviewed,' wrote the French ambassador, Bassompiere, to Louis XIII in Paris, as plans were busily laid in The Hague and Amsterdam to support every available anti-Habsburg movement, whether championed by the Bohemian nobility, the German princes or the crowns of France and Sweden. Only thus, it seemed, could the interests of the United Provinces be upheld – and in particular those commercial interests that were so influential not only in Dutch thinking but among Spaniards too. For in Madrid, likewise, the debate had been decided ultimately by the representatives of the East and West India trades, along with the Councils of Portugal and the Indies, all of whom were acutely aware of Dutch expansion during the truce, and now convinced beyond all hope of recall that Holland must be destroyed by land, in order to loosen her tentacles at sea.

Neither Olivares nor Zuñiga nor any other of their colleagues were, of course, in doubt concerning the scale of the task ahead:

Whoever looks at the matter correctly and without passion [Zuñiga observed] must be impressed by the great armed strength of these provinces both by land and by sea, their strong geographical position ringed by the sea and by great rivers, lying close to France, England and Germany. Furthermore, that state is at the very height of its grandeur, while ours is in disarray.

Yet Spain stood quite literally, it seemed, between the devil and the deep blue sea, and the current diplomatic conjuncture, at least, was eminently suited to her purposes, since the two branches of the House of Habsburg were united in action as they had never been in the reign of Philip II, notwithstanding the fact that the merging of the fate of Bohemia with the war in the Netherlands would ultimately engender a wider, all-consuming conflict in which the European supremacy of Spain would actually founder once and for all. Ironically enough, the correspondence between Madrid and Brussels reveals an almost total grasp of the intricacies of the international situation and, above all, the keenest possible awareness of the inseparability of developments in Germany, Italy, France and the Baltic. But it was to Europe's great cost that this at no point translated into any modification of Habsburg goals or, much more importantly still, even the remotest appreciation of the full consequences of a pan-continental war involving more countries and more agony over a longer period of time than anything witnessed hithrto.

Nor was it likely to, of course, when all was still being staked upon the possibility of a swift campaign, and when the fighting itself, in spite of all the heated debates beforehand, was actually renewed in such a comparatively half-hearted manner. For the Dutch, irrespective of their undoubted wealth and fervour, still had insufficient funds to launch a major assault, especially when the individual provinces, as the Dutch Council of State frequently complained, were in arrears with their contributions. So great, indeed, was the fear that Spinola might consequently seize the initiative by crossing the protective riverline, that Maurice was forced at first to withdraw from his forward positions in Cleves at Emmerich and Rees, even though there would be no shortage of private investment to provide the 7 million florins required for the establishment of a West India Company. 3 million alone, in fact, were contributed by Amsterdam, much of it by those self-same Calvinist exiles from the south, hungry to combine their zeal for God's cause with an equally healthy appetite for silver and gold. But while the interruption of Spanish bullion bound for America might indirectly assist the Dutch land army in holding its own, there was still altogether less urgency when it came to the liberation of the south that Maurice himself dreamed of. Indeed, were it not for the reluctance of the Brussels government to take decisive action of their own, the Dutch might well have been forced back onto the defensive even more decisively.

For by now the new regent, Isabella, was already a disillusioned woman, deep in sorrow at the death of her husband Albert, while the real power in the still loyal southern Netherlands – Alonso de la Cueva, Marquis and Cardinal of Bedmar – was unable to press home any apparent advantage for reasons that Isabella herself well understood:

> If we go on with the war in the Lower Palatinate [she wrote], we shall have before us a struggle of the greatest difficulty. We shall be assailed by the whole force of the opposite party and the burden will fall with all its weight upon Spain. It will hardly be possible to bring together sufficient forces to meet the enemy.

Too many troops of the Army of Flanders were currently serving as far afield as Hungary and Bohemia, and though permission was secured to recall Spinola from the Rhineland, he was required to leave two-thirds of his men behind under the command of Gonsalvo de Córdoba. As a result, the autumn campaign was at best no more than moderately successful, consisting of an attack on Sluys which achieved nothing, while Spinola, who planned to occupy Jülich, as the preliminary to the invasion of Overijssel, encountered unexpected resistance from the small Dutch garrison in the city, which did not fall until February 1622.

In the Rhineland itself, meanwhile, the truce established early in 1621, in order to allow the Protestant Union to disband, had actually been broken by Sir Horace de Vere, an English officer serving with a small contingent of 2,000 English volunteers in the employment of the United Provinces. One of the 'Fighting Veres' family with long experience of the Dutch wars, including the Siege of Jülich, Vere had found himself without money or supplies, and in a desperate bid to keep his small force in being had duly staked everything upon the reckless adventure of invading the diocese of Speier. It was a ploy that would become all too familiar over the coming decades as successive commanders were driven to sustain their armies by unleashing them upon towns and countryside, irrespective of strategic considerations or whether the place concerned was friend or foe. Nor was it new. 'Every soldier needs three peasants,' the old saying ran, 'one to give up his lodgings, one to provide his wife, and one to take his place in hell.' But in shattering the fragile lull, Vere had nevertheless not only sparked the war anew but given the current generation of German civilians their first experience of soldierly excess, and their first taste of much worse privations to come, as the so-called 'contribution system', reinforced by the growing influence of state bureaucrats and entrepreneurs, allowed rulers to field larger forces for longer periods than had ever been possible hitherto.

'Whenever we camped overnight, the head of the household had to give each of us a half thaler,' one soldier would write, 'but it was for the best, since then we were satisfied with him and let him keep his livestock in peace.' Not all troops, however, were so accommodating. 'We have to buy for the soldiers whatever they want to have,' complained one victim of the contribution system, 'including meat, wine, beer, and many other things, whatever they can think of,' while in many more cases still, the brutality of pillaging soldiers rapidly began to exceed all bounds of common humanity:

> In sum [wrote Hans Heberle describing his own experience at Ulm], it was such a miserable business that even a stone would have been moved to pity not to mention a human heart. For we were hunted like wild animals in the forests. One was caught and beaten badly, a second clobbered and stabbed, a third even shot dead, and from another were stripped and taken his little piece of bread and clothing.

Normally perpetrated by the musketeers in a regiment, who were both more mobile and lower paid than pikemen, such incidents would become increasingly common as the war went on, notwithstanding the best efforts of commanders to impose some semblance of order by means of public humiliation, whippings and in some cases execution. Nor, as the fighting gathered pace over the coming months and years, was it uncommon for the victims of soldiers' cruelty to exact penalties of their own, though, as the following account of the Scotsman Robert Munro makes clear, such acts of revenge usually incurred equally hideous acts of reprisal of their own:

> The Boores [i.e. peasants] on the march cruelly used our souldiers (that went aside to plunder) in cutting off their noses and eares, hands and feete, pulling out their eyes, with sundry other cruelties which they used; being justly repayed by the souldiers, in burning of many Dorpes [i.e. villages] on the march. Leaving also the boores dead, where they were found.

But even as Sir Horace de Vere's comparatively miniscule contingent made its way through Speier, the familiar pattern was not only underway but expanding in scope. For by September 1621 Count Ernst of Mansfeld's Protestant force was in much the same condition as its altogether smaller English counterpart. The Bohemian war was over and the countryside impoverished, while the Duke of

Bavaria had occupied the Upper Palatinate without difficulty, as Mansfeld's men festered in Pilsen. Only the chance visit of the English ambassador, John Digby, Earl of Bristol, had in fact prevented the general from surrendering altogether, though for his disgruntled troops, there remained ample scope for indiscipline, and for Mansfeld himself abundant opportunity for adding yet another black mark to his already checkered history.

Born in 1580, the thirteenth – and illegitimate – son of Peter Ernst, count of a small territory in Upper Saxony and a Spanish field marshall, Mansfeld had opted for a military career in the first place, mainly in hope of securing both respectability and reward. And though he had been raised a Catholic – and seems to have remained so – this had not prevented him from defecting to the Protestant Union in 1610, or demonstrating a flair for opportunism in other ways. For even before the Battle of White Mountain, he had been acting independently, consolidating his control over western Bohemia in the hope of obtaining a pardon and compensation. In October 1620, moreover, he had offered to surrender Pilsen in return for 400,000 florins, and even after Digby's visit, similar proposals followed from November 1621 onwards, usually coupled with demands for territorial compensation and a military command, preferably in the service of his former enemies. Plagued by heart trouble and asthma, which forced him to travel in a coach, Mansfeld embodied, in fact, some of the worst – and arguably most typical – defects of his contemporaries, wreaking turmoil in Alsace when he moved south to winter there in 1621, and further havoc in Speier, which he occupied in spring of the following year:

> The bishopric of Speier is ours [wrote one of Mansfeld's men]. We are plundering at our ease. Our general does not wish for a treaty or for peace. He laughs at the enemy. All his thoughts are fixed upon the collection of money.

Yet it was Mansfeld with whom the refugee Elector Palatine, travelling from The Hague dressed as a merchant to enlist his aid, was now forced to throw in his lot, and another adventurer of equally dubious value upon whom he would soon find himself even more reliant.

Still only 22 years of age, Christian of Brunswick, administrator of the Lutheran Prince-Bishopric of Halberstadt, was, in fact, little more than a violent youth, intoxicated by cavalry warfare and quixotically romantic in his devotion to Frederick's wife Elizabeth. Known to his Catholic enemies as the 'mad Halberstadter', he would earn a not altogether unwarranted reputation as a dangerous fanatic, sacrificing his men in repeated cavalry charges, which would eventually cost him his own arm and finally his life before he had reached his 30s. But, after service with Maurice of Nassau, he had neverthe-less succeeded in persuading the Dutch to help him raise 11,000 men, and duly ridden off to do battle for his lady Elizabeth – with 'For God and For Her' as his blazon – in defence of her husband's electorate. The intention was a concerted effort with the altogether more reliable Margrave of Baden-Durlach – a devout Protestant who had long maintained that his faith could only be defended by force of arms and who had entered the fray out of shame at the cowardice of the Protestant Union. Yet, with predictable consequences, Christian had rapidly gone his own way, moving north into Westphalia with the approach of winter, to quarter his troops in the dioceses of Münster and Paderborn and ransack the area for the gold and silver he needed for cam-paigning the following spring.

It was hardly the stuff from which the former King of Bohemia might wisely hope for better things, though when alternatives were so few he had little other choice, and rather more encouraging, at least, was news from elsewhere. For English volunteer garrisons had been established at Heidelberg and Frankenthal on the Rhine and Mannheim on the Neckar, and while James I remained unwilling to help his son-in-law in Bohemia, he now appeared rather more responsive in the Palatinate itself. Indeed, when Digby visited the English troops and lent them £10,000 on his own account, the king, in a momentary flush of enthusiasm, had repaid the debt and sent Frederick a further £30,000. When, moreover, Olivares balked at the prospect of English intervention, fearing its implications for the sea route to Flanders, James seemed uncharacteristically res-olute in the face of bribery. For Gondomar, the Spanish ambassador in London, was instructed to revive the prospect of a Spanish marriage for James's son, Charles, by adding the further enticement of the Palatinate as the Infanta Isabella Clara Eugenia's dowry, so that it might then be returned to Frederick by his father-in-law. What the ambassador had not revealed, however, was that neither Maximilian of Bavaria nor Frederick himself had been consulted. And whether it was this realisation or his kingdom's growing war fever that was responsible, James nevertheless remained untempted. The House of Commons, after all, was renewing its outcry and would soon be threatening financial action if direct intervention in the Palatinate was not forthcoming, as John Pym and others declaimed loudly about 'the religion which is being martyred in Bohemia'. And under such pressure, even James, it seemed, could not hold back indefinitely, so that in a rare attack of dignity and honour that appeared to make the prospect of war very real, he ostensibly dismissed Gondomar's enticements once and for all, informing him how 'I like not to marry my son with a portion of my daughter's tears.'

Yet a combination of Anglo-Dutch rivalry and Parliament's intransigence would again pull the King of England back from the brink and further compromise a cause in the Palatinate that was already looking increasingly forlorn. For by blockading the Flemish coast since the ending of the truce, the Dutch had interfered with English trade as well, at the very moment when rivalry between the rival East India Companies of the Netherlands and England was already coming to a head. 'I have seen the time,' complained the Dutch ambassador, Caron, in London, 'when the friends of Spain were held here as open enemies, but the king's subjects are now so irritated by these East India disputes that they take part against us.' And while English merchants grumbled against their co-religionists in Holland, so the House of Commons' foreign policy pronouncements proved most provocative of all to a monarch who firmly believed that his kingdom's international relations were his alone to determine – so much so that in January 1622 he not only dissolved Parliament, but, in doing so, rebuked all who spoke ill of 'our dear brother the King of Spain'.

For Spain, as her ambassador well appreciated, it was a rich harvest. 'It is the best thing that has happened in the interests of Spain and the Catholic religion since Luther began to preach heresy a hundred years ago,' observed Gondomar. And if Spanish success in keeping the sea route open was rightly hailed as a triumph of the first order, it was reinforced by other tidings from the Valtelline. Since its occupation by Gómez Suárez de Figueroa, Duke of Feria, in 1620, pressure had been building in France for the restitution of Protestant rights in the area, and in April 1621, as a result of the Treaty of Madrid, Spain had duly decided to comply. But the decision was swiftly followed by further aggression from the Protestant Grey Lords and appeals from the Catholic population both to Feria and Archduke Leopold of the Tyrol. The result was a crushing victory for Spain and the confirmation of the Articles of Milan of January 1622, which not only abolished the sovereignty of the Grey Lords in Bormio and the valley itself, but assigned the protection of Davos and the Lower Engadine to Leopold. Thereafter, with their interests intact and a papal force temporarily installed, Spanish forces duly salved French pride by staging a tactical withdrawal, which could nevertheless be reversed as occasion demanded.

Further to the east, moreover, the Habsburgs had survived a renewed onslaught by Bethlen Gábor and the Hungarian nobility, who had renounced their truce with the emperor on 1 September 1621 and advanced with 30,000 horsemen in an effort to overrun Upper Hungary and retake Bratislava, where Bethlen intended to hold his coronation with the crown of St Stephen that he had captured the year before. Bucquoy, in fact, had already led the Imperial armies in a successful assault on the city, but was killed in the Siege of Neuhäusel, and when Bethlen's wild cavalry, which could not conduct a sustained campaign without infantry, was joined by a force of 12,000 men under the Margrave of Jägerndorf, the scene seemed set for a decisive blow. But lack of food forced Jägerndorf to abandon the assault to go marauding for supplies, while Bethlen himself once more proved an inconstant ally, meeting Ferdinand's representatives at Nikolsburg in Moravia and agreeing a treaty in January 1622, which granted the Hungarian Estates virtual autonomy and left Bethlen himself with a pension of 50,000 florins, in return for his surrender of the crown of St Stephen and renunciation of the royal title that he had assumed in August 1620.

By then, however, the attention of all Europe had in any case turned back firmly to the Palatinate. On his journey to rendezvous with Mansfeld and the Margrave of Baden-Durlach, Frederick had actually been briefly apprehended, only to escape by virtue of his disguise, though this particular stroke of luck would prove to be another rarity. For although, in his desperation, he had ratified an alliance with the Turks in July 1620, it was already clear that the sultan was interested only in pressurising Ferdinand to adjust the truce of 1606, and when news of the Battle of White Mountain finally reached Constantinople the following January, it resulted in an understandable cooling of interest. Even more disappointingly, the subsequent military campaign swiftly faltered after Mansfeld and Baden-Durlach had achieved a fleeting victory over Tilly's army to the south of Wiesloch. For Córdoba had recognised the danger and abandoned the siege of Frankenthal to bring the Spanish army to Tilly's aid, forcing Mansfeld to withdraw with Frederick to Oppenheim, and leave Baden-Durlach to stage a brave but unsuccessful stand on 6 May 1622 at Wimpfen. Amid exploding powder wagons, which created the myth of a white-robed woman leading the Catholics to victory, the margrave had finally succumbed after ten hours of heavy fighting in front of the marshy Bölliger stream, which left little scope for retreat and resulted in destruction heavy enough to force his retirement from the war.

With Tilly's subsequent interception and defeat of Christian of Brunswick at Höchst on the Main on 20 July, Frederick therefore became totally disillusioned. The bridge at Höchst had become so clogged with Christian's wagons as he frantically manouevred into position at the enemy advance that it collapsed. And though, with typical boldness, he ordered his cavalry to swim the distance, the result was chaos and the loss of a third of his men – along, it seems, with the fine Westphalian hams that his cavalry had jettisoned with their saddlebags in making their vain crossing. Worse still, on 29 August the remnants of Christian's army were overtaken by Córdoba at Fleurus, west of Namur, on their way to Breda, though many of his cavalry still managed to reached their objective. His baggage and artillery lost, his arm hanging in shreds from wounds sustained in a cavalry charge, and the fate of the Palatinate virtually sealed, the 'mad Halberstadter' had chosen to have the shattered limb amputated on the battlefield to the sound of martial music, before issuing a commemorative medal with the inscription *Altera restat*: 'the other remains'. But for Frederick it was the supreme blow, and though Christian himself would live to fight again, the Palatine phase of the war was now reaching a close.

Instead of marching in triumph to Heidelberg, his capital, the sometime King of Bohemia actually faced the prospect of a long winter pillaging in Alsace in the company of Mansfeld's troops, which would soon become unendurable:

> As for this army [he wrote] it has committed great disorders. I think there are men in it who are possessed of the devil, and who take pleasure in setting fire to everything. I should be glad to leave them. There ought to be some difference made between friend and foe but these people ruin both alike.

And his sentiments were largely shared by the English envoy, Lord Chesterton, who attended him and reflected thus upon the decay of discipline:

> I might conceive that kingdoms and principalities for which they shall fight be in great danger and hazard … and how can it be better otherwise where men are raised out of the scume of the people by princes who have no dominion over them, nor power for want of paye to punish them, nor meanes to reward them, living only upon rapine and Spoyle as they do.

In such circumstances, Frederick soon thought only of escape – to his uncle the Duke of Bouillon who gave him refuge in the fortress at Sedan, from where he wrote to James I agreeing at last to abandon the war.

Still prone to gusts of delusion, he would remain, like Mansfeld and Christian, at large, but of little more, henceforth, than irritant value. For with no one of substance to oppose him in the Palatinate, Tilly had duly forced the surrender of Heidelberg in September 1622, of Mannheim in November, and of Frankenthal in March. In the meantime, Maximilian had set about the expulsion of Protestant clergy, dispatched Frederick's library as a gift to the Pope, and declared his right to be appointed elector in accordance with the secret arrangement made with the emperor that was already widely known across Europe, as a result of the documents captured by Mansfeld and subsequently published. Since no full Diet would ever give its approval – and notwithstanding the opposition of Philip IV who remained certain that the decision would lead to a declaration of war by

England – the transfer of title was duly sealed by what amounted to a sham convention of deputies at Regensburg on 7 January 1623, though, as a result of Spanish reservations, Maximilian's electoral powers were to endure only for his life, after which they would revert to one of Frederick's Wittelsbach heirs. Even so, it remained a triumph for the Catholic cause – and one that would be marked in Munich by lavish feasts and in Rome with a ceremonial *Te Deum* in St Peter's. Yet no Protestant prince was present at Maximilian's investiture and no new golden era of peace had in fact dawned, either in Germany or in Europe as a whole. On the contrary, the episode was a triumph for the men of arms in general and for one man in particular, who would not only achieve fame at the head of his troops but untold fortune too by reaping the profits of bloodshed on a hitherto undreamed of scale – a 'soldier under Saturn' whom the stars themselves, it seemed, had set aside from normal mortals.

6

'SOLDIER UNDER SATURN'

Of this gentleman, I may in truth write that he has a character alert, lively, eager and restless, curious of every kind of novelty, unsuited to the common manner of mankind but striving after new, untried or extraordinary ways; moreover he has much more in his head than he allows to be perceived. For Saturn in the ascendant brings contemplative, melancholy though luminous thoughts, a bent towards alchemy, magic and enchantment, community with sprites, scorn and indifference towards human ordinances and conventions and to all religions, making everything proposed by God or man to be suspected … he will be unmerciful, without brotherly or nuptial affection, caring for no one, devoted only to himself and his desires, severe upon those placed under him, avid, covetous, deceitful, inequitable in his dealings, usually silent, often violent, contentious also, not to be browbeaten … there may also be seen great thirst for honour and a striving after temporal titles and power, whereby he will make for himself many great and injurious enemies both secret and confessed.

Johannes Kepler, *Opera Omnia*, Vol. III

When Johannes Kepler first cast the horoscope of a minor Bohemian nobleman of comparatively modest means in 1607, he could hardly have foreseen the true scale of what lay in store for his client. Born 24 years earlier at the village of Heřmanice on the Elbe and orphaned at the age of twelve, Albrecht Wenzel Eusebius von Valdštejn, or Wallenstein as he is more commonly known to posterity, had been raised by his uncle, both conventionally and unpretentiously, among the Bohemian Brethren before becoming a Catholic convert in early manhood. In the interim, however, he had been sent first to a grammar school at Zlotoryja (Goldberg) in Silesia – where he had proved bold enough to complain to the provincial governor of taunts of 'Calvinist scum' in the town's streets, along with other forms of hostility, probably relating to his Czech origins – before completing his studies at the Nuremberg Academy at Altdorf in only six months, after attempts to expel him on grounds of riotous behaviour. For he had been ringleader, it seems, of a gang of students who mobbed an academic's house one night, breaking the door and windows, and was present, too, when an argument between a group of his peers and a junior militia officer led to a brawl in which the officer was killed. Deemed innocent on this particular occasion of dealing the fatal blow, he was nevertheless under suspicion only a little later when he wielded the blade in his own right, stabbing a fellow student in the foot. And this time the young hothead would not escape so lightly, spending at least two nights in jail for his recklessness, prior to a further spell of house arrest by the Academy pending expulsion: a penalty that was never actually executed, in fact, by virtue of a letter penned to the Nuremberg authorities in the culprit's own hand, into which he carefully dropped the names of two distant relatives who happened to be Imperial privy councillors.

Plainly a fellow of spirit, the young Wallenstein was equally plainly, too, a character of some resource. But there remained little, if anything, to suggest future greatness after his departure from Altdorf – ostensibly of his own accord – on the customary grand tour, which, in his case, encompassed France and above all Italy, where he stayed long enough to gain a good grasp of the language and resided reportedly in the university cities of Padua and Bologna, before returning home in 1602. Certainly, his appearance was prepossessing enough, if a twentieth-century examination of his remains, and contemporary likenesses and descriptions are any guide – being deemed 'tall of stature' at around 5 foot 8 inches, 'slender and lean', and distinguished by a high forehead, dark eyes and dark hair, which he wore short and brushed back to complement a beard of the popular Spanish style. By the age of 23, moreover, he had reputedly matured into a gentleman replete with 'good manners' and other 'fine and laudable qualities', speaking German and Italian fluently, reading Spanish, French and Latin with varying degreees of competency, though never less than adequately, and capable too, it seems, of considerable generosity. For, according to a contemporary French pamphlet, he 'was very liberal and when he gave presents he very much rejoiced and indeed was a man who gave the most to those who least expected it.' Yet in all such respects – with the exception perhaps of what one contemporary termed his 'immutable chastity' – he was no more than typical of so many of his class. And there remained a darker side even to his liberality, since his gifts, it seems, 'were golden snares which indissolubly obliged', and his aura was considered forbidding. For he was 'almost perpetually melancholic' and accentuated his sombre appearance with austere black clothing, frequently alternating, in the meantime, between icy self-control and violent outbursts which would increase as his health deteriorated after a bout of malaria in 1605, from which he would never fully recover. Already prone to gout in his 30s, a decade later he was experiencing heart problems and panic attacks, as well as nervous debility, colic and depression, all of which are likely to have heightened his morbid obsession with astrology.

Perhaps, then, only a combination of supreme ambition, the greatest good luck and, above all, a sublime gift for exploiting that luck to the limit could ultimately have propelled a man like Wallenstein to the heights. But by 1604, he had nevertheless opted for a military career, serving first as an ensign and then as a captain in one of the interminable episodes of war against the Turk on the Hungarian border. And it was during this period, too, that he almost certainly encountered a series of influential colonels, including the 45-year-old Count Tilly, who was to be his principal colleague – and indeed rival – in the Catholic armies more than twenty years later, as well as Count Heinrich Matthias Thurn of the Bohemian revolt and the Spaniard Balthasar Marradas, who was successively his superior, subordinate and opponent in the 1620s and 1630s. For like the American Civil War more than two centuries later, the Thirty Years War pitted old familiars and former colleagues against each other on numerous occasions, and from an early stage in his career, Wallenstein was already on his way to becoming part of this martial nexus. But his nomination as a colonel in his own right at the age of only 22 and the further fact that by February 1607 he was reportedly attending Mass after his conversion by Jesuits, were almost certainly of less importance in his rapid rise to prominence than something that had occurred entirely independently of his actions during his absence on campaign. For in 1604 Wallenstein's sister, Kateřina Anna, married Baron Karl Žerotin, a leading Moravian nobleman, whose sponsorship would carry him not only to Vienna and ultimately the heart of Imperial affairs, but also to a marriage in May 1609 with Lucretia of Vickov, a wealthy widow whose estates dwarfed Wallenstein's own and whose early death from plague in 1614 left him with property worth 400,000 florins.

Largely as a result of Žerotin's recommendations, the young soldier had already been made chamberlain at the court of Emperor Matthias in 1606, and a similar appointment would also follow at the court of Ferdinand of Styria, for whom he fought in the war with Venice of 1617, commanding a cavalry force and helping to relieve the Venetian siege of Gradisca. 'Herr von Wallenstein,' he had written at the time, already displaying a hint of the superb confidence that was to be his hallmark, 'will wait upon Archduke Ferdinand in the camp with 180 cuirassiers and 80 musketeers maintained at his own cost.' But it was marriage once again and, above all, the revolt of Bohemia that turned Wallenstein's rise from impressive to extraordinary. For in 1623, after the death of his first wife, he strengthened his ties to the Habsburg elite and made himself one of the richest men in Bohemia by a match with Isabella Katharina, younger daughter of Count Karl Leonhart von Harrach, an Imperial privy councillor and member of the 'Spanish faction' centred upon Emperor Ferdinand's most trusted adviser, Eggenberg. In all, she would bear him two children, a son who died in infancy and a surviving daughter, and in the process cement his position within the Imperial ruling class, though, in some respects, the marriage itself was as much confirmation as cause of his status. For even before the knot was tied, Wallenstein had exploited the disorder in his native land to perfection – by a deft combination of financial speculation, property grabbing and loyal service to the Imperial crown, which not only complemented one another, but made him increasingly indispensable as both creditor and soldier of the Imperial cause and the man who recruited and equipped its forces on a scale and at a personal profit that far outstripped his contemporaries. In truth, the armies that would come to fight under his command in the coming years were essentially no different from other German armies of the time in terms of tactics and composition, but, unlike others, he would remain the supreme entrepreneur of warfare, an administrator of superb ability capable of equipping his troops at his own expense and offering them to his Imperial master in a manner that would eventually lead the emperor to question who was master of whom.

At the outset of the Bohemian revolt, in fact, Wallenstein had been serving as commander of a Moravian cavalry force, but soon opted for the Imperial cause, brazenly appropriating the Moravian treasury for Ferdinand in the process, and raising 20,000 gulden from his own resources before borrowing a further 20,000 to raise a regiment of 1,000 cuirassiers. By February 1619, moreover, he had been appointed an Imperial colonel, and thereafter served with distinction under Bucquoy in the wars against both Mansfeld and Bethlen Gábor, joining in the victory at Záblatí in June 1619 and helping to defend Vienna during the siege of that November. But it was in the aftermath of Bohemia's subjection that the colonel finally came into his own – and not as a soldier. For although appointed to the Imperial War Council in 1620 and created military commander of Bohemia in December 1621, his main interest, and indeed skill, at this time lay in financial speculation and property acquisition, the opportunities for which were now boundless. Profiting considerably from the minting monopoly, which had begun in January 1622, Wallenstein also exploited the devalued currency to purchase the estates of fugitive Bohemian nobles, including his own Smiřický relatives, some of which he sold at enormous profit, while retaining others for himself. Ultimately, no less than sixty-six in all were accumulated, mainly between the frontier towns of Friedland and Reichenberg in north-east Bohemia, covering some 1,200km^2 of territory and including not only fifty-seven villages and castles, but nine towns – among them Gitschin, where he built himself a palace befitting a man of his exceptional status.

Yet the accumulation of such vast lands was still, it seems, only the means to a further end. For as his wealth grew, so too did his ability to win influence with an emperor whose only recourse was to fill his empty treasury by lavishly rewarding his creditors with honours. Already in 1619 Wallenstein had been in a position to lend Ferdinand 40,000 florins, but by 1620 the sum had risen by another 160,000, and in 1621, 195,000. In 1622, moreover, there was an altogether more massive loan of 527,000, followed by 700,000 in 1623, leaving the borrower hopelessly in hock and committed, beyond all hope of manoeuvre, to offering his benefactor whatever he chose. The result was Wallenstein's elevation in 1623 to the honorific rank of *Fürst*, or 'prince of the Empire', and the subsequent award of the dukedom of Friedland in March 1624. Now, some said, there remained only a kingdom or the Empire itself to satisfy the ambition of this doyen of all contemporary mercenary captains, for with further war inevitable, Ferdinand felt an increasing need for an army independent of the Catholic League, whose first allegiance lay with the Duke of Bavaria. And though he had refused Wallenstein's proposal of 1623 to raise such an army at his own expense, on the condition that he might command them, the same misgivings about the resulting increase in Wallenstein's power were now being outweighed by more intense pressures from without.

For in 1621 another giant figure of the years to come, Gustavus Adolphus, King of Sweden, had made a dramatic entry of his own upon the European stage by defeating King Sigismund of Poland, friend and loyal ally of the emperor. Launching an audacious attack on the wealthy Polish port of Riga with an army of 19,000 men and a fleet of some 160 ships, Gustavus had embarked his Protestant kingdom upon the conquest of Livonia and the creation of a Baltic empire, which would be unlikely to hold aloof for long from the religious and political tensions of Central Europe. 'What have we to expect of Sigismund,' he had boldly declared to the Swedish *Riksdag* on the outbreak of war, 'who is not only evil himself, but allows himself to be governed by that Devil's party the Jesuits, the authors of the grievous tyranny in France and Spain and elsewhere?' And with these words he had sounded a clarion call to action not only against a king directly connected by marriage to the Austrian Habsburgs but a kingdom central to the progress of the militant Counter-Reformation, which reverberated ominously for the future peace of the continent.

Dubbed 'Gideon' by Ludwig Camerarius who met him at Stockholm in November 1623, Gustavus was now, as he himself fully appreciated, the Continent's coming man in more senses than one. 'I cannot praise adequately the heroic virtues of that king,' wrote the leader of Frederick V's government-in-exile in The Hague: 'piety, prudence and resolution. He has no equal in Europe.' But while the ruler of Sweden was being hailed thus, he was not the only ruler threatening the crumbling status quo, since his Danish rival, the Protestant Christian IV, was at that very moment opening negotiations with the United Provinces and hungrily eyeing the secularised bishoprics of Halberstadt and Osnabrück. A hard fighter, inveterate drinker and cheerful father of innumerable illegitimate children – 'One could hardly believe he had been born in so cold a climate,' reflected Cardinal Bentivoglio – Christian was even harbouring hopes, it seems, of gaining control of the Elbe and Oder. And while both he and his Swedish counterpart loomed on the northern horizon, there was also the more immediate problem of Christian of Brunswick for the emperor to consider, since the 'mad Halberstadter' had spent the winter of 1622/23 in occupation of Lower Saxony, where he was well placed to attack Maximilian of Bavaria's brother in the dioceses of Cologne and Liège, or expel his brother-in-law, William of Neuburg, from Jülich.

From the Netherlands, it is true, the news for the Habsburgs was more encouraging, as the Brussels administration fortified the harbours at Ostend and Dunkirk and built light cruisers to co-operate with the Dunkirk privateers in preying upon North Sea shipping and raiding the Dutch herring fisheries. In May 1623, moreover, Spinola had sent a flotilla of fourteen flat-bottomed boats to penetrate the canals and rivers of Zeeland, taking Walcheren in the process and thereby boosting opposition to the war to new levels of intensity within Holland. Only, in fact, the hesitancy of the Catholic League in joining the assault finally prevented Spinola from delivering a potential killer blow, since Maximilian of Bavaria had no wish to risk open war with the Dutch, lest they were to succeed one day – perhaps alongside England and France – in removing him from the Palatinate. And there were enduring suspicions, too, about Spain's future policy in the Rhineland after the Spanish ambassador had refused to attend the duke's installation as elector, and Córdoba had remained behind in the Lower Palatinate while Tilly went north in pursuit of Christian of Brunswick.

In the event, Tilly had indeed defeated Christian at the Battle of Stadtlohn, just 10 miles from the Dutch border, on 6 August 1623 – and so decisively that the vanquished Halberstadter lost all but 2,000 of his 15,000-man army. Just three days later – with Christian sheltering in The Hague and blaming his colleague Baron Dodo Knyphausen for the disaster – Frederick V duly agreed an armistice with Ferdinand, leaving Mansfeld to disband his own army on the Rhine shortly afterwards. Yet what might have appeared a critical victory once again bore ramifications that undid the benefits it delivered. For while Stadtlohn left even Frederick resigned for the time being to realities and also ensured Christian's removal from a projected alliance between Bethlen Gábor, the Turks and the so-called 'Vlachs' of East Moravia, news of the battle had also wrecked all hopes of a Spanish marriage for Prince Charles of England, as it at once became clear that Spain could do nothing to restore either the Palatinate or its electoral title to the English king's son-in-law. Worse still, both Charles and his mentor, the Duke of Buckingham, now returned from an abortive venture to woo the Spanish Infanta in Madrid, bitterly humiliated and bent on revenge.

By the winter of 1623/24, therefore, it was news of the most welcome kind to the Dutch that their English counterparts were at last preparing to abandon their much talked of alliance with Spain, for morale in the United Provinces after the setback of Stadtlohn was arguably as low as it had been at any time since the murder of William the Silent in 1584. On the one hand, none of the victories dreamed of by Maurice of Nassau during the truce had actually materialised, and the initiative was firmly in the hands of Spinola. Worse still, the months of January and February ushered in a period of exceptionally cold weather that brought Spanish troops across the frozen waterways into the Veluwe to threaten Utrecht. At which point, Maurice's concern was such that Madame de 'Tserclaes was once again dispatched on her travels to seek a six-month suspension of hostilities, though this time, unsurprisingly, there was no response from Brussels, as the spring thaw brought with it not only devastating floods but a mutiny at the key strategic city of Breda for lack of pay. Under the circumstances, only the prospect of outside help offered any consolation to the beleaguered Dutch, so that news of Mansfeld's summons to London that spring with a view to providing assistance could hardly have been more timely.

Help, however, was also on its way from France, where a new figure was stirring in preparation for his own massive impact upon the course not only of his own country's history, but that of the entire continent. Born in 1585, the third son of one of the lesser nobles of Poitou, Armand-Jean Du Plessis de Richelieu had been brought up for life as a layman before entering the Church at the age of 17 upon the death of one of his elder brothers, so that he might take over the family bishopric at Luçon, from which point his rise was seemingly inexorable. For after distinguishing himself as a spokesman for the clergy at a meeting of the States-General in 1614, he was subsequently appointed Minister of Foreign Affairs by the Queen Mother, Marie de' Medici, who, upon the death of her husband in 1610, had become regent on behalf of her 9-year-old son, Louis XIII. By 1622, moreover, Richelieu had been made a cardinal and by 1624 a member of the royal council, bringing with him in tow the mysterious figure of Père Joseph, a member of the Capuchin order of reformed friars, who, with their rivals the Jesuits, were rightfully acknowledged as spearheads of the Counter-Reformation.

From the very outset, in fact, the Capuchin's influence was indisputable. 'You,' Richelieu told him, 'are the principal agent whom God has employed to lead me to all the honours which I have reached ... I beg you speed your voyage and come soon to partake of the management of affairs.' And the man whom the cardinal referred to alternately as 'little Ezekiel' and 'Tenebroso Cavernoso', while always subordinate to his master, did indeed remain a guiding influence: on the one hand an austere mystic who dressed humbly, walked rather than rode, and whose life had been transformed by reading Father Benet of Canfield's *The Rule of Perfection*; on the other, the deeply reviled *eminence grise*, a shadowy amoral diplomat for whom *raisons d'état* were merely the instrument of God's will, and who saw in the aggrandisement of France and the destruction of the Habsburgs the necessary preliminary to a great crusade against the Turks.

'I will prove to the world that the age of Spain is passing away and the age of France has come,' Richelieu boldly declared, and although that boast would take time to make good, both the rapier-like flexibility of his own Machiavellian intellect and the whispered promptings of his confidant would ensure that over the next eighteen years the cardinal not only laid down the lines of French development for the next 150 years, but came by turns to hold the whole course of European history in his hands. Unity within the state, and in this regard, the elimination of religious dissent, was the crucial first step, though in the broader longer-term task of neutralising the chain of Habsburg bases encircling his country, he was no less prepared to seek out Protestant allies than Catholic. When asked about alliance with the Dutch rebels, he was in no doubt that it would be understood by the Pope, since 'in Rome, more than in any other place in the world, affairs are judged as much by the criteria of power and interest as by ecclesiastical argument.' And in other respects too, as his *Testament Politique* manifestly confirmed, Richelieu was equally prepared to lie down with the devil in the service of God and France:

It is one thing to be a good man according to the laws of God, and quite another to be one according to those of men ... The honesty of a public minister does not demand a timid and over-scrupulous conscience, for just as through lack of conscience many injustices and cruelties may occur, so over-scrupulousness can produce many omissions and indulgences harmful to the nation, and it is very certain that those who tremble at certainties through fear of destroying themselves often destroy the state, when they could have saved both.

To sum up, it should be realised that statesmen must be like the stars, which pay no attention to the snarling of curs, nor can they be diverted from marching steadily towards the goal which they have selected for the good of the state.

This, then, was the man described by Cardinal de Retz as 'a man of his word, except when some great interest obliged him not to be' – a man who 'did good, either through inclination or good sense, whenever his interest did not lead him to do evil, in which case he knew quite clearly what he was doing.'

In 1624, however, while France was still hampered by the activity of her own Protestant Huguenot rebels and Richelieu himself was not yet sufficiently dominant to risk head-on confrontation with his more cautious fellow councillors, he would have to tread carefully, notwithstanding the fact that the new Pope, Urban VII, who had been crowned the previous year, was himself an avid opponent of the Habsburgs. 'When Your Majesty decided to take me into your Council and your confidence,' the cardinal later reflected, 'I can say with truth that the Huguenots shared the state with you, that the nobles behaved as if they were not subjects and the most powerful provincial governors as if they were supreme within their provinces …' Only when the decks had been cleared of opposition at home, therefore, might any grander enterprise abroad be confidently undertaken. And not until 1629, in fact – with the Peace of Alais and the solution of the Huguenot issue – were all obstacles finally removed.

Throughout, Richelieu had remained adamant that 'we must abandon what is to be done abroad until we have done what must be done at home.' Yet even in April 1624, as he sat at the royal council table for the first time, his ultimate goal was already clearly formulated. 'Man,' he believed, 'is immortal, his salvation hereafter; the state has no immortality, its salvation is now or never.' And on this principle, as he made clear five years later, his intention had always been that France 'might enter the states of all her neighbours to protect them from Spain's oppression', in order 'to arrest the course of Spain's progress' and thereby, at one and the same time, liberate France for further expansion of her own. Wherever war or unrest struck his Habsburg rivals, he would keep the pot boiling, intervening indirectly at first, later openly, with the object of weakening their power, and ultimately advancing France's borders to their 'natural limit', the Rhine. 'We must think,' he reflected in his *Advice to the King*, 'of strengthening our position at Metz, and, if possible, of advancing to Strasbourg, in order to have the gateway to Germany.' And while caution was still a priority, even now he was willing to probe and pressure his enemy on three fronts: by forging a marriage alliance with England; by sealing the Treaty of Compiègne, which assured the Dutch a subsidy of 400,000 écus; and above all by implementing preparations for an assault by the Marquis of Cœuvres upon Spain's vital line of communication through the Valtelline, which he considered *importantissime*.

In the southern Netherlands meanwhile, Isabella, its governor-general, was beside herself at the extension of hostilities and the growing number of Spain's enemies. 'This is a war which will last for ever,' she wrote to Philip IV in September 1624, paying little heed to the current demoralisation within the enemy camp, and emphasising instead the potential catastrophe in store for his own kingdom:

> If you do not see that the wants of our army are supplied to the minute we shall risk a disaster which will ruin all your states. I think it is my duty then to spell this out plainly for you in good time, else if war breaks out next year in Germany, and France joins in with England, Your Majesty will find yourself face to face with the most awful difficulties one can imagine, and utterly unable to wage war in so many quarters at such a fearful cost. In such a case you would not have a hope, I will not say of victory, but of escaping utter defeat and ruin.

It was an extraordinary declaration from an aged and careworn widow, but with a prophetic quality that continues to resonate down the centuries. Already reduced to largely nominal authority by the influence of Cardinal Bedmar in Brussels, Isabella would eventually be forced to pawn her jewels to meet her liabilities, and by 1629 had withdrawn her support for Bedmar altogether. But by the time of her death in 1633, though the accuracy of her prediction was already increasingly manifest to those with eyes to see, her plea would still remain unheeded.

Certainly, if French intervention was one day to deal a deathblow to Spain's European policies, that day still seemed far off to many in 1624. For while Spinola had failed at Bergen and though English hostility was fully expected to be troublesome, Frederick V had nevertheless been virtually abandoned and the Palatinate cleared of Spanish enemies. Hungary and Moravia, too, had been successfully defended, while the Valtelline did indeed remain open, allowing Spinola to march in August 1624 against Breda, a frontier fortress of great importance guarding the routes north to Utrecht and Amsterdam. If this place – the favourite residence of Maurice of Nassau, which he himself had liberated in 1589 and which had been part of his family's patrimony for all of two centuries – were to fall, might not Isabella's misgivings about the prospects of an endless war yet be proven misplaced once and for all? Unrelentingly, she continued to warn against the operation, and she was not alone, since the Spanish council of war itself harboured doubts. Breda was, after all, exceptionally well fortified and the surrounding countryside little better than a quagmire. Furthermore, Justinus of Nassau, Maurice's natural brother, had garrisoned it with 7,000 men. But Spinola had elected to restore his reputation and, knowing that Breda's burghers had laid in only the usual stocks of winter supplies, because they did not expect an attack so late in the season, would not be swayed from his course.

Nor, indeed, did the dire prognostications of the general's opponents seem justified as the assault pressed forward initially. For as the Spanish army approached, Breda mistakenly opened its gates to the hundreds of refugees fleeing before the invader, and Spinola wasted no time in confining the swollen population within his siege works. Moreover, despite the difficulty of working in waterlogged ground, his troops had proceeded within seventeen days to dig 6-foot ditches, with protective walls 5 feet high, not only to encircle the defenders at a radius of half a mile from their walls but also to protect the besieging army itself from a relieving force. Under the circumstances, Breda was effectively doomed – on three assumptions: firstly, that the besieging army was supplied and paid; secondly that it was defended against attack from another force; and thirdly on the understanding that it was not diverted from its task by being called away to deal with other matters. And it was this last condition, in particular, that deeply concerned Philip IV who warned Spinola 'to look to it that no fortress of our own is jeopardised for the sake of taking Breda.' For Maurice of Nassau was already planning the capture of Cleves, which he duly achieved in September and followed up with raids on Antwerp in both the succeeding months.

Even so, notwithstanding the chorus of recrimination from Madrid and Brussels, Spinola remained determined to persist throughout the winter, while in the Valtelline, the French expedition which had set out under the Marquis de Coeuvres in November 1624 performed its task admirably. Despite heavy snowfalls which blocked the passes, the marquis's troops had nevertheless occupied the entire valley by February 1625 and treated with meticulous courtesy those papal garrisons that had been left in temporary occupation after the earlier Spanish withdrawal. Indeed, the success of the French prompted Charles Emmanuel of Savoy to launch a lightning attack of his own on Genoa, in alliance with the Duke of Lesdiguières, the independent-minded Huguenot governor of Dauphiné. And the potential importance of this particular initiative was not lost upon those in a good position to judge, including Sir Isaac Wake, English envoy at the Savoyard court, who reflected thus upon its possible impact:

It is very certain that the Spaniards are in very great labyrinth, and their weakness doth now evidently appear to all men. They must defend Genoa or else their honour and all that they have in Italy will be buried in the ruin of that city, and when that source shall be dried up [a reference to the Genoese banks which financed the government in Madrid] and the passage cut off for their transporting of Spaniards, Neapolitans and Sicilians, their armies in Germany will not be able to subsist long.

In fact, the support of English and Venetian ships that Wake had hoped for was never forthcoming. On the contrary, the only ships to be seen by Charles Emmanuel were those of the Marquis of Santa Cruz bringing Spanish reinforcements to the port, which soon allowed the Duke of Feria to send the invaders packing. But the message of Spain's vulnerability had been sent far and wide across Europe – even, indeed, to the corridors of Whitehall where the King of England duly stirred once more for action.

Upon Prince Charles' disillusioned return from Spain with the Duke of Buckingham in early 1624, the government had in fact raised 12,000 men with whom Mansfeld was intended to recover the Palatinate. Yet the resulting campaign was doomed from the start and served not only as a further reminder that Spain was as yet far from beaten, but that Isabella's prediction of 'a war which will last for ever' seemed altogether more plausible than the quick-fire *coup de grace* dreamed of by James I. For even now, the king could not bring himself to commence hostilities with Spain, and when Mansfeld inquired how he was consequently to pass through Spanish lines, he was met with the witheringly naïve instruction 'to demand passage according to the amity between England and Spain'. Thus confounded, the general duly set out for Calais in February 1625, with no other alternative in mind than to disembark his men and march them overland to the Rhineland, though Richelieu promptly refused him passage, on the grounds that French troops had already intervened against Spain in the Valtelline and that further assistance in a hostile act might lead to an open war that France could ill afford at this time.

Nor too, of course, had Mansfeld's own reputation as a plunderer and opportunist been overlooked in Richelieu's decision to deem him an unwanted guest. And that same reputation was also to foil the general's subsequent plan of sailing up-Channel to Walcheren where he was once again denied permission to land, since Maurice of Nassau was only ready to employ him for the relief of Breda rather than countenance his free passage through the Netherlands and be forced thereafter to watch his every step. While negotiations dragged on between Walcheren, London and The Hague, Mansfeld's unhappy troops, cooped up on board ship with foul water and contaminated food, died in their thousands, leaving many of the remaining 7,000 that finally put ashore without orders or pay, to desert in large numbers to the Army of Flanders, though for Mansfeld himself, this merely involved not so much the abandonment of his mission as the delay and irritation of raising replacements. For even as his force was being steadily depleted, events in northern Germany and elsewhere made the continuation of his efforts all the more important. Duke Maximilian's investiture as Imperial elector and alarm at Tilly's continued presence in the Lower Saxon Circle had, after all, led to talk of a new Protestant alliance, and if Mansfeld could indeed muster a force, there was also the possibility that it could work in conjunction with either Christian of Denmark, who was now courting glory and profit for the Protestant cause, or even the seemingly irrepressible Bethlen Gábor, with whom it might combine after advancing down the Elbe and ravaging the Habsburg lands in Silesia. Neither sickness nor desertions nor lack of funds any more than interminable delay could therefore blunt Mansfeld's will to continue his campaign when the stakes were still so high and when the dream of ultimate success, however implausible, was still so potent.

The same giddy cocktail, moreover, was still working its spell in London where King James was continuing to be promised great developments at low cost in Germany by his ambassador. 'It seems there is fuel enough if we bring coals and bellows,' wrote Sir Robert Anstruther, though it was Gustavus Adolphus of Sweden who now stood poised to set the fire ablaze by offering to lead 40,000 men across Silesia into Bohemia and Austria, provided that two-thirds of the cost was met by the German princes along with England and the United Provinces, and with the further proviso that he be given free access to Bremen and Wismar, and the support of a Dutch fleet to patrol the north German coast in case of interference by Denmark or Poland. Flushed with his victories over the Poles and still only 30 years old in 1625, the Swedish king was in no more mood to lose the initiative now than he would be five years later when he declared to the Margrave of Brandenburg's ambassadors how neutrality was 'nothing but rubbish which the wind raises and carries away.' 'What is neutrality anyway?' he concluded at that time, 'I do not understand it,' knowing full well his subjects' conviction that they were not only heirs of the Goths and descendants of Noah's son, Japheth, but denizens of the oldest nation in the world, teachers of the ancient Greeks, and, most significantly of all, world conquerors – myths of long-standing that had been systematised by the historian and genealogist Johannes Magnus in 1554, and stoked to a new intensity by the prophecies of Paracelsus and Tycho Brahe, foretelling the imminent emergence of a 'Lion of the North', precursor of the second coming and universal peace.

Yet it would be to Gustavus's arch-rival, Christian of Denmark, that the Dutch States-General nevertheless turned, suspecting that the Swedish king was still more interested in Poland than Bohemia. And the broader ramifications of the decision were plain enough, since the mutual antagonism between Denmark and Sweden had already resulted in two major wars, in 1563–70 and 1611–13, over Danish hegemony in Scandinavia and the *dominium maris Balthici*, which now seemed threatened once more by the growing success of Gustavus Adolphus. Already by the 1590s, the rulers of both countries had abandoned attempts to settle their disputes by negotiation or mediation, so that even in peacetime the Danish government in particular had continued to spend heavily on defence. In the first twenty-five years of Christian's personal rule, which began in 1596, some 1 million thalers, for example, were expended upon the fortification of Copenhagen and Malmo, and the fortresses along the Swedish frontier. And the grounds for Danish concern were far from insubstantial. For although the Treaty of Knared had forced Sweden to pay a very large indemnity in return for territory captured by the Danes, the latter had nevertheless been obliged to recognise the right of Swedish ships to pass through the all-important Danish Sound without paying toll, at a time when their own financial strength was being increasingly compromised.

These tolls, indeed, were among the most important financial assets of the Danish crown and had been the primary source of funding at the start of the seventeenth century for what was probably one of the best and most modern navies in Europe, while the Sound itself – since both its sides were Danish territory – had long been considered private Danish property rather than an international waterway. As such, the decision to exempt Swedish shipping from payments had meant that in winning a war the Danes had nevertheless lost the peace, and now found themselves increasingly vulnerable, particularly when the ongoing strategic imperatives of the Swedes still made conflict likely sooner or later. For Sweden's solitary window to the Atlantic, at Älvsborg, was so hemmed in by Danish and Norwegian territory to the south and north that it could be easily blocked, and in wartime scarcely defended. Equally worryingly, Denmark's outlying islands – Bornholm, Gotland and Ösel – were strung out eastwards across the Baltic, cutting across the main Swedish trade routes. With the accession of Gustavus Adolphus in 1611, open conflict therefore became a permanent possibility and, with neighbouring Germany in turmoil, it became even more unlikely that the two Lutheran rulers of Denmark and Sweden could remain uninvolved from the affairs of the Holy Roman Empire indefinitely.

As Duke of Holstein, furthermore, Christian exerted a not inconsiderable influence within the Lower Saxon Circle, which he was anxious to increase.

And this was not all, since Halberstadt and Osnabrück, as we have seen, were further targets, and he was also casting avaricious eyes upon Bremen and Verden, both as a means of establishing political and fiscal control over the estuaries of the Weser and the Elbe, and as useful appanages for his younger sons. In this regard, Christian had already secured an early success by constructing the fortress-port of Glückstadt above Hamburg, which was followed five years later by Hamburg's recognition of the outright suzerainty of the Danish crown, further bolstering the Danish king's confidence and encouraging him in 1623 to expend at least 135,000 thalers from his personal fortune 'to see that my son Frederick should come to the see of Verden'. So when his council now urged moderation in response to appeals for involvement from both the United Provinces and the advisers of Frederick V, Christian's own impulses were squarely for action, not least because the indemnity of 1 million thalers paid in instalments by Sweden after the peace of 1613 had indeed provided funds for a major conflict, irrespective of the fact that, unlike his Swedish counterpart, he was no more than a talented amateur in military affairs and would have to depend upon mercenaries to augment a Danish militia more suited to defence than aggression. So far at least, Christian could indeed boast a successful foreign policy record, and this too, it seems, was more than enough to make him ready not only to pose as the saviour of Protestantism both in Germany and the Netherlands, but risk the shipwreck of his kingdom in an effort to prevent the leadership of Sweden in the same cause.

When asked by James I what he would do if the salvation of the Netherlands and the Palatinate were entrusted to another, the Swedish king's reply spoke volumes in a single word. 'Nothing,' he declared. But for Christian, on the other hand, the bait was much too tantalising to resist, even though in 1614 the United Provinces had agreed a defensive alliance with the Swedes intended to weaken the Danish stranglehold on the Baltic trade. Over 60 per cent of the commerce passing through the Sound was in fact Dutch, but in 1618 Oldenbarnevelt, the champion of his country's mercantile interests, had fallen from power, and in the same year the struggle in the Empire began. With the expiry of the truce with Spain in 1621, moreover, any prospect of prioritising trade over the necessity of military alliance finally disappeared. In consequence, Christian would become friend at the expense of the Dutch-Swedish alliance, while Gustavus Adolphus would be left to bide his time for a more opportune moment, shrewdly avoiding for the present the main European maelstrom, and settling instead for the conquest of the rich Polish ports of Memel, Pillau and Elbing, which he duly completed before 1625 was out – capturing customs dues in the process which exceeded the Swedish government's usual internal revenues.

By contrast, Christian was only elected director of the Lower Saxon Circle's military force in May 1625 after intense pressure from the Dutch upon Brandenburg and Saxony, who were reluctant to make any move without Gustavus's leadership. Nor was this the only ill omen of its kind, for in the spring of 1625 the defence of Breda seemed increasingly precarious. Across a flooded landscape Spinola's engineers had, it is true, been forced to protect their earthworks by a system of sluices and counter-sluices, which was also intended to prevent Dutch reinforcements from entering the city in barges over the fields from Sevenbergen. Lack of forage was another problem. But Breda's defenders were also in straits of their own as plague struck and Maurice himself succumbed in April, appointing his brother Frederick Henry as commander-in-chief shortly before his death. The washed-up bodies of Mansfeld's troops, who had idled in cold ships, eating foul food and drinking contaminated water, had ultimately spread pestilence throughout Brabant, and Frederick Henry's generalship – no more than Maurice of Nassau's own, had he lived – was unable to stem the inevitable for long. Accordingly, on 25 May, came Spinola's greatest victory, achieved not only against the opposition of the enemy and the elements themselves but also of his own government, and made memorable by Velázquez's celebrated canvas, *Las Lanzas* and Lope de Vega's *Triumphal Ode*.

But if news of Breda's fall was painful enough, the King of Denmark's woes were only beginning, for in the summer of 1625, whilst cautiously advancing up the Weser, he too experienced a potentially fatal fall of his own – one involving a crashing descent from his horse down an 80-foot drop. For some days, indeed, he was paralysed and taken for dead, and though he eventually recovered the use of his limbs as well as his appetite for battle, the net was nevertheless tightening around him. So far the Protestants' main enemy had been Tilly's army – financed largely by the Catholic League and billeted in Westphalia and Hesse – which had already moved north to block Christian's advance, while keeping a wary eye upon Mansfeld, who, following the loss of Breda, was raising men once more. But in the spring of 1625, at the suggestion of the League's leaders, the emperor had at last decided to raise a major campaign army of his own, entrusting the supreme command to the very man who had proposed such a force in the first place: Albert of Wallenstein, Duke of Friedland, who, with the aid of loans arranged by the Antwerp banker Hans de Witte and contributions extorted by his own troops, had raised a force of some 35,000 foot and 17,000 horse, supplied from his own lands.

The freshly-created count had taken as his proud motto the prophetic words *Invita Invidia*, 'Welcome Envy', and after his installation by Ferdinand as 'Independent General over this our Expedition dispatched in the Holy Roman

Empire', he was now in a position to seal his authority definitively, marching northwards against the unknowing Danes into the territories of Magdeburg and Halberstadt. With the acquisition of further estates in 1624, Wallenstein had come to enjoy virtual autonomy over a vast stretch of land between the Elbe and the Sudeten mountains, and here he had created a self-sufficient military supply base, in which his agent, Gerhard von Taxis, exercised minute control over each and every activity of the peasantry, directing their choice of seed and methods of farming in order to produce a surplus of cereals for his troops, while armourers, smiths and weavers imported from Flanders and elsewhere ensured that Wallenstein's warehouses became crammed with weapons and uniforms. Using the contacts he had made in his obscure years to provide 'powder from Poland, cuirasses from Leipzig, match-lints from Nuremberg and pikes from Liége', Wallenstein also ordered von Taxis to collect supplies at Reichenberg in north Friedland, where the volume of trade had soon quadrupled, before sending them north. And as the elaborate process unfolded, so the general continued to write regularly, issuing a continual stream of instructions, which even extended on occasion to the supply of manure and the cultivation of flowers for his wife.

Nor, it should be said, did he neglect his broader obligations as a dutiful landlord, organising schools, medical services and poor relief on his estates, as well as laying up surpluses to feed his people in time of famine, and controlling prices wherever possible:

> Have a keen eye in all ends and places of our duchy [he informed von Taxis] that the beer is not overcharged, also that bread and other victuals and all things else that man cannot forgo in his undertakings are bought at a cheap rate.

But it was war, its tools of destruction and its everyday necessities, that continued, unsurprisingly, to preoccupy Wallenstein most:

> The following matters I beg you to exercise *in continenti*: first pay my cousin Max 24,000 gulden for the Croats; secondly see that Herr Michna [the Imperial General-Commissioner] receive the 17,000 sacks of corn soon, so that they can be here this month; thirdly deliver to Herr Michna 2,000 hundredweight of powder, to be sent here *in continenti* by water, as well as the match-lints that you have, and make up to 3,000 hundredweight of them. Also have 10,000 pairs of shoes made for the infantry, so that later I can divide them out among the regiments. Have them made in my towns and markets and pay a fair price for them in cash. See especially that the shoes are always carefully bound pair by pair, so that one will know which belong together.

At the same time have leather prepared, for I shall shortly order a further few thousand boots to be made. Have cloth ready also, for it may be that clothes will be required.

The plan, in fact, was not only to raise a superbly equipped army for the emperor's service, but to make war a profitable business at one and the same time, whilst avoiding the indiscriminate looting which characterised armies like Mansfeld's. Sound logistics was one principle. The other involved the compulsion of towns wherever he operated to pay heavily for protection from his troops. With the money thus raised, Wallenstein would then supply his army from his base in Friedland, in the expectation that his troops, well paid and well supplied, would be better disciplined and more effective than others, yielding victory, further rewards of land from the emperor and a heady upward spiral of efficiency, profit and glory.

This, then, was the theory. Wallenstein was to bear the cost of recruitment and the emperor the cost of soldiers' pay. But if, as was so often the case, the emperor could not meet his side of the bargain, his supreme commander would have to make do as best he could. Wallenstein's colonels, meanwhile, would have to bear much of the financial burden involved in recruiting their regiments, just as they, in their turn, partly transferred the further cost of recruiting individual companies to the captains concerned. Like other contemporary armies, therefore, all officers, from captains up to the commander himself, formed what amounted to a syndicate in which every member stood to share the profits or losses and therefore naturally took into account the financial risks they were running in a typical military campaign. Since Wallenstein paid his officers well, their solidarity was assured up to a point, and reinforced by a community of risks, though for the common soldiers the story was often different, and the irregular payment of wages that were in any case low, meant that both on the march and in quarters, Wallenstein's army, notwithstanding his genuine efforts to the contrary, was as prone to desertion and the infliction of terror as other forces of the day.

The instructions issued by the emperor to his army in June 1625 laid down stringent conditions, in fact, about the protection of property and the treatment of civilians, but added the important proviso that 'nonetheless we sanction the levy in conquered places and territories of sufferable conditions and loans.' Furthermore, there was no definition by the Imperial chancery of what the term 'sufferable' meant, while the clerks in the exchequer would subsequently pretend 'that without any remuneration on the part of His Imperial Majesty it was the Count of Friedland's intention to provide his army with all its needs until such time as a state of peace might again be attained.' Under such circumstances, Wallenstein would indeed need to strike an uncomfortable balance between ensuring the discipline of his troops and employing them, in the way that his enemies claimed, as an organised horde of robbers. According to the Imperial Secretary Khevenhüller, himself no friend of the general,

> he of Friedland maintained exemplary order, so that the land was not wasted and burned, nor the people driven from hut and house; but all was cultivated and harvested … and though he pressed heavily upon the Empire, yet the soldier and the peasant lived side by side, and all commanders have learned this manner of waging war from the Duke of Friedland.

Yet Wallenstein harboured no such rose-tinted illusions, construing the army, though heavily financed by de Witte, as his own private investment, and consoling himself with the knowledge that if the emperor did not meet his side of the bargain, he would take whatever steps were necessary. In the last resort, as he himself put it, 'we must needs go *a la desparata* and take what we can get.'

Among the more notorious of Wallenstein's troops in this regard were the Croatian dragoons, who had been deployed to devastating effect at Stadtlohn, and were often mistaken for gypsies as a result of their extravagant appearance. Dressed predominantly in red and loading both themselves and their horses with silver trappings, jewels, feathers and anything else on which they could lay their hands, pillage was effectively their unchecked prerogative, since they were invaluable for foraging, and therefore frequently beyond reach of superiors. Under their colonels, Peter Gal and Giovanni Isolani, a Cypriot with property in Croatia who had made his name during the Long Turkish War, they became a byword, in fact, for whirlwind descents in unexpected quarters – both military and, equally frequently, civilian – and the results were wholly predictable. 'War must nourish war,' Isolani is given to declare in Schiller's play, and even Wallenstein's provosts, who erected gallows in every camp and carried out the sentences of regimental court martials, appear to have been hard-pressed to contain them. Not long after Isolani's men had set out on one of their many notorious missions – on the road to Eger in this particular case – Wallenstein issued a stern rebuke in response to their depredations. 'I will not have the peasants harassed!' he ordered, and in order to drive home the point personally presided over the hanging of fifteen offenders at his own camp – some of them mere boys.

But, as Wallenstein well knew, the exercise of discipline in a contemporary army was an ideal objective rather than a practical possibility. Certainly, as his camp and quarters sprang to life at Schweinfurt, it compared favourably enough to the troops of Tilly – with their ragged clothes and bright muskets – who had already crossed the Weser, without declaration of war, 'in the name of God and

His Holy Mother', and who were, at that very moment, falling 'like a tempest' upon the plain of Hanover, forcing the Duke of Brunswick-Wolfenbüttel and the Margrave of Brandenburg to complain bitterly to the emperor about their behaviour in response to the enraged opposition of the Brunswick peasantry. Defenceless men, women and children had been cut down in town and field, priests abused and martyred, people of all conditions tortured, towns and monasteries plundered, altars profaned, honourable women and maids raped in the open street, while the 60-year-old 'monk in armour' Tilly – his hair grown grey in Catholic service – had not only witnessed proceedings largely impassively, but remarked that the victims deserved the horrors visited upon them.

Yet if Wallenstein, by contrast, was more inclined to moderation where possible, he knew just as surely that if war made brutes of men, then some of their more brutish needs must be met if war was to be waged at all. The *Hurenwebel* or whoremaster, whose thick stick had belaboured generations of army prostitutes, was, on the one hand, as much a feature of his camps as any other. 1,200 of these women had followed Alba's Spanish army in the previous century, and while the policy of making life as unattractive as possible to them was necessarily continued by Wallenstein, their presence was ongoing. Likewise, though his army's chaplains were frequently dismissed for joining in with the misdemeanours of common soldiers, Wallenstein himself was known to drink and dice with all ranks, even paying the gaming debts of his officers when they became too heavy. Overall, his attitude to the moral constraints prevailing within his camps remained flexible, and a similar pragmatism applied equally to his troops' religious sympathies. More interested in their fighting quality than their faith, he freely employed Catholics and Protestants alike, and it was only after his death that orders were eventually laid down for the celebration of Mass every Sunday and feast-day, and the recitation each morning and evening of *Jesu Maria*, 'as had been the custom heretofore'.

In one of Jacques Callot's magnificent contemporary plates of the *Miseries of War*, the dice roll merrily on a drumhead beneath a tree whose branches are grimly loaded with some two dozen military malefactors. It was a scene, moreover, fully familiar to any of the troops now travelling northwards through Germany after Wallenstein's departure in August 1625, singing the marching-songs that still echo across the centuries:

> We have no care nor sorrow
> For Empire and its fate.
> Come death today, tomorrow,
> We meet it soon or late.

'God help the place where they should lay their winter quarters!' exclaimed the chief magistrate of Hodenberg, watching the long train of men and horses, baggage-wagons and artillery approaching his town. They were on their way, in fact, to a rendezvous with Tilly, which they effected without haste, but with no more trouble than some minor skirmishes near Göttingen, before reaching the last spurs of hilly country in the Harz mountains, beyond which the plains stretched northwards to the sea. And surely enough, in the middle of October, near the village of Hemmendorf, the two generals finally met – more cordially, it seems, than the mutual suspicions of their respective employers, the emperor and the Duke of Bavaria, might have presaged. Tilly's army had, it is true, been much depleted in the Siege of Niendorf on the Weser, but this did not appear to affect Wallenstein's confidence in him – or indeed his personal sentiments towards the man. 'I and General Tilly agree very well, let there be no fear of that,' he declared. 'Would to God that all His Majesty's servants were in such agreement!'

More crucially still, the two armies were much superior to any force that their quarry, the King of Denmark, could command at that moment, and Christian had wisely decided to avoid all possibility of an engagement. But Wallenstein, too, was keen for the time being to avoid the vagaries of a murderous pitched fight – something that would remain his policy, wherever possible, throughout his career, and earn him the criticism of his political enemies who were soon complaining that he was a 'general without victories'. Recognising that this was a war of attrition, inextricably linked to the shifting sands of politics, Wallenstein preferred, in fact, to keep his army intact, his lines of communication free, and the possibility of negotiation constantly open. Not all victories, after all, were won by the side who attacked first, and Wallenstein, though capable, as events would prove, of engagements every bit as spectacular as others of his time, was nevertheless ahead of his contemporaries in his mastery of forcing decisions by defensive action. It was an art, supported by efficient espionage and a remarkable talent for political prescience, that bred frequent suspicion in Vienna, and later earned him the accusation that he was a businessman first and the emperor's soldier second. True or not, however, he would spend the winter in military recuperation and political jockeying, awaiting the arrival of spring for the destruction of his foe.

In the meantime, the question of the two armies' winter quarters had been provoking anxiety in both Munich and Vienna. Tilly, with a trained eye for fat country, had selected the ecclesiastical lands of Halberstadt and Magdeburg in the east, though Wallenstein had both military and personal motives for wanting these places for his own army. To the north, of course, Christian of Denmark was also preparing for a spring campaign, and there were other fronts, too, that needed to be guarded. In Holland, perhaps also in France – since Mansfeld had been summoned to Paris to confer with Richelieu – lay potential foes of the League's army. Yet Wallenstein, with the Empire's interests in mind, had also to look east and south, to Silesia and the recurrent threat of Bethlen Gábor in Hungary, a threat which the Bavarian faction in Vienna were already employing to influence his recall. More importantly still from Wallenstein's perspective, Halberstadt and Magdeburg must be secured, if the option of a swift return to Bohemia and above all the security of his own peaceful duchy of Friedland were to be guaranteed. Accustomed to having his own way, Wallenstein would certainly have protected his personal property with his last regiment, and on this occasion, notwithstanding the growing rumbles of discontent at his upstart pretensions, he once more got what he wished. Tilly would winter in the Weser Valley, while the Imperial free city of Magdeburg – conveniently located on the broad waters of the Elbe, which allowed von Taxis to transport supplies by barge from Friedland – made ready to welcome his colleague and rival. A member of the Hanseatic League and more interested in trade than religion, though nominally Protestant, Magdeburg would require only a firm voice and the sight of Wallenstein's army to join interests with him 'in commercial and other ways'. And as the weather turned bitterly cold, the general was also able on 29 October to enter Halberstadt without opposition.

But while Wallenstein bided his time and the Siege of Breda was brought to its successful conclusion, the emperor had been both busy and successful with ventures of his own within the 'hereditary lands' of his Habsburg patrimony. Bohemia by now was in no position to make trouble, and Hungary too proved surprisingly accommodating, not least because the elected leader of the Hungarian Diet, a Protestant and former agent of Bethlen Gábor, had become a Roman Catholic and agreed to serve Ferdinand's needs. In May 1623, moreover, matters had already been improved by the renewal at Gyarmat of the Treaty of Zsitva-Török, which removed the immediate threat of Turkish invasion and, as such, permitted the emperor to be less dependent upon purchasing Magyar co-operation. In October 1625, indeed, he had even secured the election of his son, the future Ferdinand III, as King of Hungary, while in Upper Austria, which was currently governed by Duke Maximilian's Bavarian officials, he was able to impose a further fine of 600,000 florins upon the Estates for their earlier collusion with the Bohemian rebels. When the cry went up that Maximilian had already taxed them for that offence, the revolt of a desperate and disillusioned peasantry was swiftly suppressed by Bavarian troops.

For Spain, too, what had begun as a bad year in their broader empire of the New World had ended ultimately in triumph after Madrid had been plunged into panic by a daring raid on Bahia, capital of Brazil, by the Dutch West India Company in May 1624. Like the rest of the Portuguese empire, Bahia had fallen under Spanish rule during the reign of Philip II, and had grown rich from the production of sugar. As such, it was a tempting prize for a Dutch fleet of more than fifty ships that swept into the port unheralded, making a rich haul of shipping, before landing a force sufficient not only to take control of the town, but subsequently to establish its authority over the whole province – an offence to Spanish pride that was certain to provoke the most determined response possible. 'All the grandees, dignitaries, magistrates and government servants here, even those of the lowest class,' reported Tarantaise, the Savoyard ambassador, 'have determined to make a voluntary offer to His Majesty which they think will amount to 2 million ducats in all.' And within six months an armada had indeed been dispatched to South America, though even by the time of its arrival, the population had risen against its new masters, with the result that a hard-pressed Dutch garrison of some 2,500 men was duly forced to surrender in April 1625.

'God is Spanish and fights for our nation these days,' exclaimed Olivares in the wake of victory, and by the autumn of 1625, there must indeed have been moments when Spain's enemies themselves were surely left to wonder at the Divinity's national affiliation. The coalition of England, the United Provinces and Denmark remained potentially dangerous, and the French were in possession of the Valtelline, but Tilly and Wallenstein were well placed to contain the first threat, while the French government was already running into criticism at home for its action in the second case. The republic of Genoa, Spain's ally and client, had moreover been rescued from the combined forces of France and Savoy, and, almost as pleasingly, ninety Dutch and English ships, carrying some 90,000 men, had signally failed in an attempt to capture the treasure fleet from America at Cadiz. With thirty ships and many men lost, the battered expedition's return to England in November had done nothing to raise the level of enthusiasm for another foreign adventure. And nor was this the limit of the Spanish king's apparent good fortune, since the Turks had been brought to make peace, his Habsburg cousin's 'hereditary lands' were firmly under control, and the great fortress of Breda had fallen to Spinola. 'Your Highness should reflect,' wrote the Savoyard ambassador from Milan, 'how great are the vicissitudes of this world, for six months ago all the elements seemed to be uniting to bring this monarchy to ruin. Now they seem inclined to favour everything they do, and all the winds are wafting them on their way.'

7

CRISIS OF A CONTINENT

I roared, loved and romped, and what I lauded most was sin …
Seeking common whores, vagabonding, picking quarrels, cursing,
Drinking away money and blood,
Everything was splendidly good.

Georg Greflinger (*c.*1620–*c.*1677), poet and soldier

In spite of his declarations to the contrary, the Count of Olivares was still keenly aware that the *annus mirabilis* of 1625, however reassuring, offered little more in reality than a much needed breathing space. 'Blessed be God who is thus defending his cause,' he had exclaimed that autumn, and his choice of terms was instructive. For the very success of the Habsburg governments in appearing to further their goals had only increased the number and resolve of their enemies, and carried all of Europe closer to a general war of unknown duration. From his map room in Madrid, Olivares could see plainly enough that the King of France, although temporarily distracted by the problem of the Huguenots, continued to present a permanent threat to the *pax austriaca* that Spain considered so indispensable for the survival of Catholicism and the maintenance of stability throughout large parts of Europe. Likewise, the English attack on Cadiz, though an unmitigated failure, nevertheless represented an act of war, and meant that Spanish shipping could no longer shelter from the Dutch in English waters before slipping across the Channel to Dunkirk. No less precarious was the condition of Italy, with Venice forever engaged in anti-Habsburg machinations, Charles Emmanuel of Savoy infinitely unpredictable and the Pope himself now inimical to Spanish interests. But it was the Dutch and their impact upon Spain's overseas possessions and the entire economic life of the Iberian peninsula that remained the most painful open sore of all: this and the fact that statesmen and soldiers alike seemed to be losing not only their taste for peace but their appreciation of precisely what they were fighting for.

In the Valtelline, where French troops had taken over the garrisons entrusted to papal troops, Louis XIII's overall objectives seemed plain, but they also involved him in moral contortions that were not lost upon either the Holy Father in Rome or the so-called *dévots* within his government who found Richelieu's tactics so reprehensible. Despite the diplomatic treatment accorded his servants, Urban VIII had indeed protested to Louis XIII about France's flirtations with Protestants, while the *dévots* published a similar *Admonitio ad regem* which declared it sinful to encourage heresy out of envy for Spain. But the counterblast of Richelieu's ministers and the *Déclaration* of the Bishop of Chartres demonstrated all too aptly a sentiment that threatened to fan the flames of the existing conflict to unquenchable heights:

> The king [declared the bishop] made the alliance, because he willed it; he undertook war because it is just and reasonable, or better, such a war is just, because he undertook it.

Such, indeed, was the murkiness of diplomacy and the entanglements of its conduct that the very line between peace and war – let alone war and warlike acts – was itself increasingly unclear. For French soldiers had not, as yet, crossed swords at all with their Spanish counterparts, and nor, for the time being at least, were they able to do so, since the extent of France's action on behalf of the Protestant Grisons was still restricted, ironically enough, by the activity of her Protestant Huguenots at home, who had risen in 1625 under the leadership of Benjamin de Rohan, Duke of Soubise. With Languedoc in uproar and La Rochelle leading the defiance, the Marquis of Cœuvres appealed urgently for clarification of his orders in the Valtelline, while the Dutch, too, were in no less of a quandary, since, in spite of their pledge to assist France against Spain, their sailors refused to make this possible by attacking Soubise and the rebel Huguenot fleet.

This, then, was the evolving imbroglio generated by a conflict that had begun seven years earlier on the margins of the Holy Roman Empire, though in the meantime, as rulers tore their hair and the likelihood of further escalation soared, the prospects for profit and plunder had never looked better. 'He who wages war fishes with a golden net,' ran the contemporary saying, and it was not only Wallenstein who had learned this maxim well. With the capture of Heidelberg on 15 September 1622, Tilly had taken what was probably the finest prize of the

Palatine capital – the illustrious 'Biblioteca Palatina' – and presented it to Duke Maximilian, who resisted the temptation to keep it as booty, and dispatched the most precious part, including 3,500 manuscripts, to the Pope, packing the entire haul across the Alps on mules, in return for which the League's armies had received some 650,000 florins from Rome by August 1623. Further away, the Swedes too were establishing a reputation as plunderers that would swell to notorious proportions as their conquests grew. The treasures, books and artworks of the Jesuit colleges of Riga had been systematically stripped in 1621, while the authorities of Saxony, in their turn, had also been quick to exploit an Imperial order that Bohemian refugees should not be able to retain their belongings. Arriving in wagon-trains at Zittau, Pirna, Freiburg and Annaberg, the 'possessions and movables of the rebels' – most of whom were of middle-class status – were systematically stripped, allowing the princely and municipal officials to take their share, and thereby reap a healthy windfall from the gold and silver plate in particular, which was being regularly hawked at the fairs of Leipzig up to 1629.

Nor was this the only indignity to which the steady flow of refugees was subjected. Some 2,000 had made their way to the border town of Pirna alone, and sizeable Czech communities were also established at Dresden and Zittau. But as one of their number, Jan Ctibor of Prague, made clear, it was not always easy for the new arrivals to be accepted. Initially at least, the inhabitants of most Saxon cities greeted the new arrivals, who included proud noblemen and well-dressed merchants, with curiosity and sympathy, but it was not long before their goodwill dwindled. Soon, indeed, songs were spitefully mocking the 'lost band', the 'ragamuffins' and the 'rebellious wretches', while the Lutheran clergy in particular harboured growing concerns about the 'infiltration of Calvinism', since local Saxon officials could not understand what was being said in the exiles' churches. Through fear of pestilence and an increase in competition and prices, the newcomers were not permitted to settle within town walls, and not until 1627, in fact, would the Duke of Saxony and his advisers see fit to discuss the thorny issue of asylum for those of higher social status. Even then, moreover, it was not until 1650 that restrictions on their rights were relaxed, only to be reimposed in 1680.

Though some Bohemian artisans established themselves more successfully in the Erzgebirge district, producing lace and manufacturing toys and musical instruments, the same sorry tale was repeated for other victims of the conflict. The Inner Austrian Protestants, on the one hand, largely fled into western Hungary or trekked to Württemberg, Franconia and the south German imperial cities, while the Upper and Lower Austrians often made their way up the

Danube to Protestant cities like Regensburg. Many Moravians, meanwhile, went to north-west Hungary. But the striking contrast between their fortunes and those of high-ranking army officers like Johann Aldringen – who had begun his career as a clerk in the chancery of Luxembourg and in 1618 was to be found fighting as a soldier in Northern Italy and the Tyrol – could not have been more marked. By 1630, profiting wildly from the three-day sack of Mantua, Aldringen was in fact calculated to have amassed a fortune of a million florins in Italian banks. And as the skills of its practitioners became ever more marketable, so the spread and duration of the war not only increased their appetite for riches but delivered almost limitless opportunities for satisfying it. 'There was scarcely any one of rank, any well known officer or official,' wrote the Swedish Chancellor Axel Oxenstierna, 'who did not aspire to a few offices, abbeys, monasteries, domains and so on, and the more exalted the person, the greater his aspirations,' while General Karl Gustav Wrangel expressed the common attitude of his peers rather more pithily. 'If you take something, you've got something,' he observed, quoting the advice of his revered father.

But while soldiers in search of enrichment were indeed all too ready to take, there were also those preferring to make. And for them too, so long as arms and armaments and other materials of war were involved, the prospects looked equally mouth-watering as winter turned to spring in 1626. The Holy Roman Empire had, after all, been the world-leader in mining, metallurgy and metal-working, and in addition to the traditional centres, such as Nuremberg, Suhl, Aachen, Cologne, Augsburg, St Joachimstal, Eger, Essen and Solingen, new ones were now emerging in response to the war: in Dresden, Munich, Graz and Vienna. Already the Löfflers and Herolds of Nuremberg and the Schelshorns of Regensburg had primed their bell foundries for the casting of cannons and mortars, while merchants and their agents were zealously scouring the whole of Europe for investors and reliable sources of supply, particularly for sulphur, slow-match material and saltpetre, whose prices were rising steadily. Danzig, Hamburg, Bremen and Amsterdam, too, were all enjoying the beginnings of a 'Golden Age' on the sale of such items. And when the ideal equipment of an infantry regiment of some 3,000 men, including 1,500 musketeers, 300 riflemen, 1,200 pikemen and a further 200 halberdiers, consisted of the following, it is easy to appreciate why:

10 flags	20 pipes
10 partisans	1,200 sets of ordinary harness
50 halberds for the commanders	1,000 long pikes
31 drums	200 ordinary halberds

200 pairs of metal gauntlets	1,500 leather bottles
1,500 muskets	300 short muskets
1,500 musket rests	600 powder or priming flasks and
1,500 bandoliers	slow-match material
1,500 powder flasks and slow-match material	1,851 tunics

In 1625 at Würzburg, the following prices were standard charges for such items: 61 Imperial thalers for a flag, 2 Imperial thalers for a partisan (a kind of halberd), 4 Imperial thalers for a drum, 5 Imperial thalers for a pike and three thalers Imperial for a musket, while one hundredweight of powder cost 40 Imperial thalers and the same quantity of musket-shot and slow-match material 6 Imperial thalers each.

From the figures submitted by the Nuremburg cannon founder Leonhard Loewe, moreover, it is also clear that the cost of artillery was not only rising but actually much higher than in later centuries. For two so-called 'half-cannon royal', Loewe's bill listed the costs thus: 638 florins for raw material (copper, zinc and lead), 732 florins for foundrymen's wages and 1,273 florins for the services of carters, locksmiths, smiths, carpenters, ropemakers and other tradesmen. The charges of labour were accordingly much higher than the cost of the material, but for each half-cannon-royal there was also to be reckoned the cost of: 100 iron cannonballs (each weighing 24 pounds), 40 hundredweight of slow-match material, one gun carriage, one hoisting-crane, one pair of wheels, several hundred entrenchment tools (choppers, picks, spades, shovels), wagons, several dozen draught horses, and fifteen to twenty men for manning and moving the piece and constructing a field fortification to protect it. Nor should it be forgotten that the material needed per round expended cost a further 5 Imperial thalers at a time when an average of 50 rounds could normally be fired daily.

Plainly, war was big business, and merchants and agents like the Kletts of Zurich and the Stöhrs of Suhl, grew rich from its pickings, distributing wagonloads of war material from Schmalkalden, Schleusingen, Ilmenau and elsewhere. Such, indeed, were Wallenstein's needs that even he could not supply them from his own estates, leaving Hans de Witte to conclude large contracts with the Nurembergers in particular via his agent Abraham Blommaert, who was one of the major depositors of the Banco Publico, founded in 1621. With an annual turnover of up to 350,000 florins, the bank rode high on the squabbles of princes and the ambition of those who served them. And in 1625 the gunsmiths of the Thuringian Forest also reaped a plentiful harvest of their own after de Witte placed an order for the complete equipment of seven regiments. Within five weeks and against the immediate payment of an installment of 10,000 florins, the requisite breastplates, muskets, pikes and short-barrelled guns were assembled and sent to Eger, while other contractors from Suhl even delivered their goods ahead of schedule, though their demands for punctual payment thereafter led to disagreements with middlemen and pressure for Blommaert in particular.

On the edge of the theatre of war in the Netherlands and along the Lower Rhine, other highly productive centres for the fabrication of small arms also came to prominence. The gunsmiths of Essen, for instance, had already increased in number from twenty-four in 1608 to fifty-four in 1620, and sold their wares, without hint of compunction, not only to the United Provinces, but to the Spanish 'Parma' regiment, as well as the freebooting troops of Mansfeld, and the mercenaries of the Archbishop of Cologne. Around 1620, indeed, the arms production of Essen reached a peak of almost 15,000 separate items, while away to the north, Sweden too was stepping up its preparations to become one of Europe's foremost arms manufacturers. Though peopled by no more than 1.5 million inhabitants, and boasting only a few large towns, Gustavus Adolphus's kingdom owed much of its growing importance to copper, from which it derived huge profits, exporting to the whole of Europe, including Spain. Even a century later, in fact, the country's most productive mine at Falun – with a total adit length of 3.5 miles – was still being described by Carl Linnaeus, the famous scientist, as 'Sweden's greatest wonder'. 'What king possesses such a palace as this!' Gustavus himself declared upon one of his visits. And few who held shares in the Swedish trading company holding a virtual monopoly of copper production in Europe would have been likely to disagree, since not only the king, but noblemen, senior state officials, merchants and Church institutions had all invested heavily, along with Dutch business capital, to make copper, in effect, the gold of its day, as other great installations in Södermanland, Östergotland, the Mälar-Hjelmare region and the Uppland ore zone also boosted output to record levels.

Yet as miners toiled and foundries far and wide belched fire round the clock, miles away in the Valtelline at least, there was temporary respite. For as France looked inwards once more to her Huguenot rebels, and Spain dared not divide her attention from the Netherlands, token gestures and temporary resolutions rather than brass cannon and the white-hot heat of open warfare were, for a brief space, the order of the day. Indeed, an unexpected solution to the entire issue was proffered by the French ambassador, the Marquis de Fargis, a close associate of the *devots* in Paris, who now saw fit – possibly at Louis XIII's unofficial instigation – to suggest to Olivares a way out of his dilemma. Should the sovereignty of the Grisons be accepted and an annual tribute paid by the valley's inhabitants, de Fargis proposed, then the latter could be protected in their Catholicism and allowed to appoint their own magistrates. If the offending Spanish forts were finally destroyed, moreover, French troops might be withdrawn, leaving the crucial Spanish Road unblocked. Though Spain would have no formal right of access, Olivares could be satisfied of the route's availabilty. And, accordingly, the Franco-Spanish Peace of Monzón was duly agreed on 5 May 1625 – to the con- siderable indignation of the Grisons themselves, as well as Savoy and Venice, and apparently Richelieu too, who, in spite of a feigned show of fury, nevertheless inwardly acknowledged the necessity of de Fargis's unauthorised intervention. For 'everyone', as Bassompierre wryly observed, 'was more concerned to blame the workman than to demolish the work.'

As one protagonist withdrew to await its moment, however, others were girding for action anew. At The Hague in December 1625, the Dutch brought together England and Denmark in a new alliance with Mansfeld and Christian of Brunswick, and unlike the feverish crusades dreamed up by the over-ripe imagination of Christian of Anhalt, this one showed altogether more potential, since the Netherlanders had agreed to supply 50,000 florins a month for the maintenance of 30,000 infantry and 8,000 cavalry in northern Germany. On this occasion, furthermore, the plan was both simple and sensible enough to give grounds for cautious optimism. For Christian of Denmark was to engage Tilly along the Weser, giving Christian of Brunswick the opportunity to slip across Hesse into the Rhineland dioceses held by the Bavarian princes. In the meantime, Mansfeld would bypass Wallenstein's army in the Rhine Valley, raise the persecuted Protestants of Silesia and Bohemia and attack Vienna. As of old, Bethlen Gábor was also called upon to assist, though little faith was placed in his promises – or, for that matter, the assurances of the newly-crowned Charles I in England, who, in a high tide of enthusiasm that took no account of his impoverished condition, committed his kingdom to a contribution of 144,000 thalers a month.

But if the enemies of the Habsburgs had at last begun to organise themselves realistically upon a continental scale, Olivares, too, was no less wide-ranging in his own designs. At a conference held in Brussels in May 1626, plans were discussed involving not only the Habsburgs, Bavaria and the Catholic League but Poland and the Hanseatic cities. And the plan that resulted, though far from new – having first been conceived by the Count of St Clemente at the turn of the century – retained an attraction that two decades later made it worthy of consideration once more. For the possibility of destroying the Dutch economy by denying its merchants access to the Baltic trade upon which their country's livelihood largely depended, had been reinforced in 1625 by an offer to the cities of the Hanse, providing them with the monopoly of Iberian trade in

Europe, in return for the exclusion of the Dutch from their ports. The snag was that England and the Dutch already controlled the North Sea routes, and that consequently any profit from the Iberian trade was likely to be limited. Yet the suggestion derived in large part from Spain's newfound confidence in her ability to launch an effective naval force in northern waters, and if Imperial troops could indeed occupy the German coastline while the Catholic League neutralised Christian of Denmark, the Hanseatic cities might yet be persuaded to act boldly under the protection of Spanish ships.

All depended, firstly, upon the support of the Flanders government, which on this occasion did not appear to be dogged by the perennial pessimism of its governor-general who, in her correspondence with Madrid, agreed that 'it would be much in Your Majesty's service if you kept up war vessels in the Baltic Sea, as they would so hamper the trade which the Dutch carry on there that they would soon be brought to reasonable terms.' Spinola too, who had already expressed his confidence in the value of the Flanders cruisers, was confident. Indeed, his reports that 'we are continuing to disquiet the enemy and are keeping as many ships as we can at sea to do so' had been instrumental in reviving the Baltic strategy in the first place. And though Maximilian of Bavaria continued to fix his eyes firmly on the Rhineland, showing little interest in the defeat of the Dutch, even he could not ignore the potential benefits of the overall strategy concerning the armies of Denmark and Brunswick. As such, the participation of the Catholic League was assured.

Emperor Ferdinand, meanwhile, was also predictably amenable to the principle of establishing his authority more firmly in northern Germany, and to settling the religious issue once and for all in favour of the Catholic Church by the strict enforcement of the original Peace of Augsburg. The grand plan seemed, indeed, to offer the possibility of peace, stability and absolutism in one fell swoop, for if the Dutch infection were eradicated, the diseased members of the Empire would surely succumb as well. And if hard-headed Wallenstein remained predictably sceptical of such fancies, he too was prepared to serve them for the price of a Baltic duchy and the prospect of greater independence from Vienna, in much the same way that Sigismund of Poland was successfully lured by the prospect of a fleet in the Baltic to challenge Sweden's – with the result that by 1626 the expansive intentions of the Dutch and their allies at The Hague, and of Spain and her allies at Brussels had created a prospective war zone stretching from the Atlantic to the Balkans, and from the Baltic to the Danube, involving every major power in Europe save France, which had, in any case, only stood clear of foreign adventures until the siege of the Huguenot stronghold of La Rochelle reached its largely inevitable conclusion.

As the flood tide mounted, Tilly, in fact, had wintered at Hildesheim while Wallenstein concentrated upon securing the bishoprics of Halberstadt and Magdeburg for the emperor's 14-year-old son. Yet the latter had spent his time, too, not only in preparing his raw recruits and supplementing his funds with massive contributions from nearby cities, but by fortifying the bridge at Dessau on the Elbe to prevent Mansfeld or the Duke of Brunswick from crossing into Silesia. And this last gesture was triumphantly vindicated when Mansfeld subsequently appeared on cue in spring at the head of 12,000 men in an ill-fated attempt to restore his blighted reputation by storming the Dessau crossing. Rushing his best troops to meet the attack on 25 April 1626, and duly assisted by defence works that had been constructed so carefully that winter, Wallenstein easily completed the rout at a cost to Mansfeld of no less than a third of his men, leaving the loser to retreat into neutral Brandenburg, bloodied though still unbowed, and able to rejoin the fray in August, buoyed by Danish reinforcements and the familiar posturing of Bethlen Gábor, who by then was once again threatening to make one of his periodic attacks upon the emperor.

By that time, however, there was no assistance to be had from Christian of Brunswick, who had failed to raise an adequate army, and whose diseased body and dejected spirit had, in June, finally put paid to him – at the age of only 28. And nor was this the only baleful news of its kind for the Protestant cause. For as Mansfeld set off on a line curving east and south, with the intention of reaching Moravia, Wallenstein followed, carefully holding the inside of the curve to prevent any sudden breakout by his opponent into Bohemia. In doing so, in fact, the Imperial general had created an ever-widening gap between himself and his colleague Tilly, and he had not gone far before learning that Christian of Denmark had moved into this opening to force what would prove to be a fateful reckoning – though not for Wallenstein himself. For in detaching eight regiments from his force to turn the Danish king's advance, Wallenstein actually succeeded in pushing his enemy northwards, where on 26 August, after several days of heavy skirmishing in the rain, he encountered Tilly's army – primed, rested, willing and ready – at the village of Lutter am Barenberge in Brunswick.

'Fought with the enemy and lost. The same day I went to Wolfenbüttel.' Thus ran Christian IV's laconic diary entry upon his army's crushing defeat, which in spite of his own reckless courage, had resulted in the loss of half his troops and subsequent abandonment by all his German allies save the Dukes of Mecklenburg, with whom he now sought shelter – making first for Stade near the estuary of the Elbe and ultimately to Verden. What exactly had happened at the battle itself is obscured by the deluge of pamphlets published immediately afterwards by Tilly's field chancery – all of them stressing the inevitability of defeat for the heretic host who had opposed their rightful emperor. But it seems that Tilly's victory at Lutter had in fact been won largely as a result of his enemy's blunders, since the Danes had taken up a strong defensive position by the Neile and Hummecke streams and adjacent woodland, only for their king to sacrifice the advantage by leaving the front at the critical moment before battle, in order to attend to transport problems involving his baggage train. With no clear orders concerning the chain of command in Christian's absence, an unauthorised cavalry attack was staged, with the intention of silencing Tilly's bombardment as his men ate lunch. But the attack was unsuccessful and as it foundered, Tilly's troops managed to work their way through the woods and turn the Danish flanks. By the time that Christian returned, the situation was already critical, and although his royal escort charged to cover the retreat of the second and third lines, the first was unable to disengage and forced to surrender.

In total, the Danes lost up to 3,000 dead, including Philipp of Hesse-Kassel, General Fuchs and other senior officers, while 2,000 deserted and another 2,500 were captured – along with all the artillery and much of the baggage, which included two wagons loaded with gold. By contrast, Tilly's losses amounted to some 700 killed and wounded, although the killer blow, even now, was not quite delivered. For as the Danes retreated, burning twenty-four villages around Wolfenbüttel and plundering their way across Luneburg, the pursuing army found itself entering territory that had already been eaten out or destroyed. And while Lutter itself had considerably enhanced Tilly's prestige, enabling him to marry his beloved nephew Werner to the daughter of the immensely wealthy Prince Liechtenstein, Governor of Bohemia, the onset of winter would nevertheless see his campaign founder miserably like so many others of its kind. For when Christian offered the comparatively measly sum of 6 thalers to every deserter who rejoined his army, most were keen to take the bait, and, as conditions deteriorated further, even Tilly's original troops found themselves scavenging for scraps, so that some, such as the Bavarian Schönberg cavalry, resorted to systematic highway robbery in an effort to sustain themselves.

In the meantime, Mansfeld had been no more successful than Christian. Shadowed by Wallenstein for nearly 500 miles across Europe and continually barred from his objectives of Prague and Vienna, he had heard of the Danes' defeat on 3 September in Silesia while pressing on to Hungary in the hope of seeking out Bethlen Gábor. Within a week, moreover, he had done so, and at the end of the month, boosted by some detachments supplied by the Turks, turned with his unlikely friends to face the Imperials. But while skirmishing occurred near Neuhäusel throughout the late autumn, a decisive engagement of any kind was beyond either side, since Wallenstein's troops had suffered heavy privations of their own during their rapid march through Hungary, and Bethlen lacked not only guns, but the will to continue, following news that the Turks had suffered a massive defeat in the Near East. After a siege lasting almost a year, the Ottoman army had failed to recapture Baghdad, taken by the Persians in 1624, and this would prove the final straw for their would-be ally, since the Prince of Transylvania was now not only deprived by Tilly's victory at Lutter of aid from the west, but bereft of support from the east, leaving only one available option. 'I see that I must make peace' was Bethlen's immediate and predictable conclusion, enabling Wallenstein to seek not only fresh promotion after his apparent success but a free hand for his next campaign, as Mansfeld, by contrast, set out on his last journey, perhaps with Venice as his ultimate goal, only to die from consumption in the hills near Sarajevo on 25 November. Though merely 46 years of age, the soldier of fortune had been crippled by asthma, heart trouble, typhus and the advanced stages of tuberculosis for some time. But he insisted, it seems, upon meeting his end with suitable panache, propped up by his aides into a standing position and wearing full armour for his final breath, which was taken some two weeks before his closest comrade, Duke Johann Ernst of Weimar, himself succumbed to the plague.

By now, in fact, Bethlen too was ill and although he would avoid the final summons of the grave until 1629, his campaigning days were over. Yet in Vienna Wallenstein still faced bitter criticism for failing to deliver a decisive blow at that stage, despite pursuing his ailing quarry into Hungary, and notwithstanding the fact that in other respects he had conducted his campaign comparatively successfully, protecting the Austrian heartlands, neutralising the emperor's enemies and eventually helping to drive them from the field. On 30 September, his vanguard had actually made contact with Bethlen's outriders and by evening the main armies had met and taken up positions, only for the Transylvanian's lighter and more mobile force to slip away during the night, after which a wild goose chase across the Hungarian plains offered not only little chance of success but a fair prospect of disaster if Bethlen led him too far from his base and supply lines. As such, Wallenstein's decision to abandon pursuit was unquestionably the right one, though the necessity of wintering his sick and starving army in Moravia and Silesia well into December until the threat from his opponent had finally dissolved, only increased the sniping of the armchair strategists in Vienna, who now renewed their assault on the 'general without victories'.

It was no coincidence, of course, that the chorus of calls for Wallenstein's discharge as supreme commander, which included the voice of the Spanish ambassador, should have reached such a crescendo at this point. For resentment at the general's meteoric rise was already deep-seated and, despite prohibitions from Vienna, he had nevertheless quartered his troops in regions where not only were Imperial estates numerous, but also those belonging to some of the most important members of the Austrian nobility. From Wallenstein's perspective, his detractors were nothing more than 'women, clerics and rascally Italians', and his own sense of injustice was heightened by the imprecise financial arrangements upon which he had raised his force for the emperor in the first place.'It is sufficient for the emperor,' he wrote, 'that I have provided him with an army the like of which no-one has had before, and for which he has still not laid out a single far-thing.'And to compound his frustration, the Imperial War Council in Vienna was still under the influence of those lordly, leisurely, Spanish-trained cavaliers whose old-school attitudes were wholly out of line with his own altogether more robust approach to organisation. Together these envious and self-interested place-seekers had blocked Wallenstein's choice of a Protestant field marshal as his deputy, and now they gnawed away at any credit he had gained from his victory over Mansfeld at Dessau by magnifying Tilly's success at Lutter. Why, they asked, had the Duke of Friedland delayed in following Mansfeld south and failed to mount a winter campaign against Bethlen, irrespective of the strategic realities involved? Why, some even argued, was the mighty duke's army actually necessary at all?

And this last question raised broader queries about Wallenstein's intentions that merely increased the clamour for his dismissal not only in Vienna, but more generally among the Catholic princes of the Empire and in particular Maximilian of Bavaria, whose undoubted loyalty to Ferdinand II and the Imperial institutions was in constant conflict with his fear that both might acquire sufficient real power to subordinate the principalities to an incipient absolutist state. According to an anonymous memorandum, thought to have been written by Count Valeriano Magni, an aristocratic Italian-born Capuchin monk who had been raised in Bohemia and become long associated with Wallenstein, this was indeed the general's – and by implication the emperor's – objective. And this memorandum was duly dispatched to Maximilian within days of a meeting between Count Karl Harrach, Ulrich von Eggenberg and Wallenstein on 25 November, at which discussions allegedly took place to maintain Wallenstein's command, with a view not so much to defending the Empire as oppressing it, so that power might shift decisively to the centre at the expense of territorial rulers.

It was a potent allegation, which not only explains the ongoing resentment towards the general himself but throws further light, no doubt, upon the curious ambivalence of Maximilian's approach to the war he now waged. Yet the real motive underlying the meeting at Harrach's castle at Bruck an der Leitha, some

30 miles east of the city, appears to have lain elsewhere. For where Wallenstein's enemies saw intrigue and ambition, Harrach and Eggenberg thought only of necessities, fully aware that while Denmark and Bethlen were vanquished, Sweden, France, England and Holland were waiting in the wings. Should the general therefore voluntarily withdraw from his command as they now feared, the army upon which the Empire's safety still depended would surely disintegrate. He was, after all, not only its leader but its paymaster – as he himself well knew – and, as such, still held a winning hand, as the terms of his re-appointment, which were eventually issued on 21 April 1627, resoundingly confirmed. For far from suffering disgrace, the general was offered the command not only of his own army, but of all Imperial forces wherever they might be, as well as a larger force to be funded by a 'contribution' or direct tax paid by Bohemia, allowing him to plan for the campaign of the coming months without the faintest misgivings.

Though the groundswell of antagonism was only magnified by the arrangement, it was nevertheless a triumph of the first order and one which had been sanctioned in full consultation with the emperor, who, with whatever reservations of his own, had nevertheless accepted Wallenstein's primacy as a necessary sacrifice for the broader cause. For less than a year earlier, the forward march of Imperial victories had been seriously threatened by the greatest popular uprising to occur in central Europe since the Peasants' Revolt of 1525, as Upper Austria dissolved once more into a state of near anarchy. Throughout the winter, in fact, millenarian expectations of the fall of Antichrist had spread widely, reigniting a revolt which had been stifled only months before and inflaming alike the victims of famine and religious persecution, so that when the entire population was required to attend the Easter Mass, the results were predictable. Abraham Scultetus, the Calvinist preacher at Frederick V's coronation, was duly smuggled into the country by Christian of Denmark's agents to encourage Protestant resistance, and when Protestant books were forcefully confiscated by house-to-house searches, some 40,000 rebels from a population of 300,000 took to the field between May and July. Though religion was the principal cause, other issues also ensured that Catholic peasants would fight alongside Lutherans, as the rebels raged in their verses and manifestos not only against 'severe oppression of conscience' and 'the duplicity of the Jesuits', but about 'thieving by the governor and swindling by the officials ... and the excessive weight of taxation'. 'It is these,' ran one such declaration, 'that have brought about in this country the uprising of the peasants.'

Inspired by their leader Stefan Fadinger, a wealthy farmer, and his brother-in-law, the innkeeper Christoph Zeller, the revolt had begun prematurely after a brawl with Bavarian soldiers in Lembach on 17 May 1626. But with the assistance of many nobles, whose military experience was indispensable for success, and under the charismatic leadership of Fadinger, whose magnetic personality made him a folk hero for many generations thereafter, the peasants initially held their own, seizing several towns and laying siege to Linz, the capital, before Fadinger's death in skirmishing, alongside Zeller, engendered a crisis of confidence. When Emperor Ferdinand therefore offered to pardon all who submitted to his laws, the majority went home peacefully, though such apparent leniency proved intolerable to the Duke of Bavaria himself, who arrived with a force of 8,000 men to provoke a new rising in September, which had been decisively crushed by spring. Upon their advance, Maximilian's troops had in fact been routed within days by the peasants in the mountains along the frontier, but by November the duke's army had been reinforced by a further 4,750 men under Count Gottfried Heinrich Pappenheim who swung the balance in four hard-fought battles south of the Danube.

Some 12,000 rebels were killed in the process, while Fadinger's corpse was exhumed for hanging, before a decree of May 1627 compelled all Protestants to choose between conformity and exile. But notwithstanding the brutality of its suppression or, more importantly still, the scale of its magnitude, the rebellion seems nonetheless to have served as a curious filip to Ferdinand's self-confidence. For by September a new constitution had been promulgated in Bohemia which made no reference to the Letter of Majesty and confirmed the kingdom's dependence upon the administrative hierarchy of Vienna. The monarchy was declared hereditary, eliminating Bohemian claims to elect their king, and while the Bohemian Estates retained the right to vote on taxation, the right to free assembly was also lost, along with control of the formerly hereditary great offices of state. Henceforth, only Jews were to enjoy special religious dispensations in arrangements that were extended to Moravia the following year and would remain in force in both places until the revolution of 1848. As such, the emperor's victory seemed virtually complete, and after the victories over Christian IV and Bethlen of 1626, a well-paved path to further triumphs now seemed largely assured under Wallenstein's auspices.

In Madrid, however, the high optimism of the previous year was soon frozen solid by an icy gust of insolvency that temporarily paralysed the government's projects. In January 1627 Philip IV had outlined to regent Isabella his plans for the coming year, which reflected his confidence. The Palatinate was to be held by Bavaria, notwithstanding Duke Maximilian's almost congenital distrust of Spanish ambitions; an armed watch would be kept on French activity, especially in northern Italy; the Hanse towns were to be recruited as allies and bound to Spain by commercial treaties; the war with England and the United Provinces would be prosecuted with renewed vigour; and Poland was to be encouraged to greater efforts against Sweden. But Olivares was keenly aware that these undertakings could not be financed merely by renegotiating Spain's debts, and that Castile in particular was no longer able to bear the burden alone. Prices were continuing to rise steadily under the combined pressure of poor harvests and currency debasement, while Castile's productive forces were being crippled by an inequitable system of taxation that was further heightening the risk of unrest in the towns — all of which meant drastic action was necessary, particularly if opposition to the count-duke's 'grand design' in the Baltic was to be silenced.

As late as June 1626, there had been strenuous resistance to a declaration of war against Denmark, 'because we find ourselves with so many inescapable enemies, it does not seem right to seek more deliberately,' and by the following year King Philip was still being warned how 'there is nothing in theology which obliges your majesty to send his armed forces against heretics everywhere.' Olivares too, for that matter, was of the opinion that the Habsburgs should learn to live with the Lutherans, and he entertained no illusions either about the possibility of bringing back the United Provinces into allegiance to Spain. Those days were long since gone. But he remained convinced that 'not for anything must these two houses [of Habsburg] allow themselves to be divided,' and he also believed no less firmly that the Dutch, by a combination of economic and military pressure, might be brought to negotiate an altogether preferable and more permanent peace than the one embodied by the truce of 1609, which he considered disastrous for Spanish interests. If, indeed, the Holy Roman Emperor could be persuaded to join the war against the Dutch, perhaps by persuading him that a final settlement in Germany depended upon the pacification of the Netherlands, the entire continent's problems might be solved at a stroke.

The bedrock of such a masterplan, however, remained Spain's own solvency and the rescue of Castile from the mounting spiral of debt that was threatening to consume her. Sensitive to the existing grievances of non-Castilians who neither saw their king nor enjoyed his patronage, Olivares therefore suggested the creation of a more broadly-based administration to replace the one currently dominated from Madrid, in return for which Spain's other kingdoms would agree to increase their financial contributions and raise their own reserves of troops under a so-called 'Union of Arms'. But Castile's lifebelt was to prove a vain hope, perceived by her intended rescuers, with more than a little justification, as an open invitation to a wider disaster — one in which they themselves were likely to be sucked down into the bottomless vortex of Madrid's mismanaged finances. Even when the failure of the English raid upon Cadiz engendered a short-lived mood of national unity in the face of danger, the Cortes of Aragon,

Catalonia and Valencia had each refused their aid, so that by January 1627 there
was no other alternative than to settle the issue of the government's bankruptcy
by further borrowing, which Olivares reluctantly achieved by playing off a new
group of Portuguese financiers against the Genoese, who for nearly a century
had monopolised the business of lending to the Spanish crown.

France in the meantime, after forging friendship with England by the
marriage of Charles I to Princess Henrietta Maria, had nevertheless drifted into
war with her would-be ally over the rights of English Catholics and English
aid to the Huguenots of La Rochelle, as a result of which Richelieu even
mooted the possibility of joint naval action with Spain in the Channel. And it
was only this temporary relief from French hostility that made Spain's financial
predicament manageable at all, after Spinola, appreciating that the initiative
lay once more with the Dutch, duly opted for inaction in the Netherlands,
enabling Frederick Henry, Maurice of Nassau's half-brother and successor, not
only to launch his first major campaign, but to do so in a way that revealed his
skill as a remorseless, if cautious, director of siege operations, taking Groll, a
powerfully defended fortress in Overijsell which the Spaniards had occupied
since 1606. Though still, perhaps, of greater distinction as a diplomat than as a
soldier, the new Dutch leader was plainly no less committed to the war than
his predecessor, deeming it a means of increasing his authority as stadholder
and of centralising the government. And in this latter regard too, urged on
by his ambitious wife, Amalia von Solms, he was not only prepared to flout
the republican and separatist sympathies of the provinces, but to risk further
hostility in his own Calvinist heartlands by courting a Franco–Dutch alliance,
the implications of which for Spain were all too obvious.

'If the Prince of Orange and the rebels,' wrote one Spanish official based in
Brussels, 'were not kept by their fanatical intolerance from granting liberty of
worship and from guaranteeing of churches and Church property to the priest-
hood, then a union of the loyal provinces with those of the North could not
be prevented.' And with the political temperature lowered in any case after the
fall of Oldenbarnevelt, Frederick Henry's hand had been further strengthened
by a policy of unofficial religious toleration for the so-called Remonstrants –
supporters of the anti-Calvinist ideas of Jacobus Arminius. Now reaping the
benefits of greater unity at home and the troubles of Spain, Frederick Henry
could indeed look forward to the future with renewed confidence less than two
years after the fall of Breda had dealt such a grievous blow to Dutch morale. For
the town's capture had in any case proved a pyrrhic victory for its conquerors,
as taxation at home doubled between 1621 and 1627 partly to cover the cost of
its defence, and the overall expense of the Dutch War continued its climb from

1.5 to 3.5 million ducats. If, therefore, Spain's 'grand design' for the Baltic could indeed be thwarted and the success of Wallenstein's Imperial army pre-empted, there might yet, it seemed, be everything to play for.

But the last condition, in particular, soon seemed increasingly implausible as 1627 unfolded, and Wallenstein squared for action. Now in control of a larger fighting force than ever and with the support of both the Catholic League's army, under Tilly, and the court of Spain, which had won him over to the idea of establishing Imperial garrisons in the Baltic, he first sent troops to strengthen the defences of Hungary and to reinforce Sigismund in Poland, since the Swedes – 'in whom we shall find a worse enemy than the Turk' – had advanced through Polish Prussia to the estuary of the Vistula. Thereafter, he successfully cleared the survivors of Mansfeld's army out of Silesia and marched north to join Tilly in Lower Saxony, to deal with the Danes who, as it transpired, were in no effective position to resist after the Dutch had abandoned their king as a poor investment and the English not only defaulted on their promise of financial support but redirected their fleet to the aid of La Rochelle instead of Stade on the Elbe, where they might have rendered invaluable assistance. Desperately dispersed into a series of fortified towns, including Boizenburg where a force of 800 Scots is said to have repulsed Tilly and inflicted 2,000 casualties against all odds, the forces of Christian IV nevertheless awaited the inevitable, as Wallenstein joined up with Tilly's force just north of Lauenburg on 5 September and overran Holstein in no more than two weeks.

Nor was the final blow long in arriving, for on 26 September the Danish camp at Heiligenhafen dissolved in panic under Imperial bombardment. Only 1,000 from a total of 6,000 troops were fortunate enough to escape in their ships, and most of those who surrendered promptly enlisted in Wallenstein's army, seeking pay and the simple comforts of soldierly life, with which their former leader had signally failed to provide them. On 16 October, moreover, the fall of Rendsburg completed the triumph by opening the Danish peninsula itself to the emperor's whim, wheupon the native peasant militias promptly saw fit to oppose their own Danish authorities, and the local nobles either failed to answer Christian's appeals, or fled at the Imperials' approach. As the remnants of Christian's army finally evacuated from Ålborg to their home islands, a further 3,000 cavalry were left behind, and while Wallenstein revelled in the knowledge that he was now no longer the 'general without victories', there was further good news to cheer him. For only two days after the victory at Heiligenhafen, Tilly had been laid low by a musket ball at Pinneburg, forcing him to convalesce for the rest of the campaign, and thereby leave his counterpart to assume control of both invading armies.

With Lower Saxony now at the mercy of Emperor Ferdinand and his allies, and Mecklenburg swiftly subdued, along with Holstein, Schleswig and Jutland, the rewards of war awaiting the Imperial generals were predictably rich. Count Heinrich Schlick and Count Jean Merode were assigned portions of Magdeburg and Halberstadt, while other lands were distributed to meet the army's mounting pay arrears. But it was Wallenstein, understandably, who once again bathed most remarkably in the warm glow of Imperial gratitude. Already in May 1627 he had received the Silesian duchy of Sagan in lieu of 150,850 florins owed him by the emperor, and now rumours were already circulating of his elevation to the two duchies of Mecklenburg, which was duly confirmed in February 1628, some two months or so before he was also designated 'General of the Oceanic and Baltic Seas' in anticipation of the next overriding objective: the realisation of Spanish and Austrian ambitions along the north German coastline, which would hopefully seal the fate of Dutch resistance once and for all.

That a mere duke of Friedland should have been awarded the titles and territories of two Imperial princes was, of course, provocative enough in its own right, but its ramifications as an unwarranted, over-hasty and indeed threatening exercise of Imperial authority were, arguably, far more significant still. Maximilian of Bavaria's appointment to Frederick V's title, with the support of four electoral votes, had of course been met with widespread disapproval, but the presence now of Wallenstein's troops in Pomerania, Holstein, Württemberg, Anhalt and parts of Brandenburg raised altogether darker fears that further venerable ruling houses were also liable to lose their possessions at the emperor's whim: fears, moreover, that Wallenstein was actually keen to foster, in order to distract criticism from his own promotion. Tilly, he suggested, should become Duke of Calenberg, while Wolfenbüttel might be offered to Pappenheim. And all the while that such bargaining was underway, the growing clamour from the ecclesiastical princes and religious orders for the restitution of church property only served to increase the broader anxieties of Protestants about the emperor's silent intentions. If Ferdinand was now so firmly in the ascendant, what was to stop the destruction of the principles of the Peace of Augsburg altogether? And what, for that matter, were the prospects for the Imperial constitution itself under an emperor upheld by Wallenstein's mighty grip – a concern hardly less prevalent among German Catholic rulers than Protestant ones, and one voiced too by the Flemish envoy in Brussels to Isabella who warned that unless she and Philip IV secured Wallenstein's dismissal, 'they would confirm the very general belief that His Majesty has a secret understanding with the emperor to set up a universal monarchy and to make the Empire hereditary.'

When an electoral congress took place at Mühlhausen in October 1627, therefore, the tension was already palpable. Duke Maximilian, in particular, had watched the expansion of Wallenstein's army with growing unease, fearing its potential use by Ferdinand in the Dutch War. But he harboured other misgivings too, not the least of which involved the integrity of his own army, as officers of the Catholic League defected to Imperial service. Indeed, the military balance prevailing before 1625 had by now been entirely reversed, as Tilly found himself with three times fewer soldiers than Wallenstein, to whom Ferdinand regularly sent orders without consulting Maximilian. Yet the Mühlhausen congress had been called, in part, to settle the Palatinate question definitively, and the duke's desire to convert his status there from a purely personal title to a hereditary one obliged him to mute any criticism of the emperor. Saxony, after all, had recognised the transfer of title in 1624, while Brandenburg accepted it in its treaty with Ferdinand in May 1627. As such, all seemed well set for final confirmation, provided that the emperor's consent was assured by a suitable Bavarian silence on the activities of his military commander-in-chief.

The same did not apply, however, to the electors of Saxony and Brandenburg who were outspoken in their condemnation of Wallenstein's exactions in their own territories. Nor, it seems, were members of the Catholic League or those archbishop electors present any more inclined to keep silent, for while they, like Maximilian, were anxious for Tilly to invade Denmark, they left no doubt either that Ferdinand's requests for aid, not to mention his known desire to have his son elected King of the Romans – thus guaranteeing the young man's eventual succession to the Imperial title – would be roundly rejected unless Wallenstein's powers were swiftly curbed. Yet without the Duke of Bavaria's unequivocal backing, any faint hopes of prevailing swiftly evaporated for the emperor's opponents. Instead, Maximilian struck an eminently judicious balance between condemning the worst excess of Wallenstein's subordinates and condoning the emperor's political agenda. As a result, the duke's status as hereditary elector of the Palatinate was duly confirmed on 12 November and followed by his enfeoffment with the whole Upper and eastern half of the Lower Palatinate on 22 February 1628, in return for abandoning the Bavarian occupation of Upper Austria after a suitable guarantee of war costs, set at 13 million florins, had been agreed.

Ironically, the electoral transfer had run parallel to Wallenstein's own enfeoffment with Mecklenburg, and the realisation of Maximilian's long-term dream would indeed be bitterly compromised by the cost of his silence at Mühlhausen. For in securing the Palatinate, he had been reduced to the role of a bystander as Wallenstein assumed command of the Catholic League army as well as his own, and staged a triumphal progress through the Jutland peninsula, where by Christmas he had 60,000 men in winter quarters. To add salt to the wound, Wallenstein's other troops in Mecklenburg now controlled 100 crucial miles of coastline from Lübeck to the mouth of the Recknitz, which included the ports of Wismar and Rostock, and provided him not only with a base from which to execute Olivares's Baltic Plan, but a new nucleus for his personal empire outside Friedland and at the heart of continental commerce. Acknowledging the King of Denmark's ongoing power at sea, he considered it advisable to fortify the Mecklenburg fleets and establish a further fleet in the Baltic under the pretense of support for Spain. But his first priority remained the defeat of the Danes for his own purposes, and, to this end, he played his double game of duty and duplicity, service and self-interest, with characteristic mastery, writing urgently to Isabella in Brussels to secure the dispatch of the Dunkirk fleet.

Nor, in advancing his own objectives, did Wallenstein display any less boldness and enterprise than ever, even proposing at one point the cutting of a canal at Kiel to facilitate Spanish access to the Baltic. And he was equally diligent in his dealings with Gabriel de Roy, the Spanish naval and commercial expert, who had been sent to Wismar to superintend operations with the Hanseatic League, whose good offices remained pivotal to Spain's plans, as well as Wallenstein's own. At the end of 1627, the Genoese envoy reported that the Hanse towns, 'though they may sympathise with their Protestant brethren, are trembling at the emperor's good fortune and so will probably bow before his commands.' Moreover, the prospects of co-operation had been boosted by an offer of support from Duke Frederick of Gottorp just prior to a conference held by the League at Lübeck in 1628. In return for access to the Indies of precisely the kind now under offer to the League's towns, Frederick duly offered to help thwart the Dutch, and since Bremen largely backed him, the scene was set, it seems, for more general compliance, especially when Wallenstein himself offered to buy or build twenty-four ships of his own, using de Roy's money, to match the twenty-four required from the members of the Hanse as part of the arrangement.

But neither Wallenstein nor de Roy had counted upon the unwelcome impact of the Imperial ambassador, Count Schwarzenberg, whose needlessly aggressive manner at Lübeck was one of a number of reasons ensuring the meeting's failure. Ultimately, there were simply too many Protestants at the conference, too many exiles from Roman Catholic states and therefore too many influential parties with grievances against the emperor's servants, so that when Schwarzenberg opted for bluster rather than tact with an audience facing considerable risks, the outcome was assured. Sweden, Denmark and the United Provinces were, after all, considerable foes for an organisation that had already seen its best days, as was demonstrated soon afterwards when the Dutch reinforced the garrisons at Elsinore and Helsingborg and effectively closed the Sound. And Wallenstein's recent victories on land were no guarantee either of further success in a naval campaign, especially when his own ships were still a pipedream, and the gunboat flotilla maintained by the Habsburgs on the Danube had little potential in high seas warfare. Only the Poles, in fact, had scored a minor victory against the Swedes – in the Danzig lagoon in November 1627 – but their first fully effective sea-going warship had not been launched until 1622, and the eleven built since, along with fifteen now being fitted out, were not nearly enough, under the circumstances, to convince the doubters.

By the time that Wallenstein was appointed 'General of the Oceanic and Baltic Seas', therefore, the contradiction in his title was already manifest, for while generals might capture ports, only ships could control the all-important waters flowing round them. Yet in spite of his detractors and well-merited reputation for hard-headed pragmatism, he would nevertheless continue to increase the size of his army and draw up ambitious plans for an attack upon Stralsund, an important Hanseatic port of 15,000 inhabitants lying close to the eastern frontier of Mecklenburg which controlled communications between the Pomeranian coast and the island of Rütgen. And the decision would prove fateful. For in 1627, fearful of Wallenstein's approach, the town's magistrates had employed a team of Swedish engineers to construct a new chain of powerful fortifications, and increased the militia to almost 5,000, so that when Rostock and other places agreed to pay Wallenstein contributions to avoid having soldiers billeted, Stralsund categorically refused. Though its wealthier citizens had considered it cheaper in the long run to submit, the majority nevertheless remained resolute, and they did so, moreover, firm in the belief that the King of Sweden would act as their protector – a prospect that Wallenstein was unwilling to countenance under any circumstance. 'It must be stopped at once,' he told Hans Georg von Armin, his commander in the field, 'and you must conclude with them by force so that they may not avail themselves of the assistance of the enemy.'

But the enemy was already at work. For although Christian IV had few troops to spare, and notwithstanding the Danes' antipathy to their long-standing rival, he had signed an agreement with Sweden guaranteeing that both powers would defend Stralsund if she were attacked. And Gustavus Adolphus was indeed both eager and ready – not only for this particular task but a mission of altogether broader scope and significance. 'All the wars which are going on in Europe,' he had by now decided, 'are linked together and are directed to one end', which he interpreted quite unequivocally as the defeat of the Reformation in Europe and the triumph of Habsburg hegemony. As early as 1621, indeed, he had written with notable prescience to the Duke of Mecklenburg who at that stage appeared indifferent to the Elector Palatine's fate. *Hodie illi, cras tibi* – 'Today him, tomorrow you' – Gustavus had warned; and with Mecklenburg, as predicted, now gone, he consequently lost no time in countering the threat to Stralsund by sending in 5 tons of gunpowder, before proposing the new alliance to Christian:

> I now see with little difficulty [he wrote] that the projects of the House of Habsburg are directed against the Baltic; and that by a mixture of force and favour the United Provinces, my own power and finally yours are to be driven from it.

Nor, after his defeats on the mainland, could Denmark's ruler realistically refuse, especially when Stralsund stood on a triangular promontory connected by a causeway with the mainland, virtually surrounded by sea, and the assistance of the Swedish and Danish fleets was not only critical to its survival but virtually assured of success. For, as the enemies of the Habsburgs commented gleefully, 'the Eagle cannot swim', and Wallenstein still needed at least a year to construct his own fleet after the Hanseatic League had refused to commit and Sigismund of Poland had declined to transfer his squadron to Wismar until Spanish vessels had entered the Baltic.

As such, Wallenstein's hopes for a speedy and decisive resolution lay almost exclusively in the anxieties of the rich patricians controlling Stralsund's town council, who did indeed attempt to capitulate when the enemy commander, Hans Georg von Arnim, first pressed home his attack. But the fighting spirit of the citizenry was not to be quenched so easily. On the contrary, buoyed by a heady combination of physical danger, religious conviction and the assurance that help would not be long in coming, the doughty townsfolk, guided by the radical lawyer Johann Jusquinas von Gosen, took the law into their own hands and forced Arnim to opt for a siege. Even before the siege began in earnest in May 1628, moreover, seven companies of Scottish veterans in Danish service had duly arrived, to be followed shortly after by some 600 Swedes, who further swelled the ranks of the town's 2,450-strong militia, and 1,000 mercenary recruits. By comparison, the enemy's force numbered only 8,000, and after Gosen's militants had burnt down the suburbs and seized Dänholm island at the south-east entrance to the harbour, the swift victory sought by Wallenstein seemed increasingly unlikely, even after his own arrival with 25,000 further besiegers in July and the commencement of an intense bombardment in which, we are told, a single shot decapitated fourteen defenders. 'Who doubts this,' wrote Robert Monro, a commander with Sir Donald MacKay's Scottish contingent, 'may go and see the reliques of their braines to this day, sticking to the walls.'

Yet in spite of such carnage, Stralsund's defenders not only beat off successive Imperial assaults, the heaviest of which had occurred on 27–29 June, but continued to attract further reinforcements not only from Scotland, Denmark and Sweden, but Germany too. Gustavus Adolphus, it is true, was still campaigning in Poland, and Denmark's own position remained hopeless in the long term. But the siege was already proving a potentially devastating political blow, as criticism of Wallenstein grew in proportion to his demands for extra men – whose numbers already stood at 130,200 – and the Empire also found itself loaded with additional payments for the forces of Spain and the Catholic League in the north-west. Already, at Mühlhausen, the Catholic electors had criticised both the level of taxes imposed by Ferdinand's generalissimo, and the way they were distributed. 'His war taxes guarantee exorbitant rates of pay to regimental and company staff officers,' they claimed, pointing out that Lieutenant-General Arnim alone received 3,000 florins a month. And there had been further censure for Wallenstein's practice of selling commissions 'for up to four regiments at a time to anyone offering his services, including criminals, foreigners and those ignorant of military administration', as well as the destruction caused within the electors' own domains. 'Territorial rulers,' his critics raged, 'are at the mercy of Colonels and Captains, who are uninvited war profiteers and criminals, breaking the laws of the Empire.'

Now, however, the ugly prospect of military failure had heightened the chorus of complaint at the very time that another siege many miles from the Baltic was also taxing Habsburg resources to the limit. For since 1612, Charles Emmanuel, Duke of Savoy, had been nursing an ambition to acquire Montferrat, which controlled the route from Genoa to Milan and belonged to the Duke of Mantua. So when the latter died in 1627 and left his territories to the Duke of Nevers, whose son had married his niece, the way lay open for a counter-claim. Hoping indeed to profit from a conflict, Charles Emmanuel advised Olivares of an alternative candidate, the Duke of Guastala, who might prove more amenable to Spanish control than a French interloper, and offered into the bargain to take the field in alliance with Spain. Since Mantua, moreover, was an Imperial fief, Ferdinand too was able to further the scheme by ordering its sequestration pending a decision, though it was known that his own second wife, who came from the ducal family of Mantua, favoured the French candidate.

Not wishing to antagonise either the emperor or indeed Louis XIII, and fully cognisant of Charles Emmanuel's penchant for duplicity, Olivares had in fact initially counselled caution, warning Philip IV that 'though my greatest wish in the world is to see Your Majesty the master of Montferrat, I cannot find any way to justify you in dividing it with Savoy.' But the count-duke's prudence was not reflected in the action of Gonzalo Fernández Córdoba. Formerly the Spanish commander in the Palatinate, Córdoba was now in control of Milan, the base from which Spain dominated northern Italy, and the starting point of that vital system of military corridors which ran by way of the Valtelline to Central Europe, or up the Rhine to the Netherlands. And the prospect of safeguarding the route from Milan to Genoa by a brilliant *coup de main* now proved impossible to resist. If the almost impregnable fortress of Casale in Montferrat could be captured, Córdoba reasoned, not only would the reputation of Spanish arms be considerably enhanced, her control over the Lombard plain would be effectively unchallengeable.

Alarmed by the Duke of Nevers' arrival in Mantua in mid-January 1628, and under heavy criticism at home for the alleged failures of his government, Olivares therefore acceded to his general's urging and, in doing so, found himself impaled once more upon the age-old Spanish dilemma: Flanders or Italy. If the Siege of Casale was rapidly concluded, the momentum enjoyed by the Habsburg cause might well become irresistible. If not, the diversion of scarce resources from the Army of Flanders might drastically undermine the struggle against the United Provinces and in the process risk even the loyalty of the now desperately war-weary southern Netherlands. For seven fat years, in fact, the governments of both Spain and Austria had enjoyed the initiative and savoured the pickings. Bohemia and dissenters within Austria had been brutally but effectively brought to order, the Catholic cause in northern Germany had trampled all before it under the heels of Wallenstein's army, and the Palatinate had been occupied by the troops of Spain and the Catholic League. By contrast, German Protestantism had lain beleaguered, while the standard-bearers of the cause of resistance, the rebel Dutch provinces, had of late managed little more than grim survival. Frederick Henry's capture of Groll was small compensation for Spinola's victory at Breda; Dutch merchants were now threatened with the loss of their Baltic trade; and the coalition of Protestant powers, so crucial to any reversal of fortunes, remained singularly ineffective.

Yet so far-reaching was the range of Habsburg policy across the whole of Europe, so all-embracing its scope, so successful its progress to date, that even the allies of the Habsburgs were becoming as alarmed as their enemies. Furthermore, an explosive coincidence of political and military factors was now imminently threatening to merge Europe's several conflicts into a single all-embracing conflagration. For the Imperial advance to the Baltic had not only made bedfellows of Denmark and Sweden, but emboldened Poland to offer support to Ferdinand. In the meantime, full-scale French intervention in Italy waited only upon the imminent suppression of Huguenot opposition in

La Rochelle, which England vainly wished to prevent. Such, indeed, was the tangled web of mutual self-interest and rivalry, and such the stakes and passions involved that no event in far-off Stralsund or Casale, or indeed any number of other emerging flashpoints, could fail to have massive ramifications elsewhere. La Rochelle, Danzig, Magdeburg, Mantua, 's-Hertogenbosch in Brabant would all before long assume equivalent importance. All, like Stralsund and Casale, were to become notorious victims of siege warfare, and the fate of each city would determine whether one or more powers would be free to intervene elsewhere. Fuelled by religion and what amounted to incompatible visions of Europe's destiny, and fanned at the same time by ambition, bigotry, suspicion and the all-consuming militaristic ethos of the day, the war that had begun ten years earlier in Bohemia was now no longer containable. For while the necessity of peace grew stronger by the day, so too did the hunger for war without limit.

8

'LION OF THE NORTH'

For though he had bin no king he was a brave warrior, and which is more, a good man, magnificent, wise, just, meeke, indued with learning, and the gift of tongues, and as he had strength of body, and a manlike stature, he had also the ornaments of the mind, fitting a brave commander. O would to GOD I had once such a leader againe to fight such another day; in this old quarrel! And though I died standing, I should be persuaded I died well.

Robert Monro, *Monro his expedition with the worthy Scots regiment called Mackays* (1637)

In the high summer of 1628 all Europe's gaze was firmly fixed upon what the Pope had so colourfully designated 'the synagogue of Satan'. La Rochelle, last bastion of Protestant Hugenot resistance in France, was, like far-off Stralsund to the north and the fortress of Casale in Montferrat, fighting for its life, and, like them too, holding the fate of a continent in the balance. One year earlier, with strong encouragement from England, its inhabitants had revolted, but by November Richelieu had forced the withdrawal of the Duke of Buckingham from the Ile de Ré, and on 11 May 1628 successfully repulsed the English fleet. Taunted by besieging soldiers brandishing chickens impaled upon their pikes, and cut off from all prospect of help by a 1,500-metre wall constructed across the harbour upon sunken ships at the cardinal's personal directive, the starving defenders had nevertheless remained defiant under their determined mayor, Jean Guitton. But while Richelieu's army rose steadily to more than 25,000 men, the Rochellois had dwindled from 27,000 to 8,000. Nor was the toll from famine and plague the limit of their torment, for when hunger finally weakened their resistance beyond recall, they were faced with a demand for unconditional surrender. From first to last, Richelieu had conducted the siege in person, and in doing so demonstrated a brilliance that showed how much the army lost when he ultimately evaded the military career intended for him. As the struggle intensified, he had ordered the construction of 7.5 miles of siege-works and twenty-nine separate fortifications. And he would not be swayed by sentiment any more at the end than he had been throughout, so that when Louis XIII finally entered the city on the first day of 1629, he found the inhabitants more like scarecrows than human beings after fourteen months of acute suffering.

In the early stages of their revolt, the Huguenots had not only sunk most of the cardinal's new fleet at Blavet but forced him to withdraw French troops from the Valtelline. And the subjugation of La Rochelle was now marked by the systematic destruction of all other vestiges of resistance as Richelieu's troops proceeded to sweep down the Rhône Valley in a resolute show of strength, seizing one stronghold after another from the remaining Huguenot rebels committed to a desperate last stand under Benjamin de Rohan, Duke of Soubise, in Languedoc. With the fall of Montauban, de Rohan's final fortress, victory was complete, and one of the more momentous of the many treaties ending civil war in France duly followed on 28 June 1629. By the so-called 'Grace of Alais', the Huguenots were allowed complete freedom of worship wherever their churches were already established and protected from discrimination in their careers. But Richelieu's generosity, born as it was from a wish to permit the speedy resumption of his designs in Italy, was also tempered by a firm determination that Huguenots should never again challenge the authority of the state. In consequence, their political and military privileges were destroyed by the abolition of their separate law courts and assemblies, and by the destruction of their former strongholds.

In two respects, at least, the man who had spawned the revolt in the first place was at one with his nemesis. Escaping to Venice with four crates of books, which included works by Machiavelli and Guicciardini, Benjamin de Rohan spent his enforced leisure far from the smoking ruins of La Rochelle, writing about politics, and in doing so made clear that his loyalty to the Huguenot cause, while not in doubt, had not uniquely inspired his rebellion. He rationalised his action, in fact, by a visceral hatred for Spain – whose 'interest is to persecute Protestants in order to aggrandise themselves on the spoils' – while contending likewise that France's own best interest lay in 'understanding the poison which results'. And just as de Rohan's antipathy to Madrid mirrored Richelieu's own, so his broader approach to politics and war also bore a close affinity to the cardinal's. Appreciating that neither were spheres where Christian ethics played any significant part, he openly acknowledged that he was living in a world of 'revolutions' for which there were no eternal 'rules' or any immutable standards. 'It is the vice of irresolution and a weakness of courage,' he wrote, 'that holds us back, rather than true compassion for the sufferings of others … it is thus that we then try to cover our vices with the meanest virtue [pity].'

Plainly, the imminence of total war was already breeding iron in the soul and entrenching the same kind of flint-faced indifference to moral niceties that was by now commonplace across a continent. The age of geopolitics had been born, and nowhere were its mechanics more richly embraced or exquisitely practised than in Paris, where Richelieu triumphantly introduced his seminal memorandum on the international situation with the words 'Now that La Rochelle has fallen'. For by clearing at last the political decks at home, the way was finally open 'to arrest the course of Spain's progress', and it was to France's good fortune that the preliminary groundwork for this task had already been undertaken in Montferrat. Notwithstanding snowdrifts, avalanches, a 6-metre high barricade and the presence of 4,000 Spanish and Savoyard troops, Richelieu had in fact brushed aside the resistance of Charles Emmanuel of Savoy, and forced the pass of Susa in February 1628, concluding an agreement only two days later, by which France would be allowed to garrison Casale. And though his army still numbered considerably less than 40,000, he then sent 3,000 of them down the Po to reinforce the beleaguered fortress itself, lifting the defenders' spirits, and in the process shattering the hopes of the man who had masterminded the siege from the outset. For by 19 March, discouraged by the desultory response from both Madrid and Vienna, General Córdoba had acknowledged his failure and taken his army with him.

The victory was not, of course, a killer blow, but rather, as Richelieu hoped, the onset of death by a thousand cuts to Habsburg pretensions. Neither side was ready for a full-scale confrontation, and the War of the Mantuan Succession was therefore contained for the time being by an arrangement which left Charles Emmanuel and the Duke of Nevers in control of their respective portions of Montferrat. But Olivares would warn the papal nuncio with uncanny prescience that if a French army were ever to cross the Alps, a war of thirty years would ensue, and even before Casale had been abandoned, the Habsburgs had been denied victory at Stralsund too. For while Wallenstein had blustered that 'the town shall yield though it were bound by chains to heaven', Danish and Swedish control of the coast had indeed rendered his words empty. Comfortably supplied and succoured by the King of Sweden's protective wing, Stralsund could plainly hold out indefinitely, and the siege was duly lifted by Wallenstein on 31 July, employing the face-saving formula that the Duke of Pomerania had requested his withdrawal, though in keeping out the Imperials, Stralsund had in fact acceded to 187 years of Swedish occupation. Worse still from the Habsburg standpoint, the Hanseatic League not only subsequently rejected the planned naval agreement, but even refused Wallenstein the opportunity to buy ships and stores in future.

Only the stubborn refusal of Christian IV to leave well alone provided any consolation, in fact. For in an attempt to recover a foothold on the mainland, he landed with 7,000 men at Wolgast on the Pomeranian coast east of Greifswald, with the result that Wallenstein succeeded in trapping him on 24 August, just as had happened at Heiligenhafen the year before. On 2 September, Wolgast's defences were successfully stormed, and though a cohort of Christian's troops eventually offered stout resistance behind a stretch of marshland, enabling their king to escape by sea, some 1,000 nevertheless died and 1,100 were captured. The Danish army, which had been rebuilt by extending conscription to Norway, had thus been dealt another withering blow, and, much to Wallenstein's relief, his opponent's projected march on Mecklenburg had been thwarted, though even now Christian was unprepared to surrender. Instead the tortuous peace negotiations, which had already been underway at Lübeck for some months, continued on their weary course and followed the fashion of the times, whereby each side made wildly unrealistic demands and responded to proposals only after the maximum possible delay, in what amounted to little more than a stately qua-drille, conducted all the while amid endless quibbles over protocol rather than substance, in the hope that some timely success or other of their commanders in the field might thereby improve their negotiating positions.

For Emperor Ferdinand and his thwarted general, therefore, there was frustra-tion in plenty, but for Olivares, too, the autumn of 1628 had brought only bad news. During the year, manifestoes and satires had circulated in Madrid urging Philip IV to rid himself of the count-duke, and though the king showed no inclination as yet to follow the advice of the majority of his council of state, who had succumbed to Spinola's preference for peace in the north and war in Italy, tension continued to mount. The king, indeed, had talked of leading an army in person to Italy, and when Spinola left Brussels for Madrid, his purpose was to make clear that unless Spain could afford to finance a series of major offensives against the Dutch, it would be better to abandon the war altogether. In particu-lar, he explained that a full-scale attack in the Netherlands could mean nothing but a series of major sieges, occupying many years and costing millions of ducats. Nor was Olivares' scorn for the general remotely convincing. The Romans, he claimed, had conquered the world with 100,000 men, while Spinola was unable to contain the Dutch with 90,000. But while Olivares was declaiming grandly, the Dutch privateer and national hero, Piet Heyn, was already engaged in destroying a third of the ships engaged in the Spanish West Indian trade at the Battle of Matanzas Bay off Cuba.

With the consequent rush of booty, valued in Holland at 11 million florins, the balance had once more swung wildly, and, as the directors of the West India Company celebrated Heyn's victory by declaring a dividend of 50 per cent, so the Dutch government planned for a new offensive against the southern Netherlands in the spring of 1629. The target was 's-Hertogenbosch, Brabant's second most important city after Antwerp, lying between two rivers, surrounded by swamp and defended by three strong outworks, which Frederick Henry, with the unprecedented number of 128,000 men from the Dutch citizens' militia at his disposal, duly invested on 1 May. Just as Spinola had done at Breda, the besiegers constructed an imposing system of dykes and trenches, supplied in this case by boat from a secure base on the Maas at Crèvecourt. And as the operation proceeded, the Habsburgs retaliated by sending two columns – one of 10,000 Imperials, the other from the Army of Flanders – deep into Dutch territory. By a curious quirk of circumstance, moreover, the latter was commanded by Henry van den Bergh, nephew of William of Orange, and first cousin to Frederick Henry.

But van den Bergh, unlike his illustrious uncle, did not enjoy either the skill or indeed the luck of the truly great tactician. For, after observing the steady development of the siege, he mistakenly opted to distract the Dutch from their quarry by attacking in an entirely different quarter. Aided by a contingent of 20,000 men from Wallenstein, which had been sent with considerable reluctance, he duly crossed the riverline at Arnheim in July to relieve Amersfoort and Veluwe, yet found his opponents not only resolved to persist in their original plan but ready to raise a second army for the attack of Wesel, the indispensable link in the chain connecting the invading army with its base. Though Amersfoort, only 40km south of Amsterdam, resisted throughout August, Wesel was taken by storm earlier in the very same month, after which the fate of 's-Hertogenbosch was itself effectively sealed. By 18 July, in fact, the Dutch had already taken the city's outworks and were only 25 metres from its main wall, though it would take the explosion of a huge mine to breach that wall on 10 September and finally bring the garrison's five-month-long resistance to a heroic end. One week later 's-Hertogenbosch had indeed submitted, thus compelling the uncomfortably isolated Habsburg forces at Amersfoort to surrender in disorder.

Nor was this all, since in Flanders and Brabant there was serious unrest. The failure to save 's-Hertogenbosch, coupled with the ever-increasing burden of taxation, was blamed upon Spanish influence in general and Cardinal Cueva's in particular. And as the common people began to stir in dissent, so too did great nobles, like van den Bergh himself, who were now as discontented with rule from Madrid as their grandfathers had been seventy years earlier. Indeed, only Cueva's dismissal and the threat to its freedom of worship from the Calvinist States-General in Holland was enough to maintain the south's loyalty – and only then by the slenderest of threads. 'Never,' reported one Spanish observer from Brussels, 'have these provinces been more bitter in their enmity towards Spain.' And as Madrid reeled from its most serious defeat since the Armada, the victorious Dutch proceeded to send 12,000 troops along the Rhine, capturing the remaining Spanish outposts and preventing the dispatch of reinforcements to Italy, where conflict was once again flaring. Henceforth, as Spain abandoned its German positions to the charge of the Catholic League's armies, the demarcation between the war in the Empire and that in the Netherlands would be re-established more and more distinctly, with the result that the League and Tilly, its general, would now be left to shoulder the burden of defending the Catholic cause in Germany almost alone, and the principle reason was simple. For during the course of 1629, thanks to the tireless diplomacy of the Count-Duke of Olivares, both branches of the House of Habsburg were about to become fatally involved in a major war with France in Italy.

Not surprisingly, the presence of the French beyond the Alps was a source of greater concern to Emperor Ferdinand than the course of the war in the Netherlands, and in the summer of 1629 he revoked the permission he had granted Wallenstein to deploy part of his army against the Dutch. Instead, his troops were ordered to Italy, where the Mantuan question and the insult to Spanish honour created by the unsuccessful siege of Casale were to be settled once and for all. Wallenstein, in fact, had admonished Ferdinand not to imperil his position north of the Alps by adventures below them. 'Let there be peace in Italy and there will be peace with France,' he urged. But Ferdinand was determined to enforce his prerogative, and in September 1629, bolstered by Imperial support, Spanish troops duly began the siege of the city of Mantua. This time their leader was Spinola, since Córdoba had been court-martialled for his unauthorised intervention at Casale, and Imperial forces under Wallenstein's assistant, Count Merode, had already occupied the Valtelline by the time of his arrival. The Army of Lombardy too, which now lay at Spinola's disposal, had been bolstered by support from Parma and Tuscany, as well as additional Neapolitan recruits, while a further 30,000 Imperial troops under Count Ramboldo Collalto were soon pouring through the Valtelline towards Mantua after Denmark had finally agreed peace terms at Lübeck in June.

That spring in fact, tireless as ever, Christian IV had renewed the unequal struggle against Wallenstein, landing on the east coast of Jutland with the

intention of a joint enterprise alongside British and Dutch troops against
Nordstrand. Once more, however, he succeeded only in ensuring his own
entrapment, though Ferdinand, on the advice of Wallenstein and in the interests
of winning Christian as a potential ally against Sweden, was willing to prove
generous in victory, so long as Danish pretensions in Germany were abandoned.
Denmark, after all, remained unbeatable at sea, and the successful prosecution
of Imperial commitments in Italy precluded all possibility of distractions
elsewhere. And while Richelieu proceeded to condemn Christian as a coward
for accepting its terms, the outcome of the Peace of Lübeck remained effectively
irresistible, painful as it was for the Danish king to renounce his family's claims
to the disputed bishoprics in Westphalia and Lower Saxony, and to recognise the
emperor's sovereignty in Holstein – leaving Ferdinand free to pursue his ends
against France over Italy.

It was true, of course, that the collapse of Danish resistance was not without
compensations of a kind. For Pope Urban VII was so enraged by the massive
demonstration of Habsburg power in northern Italy that France's Catholic *dévots*
could no longer successfully oppose Richelieu's plans to intervene on behalf of
the Duke of Nevers. Yet intervention in Mantua remained problematic, not
least because the presence of 18,000 French troops on the Savoyard frontier
had already failed to deter the Habsburgs, and the French army as a whole
was no more than half the size necessary for guaranteed success. The arrival of
7,000 Venetian auxiliaries had, in fact, failed to stop the Imperials overrunning
the Mantuan countryside in October, and Casale too was now being subjected
once more to blockade, so that when Richelieu finally advanced in person in
February 1630 along the road immediately south of the Susa pass, capturing
Pinerolo on 31 March, the outcome of his gamble remained far from clear. For
by September, notwithstanding the defeat of the Duke of Savoy's main army at
Avigliana just west of Turin two months earlier, disease had accounted for some
20,000 French troops, obliging them to suspend operations until the arrival of
reinforcements, and in the meantime the Imperial siege of Mantua appeared to
be proceeding to plan.

Certainly, the condition of Mantua's defenders continued to deteriorate
rapidly, as Emperor Ferdinand's generals pressed home their assault on what he
continued to consider his imperial fief. Faced, on the one hand, with a French
threat to his dukedom of Savoy and an Imperial threat to what he perceived
as his own rightful inheritance, Duke Charles Emmanuel was in fact facing
inevitable defeat, but not, it seems, before Mantua had paid the heaviest of
prices. For plague had appeared in Lombardy during 1629 and, after a lull over
the winter, the outbreak grew more virulent with the warmer spring weather,

especially within the city itself where the population of over 30,000 had been further swollen by an influx of refugees. By mid-July, indeed, only 700 soldiers remained fit for duty, and, as all hope waned, the Imperials duly crossed the San Giorgio bridge on 16 July, supported by additional troops in boats, to complete the city's capture in an orgy of pillaging lasting three days and nights, in which the generals, Collalto and Aldringen, helped themselves to the duke's fine art collection, and the rest of the booty amounted to some 18 million ducats – no less than twice the annual revenue of the kingdom of Naples.

At least 10,000 inhabitants had died during the siege and no more than 9,000 remained in the city afterwards. Charles Emmanuel, meanwhile, merely attributed the outcome to the ineffable operation of God's will. Whether France or her opponents would eventually prevail in Savoy, of course, was still unknown, but his own defeat was no longer at issue, and events in Italy were, in any case, being swiftly overtaken by the broader tide of events in other areas of the European maelstrom. For even before Mantua's fall, Emperor Ferdinand had taken the fateful decision to publish a single sheet of paper bearing no more than four columns of small print and his own signature, which would inflame his territories anew and undo at a single stroke the numerous successes he had enjoyed over recent years. Secretly printed in Vienna and distributed to the Directors of the Imperial Circles and the major German princes, with instructions to publish multiple copies simultaneously on 28 March 1629, the so-called 'Edict of Restitution' was intended, in fact, to complement the Peace of Lübeck by effecting a general settlement of the Empire's problems. But what was purported to bring harmony by resurrecting the 'authentic' interpretation of the Augsburg Settlement of 1555 would prove both unrealistic and one-sided, and provocative in the extreme, since it involved nothing less than the recovery of those ecclesiastical lands lost to Protestantism over more than seventy years and the outright prohibition of Calvinism once more.

The decision flowed naturally, in many respects, from the general re-imposition of Catholic authority ongoing since 1620. From many perspectives, indeed, it was born from the very success that was now about to undo that success. The process of Counter-Reformation had, of course, been controversial throughout as it spread steadily from the Habsburg and Palatine lands to embrace broad swathes of Franconia and the Rhineland after 1623. But it had proceeded inexorably and upon a tide of victories since the outset of the war that convinced its crusaders of God's favour and the need to carry their cause to ultimate and uncompromising victory. Events like the apparently miraculous survival of the victims of the defenestration of Prague, or the fall of La Rochelle, were all ardently presented as part of an unfolding divine plan, not only by Adam Contzen, Jesuit adviser to Maximilian of Bavaria, but, even more influentially, by Ferdinand's own personal confessor, William Lamormaini. For both, the long-overdue return of lost ecclesiastical lands to Holy Mother Church was to be 'the great gain and fruit of the war', and by the end of 1628 their objective was being eagerly embraced in both Munich and Vienna.

> Just as up to now we have never thought to let pass any chance to gain the restitution of church lands [Ferdinand told Peter Heinrich von Stralendorf, his Imperial Vice-Chancellor] neither do we intend now or in the future to have to bear the responsibility of having neglected or failed to exploit even the least opportunity.

Even before this, moreover, Maximilian was echoing precisely the same kind of providentialism pedalled so remorselessly by both Contzen and Lamormaini. For on 7 September 1627, in a dialogue with the Archbishop of Mainz who was potentially a major beneficiary of restitution, the duke made clear where his own preferences lay. 'We see,' he confided, 'that the opportunity presented to us by God should be accepted and the course pointed out by him continued.'

Lamormaini, in particular, had been key in encouraging a process that had already been underway informally for at least six years. The initial targets were the most vulnerable, like the Protestant knights of Franconia who were obliged to expel pastors from their estates and resubmit them to the control of the Catholic authorities of Bamberg and Würzburg. Troops, too, had been used in some cases to recover individual monasteries, and by February 1627 the bishops of Konstanz and Augsburg were sufficiently confident to open a series of reclamation cases against Württemberg, the first major Protestant territory to be affected. But after the Battle of Lutter, in particular, Lamormaini felt sure of his ground and pressed his case for what he proclaimed to the emperor was a 'glorious enterprise' – oblivious, it seems, to the fact that the ill-fated Spanish Armada of 1588 had been similarly dubbed. Some 2,500 Masses a week were promised by Mazio Vitelleschi, the Jesuit Superior General in Rome, in support of the proposed edict, and such was Lamormaini's self-assurance that by January 1628 he had already alerted Vitelleschi to the need to prepare missionaries for the territory to be recovered imminently from the Protestant foe. Forceful, wilful and austere, the emperor's confessor had originated from Luxembourg and joined the Society of Jesus at the age of 20, before becoming rector of Vienna University in 1623 and arriving at Ferdinand's court the following year. And he was now so jealous of his dominance that he had arranged for all Jesuit correspondence to Vienna to flow through him.

By 1629, indeed, Lamormaini had become almost a stereotype of the malev-olent Jesuit conspirator so caricatured and reviled in Protestant propaganda. Yet his effectiveness was not in doubt as ministers in Imperial service like Trauttmansdorff and Eggenberg shuffled uneasily but in silence over the edict's likely ramifications. The former had manifested reservations about the policy during a visit to Munich in early 1628, but remained largely tight-lipped there-after, while the latter had been frequently ill during the winter and lamented to the Bishop of Mantua in mid-March 1629 how the emperor no longer con-sulted him. Nor was Wallenstein happy with the turn of events, fearing that the decision to take Church lands from the Protestant princes who had not so far opposed Ferdinand would incite hostility at the grass roots and promote religious conflict. But he too made no attempt to prevent the measure, and only Collalto, President of the Imperial War Council, offered outright criticism of any kind, when asked, by pointing out that the measure was not only likely to incite religious war in the long run, but to undercut intervention in Italy, which was the rightful priority.

As such, Lamormaini's triumph was assured and three days after its publication, he hailed the edict in a letter to Cardinal Francesco Barberini as 'a deed truly worthy of this Emperor'. 'No Roman Pontiff since the time of Charlemagne,' he declared, 'has received such a harvest of joys from Germany, so that we can call Urban VII truly blessed, since he witnesses such gains for the Catholic reli-gion.' The bishoprics and archbishoprics of Lower Saxony and Westphalia were to be affected immediately, as were some 500 monasteries, convents and other Church properties secularised by a host of Protestant rulers since 1552. The Duke of Württemberg alone was to be deprived of the lands of fourteen large monasteries and thirty-six convents, representing a third of his duchy's wealth, while the dukes of Brunswick faced demands only slightly less exorbitant. At the same time, several free cities, such as Augsburg and Dortmund, were once again required to accept the authority of a bishop. And as Paul Laymann, a leading theologian at the Jesuit University of Dillingen, attempted to smooth the way with his tract *Pacis Compositio* ('The Way to Peace'), which arrived on the stalls of the Frankfurt bookmarket on the very day the edict was published, one surviving version printed in Würzburg was already on its way to being defiantly inscribed on its title page. '*Radix omnium malorum*', the anonymous inscription reads: 'the root of all evil'. Yet Lamormaini, bolstered by unwavering certainty in the ineffable operation of God's cosmic design, remained unwavering. If the Lord were to provide Ferdinand with ten more years of life and keep him from war in Italy, he informed Barberini, all Germany would be led back safely to the consolations of the one true faith.

The muted fears of the edict's critics were well founded, however. For although there had been widespread expectation that the courts would continue to issue judgements on a case-by-case basis, both Ferdinand and Lamormaini considered the new arrangement definitive, allowing no exceptions and confirming once and for all what was curiously deemed the 'clear letter' of the 1555 peace, irrespective of the deliberate ambiguity of the Augsburg Settlement in the first place. In effect, Ferdinand's edict merely stated the extreme Catholic interpretation, excluding Calvinism and demanding the return of all land lost since 1552. And in doing so, of course, it not only struck a bolt through Protestant hearts, but raised broader anxieties about the safety of the Imperial constitution itself, since it remained highly doubtful whether Ferdinand possessed the legal authority to make such a sweeping unilateral decision at all. Not only John George of Saxony but even Maximilian of Bavaria, wary as always of any impingement upon 'German liberties', had recommended that the matter be laid before the Imperial Diet. Yet Ferdinand had decided to press ahead on his own, and on 24 March authorised the use of force by both Tilly and Wallenstein.

Nor was it simply the current edict that sent a shudder through the rulers of Saxony and Brandenburg in particular. For although the territorial Church lands of both were safe as yet, having been secularised long before 1552, there seemed good reason to fear that a future edict might one day challenge even their immunity. Not least of all, some of the former Church properties now being reclaimed in other areas had actually become Lutheran prior to 1552. Indeed, out of forty-five Imperial cities affected up to 1631, only eight had clearly broken the post-1552 moratorium on further Protestantisation, while one, the city of Lindau, had actually been Protestant since 1528. Equally worryingly, Paul Laymann's *Pacis Compositio*, which was rightly perceived as bearing the unofficial stamp of Imperial approval, seemed clearly to signal the way ahead. 'Whatever is not found to have been explicitly granted,' the tract proclaimed, 'should be considered forbidden.' And the explosive potential of Laymann's claim, in effect, that Protestants should return everything held without a formal title was soon manifest well beyond the confines of the Empire itself. For when Gustavus Adolphus arrived in Germany the following year, he lost no time in announcing his intention of executing three men whose names began with the letter 'L' – one of whom was indeed the author of *Pacis Compositio*.

There remained, too, one further compelling reason for the level of disquiet evinced in Brandenburg and Saxony at this time: the size of the Catholic armies massed close to their borders, and in particular their role in enforcing the edict. Tilly and his Catholic troops were, on the one hand, steadily assisting the duly appointed Imperial commissioners in the dioceses of Osnabrück,

Bremen, Verden and Hildesheim, as well as in key cities like Augsburg, and if Wallenstein's forces were initially less active, it was only because of their involvement at Stralsund. Before long, moreover, they would indeed be taking up the cause. For, although an unenthusiastic champion of the Counter-Reformation, Wallenstein was unequivocally committed to enforcing the wishes of the ruler from whom his own authority derived. And soon enough, therefore, throughout Swabia and Franconia, his forces were implementing the edict with decided gusto, prompted in no small part by the further knowledge that Ferdinand had reserved not only Halberstadt and Bremen but Magdeburg, too, for their leader's own family. Anxious to win over the towns of the Hanseatic League, Wallenstein had tried to reassure them that the edict would not apply to them. But elsewhere he was now more than happy to affirm his unerring loyalty to the imperial mission in regular angry outbursts against his detractors, proclaiming how 'he would teach the electors manners' on the grounds that 'they must be prepared to serve the emperor, not the emperor them', and making clear his dislike of Duke Maximilian in particular. 'I am accustomed to serve the house of Austria,' he asserted disdainfully, 'and not to be harassed by Bavarian servitude.'

But while the mighty general was enforcing Ferdinand's will and complaining how 'I wage more wars with a few ministers than with the enemy', even the emperor's Catholic allies remained circumspect. Pope Urban's reply to Lamormaini's news of the edict had been carefully crafted, congratulating Ferdinand that 'heresy will have learned that the gates of hell do not prevail against the church ... and the arms of powerful Austria.' Yet he fell short of delivering a full endorsement, which he could not provide, of course, without recognising for the first time the original validity of the Peace of Augsburg. And papal reservations were further compounded by the exclusion of nuncios from the supervision of the actual process of restitution. Later, indeed, Urban would declare that he had never approved the measure, and early in 1631 the Capuchin theologian Diego de Quiroga would actually arrive in Vienna as confessor to the Archduke Ferdinand's wife, to become part of what appears to have been a concerted effort to remove Lamormaini from influence. Certainly, there had been serious opposition to the edict in Madrid where concessions to the German Lutherans had long been advocated as a means of pacifying the Empire, and from where Philip IV now urged the emperor to 'find a more suitable outlet for his piety and zeal.'

Once unleashed, however, the genie could not be so easily returned to his bottle, and it was with suitably prophetic gravity that Magdeburg's mayor, Johann Dauth, remarked to his travelling companion around this time how they were unlikely to see peace in their lifetime, since the tentacles of war were

yet again stirring beyond the Empire as well as within it. To strengthen his position against the Swedish invasion he feared, Wallenstein had on the one hand
chosen to reinforce Sigismund of Poland in his war with Gustavus Adolphus,
and also recruited as extensively as possible throughout northern Germany.
So jealous was he, moreover, of detaching any section of his great army for
deployment in the Mantuan or Dutch wars, that the emperor too had become
increasingly suspicious of his intentions. By 1630, according to his own army
lists, Wallenstein's troops numbered 129,000 foot and 21,000 horse – an increase
of 17 per cent over the previous year – and the cries of disapproval from his
critics consequently showed no sign of abating, as the outburst from the new
Archbishop of Mainz at a meeting of the Catholic League at Mergentheim in
December 1629 made all too resoundingly clear:

> Since the Duke of Friedland has up to now disgusted and offended to the
> utmost each and every territorial ruler in the Empire, and although the present
> situation has moved him to be more cautious, he has not given up his plans to
> retain Mecklenburg by virtue of his Imperial command.

If Wallenstein remained in possession of Mecklenburg, the archbishop maintained, there could never be peace in the Empire, and with the Margrave of
Brandenburg in fear of his independence, and the Duke of Bavaria objecting
that the League's army had passed wholly into Wallenstein's hands, the com-
ments of the emperor's own brother that 'we shall repent in the end' the general's
'excessive power' seemed all too valid.

Yet while Gustavus Adolphus loomed in the north, Wallenstein remained, for
the time being, a necessary evil. In the summer of 1629, his kingdom exhausted,
Sigismund gratefully accepted a six-year truce, which left the Swedish king free
to intervene in the Empire at a time of his choosing, since he now possessed the
necessary bridgehead at Stralsund, and the Dutch, too, were even more keen to
cultivate his allegiance, not only in the expectation that he would prove an altogether more effective ally than Christian IV, but because the two countries were
already bound by strong economic ties. Älvsborg, for example, by virtue of its
position north of the Sound, supplied timber and hemp to the Dutch stockyards,
and was almost a Dutch colony, while Sweden's metallurgical industries, in their
turn, depended upon Dutch engineers and Dutch capital. Dutch agents, too, had
even been appointed to advise Gustavus how to organise and collect export dues
in the ports he had captured along the Polish and Lithuanian coast. But most
importantly of all, Amsterdam was the market for most of Sweden's exports, and
though the war with Sigismund displeased the Dutch, since it disrupted their

vital trade in Polish corn, even this had served the Swedish king's purposes. For rather than risk his friendship, his Dutch suitors had helped him gain victory, so that the war could be brought to a swift end.

France too, moreover, had lent a hand in this process as part of their efforts to give encouragement to the emperor's enemies throughout Europe. As a Roman Catholic, of course, it had been difficult to deny Sigismund's pretensions to the throne of Sweden outright. But Richelieu's agents were nevertheless able to present him as little more than an Imperial cat's paw, and the Polish king proved more than ready to abandon what was proving an increasingly unequal struggle. Disgruntled at Spain's failure to establish his kingdom as a naval power in the Baltic, and demoralised by Sweden's capture of the Prussian ports of Memel, Pillau and Elbing, Sigismund therefore welcomed French proposals for a temporary abandonment of hostilities, and the result was the agreement made at Altmark in September 1629, whereby Livonia was granted to Gustavus Adolphus for the six-year duration of the truce, along with the right to collect the customs in the Prussian ports. Already, in December 1627, only the advice of Axel Oxenstierna, the Swedish Chancellor, had prevented Gustavus Adolphus from intervention in Germany, on the grounds that the war with Poland should be settled first. Now, however, the reins were released, and by January 1630 Oxenstierna was already speaking to the English ambassador, Sir Thomas Roe, 'of the forthcoming campaign'.

At Stralsund, as in the Caribbean and Brabant, then, the tides of war had turned against the Habsburgs, and now, it seemed, for the Holy Roman Emperor who had only just convinced himself of the prospect of ultimate religious victory in Germany, there loomed the imminent arrival of a foreign host within his own territories. Nor was the news from Casale any more encouraging, for on 25 September 1630 Ambrogio Spinola, the besieging commander, had died from the plague, uttering at the last, it is said, the words 'honour' and 'reputation'. He had landed at Genoa just under a year earlier to take up the role of plenipotentiary and general at the age of 61, and had travelled, at the suggestion of Peter Paul Rubens, in the company of Diego Velázquez, with whom he visited Milan, Venice and Rome to see the most famous paintings of the day. But his struggles with Olivares and years of military service in the Netherlands and elsewhere had taken their toll, and Casale would not succumb to his reputation alone. A brilliant field commander, whose daring in battle was often employed to outflank his opponents and catch them off guard, he was not a great technical innovator. Nor had his use of rapid movement and pell-mell actions been of advantage in the final task confronting him. Though skilled at picking out an enemy's weakest spot and applying force there to achieve victory, Casale would prove, in fact, one

challenge too many, and in the spring of 1630, as Spinola assumed the consolations of his grave, the Spanish army accordingly withdrew to Milan, while the
French advanced to seize control of Pinerolo.

Yet Imperial troops had succeeded in taking Mantua, and the balance of force
in that particular theatre of war remained unresolved. Were the siege of Casale
to be renewed, as it could at any time, French reinforcements would have further
to march than Spanish troops from Milan, and the fact that Louis XIII had fallen
ill with dysentery also restricted Richelieu's freedom of action. Still the *dévots*
and other anti-cardinalists were snapping at his heels, and, under papal pressure, he had little alternative other than to persuade the Habsburgs to accept a
truce in northern Italy, pending the outcome of an electoral Diet in session at
Regensburg, to which he dispatched the ever-dependable Père Joseph, along
with Leon de Brûlart and a number of his other best agents. Their intention,
under cover of peace negotiations, was to undermine the emperor's position by
rallying the Roman Catholic electors to the defence of their 'German liberties', so that one Frenchman, in his enthusiasm, even appears to have told the
Archbishop of Trier how it was Louis XIII's express wish 'to deliver Italy and
Germany from the oppression to which they had been reduced by the manifest
violence and ambition of the house of Austria.'

Certainly, it was an aptly provocative ploy, since the meeting at Regensburg
had been summoned in the first place to resolve the widening gulf between the
Imperial electors, and a roll-call of those who attended in person leaves little
doubt about the meeting's importance. For not only was Ferdinand himself
present, but all the Catholic electors, along with the papal nuncio and diplomatic
representatives from Spain, Venice, Tuscany and England, as well as the party from
France. Even the electors of Saxony and Brandenburg, who refused to appear in
person because of their opposition to the Edict of Restitution, nevertheless sent
delegates to sit among the 2,000 or so participants and observers, who were fully
aware of the significance of what was about to unfold. For Ferdinand needed
not only to gain approval for his financial and military aid to Spain in the war
against the Dutch Republic, but to enlist support against the threat of French
and Swedish aggression. And this was not all, since there was also a need in the
immediate future for the emperor to secure his son Ferdinand's election as heir
to the Imperial crown itself by making him King of the Romans.

The prime concern of the electors, however, was merely to secure the removal
of Wallenstein, which they formally demanded on 16 July, after a week of delib-
eration, and finally achieved on 13 August. In this, moreover, they were actually
assisted by the apparent indifference of the quarry himself. For while de Witte,
his financier, took his own life at the news, Wallenstein by contrast appears to

have greeted his dismissal with surprising resignation. Weary and disheartened by the deepening financial crisis in which he found himself and no doubt consoled in some degree by the knowledge that Friedland and Mecklenburg remained under his control, he received the emperor's letter at Memmingen, where he had spent the summer. With concerns about his possible reaction, it had been borne by two of his better friends, though one of them, Baron Gerhard Questenberg, recorded that the general's actual response was both courteous and without trace of recrimination. 'I thank God to be freed from the net,' he is said to have uttered. And the following day he expressed similar sentiments to his comrade-in-arms Collalto:

> I am glad to my innermost soul about what they have decided in Regensburg, as it means that I can escape from this great labyrinth.

Among the many 'what if' scenarios that had helped to lay him low were concerns about his army's reliability in the event of a Swedish invasion. Above all, if the Swedes were to gain a foothold within the Empire, could the large number of Protestants among his officers and men be relied upon? But now, it seemed, the threat from Gustavus Adolphus was no longer a burden he would have to bear.

With persistent stomach problems as well as gout having necessitated a three-week cure to take the waters at Karlsbad en route to Memmingen, Wallenstein's passivity may well indeed have been entirely understandable. But an alternative account of his meeting with the emperor's two messengers, provided by the diplomat Franz Christoph von Khevenhüller, provides an additional dimension to his reaction:

> The duke received them graciously and politely, and as they sought to deliver their message in the best manner they could think of, he broke in. Taking a Latin document from the table, which he read out, and in which his own, the emperor's and the elector of Bavaria's horoscopes were set down, he responded: 'Gentlemen, you can see for yourselves that I knew your mission from the stars, and that the elector of Bavaria's spirit dominates the emperor's. Hence I cannot place any blame on His Majesty, although it pains me, and I will obey.'

Over the past year, of course, Wallenstein had been increasingly obliged to employ his army in pursuit of policies of which he disapproved, while his repeated warnings about the danger from Gustavus Adolphus were ignored. But only one day after the decision to dismiss him at Regensburg, de Witte, who had been growing increasingly desperate at his inability to meet his own commitments to his business partners, had written to the general to inform him that he could no longer provide him even with the monthly financial allowance that had hitherto been available for his own personal use. And the news of such an indignity, added to the heavy weight of Wallenstein's well-documented antipathy towards Duke Maximilian, may well have proved the final straw and rendered his decision to retire to his estates in Bohemia altogether more 'painful' than his apparent response to Questenberg may have suggested.

Certainly, the emperor got precious little in return for the sacrifice of his former favourite at Regensburg. Though the electoral meeting continued well into the autumn, no election of a King of the Romans took place, no support for the war in the Netherlands was forthcoming, and Ferdinand found himself forced, too, to guarantee that 'no new war will be declared other than by the advice of the electors'. The Spanish in the meantime, having failed to prevent Wallenstein's dismissal, succeeded in blocking Maximilian's wish to succeed him, only by delivering the poison chalice to Tilly, who was at once forced to reduce his army, in principle, by up to two-thirds – merging the surviving Imperial units with his own – and to manage upon funds insufficient even for these reduced forces, which required some 5 million thalers annually for their sustenance. Even by August 1630, in fact, when Magdeburg declared its open defiance of the emperor, the consequences would be clear. For as the bulk of Tilly's forces were concentrated at the subsequent siege, local resources were quickly consumed, and without Wallenstein's contribution system, the troops were soon restless. Indeed, Ferdinand's only victory at Regensburg was a pyrrhic one: the maintenance of the Edict of Restitution in unaltered form, notwithstanding the firm belief of his Catholic allies, led by Bavaria, that some form of relaxation was advisable.

According to one account of an interview between Maximilian and Lamormaini, provided by the anti-Jesuit Catholic polemicist Kaspar Schoppe, the edict's full implementation was now being equated with the very salvation of the emperor's soul itself:

> [Lamormaini] closed his eyes and answered … the Edict must stand firm, whatever evil might finally come from it. It matters little that the emperor, because of it, lose not only Austria but all of his kingdoms … provided he save his soul, which he cannot do without the implementation of the Edict.

But if Ferdinand's seat at God's right hand was indeed by now assured, the Regensburg meeting could hardly have proved more damaging in other respects. For by retaining the Edict of Restitution, he had exacerbated Protestant-Catholic divisions while creating what amounted to a critical paralysis of power within the Empire, as a result of his decision to make any declaration of war dependent upon consultation with the electors, at the very time when the threat from abroad had never been higher. The French envoys, led by Père Joseph, had, it is true, been frustrated by the sensational news of the fall of Mantua on 18 July, and were ready thereafter to accept peace terms confirming the succession of the Duke of Nevers, even on the assumption that Spain be guaranteed possession of Casale and Pinerolo, and that all assistance to Ferdinand's enemies within the Empire should cease. Yet even this was to prove cold comfort, since Père Joseph and his colleagues had acted independently and, upon learning of its terms, the French king's reaction to the Treaty of Regensburg was unequivocal. It was impossible, he declared, to have its terms 'read out to me except with extreme displeasure' and had refused to ratify the treaty within only weeks. And in the meantime, barely before the meeting at Regensburg was fully underway, Sweden's very own 'Lion of the North' had already made his first advance upon Imperial soil against an army soon to be deprived of Wallenstein, and an emperor who remained stubbornly unimpressed by the military reputation of an adversary resting only, or so he believed, upon tinsel victories over lowly Poles.

Undoubtedly, the most astonishing aspect of the whole Regensburg saga is that it should have been played out with almost total disregard for the threat presented by the Swedes and their king. Ferdinand had sent his opening agenda to the electors on 3 July, in fact, and only three days later Gustavus Adolphus landed on the Baltic coast of Pomerania at Peenemünde on the island of Usedom with a comparatively small force of 13,000 men, quickly joined by a further 4,000 from Stralsund. He arrived, it is said, with maps extending no further than the Saxon frontier, and his precise objectives, written by the diplomat Johann Adler Salvius and published in German and Latin at Stralsund in June 1630, remain obscure. Certainly, he expected the emperor to withdraw from northern Germany without himself evacuating Stralsund. But the manifesto was a propaganda vehicle intended to justify his intervention only in the broadest terms, and its very vagueness typified Gustavus's other pronouncements, which were in any case sometimes contradicted by Oxenstierna, his chancellor. Protestantism, indeed, was not alluded to at all, for fear of alienating Sweden's French allies, though it featured prominently thereafter and was clearly central to the king's adopted image from the outset. For in a print issued shortly after his landing, Gustavus poses heroically in full armour while the hand of God reaches from a cloud to give him the sword of divine justice to smite all Catholic tyranny.

Yet Oxenstierna himself would later admit that religion was merely the pretext, while Gustavus himself confided that if it had been his primary motivation, he would have declared war on the Pope in person. Instead, it seems, the underlying rationale for Swedish intervention was actually *assecuratio* or security, for although the Imperial navy was impotent and the army soon to be scaled down, Gustavus was determined to grasp this prize opportunity to ensure that no emperor would be able to pose a threat in future. As such, Swedish interests lay not only in reversing the recent revival of Habsburg power, especially in northern Germany, but in revising, at one and the same time, the Imperial constitution by emasculating the emperor. Couched in humanist apologetics proclaiming assistance to the weak, Gustavus's propaganda therefore championed him as the guardian of German liberties and the restorer of the Empire's constitution to its 'proper' state, though the most notable work of this kind, produced by Bogislav Philipp Chemnitz – burned, in a symbolic gesture, by Ferdinand's official hangman – blatantly misrepresented the constitution by presenting it as an aristocracy in which the emperor was merely a first among equals.

'Satisfaction' – or in other words the indemnity required from the Protestants of north Germany in return for their salvation from the Edict of Restitution and the Counter-Reformation – was by contrast another, if less obviously noble, Swedish priority which rested in part upon the recently published suggestion by Hugo Grotius that Gustavus was, in effect, morally free to exact what he pleased, so long as conquered peoples were treated humanely. Likewise, there was also the issue of what was euphemistically described as the army's 'contentment', since Sweden would need to pay off its troops at Germany's expense, on the principle, as one observer remarked, that 'it is better to tie the goat at a neighbour's fence than one's own', even though broader economic motives – beyond largely defensive ones – appear to have featured minimally in the Swedish king's thinking. Certainly, little effort was later made to integrate his German conquests into a Swedish-controlled market, and when he fell on his knees on the beach at Peenemünde, invoking the mercies of the God of Battles as the first echelons of his army waded ashore, the only gold Gustavus sought directly remained that earmarked for his troops. The overriding priority for the moment, he had told Oxenstierna as early as April 1628, 'was to strengthen the army by ruining the enemy'. 'If we cannot say: *bellum se ipsum alet* [war must pay for itself], I see no way out of all that we have engaged in.' And the same approach which had underlain the war with Poland would now drive the coming conflict with the emperor.

None of which suggests, of course, that Sweden was either economically unambitious or anything less than a coming economic power in her own right – one that could dispose of far more resources than those available to Christian IV, and one more than worthy, too, of provoking greater urgency from Ferdinand. Untouched, like the rest of Scandinavia, by Roman civilisation, cut off by physical barriers and deeply rooted in its own Viking culture, Gustavus's kingdom had remained largely detached from the main lines of European development, marginalised by geography at the outer edge of the primary trade routes until the sixteenth century. In 1397, indeed, it had lost its independence altogether as a result of the Union of Kalmar by which the whole of Scandinavia was united under Denmark. But in 1520 the nobleman Gustavus Vasa had led a popular revolt and three years later was elected king by the Swedish *Riksdag*. By 1536, moreover, the state Church had become Lutheran, and only one year later a war with the Hanseatic League freed Sweden from the commercial control of Lübeck. By 1544 both a national army and hereditary monarchy had been created, and under Eric XIV the acquisition of Estonia in 1561 bestowed upon the kingdom control of the Gulf of Finland. Nor had even the turmoil caused by the temporary succession of King Sigismund III of Poland in 1592 served to arrest Sweden's development, for in 1599 the interloper was duly deposed by the *Riksdag*, who declared him a 'Papist, oathbreaker, and enemy of the realm', and succeeded by Charles IX, father of Gustavus Adolphus.

Though Charles had been menaced thereafter by Denmark, which coveted his kingdom, and Poland, which now claimed through Sigismund the Swedish throne, he nevertheless intervened with some success in Russian affairs, where the state of Ivan the Terrible was dissolving amid the civil war known as 'the Time of Troubles', and succeeded too in both improving the army and encouraging manufacture and commerce. Indeed, Denmark had been so alarmed by Charles' creation of the new port of Göteborg that she declared war upon Sweden only a few months before his death. And it was not without good reason that the Danes had eyed Sweden's growing prowess with such concern, and with a respect that seemed to elude the Holy Roman Emperor so entirely in the summer of 1630. For Sweden had by then become the principal European supplier of copper, producing 2,600 tons a year, and could thus procure on the Amsterdam Exchange a constant supply of foreign currency to augment her war efforts. While 5,000 tons of iron had been produced in 1620, moreover, 20,000 tons a year were in production by the end of the decade, servicing, with Dutch help, a flourishing arms industry. Even more lucrative were the customs duties now available in the Baltic Provinces, and since the Truce of Altmark, the rich revenues of the Prussian ports.

'The King's Majesty,' observed Oxenstierna, 'controls and steers mines, commerce, manufactures, and customs, just as a steersman steers his ship.' Regulation made taxation easier, trade with foreigners was confined to thirteen towns, and internal trade to market towns. Industrial standards, on the other hand, were supervised by reorganised guilds, while chartered companies were given a monopoly of foreign trade not only in copper and iron, but corn and salt too. And as Sweden's progress proceeded, Dutch and French traders and technicians – notably Louis de Geer, a Liègeois Calvinist from Amsterdam – continued to play a key role, so that for a time the Dutch, in particular, effectively controlled the economic life of the kingdom. Yet the price was worth paying, for as foreign investment flowed in, so Sweden's self-sufficiency developed in tandem, and when Gustavus set out for war in 1630, the army he took with him had been entirely fitted out from Swedish sources. Though the bulk of his infantry would remain mercenaries – many of them Scots – conscription from the age of 15 to 50 had also ensured that the cavalry and artillery detachments at the heart of his force were predominantly native Swedes.

For artillery, in particular, had come to assume a special significance for Gustavus, since the object of his many military innovations was to make the army he led as flexible and mobile as possible. To this end, he pioneered the use of easily portable and relatively quick-firing cannon by employing to devastating effect his famous 'leathern gun', a regimental 3-pounder with a very thin bronze barrel, bound with rope and mastic enclosed in a sheath of hard leather. Developed before 1627, it had been succeeded in 1629, by an all-metal 4-pounder that could be moved by three men or one horse, and would prove altogether more effective on the battlefield than the ponderous 24-pounders available to the Imperial and Catholic League armies. For not only could more lightweight cannon keep pace with the advancing infantry, they could also be crewed by as few as two gunners, while the splendid heavy-calibre guns of the enemy – embossed with the Imperial eagle and emperor's signature, and among the most beautiful in Europe – would, in any case, prove unavailing against the resolute onslaught of Swedish brigades. Organised in seven-gun ditch batteries, they were capable of sweeping away entire ranks, but as one Spanish observer noted upon seeing them in action against a measured Swedish advance, they were 'never able to disorder it, though many a shot was made'.

In other areas, too, the Swedes were not only battle-honed but primed for further success by the novel tactics of their king, who had built upon the advances in military theory associated with Maurice of Nassau in particular. His greatest achievement, arguably, was to revive and adapt the role of the infantry, who had become accustomed to scrumming together in massive formations, whether in defence or attack. Now, however, by grouping them in smaller units and providing them with meticulous training, he enabled them to change front and to move their ground with remarkable speed and efficiency. And since smaller units were more exposed to attack, he positioned groups of cavalry among them, and trained his musketeers to fire and reload three times as fast as other armies. As a result, instead of great blocks of pikemen, surrounded by an unwieldy collection of musketeers, Gustavus organised his army in two or three lines, each line not more than six deep. The lines were broken, too, into a 'chessboard' formation of small alternate blocks of pikemen and musketeers, with gaps between, through which the cavalry could operate freely and to devastating effect. Ordered to advance slowly before galloping the last 50 yards and employing their swords, Swedish cavalrymen found themselves protected by musketeers armed with matchlocks rather than arquebuses, and arranged in ranks so that while one rank was firing, the rest were preparing to fire or reloading, allowing for a relatively continuous rate or, alternatively, the notoriously deadly 'Swedish salvo', which entailed the simultaneous discharge of a unit's muskets at as little as five to ten paces, followed by close-quarter carnage with sword and musket butt.

Other innovations, such as field chaplains, the introduction of rudimentary uniforms (blue and yellow, or blue with red facings), charge wired to the shot, and so on, were all to be adopted throughout Europe during the years ahead, testifying to both the professionalism and imagination of the Swedish army and its leader, though no single factor would count for more perhaps than the charisma of that leader himself, who still carried a musket ball in his neck, received by courtesy of a Polish sniper at Dirschau in 1627. Now aged 36, Gustavus had succeeded to the throne in 1611 at the height of the conflict with Denmark, but his father was in no fear for the teenage boy's prospects. 'Ille faciet' (He will do it), Charles IX had uttered on his deathbed, placing his hand upon his son's head. And he was not disappointed. For both Charles and his German wife, the daughter of Duke Adolphus of Holstein-Gottorp, had imbued him not only with absolute confidence in his own abilities, but an unwavering conviction in the unchallengeable virtues of the Protestant faith. By the age of 12, in addition to German, Gustavus had learned Latin, Italian and Dutch, 'as if born to them', and would later acquire English and Spanish, as well as some Polish and Russian – to which was added as strong a dose of the classics as comported with the requisite princely training in sports, public affairs and the all-important arts of war. Tutored by Johann Schroderus, or Skytte as he is better known, he became well versed in Ciceronian rhetoric, law and history, and developed a passionate interest in all those fantasies associated with Sweden's heroic past. Significantly, too, he was encouraged to approach the military art not only through its history – by an acquaintance with Caesar,

Vegetius, Aelian and Frontinus – but on the theoretical level, too, by the study of mathematics, optics and mechanics, as well as the new Dutch style of fortification expounded by Simon Stevin.

When Skytte had taught him all he knew in this sphere, Gustavus had been provided with a two-month intensive course from Jakob de la Gardie, on leave from the Swedish armies in Livonia. And all the while that the most romantic figure in Swedish history was savouring his hands-on experience of the crafts of war and revelling in tales of his kingdom's legendary history, he was continuing to develop as both a ruler and leader of men. For at the age of 9 he had already begun to attend sessions of the *Riksdag*, and by 13 was receiving ambassadors. At 15, indeed, as Duke of Västmanland, he was ruling a province and at 16 fighting his first battle against the Danes, before proceeding in 1615, at the age of only 20, to direct the Siege of Pskov in person – by which time he was already renowned not only for his courtesy, generosity, bravery and mercy, but for his good looks and extraordinary physical presence. A huge man, with broad shoulders, golden hair and tawny beard, he was known in later life by his Italian mercenaries as *il re d'oro*: the golden lion.

There was, it is true, an impulsiveness about him that he himself recognised and that the English envoy, Sir Henry Vance, reflected upon in 1632:

> ... he hath often told me, ... That he would give all he had to be Master of his Passions; but that when he begins to be moved, he hath something rises in his Brain that makes him forget what he saith or doth; that this he finds in himself, and the Inconveniences that grow thereof, as soon as he is posed again; but yet he cannot get it mastered, though he hath often designed the same; and therefore he hopes God and all the world forgive him.

Nor was this same streak any less apparent to the man who played such a crucial role in partnership with him. For when Gustavus once remarked to his chancellor how 'if we were all as cold as you, we should freeze', Oxenstierna was quick to reply: 'And if we were all as hot as Your Majesty we should burn.'

But the combination of phlegm and choler was, of course, precisely the secret of the two men's partnership, and for Oxenstierna the qualities of the king, who remained his junior by eleven years, were beyond all dispute. Though a Calvinist in a predominantly Lutheran kingdom, Gustavus had already galvanised his people by a proven track record of military success, and a potent gift for stirring rhetoric of the kind he had demonstrated in his address to the *Riksdag* upon launching his current campaign:

The papists are on the Baltic. They have Rostock, Wismar, Stettin, Woolgast, Griefswald and nearly all the other ports in their hands. Rügen is theirs and from Rügen they continue to threaten Stralsund; their whole aim is to destroy Swedish commerce and soon to plant a foot on the southern shores of our fatherland. Sweden is in danger from the power of the Habsburg; that is all, but it is enough; that power must be met swiftly and strongly.

Oxenstierna, moreover, was at one with his king's interpretation of events. Indeed, even many years later, when it would have been only too easy to dissociate himself from responsibility, he still affirmed the necessity for war at this time:

It is certain that, had his late Majesty not betaken himself to Germany with his army, the emperor would today have a fleet upon these seas. And if the emperor had once got hold of Stralsund the whole coast would have fallen to him, and here in Sweden we should never have enjoyed a minute's security.

Throughout, in fact, all would depend upon swift, resolute, fearless and decisive action under the guidance of a leader of uncommon gifts. And now, it seemed, precisely such a leader had been provided by Providence to lead Sweden to her greatest moment on the stage of European history:

He was [wrote Bogislav Philipp Chemnitz, the official Swedish historian of the campaign now underway] careful in his deliberations, prompt in his decisions, undaunted in heart and spirit, strong of arm and ready to command and fight … Nobody could better appraise the enemy, judge accurately the chances of war, and quickly reach an advantageous solution on the spur of moment.

But he was also, Chemnitz might well have added, a man of extraordinary political vision, able to perceive connections between events and plot courses of action to exploit their linkage. 'All wars in Europe hang together' remained his watchword. And if, for some reason, they did not already, Gustavus Adolphus, King of Sweden and 'Lion of the North', was now about to ensure they did.

For, as the 'Lion' marched forth from Peenemünde, styling himself *Restitor Germaniae* and writing to Oxenstierna to tell him how he hoped 'to touch off a rocket of universal rebellion throughout Germany', Ferdinand did nothing to nip his invasion in the bud – notwithstanding the fact that on 20 July the city of Stettin opened its gates to the invaders. Indeed, for the next four weeks, while the parties at Regensburg kept their sights on Wallenstein, Gustavus was given a free hand both to consolidate his position in Pomerania and frantically recruit troops for the next stage of his onslaught. For reasons unknown, the commander of the large Imperial forces assigned by Wallenstein to protect the area against the very kind of landing now in progress did not abide by the plan to stage an early attack upon the Swedes. Instead, he opted for a strategy of passive containment, and by the time this news reached Memmingen the decision to remove Wallenstein had already been taken. Yet no replacement had as yet been appointed, with the result that no commander-in-chief was in place to direct the campaign for the rest of the season. When Ferdinand notified senior commanders of Wallenstein's dismissal on 13 September, moreover, some began to break up their regiments of their own accord, while men deserted in large numbers, only too glad to receive alternative employment with the renowned Gustavus.

So it was small wonder, perhaps, that talk of Wallenstein's recall was circulating even before the ripples caused by his dismissal had died down. Within two months, indeed, Ferdinand was writing to him again, and displaying no hesitation to ask his ex-general's advice on both military and political developments. But while Wallenstein responded in a professional manner from his Bohemian retreat, he resolutely ignored hints that he should come to Vienna, which Eggenburg attributed to his 'infirmity, lack of inclination and apprehensions about being pressed to serve again'. Nevertheless, many senior officers, too, maintained a correspondence with him that further implied that his career was not over, and in January 1631 his cousin Max confided to him how 'Prince Eggenberg tells me that His Majesty and all the councillors already recognise what they have lost in you.' By that spring, moreover, one of the very men who had first brought news of his dismissal, Gerhard Questenberg, was inclined to even greater frankness:

> We realise the wrong we did, and we regret it. Now people are seeing whether or not you were right with your extravagant recruitment, and what we have come to in such short time with our penny-pinching economy.

For the destructive progress of Gustavus Adolphus and his army had, of course, swiftly demonstrated the folly of the emperor's decision to yield to pressure to dismiss his generalissimo and disperse his army. As Ferdinand and the electors went home from Regensburg in the autumn of 1630, the King of Sweden had, in fact, some 40,000 men at his disposal, swollen by the influx of deserters from Imperial ranks, and was secure for the winter. And while the Catholic electors might believe, like Gustavus himself, that the coming campaign would be fought in the north, far away from their own territories events were to prove otherwise for one good reason above all others. For the King of Sweden was at bottom neither crusader nor strategist, but like so many of the participants who prolonged the war across Europe, a military adventurer, fighting for fighting's sake. With no precise objectives in mind, there were consequently no specific restraints to the scale of his conquests, leaving him free to chase the horizon as opportunity arose and on whatever pretext best served. Within a year, the Swedes had taken Mainz and six months later they were in Bavaria itself.

9

MAGDEBURG AND BREITENFELD

The Swedes have come,
Have taken everything,
Have smashed in the windows,
Have taken away the lead,
Have made bullets from it
And shot the peasants.

German children's song

Not quite everything Gustavus Adolphus touched turned into gold. The largely peasant population of Sweden was hard-hit by the continuing recruitment of troops during the 1620s, and no effort had been spared to convince them of the urgency of the struggle against the 'papal yoke' which was drawing ever closer and with ever greater menace. Not only were a growing number of 'White Books', 'Relations' and 'Newspapers' distributed among the king's subjects, but the clergy, who were particularly loyal to him, also did their utmost to strengthen the steadfastness of the young peasant generation in defence of national security and the reformed religion. Most spectacular of all, however, in popularising the divine plan for ultimate Protestant victory was the launch in August 1628 of a three-masted warship of 1,400 tons, intended for the coming German war. Embellished on its bows with the head of a 1-metre-high lion – the heraldic beast of the Vasa family – and bearing on its stern, which was as tall as a house, carved images of Roman emperors from Tiberius to Septimius Severus and the Jewish hero Gideon, to whom Gustavus was frequently compared, it was intended as a striking affirmation of Sweden's prowess and that of her ruler. Sadly, however, as the vessel set out from Stockholm on its maiden voyage, it keeled over and sank less than a mile from shore – a victim of the instability that its builders had been too intimidated to inform the king about.

Yet the loss of one of the most powerfully armed vessels in the world did nothing to hinder the dispatch of the military expedition and fleet that set sail two years later from Älfsnabben. Nor were failures of similar proportions much in mind as the Swedish army set about its task, even when minor reverses occurred along the way. Like many of the people of northern Germany, the citizens of the town of Pasewalk had breathed a sigh of relief at the Swedes' approach and welcomed the arrival of their first contingents with joy. But when Imperial troops made a rare show of effective resistance and re-captured the town, the premature jubilation proved short-lived. For the town was burnt in a cruel act of retribution on 7 September 1630 and its inhabitants left to dwell upon the '*Laniena Pasawelcensis*' or 'Sad Song of Complaint' composed in memory of the fearful events they had experienced. Requiring two dozen verses to encapsulate the horror of the victims, it was sung to the melody of 'Come here to me, saith the Son of God'.

Even so, such 'victories' against the Swedes remained few, as the so-called 'people of midnight' continued on their own 'Gothic expedition' of mayhem under the man now depicted by his Imperial enemies as Alaric. And if the Swedish invasion of Pomerania was to prove portentous for the Habsburgs, so too would the outcome in November 1630 of a crisis at the French court. For since his appointment in 1624, Richelieu had been constantly threatened by the intrigues of both Marie de Medici, the queen mother, and Anne, the king's wife, as well as Gaston his brother. Described by her own husband as 'completely obstinate', held fast under the spell of her Italian favourite, Concino Concini, and later derided by Saint-Simon as 'proud, jealous, excessively dull, always under the scum of the court', the queen mother had in fact been a particularly corrosive influence upon her son since he had succeeded to the throne, bitterly resenting all competitors for his ear and, above all, the growing influence of the cardinal. As the target of her displeasure appeared to go from strength to strength, moreover, Marie de Medici patiently awaited her moment, which duly emerged during the summer and autumn of 1630 as her son's illness kept him apart from his minister. For while Louis respected Richelieu's ability, loyalty and indefatigable service, his lonely and neglected childhood had rendered him both weak and indecisive, and particularly vulnerable to the violent clash of temperaments continually generated both at court and within his own family.

As friction increased, furthermore, the struggle for power had come to centre upon the entire direction of French foreign policy. For while Marie advocated peace and the need to reduce the concessions granted to Huguenots by the Grace of Alais, Richelieu had been steadily seeking to establish France's international reputation as Spain's foremost rival. Like King Louis himself, in fact, the cardinal had balked at the Treaty of Regensburg, arguing that, if it were accepted, 'all foreign nations would regard an alliance with us as useless because of our unreliability.' But the queen mother had found another lever over the choice of a new commander for the army in northern Italy, and on 10 November 1630, after a violent and emotional scene during which Marie and Richelieu confronted each other in the king's presence, it appeared that she had indeed emerged victorious. For Maréchal Louis de Marillac, the queen mother's nominee, was appointed as planned, while Louis retired to his hunting lodge at Versailles and the cardinal's opponents toasted their triumph.

But the king's emotional exhaustion did not last, and his temporary escape from his mother's clutches resulted in a remarkable volte-face, as a result of which Marillac was arrested and Richelieu found himself both saved and newly strengthened. For the so-called 'Day of Dupes' not only confirmed King Louis' endorsement of Richelieu's policies but relieved the monarch from the tyranny of his mother once and for all. Upon being summoned to Versailles and raised from his knees to be reassured, the cardinal's relief was palpable. 'I shall have no greater happiness in the world,' he informed Louis later that evening, 'than in making known to Your Majesty by ever-increasing proofs that I am the most devoted subject and the most zealous servant that ever king or master had in this world.' And by July 1631, after a period of house arrest in her château at Compiègne, the queen mother had indeed been forced to escape to the Spanish Netherlands – never to return to France again – leaving Gaston, Duke of Orléans, to join her shortly afterwards. Sporadic plotting, it is true, would continue, and the intrigues of the Marquis of Cinq-Mars in 1638 would in some respects prove the most dangerous of all. But as November ended in 1630, it was manifestly clear to both the royal family and the most powerful French magnates that they must submit to the king's will, as expressed by his chief minister, or face exile and perhaps death of the kind that now awaited Marillac.

France, then, was pacified at last, though the diametrical opposite was now true for Europe as a whole, since the collision course that Richelieu had set with the Habsburgs was henceforth free from all obstacles. In the process, the Dutch had been provided with an ally more important than themselves at the very moment that Sweden stood ready to make her entrance, though the success of the Dutch in foiling the Zeeland raid of the late summer of 1631 actually confirmed that events in the Netherlands would subsequently assume less importance for the rest of Europe. Buoyed by the fact that their control of the

Rhenish Palatinate allowed them to ship reinforcements down the Rhine to
the Palatinate for the first time since 1543, the Spanish had sent 6,000 men in
a flotilla of thirty-five ships to attack the islands of Zeeland, with the intention
of outflanking their enemy and avoiding the time-consuming and costly effort
involved in their familiar attempts at siege warfare. But their first attempt at
landing was foiled, and when a Dutch fleet caught up with the invaders in the
Slaak near Tholen island, it sank their ships and took most of the troops on
board prisoner. Now, with the irruption of France and Sweden into the conflict, the continent's political fault lines would never again be quite so directly
polarised between Madrid and The Hague, particularly as Spain's misfortunes
had plumbed new depths with the successful landing of 8,000 Dutch troops at
Pernambuco, the centre of the richest sugar-producing region of South America.

Nor had other developments assisted the Habsburg cause. For on 23 January 1631,
as if to underline the shifting centre of gravity of the escalating conflict, Sweden
and France agreed at Bärwalde to act together against their common foe 'for
the restitution of the suppressed Estates of the Empire'. France would provide
400,000 thalers annually for five years and acknowledge publicly her alliance with
the Swedes, while Gustavus Adolphus was simply obliged to refuse all offers of a
separate peace before the treaty expired and to guarantee freedom of worship in
all Roman Catholic areas falling under his sway. Subsequently and separately, he
also agreed to respect the neutrality of Bavaria and the Catholic League. And the
resulting French subsidy – though comparatively modest at substantially less than
the yield of the Prussian port tolls – was nevertheless not only timely but, under
the circumstances, more than adequate compensation for any tolerance extended
to the Beast of Rome, since the cost of maintaining not only forces in Germany
and Livonia, but a further 20,000 troops in Finland and their own territory was
already proving exorbitant for the Swedes.

Gustavus had gone to war in the first place, after all, on the assumption that
the bulk of his army's needs would be met by occupied territories. But until
August 1631 these were simply not extensive enough to carry the load. During
the second half of 1630, in fact, they had provided only 35,000 thalers a month,
and nor could the Baltic provinces, already picked clean by successive armies of
occupation, shoulder the burden for long. Even a previously unscathed area like
the county of Memel, for example, which was temporarily ceded to Sweden
in 1629, had been devastated within a year by the seventeen cavalry companies
billeted on it, and its condition was far from untypical. Where, before the occupation, there had been 154 horses, 236 oxen, 103 cows, 190 pigs and 810 sheep,
by 1631 there were merely 26 oxen and 1 cow, and even the Swedish authorities
were describing the area as 'laid waste'. But now French gold was available to

help make good the shortfall, as copper Swedish cannon cut swathes in France's enemies. It was, in effect, an arrangement made in heaven – and an ecumenical one at that – or, from the Habsburg standpoint of course, a pact conceived by the Lord of Darkness himself. But whatever the perspective, it was certainly a development of the gravest consequence not only in Vienna and Madrid, but among those German princes, too, who had hitherto steered a successful, if uneasy, course between their Protestant faith, their loyalty to the Empire and their understandable preference for peace and personal security.

'The King of Sweden,' wrote Richelieu, 'is a sun which has just risen: he is young but of vast renown. The ill-treated or banished princes of Germany have turned towards him in their misfortune as the mariner turns to the Pole Star.' John George of Saxony, however, had other views. As deeply disturbed by the Swedish invasion as he had been by the Catholics' uncompromising stand on the Edict of Restitution, he therefore commissioned Hans Georg von Arnim, a former officer in the Swedish army who had transferred his services to Wallenstein in 1625, to recruit whatever troops were available in northern Germany, and then proceeded to summon a convention of Protestant princes at Leipzig in February 1631. In all, invitations were issued to some 160 states and the response was overwhelming, for not only did every major Protestant prince, with the exception of George of Hesse-Darmstadt, attend, but also representatives from several Imperial cities. Most important of all, perhaps, George William of Brandenburg, the effective leader of the German Calvinists, was also present, and it was he and his advisers who drafted proposals for a defensive Protestant alliance, designed to protect the princes' rights against any party endangering them, be they the emperor or the King of Sweden himself.

Brandenburg's alliance with Ferdinand since the Treaty of Königsberg of May 1627 had, after all, been nothing more than a marriage of convenience from the outset, forced upon its ruler by the timidity of his territory's powerful Lutheran Estates and the influence of his principal adviser, the Catholic Count Adam of Schwarzenberg. But the majority of George William's counsellors were, like him, Calvinist, and events in any case had long since rendered the allliance untenable. For now, in the wake of the Edict of Restitution and the Swedish invasion, the need was for a resolute stand against both Ferdinand and Gustavus Adolphus. Indeed, the Swedish aspect of the 'Leipzig Manifesto', which the Brandenbergers presently drafted, was the direct corollary of their Imperial policy. Both aimed to preserve the integrity and the constitution of the Empire in general, and the rights and liberties of Protestant states in particular. Both, too, were designed to create a neutral third force between the armies of the Empire and the Catholic League, and those foreign armies – Swedish or indeed other – who were threatening a seemingly endless escalation of the conflict. Some 40,000 troops were to constitute a purely defensive *Leipziger Bund*, recruited and funded by individual Imperial Circles and co-ordinated by a committee over which John George of Saxony was to preside in an effort to 'uphold the basic laws, the Imperial constitution, and the German liberties of the Protestant states'.

All hinged, however, on possible concessions from the emperor, particularly over the Edict of Restitution, which even a congress of the Catholic League at Dinkelsbühl in May had agreed to press for under the influence of Maximilian of Bavaria. But the comparative slowdown in Swedish progress since the capture of Stettin, and the ongoing legitimist sympathies of Duke John George, which had cost him much sympathy at Leipzig, still persuaded Ferdinand to overestimate his position, in much the same way that Richelieu had appeared to overrate the appeal of Gustavus Adolphus to the German princes. And in consequence the historic opportunity offered by the Leipzig convention was largely wasted. Indeed, the stubbornness of the emperor served merely to erase once and for all the indecision of those present. For Gustavus himself had already made clear to his Brandenburg brother-in-law that harsh choices were sooner or later inescapable:

I don't want to hear about neutrality. His grace must be my friend or foe … This is a fight between God and the Devil. If His grace is with God, he must join me, if he is for the Devil, he must fight me. There is no third way.

And as the intransigence of the emperor became clear, it was not long before preparation for such choices began in earnest. On the one hand, the fugitive Mecklenburg dukes and Margrave Friedrich V, son of the outlawed Georg Friedrich of Baden-Durlach, joined Hesse-Kassel in stirring restlessly, while elsewhere Landgrave Wilhelm V, in conjunction with Wilhelm and Bernard of Weimar, was soon assembling 7,000 men in his fortresses of Kassel and Ziegenhein, at the very time that Regent Julius of Württemberg felt compelled to pack off young Duke Eberhard III and his two brothers on a grand tour, and to consign their mother to the safety of Urach Castle, as his militia began evicting Imperial garrisons.

All remained cautious, reluctant to side openly with Gustavus until he had proved himself capable of ensuring their defence against the emperor's retribution, and hoping in the meantime for a more forceful stance from Saxony, in the vain expectation that Ferdinand might yet bend to pressure. But while the emperor's Protestant critics hesitated, one Catholic prince, at least, was grasping the most unexpected of nettles, for in May 1631, Maximilian of Bavaria actually saw fit to commit himself to the Treaty of Fontainebleau with France. Superficially, Maximilian appeared to have gained more than any other from Wallenstein's dismissal, since Tilly, the League's general, now commanded the Imperial army too, paving the way, it seemed, for the Duke of Bavaria to regain the military dominance over Ferdinand that he had formerly enjoyed. But besides safeguarding his rights and interests as a German prince and Roman Catholic, Maximilian was equally concerned with protecting the electoral title and lands he had recently acquired, and rumours were circulating that Spain had, in fact, secretly promised Charles I of England that both the Palatinate and the electoral title that went with it would eventually be restored to his brother-in-law, Frederick. Fear of Wallenstein, at the same time, had been replaced by fear of Gustavus Adolphus – who had declared his intent to restore Frederick's son to the Palatinate – and this, likewise, had only been compounded by mounting concerns over Habsburg ambitions and France's geographical proximity.

After the Treaty of Bärwalde in January 1631, France's alliance with Sweden effectively left Maximilian with no choice other than to explore radical new ways of safeguarding his rights and interests, although Père Joseph had already made clear to Richelieu from Regensburg three months earlier that Bavaria was prepared to consider discussions. Adam Contzen, too, the duke's Jesuit confidant, had been urging a treaty with France since the spring of 1629 in the hope that such an alliance would further the Catholic cause in Europe as a whole by helping to create a united Catholic front of the sort that could never emerge while Habsburg-Bourbon rivalry continued in its present fashion. And just as at Leipzig, some Catholic princes were also now intent upon the creation of a neutral third force, standing apart from Imperial pretensions and acting as a buffer between the emperor and his foreign enemies in an effort to arrest the further spread of war. In complete secrecy, therefore, it was duly agreed at Fontainebleau that neither France nor Bavaria would attack each other or assist each other's enemies, and that Maximilian's claims within the Palatinate and constitutional obligations to the emperor and the Empire would be respected – meaning that Bavaria would nevertheless be free from aiding France against the Habsburgs.

Both sides recognised, in effect, that the treaty was effectively unenforceable, and Richelieu had ultimately acceded to Maximilian's position over his electoral rights and constitutional obligations only with the utmost reluctance. But the Fontainebleau agreement represented at the very least a statement of mutual good intentions at a time when the cardinal was continuing to probe Imperial pressure points and the duke was finding himself increasingly embattled. For Tilly, his general, was presently faced with a desperate struggle to meet the

Swedish threat, having 'no cannon in a condition to be used, no ammunition, no picks and shovels, no money and no food'. Without payment in advance, Wallenstein was refusing to provision him from his warehouses in Friedland and Mecklenburg, and when Gustavus surprised George William of Brandenburg in late April by marching directly upon him at Spandau, in an effort to terrify him into a treaty of alliance, Tilly was left with but one choice. Believing Magdeburg to be well stocked with supplies, he would descend upon the city in April and fill his soldiers' bellies at leisure – thereby helping to precipitate, though he did not know it at the time, the worst calamity to befall any community during the war: one that would reverberate horrifyingly throughout Europe and swiftly come to exemplify a conflict defying all accepted moral bounds.

Ironically enough, Magdeburg's complex internal politics were, in fact, a microcosm of the tangled web of issues underlying the whole war within the Holy Roman Empire. It had embraced the Lutheran Reformation in 1524, but it was also part of the similarly named bishopric which only passed into Protestant administration in 1545, and despite sharing a common faith thereafter, the so-called 'archbishop-administrator' and ruling oligarchs were nevertheless frequently at odds over the latter's desire for greater autonomy as an imperial city. To complicate matters further, the cathedral chapter consistently chose princes from Brandenburg's ruling Hohenzollern dynasty as archiepiscopal administrators, which became increasingly problematic after the dynasty's conversion to Calvinism in 1613. And the tendency of many in the chapter and city to favour closer ties with Saxony, home of the Reformation, at a time when Saxony's duke hoped to displace Brandenburg as Magdeburg's ruler, only added fuel to the fire. To cap all, while the citizens were uniformly Protestant, a Catholic minority remained in the countryside and among the cathedral canons, in addition to the monks of the nearby Premonstratensian monastery of Jericho on the banks of the Elbe near Magdeburg, feeding Catholic hopes that one of the Empire's oldest and most prestigious archbishoprics might yet be recovered for the Church.

A bad situation had been made immeasurably worse in 1625, however, when the current archbishop-administrator, Christian Wilhelm of Brandenburg, declared for Denmark late in the year, and in doing so played directly into the hands of Emperor Ferdinand, who deposed him and instated his own younger son, Leopold Wilhelm, on the assumption that Wallenstein would enforce his election, having already occupied nearby Halberstadt the same year. From its vantage point on the Elbe, which flows from Bohemia across northern Germany into the North Sea, Magdeburg remained, of course, a key strategic priority, not least because Wallenstein's army at that time depended upon the river to transport grain and other supplies from Habsburg lands. But it was for this very reason too, ironically enough, that the general had been reluctant to impose Leopold Wilhelm, knowing full well that once the Habsburg prince was installed as archbishop, any local revenues would be used for his maintenance rather than the army's. In consequence, Magdeburg had been blockaded rather than besieged during 1628, and this remained true even after the Edict of Restitution formally confirmed that the archbishopric be restored to Catholicism. For the city was, after all, a member of the Hanseatic League whose good offices were so crucial for Wallenstein's 'Baltic Design'.

Such studied restraint was at once no longer feasible, however, when Christian Wilhelm, still claiming his former status, returned on 27 July 1630, slipping through the surrounding cordon of Imperial troops to storm the town hall with a handful of supporters. Hitherto the cathedral canons and city councillors had placed their hopes in Saxony, but now, as other options evaporated, their hands were forced in Sweden's favour, making Magdeburg the Swedes' only outright ally in arms. As a guarantee against any further change of allegiance, moreover, Gustavus duly sent his trusted colonel, the Hessian nobleman Dietrich von Falkenberg, into the city, disguised as a boatman, where he eventually took command in October. Blessed by a brief interim, since the Imperials under Pappenheim had only 3,000 infantry at their disposal for the time being, Magdeburg would therefore await Tilly's arrival and prepare for its coming ordeal as best it might – its civic guard, militia and hapless inhabitants now entrapped within its walls.

At this stage, in fact, Tilly's personal preference remained an all-out offensive to drive Gustavus into the sea, though the Treaty of Bärwalde ensured Maximilian's refusal, and his assistant Pappenheim was therefore merely sent a further 7,000 troops to tighten the stranglehold on Magdeburg. In the meantime, however, Gustavus was himself committed to protecting the city as a signal to other potential allies of his resolve. He had intended, indeed, to have 100,000 men at his disposal by the beginning of 1631, only to find his plans hopelessly wide of the mark, since he could muster no more than a fifth of that number – a third of whom were sick – plus a further 18,000 in garrisons. But he could not forgo his obligations lightly, and in consequence all depended upon native German recruits, who were unlikely to enlist without a major military success as inducement, after Gustavus's southward advance into Brandenburg in January 1631, and sacking of Küstrin and Frankfurt-on-Oder in April had still proved unconvincing. Blocked initially by the Küstrin garrison, he had actually been forced to head west across Pomerania into Mecklenburg, with Tilly in pursuit, and lost 750 Swedish defenders when Neubrandenburg was stormed on 13 March. Nor had Swedish attempts to present the episode as a slaughter conducted during a church service yielded much fruit either, though Gustavus would have his revenge at Frankurt-on-Oder when 1,700 of the 6,400-strong garrison were killed in reprisal. For while Landsberg was seized only two weeks later, securing eastern Pomerania and the Lower Oder for the Swedes, extra recruits were not forthcoming, by which time Tilly had in any case arrived at Magdeburg as planned, bolstering the surrounding troops to 25,000, and posting another 5,000 at the critical Dessau Bridge.

With such a force in place, Gustavus now had no realistic hope of bringing relief, especially after his opponent had succeeded in taking Magdeburg's outworks on 1 May to begin the siege in earnest. At that stage, the defenders within had only 2,500 regular troops, backed by 5,000 armed citizens of whom only 2,000 were adults, making it no surprise that the suburbs should have fallen within two weeks. And to compound Magdeburg's predicament, its population of around 25,000 had already been reduced by a plague outbreak five years earlier and equally demoralised by long-term economic decline. As a result, many of the city's councillors had been lukewarm about the Swedish alliance in the first place and were soon pressing Falkenberg to accept Tilly's repeated offers for honourable surrender, which were roundly refused by the defending commander on the grounds that relief was imminent – notwithstanding the fact that when the decisive assault was eventually launched at 7 a.m. on Tuesday 20 May, Gustavus was still 90km away at Potsdam, powerless, as the enemy well knew, to raise so much as a finger on the stricken city's behalf. Manifestly, it was a recipe for disaster. And so indeed it proved, as 18,000 Imperial and League troops – suitably fortified by a generous wine ration distributed by Pappenheim to boost morale in the face of a broken and forsaken foe – duly descended upon Magdeburg at a prearranged signal from five directions, with bloody retribution, the lure of booty and the prospect of utter free rein in their hearts.

Only one year earlier, the politician who had played such a pivotal role in sparking the conflict in the first place, Christian of Anhalt, had died at home in bed of natural causes after appealing for mercy to the emperor in 1624 and being allowed to return to his principality. And now it was his son and successor, Christian II, who was left to reflect on Magdeburg's fate. 'It recalls to me,' he observed next day, 'the destruction of the city of Jerusalem,' though Pappenheim's report of 21 May captured more forcefully than any, perhaps, the full nature of the horror that had steadily unfolded:

> I believe that over twenty thousand souls were lost. It is certain that no more terrible work and divine punishment has been seen since the destruction of Jerusalem. All of our soldiers became rich. God with us.

Though Tilly had not intended its destruction, hoping indeed that it might be used as a base for his own operations, Magdeburg had in fact become the helpless victim of common soldiers whose pent-up fury and animal passions were simply beyond the control of senior officers. According to the best known account of the episode provided by Otto Guericke, a city councillor keen to apportion blame among Falkenberg and the Catholic clergy, 'who had long awaited such an opportunity', Magdeburg's military commander was taken by surprise when the Imperials soon broke in around 8 a.m., and the result was an orgy of violence and excess that neither he, the city authorities, nor his Imperial counterparts could staunch.

Still expecting Tilly to continue negotiations, Falkenberg was, in fact, yet again arguing with city councillors when word arrived of the onslaught and the latter fled the town hall to attend to their families. Hampered by lack of ammunition, all depended upon holding the walls, and for a brief period the defenders offered stout resistance, particularly at the small bastions constructed in front of the Ulrich and Strotdorf Gates, and upon the hornwork – a complex type of fortification composed of two half-bastions connected by a curtain – constructed before the Kröcken Gate. But neither heroism nor the enthusiasm generated by mortal fear itself were enough to postpone the inevitable indefinitely, as two companies of Croats rode through the low water by the riverbank to work an entrance through a side portal on the poorly fortified Elbe front, spreading panic in the process and helping the Imperials take control of the rest of the bank as far as the Neustadt – the newest part of the city. After which, as Guericke's account makes clear, Magdeburg's fate was effectively sealed:

Then General Pappenheim brought a good number of troops onto the rampart by the Neustadt, and from there into the alleys of the city, and von Falkenberg was shot and fires were set in every corner. Then the city was lost, and all resistance came too late and was useless. For although citizens and soldiers in some places tried to put up some opposition and come to arms, meanwhile the Imperials always had more and more troops to help them, as well as enough cavalry ... and finally they opened the Kröcken Gate and let in through it the entire army of the Imperials and Catholic League, made up of Hungarians, Croats, Poles, Heyducks [a class of Hungarian mercenaries], Italians, Spaniards, French, Walloons, Lower and Upper Germans etc. Thus it happened that the city, with all of its inhabitants, fell into the hands and under the power of its enemies, whose fierceness and cruelty came partly out of a hatred of the adherents of the Augsburg Confession [Lutherans], and partly from the fact that people had shot at them with crossbar shot [bullets with an iron spike in the middle of each ball] and other things from the ramparts, belittling them and leading them to become enraged. Then there was nothing but murder, burning, plundering, torment and beatings.

In particular, Guericke tells us, 'each of the enemies sought more and greater booty'. And as the booty ran out, so the troops resorted to ever greater violence for brutality's sake:

When such a party of looters entered a house and the head of the household had something he could give them, then he could use this to save and preserve himself until another soldier, who also wanted something, came along. Finally, however, when everything had been given out and there was nothing left to give, then the misery really began. For then the soldiers began to beat, frighten, and threaten to shoot, skewer, hang, etc., the people, so that even if something had been buried under the earth or locked away behind a thousand locks, the citizens would still have been forced to seek it out and hand it over. Through such enduring fury – which laid this great, magnificent city, which had been like a princess in the entire land, into complete burning embers and put it into such enormous misery and unspeakable need and heartbreak – many thousands of innocent men, women and children were, with horrid, fearful screams of pain and alarm, miserably murdered and wretchedly executed in manifold ways, so that no words can sufficiently describe it, nor tears bemoan it.

What Guericke refers to as 'this dismal time' lasted, it seems, 'not actually much more than two hours', but what cannon, musket shot and human hand did not achieve in that brief space, fire completed thereafter, for 'by ten o'clock in the evening the entire city, including the beautiful courthouse and all the churches and cloisters, had been reduced to ashes and heaps of stone', forcing even the attacking army to retreat, 'lest it incinerate itself'. Originally ordered by Pappenheim, so Guericke suggests, 'in order to perturb and frighten the citizens and inhabitants', the setting of fires had subsequently 'been used by the common soldiery without discretion or pause' until the flames 'took the upper hand by means of the sudden appearance of the wind'.

Thus this renowned and genteel city, the ornament of the entire land, went up in smoke in a single day, and its remaining inhabitants, with their wives and children, were taken prisoner and driven out by the enemy such that the shouting, crying and howling could be heard from far away, and the seething embers and ash from the city were transported by the wind as far away as Wanzleben, Egeln, and other places.

The fact, of course, that Wanzleben is a town 10 miles south-west of Magdeburg, and that Egeln lies some 7 miles further on, gives ample testimony to the intensity of the inferno. But on one point at least, Guericke's account requires rectification. For, according to Count Gronsfeld, a fellow general who had no particular reason to tailor the truth, Pappenheim confided that he had initially ordered the firing of no more than a single house, with the intention of flushing out some musketeers who were barring his troops' entrance to the city. Zacharias Bandhauer, on the other hand, who, as superintendent of the Catholic monastery, was inside the city, suggested that Pappenheim's main intention was to create a smokescreen for his men crossing the wall, while Captain Ackerman of Pappenheim's regiment attributed the outbreak to the firing of two houses in an attempt to force a group of defenders from the city's walls by encouraging them to fight the flames instead.

In any event, the time-honoured myth of Protestant propaganda that the 'Magdeburg Maiden' – a play on Magdeburg's name which literally means 'Maiden's castle' – was purposely put to the torch by the attacking commanders seems largely untenable. And neither, for that matter, does Guericke make any reference to the effect of the explosion of an apothecary's house used to store gunpowder, after which the fire spread particularly quickly, or, more importantly still perhaps, the worthy efforts of some participants to ameliorate the suffering. For amid the mayhem there were also some remnants of military discipline and even common humanity, which went largely unrecorded in most contemporary accounts. Certainly, by the time that Tilly entered and ordered a halt to the burning and pillaging, many of his men were wildly out of control, but enough remained under orders to save the cathedral where 1,000 people had taken shelter, and the Premonstratensians also protected 600 women in their monastery, which was fortunate enough to escape the flames. Yet, for all its understandable one-sidedness, Guericke's account still captures like no other the overwhelming essence of events, as 1,700 of Magdeburg's 1,900 buildings were destroyed and some 20,000 civilians met their death, along with at least 300 besiegers killed during the assault, besides another 1,600 wounded. As harrowing testimony to the scale of destruction, a census of February 1632 revealed only 449 inhabitants remaining, and more than a century later a large part of the city remained buried in rubble.

Other survivors too, like the family of Christopher Thodänus, a Bohemian who became a school teacher in Magdeburg in 1613 and subsequently pastor at St Catherine's Church, all carried lasting memories of their ill-treatment. Everything in Thodänus's home, it seems, was either 'smashed up' or 'taken, pocketed and carried away' before the plunderers were finally 'satisfied' by a further 2 thalers and 2 silver spoons 'which the maid had hidden in our house'. But this, as Thodänus makes clear, was by no means the end of his family's ordeal:

> Soon afterwards several more men arrived, among them one who looked like the devil himself, with two muskets and in his mouth a ball in each of his cheeks. He looked at me with a grim expression and said: 'Priest give money!' That was always their solution. When, however, I excused myself that I had no more upon me, and that this wasn't my house, he was not satisfied, but rather aimed a musket at me. But when the match refused to catch fire, he blew upon it and pulled. In the meantime, my wife plucked up her courage, struck his musket upwards so that the ball flew over my head into the wall. She then held him by the arms so that he could not move. And because he demanded money, but we had no more of it, he said: 'Give me silver instead.' Then it occurred to her that she still had silver hooks on her bodice, which she cut off and gave to him. He stood before her, watching, but did not lay a finger on her.

Another lucky escape had also been reserved for Friedrich Friese and his father, Daniel, who had moved to Magdeburg in 1628 to take up the post of Senior City Clerk. Having already been threatened and attacked by two musketeers who 'craved money' and were finally bought off by a suitable sum, as well as clothes, utensils and shoes, the Friese family were then confronted with four more musketeers who 'hit and punched father hard' before leaving with 'some of our jewellery and other precious things'. By the time that the parents and children had taken shelter in an outbuilding of their yard, Imperial soldiers were already 'shouting and charging about' the neighbouring dwelling 'like bad spirits':

> They cried, swore and blasphemed for booty and money without end. We heard all this as we sat in our coal shed as quiet as mice. After a while father got out to see what had happened. The soldiers soon saw him, screamed and ran towards him. Mother heard the shouting and also ran out and we children all followed. There were about seven soldiers, all with burning matches. They spoke a foreign tongue and no one understood what they said. They kept putting out their hands for money. Excuses were no good, father could say what he liked. They didn't understand, but fired at him twice in the house.

God mercifully ensured that the shots didn't strike father. The bullets buried themselves in the wall. Father and mother fled into the main room. One of them who was probably an officer lunged at father with a halberd. At that moment, father went through the door and the rogue hacked a large piece out of the lintel above the door. In this way father was mercifully preserved by God. Finally, father spoke to the officer in Latin, saying that the soldiers had taken everything from him, and he had nothing to give but clothes, linen, tin and the like. The madmen and furies were quietened a little with this, but the officer still wanted money; as soon as he got this, he would lead his men away. Now we still had a small box in a part of the house with pearls and a few other things, [as well as] our, the children's, godparent money and the like. Mother remembered this. She led the officer upstairs, but the soldiers remained downstairs and ate the fine breakfast that lay on the table. We gave the officer these things with the earnest plea that he should let us go and help us to get out; we were eager to ransom ourselves. But he was not to be induced and turned very fierce. Finally, he let us go and took father's best cloak with lace and satin cuffs, that he wore on best occasions … The soldiers ran about the house, smashing and searching everything for nearly half an hour, but none of them came into the stables, because this was so full of manure and straw, that no one could get in easily.

Even Catholic accounts made little attempt, in some cases, to conceal the horror. Though emphasising that Magdeburg 'had given great cause' for its 'great misfortune' as a result of its 'disloyalty for many years', Zacharias Bandauer, the prior of Magdeburg's Premonstratensian monastery, for instance, expressed his 'regret' at the 'latitude' afforded to the soldiers, and left us the following account not only of a particularly inhuman episode, but of Tilly's reaction to it and subsequent inability to exact appropriate justice:

A terrible deed took place on Saturday, the 24th of May: six godless soldiers raped a girl of 12 or 13 in the churchyard of Our Lady so that she died by their hands. When this was brought to the attention of Mr Sylvius, he decided to inform His Excellency Tilly, so that such vices could be avoided. Because none of the clerics dared do this, Mr Sylvius finally went himself to Tilly in his quarters where he found him sitting at his desk. When he saw Mr Sylvius standing before the door, he asked him in French what good news he brought. He went in and said: 'Your Excellency, I don't have anything good to say. Your baggage attendants have raped a girl of 12 in our churchyard so that she died. If Your Excellency does not counter such evil and stop it with a stringent order,

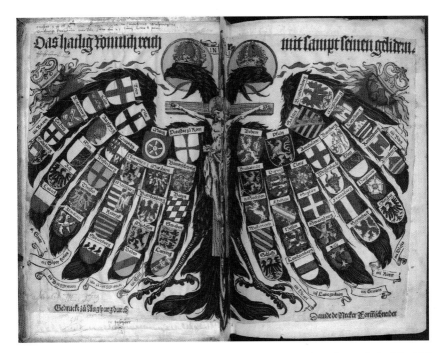

Depiction of the double-headed eagle by Hans Burgkmair the Elder. The symbol of the Holy Roman Empire, with the coats of arms of the emperor's secular and ecclesiastical electors and some of the individual rulers who owe allegiance to him, including margraves, landgraves, burgraves, counts, knights and lesser noblemen. Imperial Free Cities, such as Augsburg, Aachen, Cologne, Regensburg and Lübeck are also included, along with places like Magdeburg, which was horrifically sacked in May 1631. A distinguishing feature of the Holy Roman eagle was its frequent depiction with halos, as seen here.

Fishing for Souls by Adriaen van de Venne. In this crowded canvas painted in 1614 by Adriaen van de Venne, Christ's words, 'I will make you fishers of men', are employed as an ironic text for the whole contemporary religious situation in Europe. The Peace of Augsburg of 1555 had achieved a truce in Germany, but it was a settlement between two irreconcilable opposites that could never last indefinitely. Here Protestants and Catholics face each other across a river, as clergy from both banks attempt to drag naked men and women into their boats. Over one and all, but universally disregarded, shines the rainbow of God.

Portrait of Emperor Rudolf II by Hans von Aachen, c. 1590. The time-honoured Habsburg imperative to create a unified Christian empire had not altogether vanished from Emperor Rudolf II's thinking, but it was largely superseded by more personal priorities: the patronage of artists and natural philosophers; an overwhelming passion for alchemy and astrology; and above all a compulsive need to collect, whether it be minerals or gemstones, past masterworks by Dürer and Breughel, or wild animals like the lion and tiger that were allowed to roam free around the Hradčany Palace in Prague, to which he relocated the Imperial court in 1583.

The Defenestration of Prague. On 22 May 1618 a group of Protestant Bohemian noblemen, wishing to bring to a climax their quarrel with the Holy Roman Emperor over their religious and constitutional rights, seized two Imperial governors, Martinitz and Slavata, and threw them from the top-floor window of Prague's Hradčany Palace, pictured here. For good measure, their secretary was flung after them. Though all escaped serious injury, the flame of revolt was nevertheless lit, making the chain reaction responsible for the outbreak of the Thirty Years War inescapable.

The Winter King – Portrait of Frederick V by Gerrit von Honthorst, 1634. Frederick V, Elector Palatine, was 27 when Bohemian rebels offered him their kingdom's crown. For a year the 'Winter King' enjoyed the empty honours of royalty before defeat at the Battle of White Mountain in November 1620 robbed him not only of his new title but ultimately his ancestral estates of the Palatinate.

Ferdinand II, the Habsburg Emperor elected shortly after the Bohemian revolt broke out, devoted his whole reign to the conflict that followed, but victory eluded him. Count Tilly, the only effective general he could trust, died in 1632 after crushing defeats by Gustavus Adolphus. Wallenstein, on the other hand, seemed to be as dangerous a friend as any foe. Even Ferdinand's greatest success, the Peace of Prague in 1635, brought him no more than the lasting opposition of France. He died in 1637, his difficulties no nearer solution.

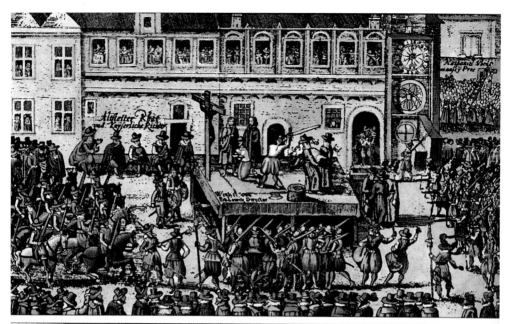

Verzeichnus was gestalt der Graff von Schlick vnd andre hohe vnd Niderstands Personen hingericht vnd vollzogen werden.

Above: **Contemporary woodcut depicting the Old Town Square execution of Protestant aristocrats in Prague, 1621.** On 21 June 1621, the most notorious execution in Czech history took place in the packed Old Town Square of Prague. At five in the morning, twenty-eight Protestant rebel prisoners, including some of the most prominent members of Czech society, many in their sixties and seventies, were led under heavy guard to the execution platform. Johannes Jessenius, rector of Prague's university, who had long polemicised and machinated against the Emperor, was beheaded and quartered after his tongue had been cut out, while the rest were dispatched in a protracted ritual, which lasted around four hours and necessitated the use of four separate swords for Jan Mydllar the executioner to accomplish his grisly task.

Left: **Maximilian of Bavaria by Joachim von Sandrart, 1643.** As leader of the Catholic League, Maximilian of Bavaria's support was vital to Emperor Ferdinand. It was gained by lavish payment in money and the promise of Frederick V's lands and electoral title when the revolt was over. The duke's jealousy of Wallenstein harmed the Imperial cause, and led to his own duchy being overrun by the Swedes, though by the end of the war he was one of the few to emerge in profit, dying three years after the conclusion of hostilities.

Jean Tserclaes, Count of Tilly. Born in Liège in 1559, Jean Tserclaes, Count of Tilly, was arguably one of the more noble representatives of the Counter-Reformation. A pupil of the Jesuits, he had originally wished to enter the order in his own right, before deciding to serve its ideals as a Christian warrior. At all times, he proved true to his reputation as a 'monk in armour', despising the low pleasures of most contemporary officers and advancing his faith by an unswerving dedication to the arts of war rather than the wiles of politics, though his troops were eventually responsible for the notorious sack of Magdeburg in 1631. Today he is still honoured in Munich as Maximilian of Bavaria's leading general by a bronze statue in the *Feldherrnhalle* on Odeonsplatz.

Albrecht von Wallenstein by Anthony van Dyck, 1629. Known more commonly to posterity as Wallenstein, Albrecht Wenzel Eusebius von Valdštejn was a Bohemian military leader who rose to become both supreme commander and chief military contractor of Ferdinand II's Imperial armies. As a result of the huge economic infrastructure established at his estates in Friedland, he was able not only to equip his own forces but to offer considerable loans to Ferdinand, leaving the borrower hopelessly in hock and committed, beyond all hope of manoeuvre, to offering his benefactor whatever he chose, until the emperor had him assassinated at the town of Eger in 1634.

Gustavus Adolphus of Sweden at the Battle of Breitenfeld, 1631. Gustavus Adolphus was considered by von Clausewitz and Napoleon Bonaparte, as well as George S. Patton, to be one of the greatest generals of all time. Before his death at Lützen in November 1632, he had swept into Germany at the head of the most efficient army in Europe, since its nucleus was conscript rather than mercenary. A figure of great charisma and fascination, he took a lively interest in a whole range of topics from navigation to the decipherment of runes.

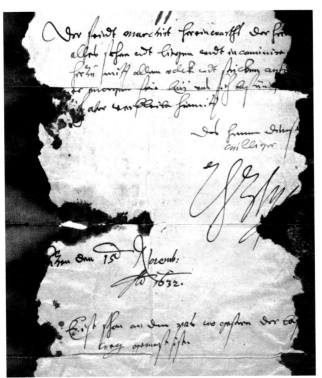

Around midnight on 15/16 November 1632, General Gottfried Heinrich Graf zu Pappenheim was awoken from his slumbers to receive an urgent summons to return with all haste to Wallenstein's headquarters. Only two hours later, he was on his way with three cavalry regiments to the historic engagement at Lützen. The *generalissimo*'s orders – which still exist soaked in Pappenheim's blood – left no doubt about the scale of his predicament: 'The enemy is marching towards us. Your honour shall drop everything, and route himself hereto with all troops and guns, to be with us early in the morning … [The enemy] is already at the pass where yesterday the road was bad.'

The Siege of La Rochelle by Henri Motte, 1881. Born in 1585, the third son of one of Poitou's lesser nobles, Armand-Jean Du Plessis de Richelieu had been brought up for life as a layman, before entering the Church at the age of 17 upon the death of one of his elder brothers. This detail of a painting by Henri Motte depicts the cardinal at the Siege of La Rochelle against the Huguenots, appropriately enough in full armour, since his willingness to wage war to the limit in pursuit of political goals was unwavering.

Soldiers Plundering a Farm During the Thirty Years War by Sebastian Vrancx, 1620.
'The day a man picks up his pike to become a soldier is the day he ceases to be a Christian,' remarked Francisco de Valdés, a general in the Spanish Army of Flanders during the Eighty Years War with the United Provinces of the Netherlands. The plundering of a farm depicted here in 1620 by the Flemish artist Sebastian Vrancx would become an everyday reality for thousands of innocent civilians in Germany over the next twenty-eight years. In the county of Memel, to take but one example, there had been 154 horses, 236 oxen, 103 cows, 190 pigs and 810 sheep before the Swedish occupation of 1629. Two years later there were merely 26 oxen and 1 cow.

Left: Though its use on the battlefield after 1640 was practically unknown, nostalgia for knighthood and chivalry still gave full armour a romantic prestige, which explains its employment in so many paintings of the period. The style displayed here was commonly worn by lancers, as well as cuirassiers who carried two pistols in holsters on either side of the saddle instead of a lance. Examples of such armour surviving today frequently exhibit pistol dents, not necessarily incurred in battle, but created by testing or 'proving' at the time of manufacture. Catholic armour was usually all black or all white.

Below: **The Ratification of the Treaty of Münster by Gerard ter Borch, 1648.** After seemingly endless negotiations the treaties constituting the Peace of Westphalia were eventually signed. This commemorative painting shows the scene in the Rathaus of Münster on 15 May 1648 when delegates from Spain and the Netherlands finally settled terms. The men with their hands raised are Dutch representatives, while on the other side of the table, holding a copy of the oath and with their hands on a Bible, are the Spanish plenipotentiaries. The treaty was read aloud, first in French and then in Dutch, after which both groups swore an oath and the Spaniards kissed the crucifix.

the Lord God will take victory from Your Excellency and give it to the enemy, the Swedes, and that will happen shortly!'

Tilly was shocked when he heard this. He stood up, went to the window and tears came to his eyes. He asked who and where the soldiers were. Because Mr Sylvius did not know, His Excellency immediately had the drummers publicise that such pranks [*sic*] were forbidden on pain of death. The culprits were already on their way and were not seen again.

For the most part, however, Catholics responded to the fall of Magdeburg, as might be expected, with joy. To sack a town that resisted surrender was, after all, standard military practice for the day, nor, if truth be told, were the individual episodes of brutality especially exceptional in their own right: only the scale upon which they occurred. So when news reached Mainz in June, the reaction of the winning side, as described by Nicholaus Michaelis, a Calvinist pastor in nearby Hechtsheim, was precisely what might be expected:

> All Protestants were terribly saddened and appalled by the wretched downfall of the city of Magdeburg, but the papists rejoiced and were glad. At Mainz, there were joyful gun salvoes because of the capture of the city of Magdeburg … They marched in procession to the Church of Our Lady with drums and pipes, and gave thanks to her for such a victory, as if the blessed Virgin Mary up in heaven had such a murderous bloodthirsty heart as the papists who cannot get enough of innocent human blood here on earth. It is said that some sixty thousand souls lost their lives at Magdeburg.

The gloss – not to mention the inflationary effect of the rumour mill – is, of course, palpable. But it was not merely humble figures like Michaelis who felt the need to place the mark of their prejudices on events. For the burning or plundering of a village was one thing, the annihilation of a substantial urban centre – and a capital of Protestantism at that – quite another. In all, therefore, no less than twenty newspapers, 205 pamphlets and forty-one illustrated broadsheets describing the tragedy were published in 1631 alone, circulating all over Europe, so that observers in London, Paris, Amsterdam, Stockholm, Rome and Madrid, as well as in the princely courts of Germany, were made acutely aware of how the emperor appeared to treat his German subjects.

And for Gustavus Adolphus especially, of course, this battle of polemics was hardly less important than the contest of sword and cannon facing him imminently, since Magdeburg's destruction – which he lamely attributed to the city's inadequate defence spending – was a potential public relations disaster, exposing the Swedish king's inability to protect his German allies. Worse still, as the course of the war continued to pendulate, the emperor had now decided, in a long-overdue effort to meet the Swedish threat, to withdraw his army from northern Italy, after a separate peace with Richelieu at Cherasco in June, by which the Duke of Nevers was granted not only Mantua but also the fortresses of Montferrat and Casale. Plainly, Ferdinand was at last prepared to bite any bullet or swallow any pill, however bitter, in an effort to deal with Gustavus once and for all. And with this in mind, fresh from his triumph at Magdeburg and buoyed by reinforcements from Italy, Tilly was accordingly ordered to march north-eastwards to deliver the Swedish foe a resounding, irresistible and killing blow. He was to destroy at a stroke the reputation of Sweden's upstart king and allow the two-headed Imperial eagle to pluck out the eyes of the lion once and for all – or so, at least, his emperor fondly hoped.

For the widely publicised fate of Magdeburg – previously administered by George William of Brandenburg's uncle, Christian William, and just across Brandenburg's borders – had finally brought Sweden the alliance it had been seeking, assisted albeit by the overwhelming presence of 21,000 Swedish troops outside Berlin and the training of Gustavus's renowned artillery upon the elec-toral palace itself. Suitably cowed, George William not only threw in his lot with Gustavus on 21 June 1631, but did so with the additional offer of a payment of 30,000 reichsthalers a month. And this was not the only encouraging news for the emperor's enemies, since the sack and burning of Magdeburg had actually left the victors with nothing more than ashes. Finding it impossible to feed and house his armies in the ruins, it was therefore essential for Tilly to move them elsewhere. Yet because of the entente between Bavaria and France, Duke Maximilian was forbidding him to challenge Gustavus in the field, at the very moment that Saxony seemed closed to his troops, lest any advance drive its ruler into the Swedish camp. Away to the south, moreover – in Württemberg and Baden – Protestant princes were proceeding to arm under the terms of the Leipzig convention, and thereby threatening to block the return of Imperial troops from Italy, while nearer at hand, William V of Hesse-Kassel, undaunted by the catastrophe of Magdeburg, was also preparing to take the field.

Instead, therefore, of a menacing Imperial force impending over him, the King of Sweden unexpectedly found himself confronted with what appeared to be a temporary military vacuum, and like the great military commander he undoubtedly was, he did not fail to exploit it, setting forth, after the frustrations of the previous weeks, from Brandenburg at the end of June, before taking Tangermünde on 2 July, which left him across the Elbe in force and into a cru-cial new supply area: central Germany itself. Now, for the first time, his armies had marched off the maps which he had first brought with him from home. Nor would they stop. For on 10 July he moved down the river to Werben, where, in a great loop of the Elbe, he constructed a huge fortified camp, which ten days later lodged 21,000 men within it, with reinforcements expected. His hope was to pre-empt a pitched battle with Tilly before the Imperial reinforcements arrived from Italy, and in this, too, he was assisted by his opponent's urgent need for supplies, since Maximilian's imprecations had been unable to halt Tilly's advance in Gustavus's direction, heartened as the aged general now was by the arrival of his own reinforcements from south Germany under Fürstenberg. Indeed, by late July and early August, skirmishing was already underway, and with another 24,000 troops expected, in addition to other men still collecting at Cologne, Tilly, too, was now in quest of a decisive victory.

Yet when the victor of Magdeburg came up against Gustavus's field forti-fications at Werben, the omens were not encouraging: his cannon made little impression; in the engagements outside the camp he could show no advantage; and in a significant encounter near Burgstall his cavalry suffered a sharp defeat. On 29 July, in fact, he ignominiously withdrew, leaving his foe to reflect with rightful satisfaction upon what amounted to a turning-point. For until his arrival at Werben, it had seemed that the best Gustavus might hope for was to be able to maintain himself in the Baltic coastlands. But with the advance to the Elbe and the successful consolidation of his position astride it, the situation altered markedly. Henceforward he would enjoy altogether more room for manoeuvre, better hopes of supply and recruitment, a nearer approach to the areas where allies were most likely to be found, and a corresponding stiffening of the morale of those princes whom the fate of Magdeburg had daunted. In a gesture of great symbolic significance, the exiled dukes of Mecklenburg were duly restored to the capital from which Wallenstein had evicted them, while one, Duke John Albert II, accepted a command in the Swedish army, as did Duke Bernard of Saxe-Weimar. Not to be outdone, William V too, who had only been saved from annihilation at Tilly's hands by Gustavus's sudden descent upon Tangermünde, now effectively surrendered Hesse-Kassel's sovereignty to Sweden 'until we have achieved our aims'.

The tide, then, was indeed turning – and with a growing surge that could not have escaped either Tilly or the emperor. But, even now, only one Protestant prince could provide Gustavus with the troops required for him to prevail in what promised to be the greatest and most significant all-out pitched battle of the war to date. That prince was John George of Saxony, whose German policy, by the beginning of August, lay in the kind of abject ruin that surpassed even his considerable powers of self-deception. The viability of the resolutions agreed at the Leipzig convention had of course been shattered at Magdeburg, and his leadership wholly undermined. He too thereafter no longer dreamed that tactics of moderation could permanently exempt him from the operation of the Edict of Restitution or the exactions of the Imperial armies. For despite his protestations that the troops he was raising were for defensive purposes only, Tilly was now brusquely demanding their disbandment and calling for the right to cross the Saxon frontier in search of food, leaving no other choice than to accept the inevitable and strike a suitably belligerent note. 'Now,' declared John George, following an ultimatum delivered by the general on 14 August, 'I see that Saxon sweetmeats so long spared, are to be eaten. But you may find that they contain hard nuts that will break your teeth.'

Accordingly, on 2 September, just one day before Tilly did indeed lead his army across the border to feast on 'Saxon sweetmeats', the Duke of Saxony duly concluded an alliance with the King of Sweden 'for as long as the danger from the enemy shall continue'. He would, in fact, accept Gustavus's absolute direction for specific operations agreed between them, but in other cases pledge himself only to conform to Gustavus's plans 'as far as possible'. And in other respects, too, there was careful hedging of bets as Saxony's ruler cannily retained his own army and generals, and in particular the services of Hans Georg von Arnim, who was to be placed at the king's disposal for the time being, but would actually prove a thorn in Sweden's side for years to come. As such, the alliance was plainly one exacted by necessity and outrightly repugnant in many essentials to both contracting parties. On the one hand, John George found himself yoked to the King of Sweden's chariot wheels, while Gustavus found himself saddled with an ally over whom his control was by no means assured, and to whom there remained an unspecified, and therefore dangerous, measure of military independence. But Tilly was marching on Leipzig in good order, and, for all the new arrangement's shortcomings, the Swedes had the precious addition of 18,000 – albeit untried – Saxon recruits. As a result, numerical superiority was at long last with the Protestants, and the time ripe to give battle.

Nor would the long-awaited encounter – at what would prove to be the village of Breitenfeld, a little to the north of Saxony's capital – be long in coming. For in the low-lying haze of the early autumn morning of 7 September, 1631, up to 42,000 Swedes and Saxons duly deployed for action against an enemy numbering around 35,000 – some 7,000 of whom had just arrived, tired and weary, from Mantua – in a pivotal confrontation between not only rival ideologies that had divided Europe between them, but opposing theories of warfare that would now be tested in the white heat of actual combat. On the one hand, the time-honoured universalist dream of religious and political uniformity represented by Roman

Catholicism and the Habsburg dynasty stood poised for what promised to be a decisive reckoning with its nemesis: the revolutionary new challenge of dynamic fragmentation along national and religious lines, championed first by the Dutch and, more recently, Bohemia. And in the process, the traditional *tercio*, or large square military formation, dating back to the Greeks and perfected by Spanish infantry regiments in the sixteenth century, would be duly pitched against the 'scientific' pretensions of the new 'linear', longer, thinner-lined, 'battalion' style of fighting, most often associated with the innovations of Maurice of Nassau, and adapted, with devastating effect, by Gustavus Adolphus into the so-called *skvadron* – seventy-six men wide and six deep, and consisting of a total of 556 men, divided into 264 officers and pike, 192 battalion musketeers, and 100 detached musketeers, supported by skirmishers in front. If Imperial forces under Tilly were to emerge triumphant, Germany's princes would be deterred from following the example of Brandenburg and Saxony, and a massive, perhaps definitive, blow struck for the forces of the Counter-Reformation. Should the laurels be Sweden's, however, all Germany would lie before her armies, as Protestantism rejoiced at the most stunning blow struck to date in its defence.

With so much at stake, it was curious, perhaps, that the martial panoply on display was not uniformly impressive as both sides gathered for action. Certainly, the 18,000 Saxons present looked suitably resplendent in their brand new – as yet untarnished – uniforms, but the 24,000 Swedes on hand presented a notably unkempt contrast, 'having lyen over-night on a parcel of plowd grownd', so that, according to Robert Monro, they were 'so dusty, they looked out like kitchen-servants, with their uncleanly rags'. Nor, it seems, had all of the Swedish host been wholly enthused at the prospect of battle, for in the two days between their initial muster at Duben and their deployment at Breitenfeld, no less than 10 per cent of the infantry had disappeared – taken sick or deserted. The worst offenders, it seems, were Swedish conscipts, who lost 15 per cent of their number, and surprisingly enough the normally bellicose Scots who suffered losses of 5 per cent. But the rest of the Swedes, unlike their finely drilled and accoutred Saxon counterparts, who had been in training only since April, were nevertheless 'old experimented blades', well used to battle and, more importantly still, familiar with the taste of victory. On the morning's final march to Breitenfeld, they had been harassed by Croat detachments and also skipped breakfast, since their king was eager to give battle. But they remained both resolute and confident in their numerical advantage, which had in fact been exaggerated by Tilly's scouts and encouraged him to delay, much to the disapproval of Pappenheim, who saw the Saxons, not altogether unreasonably, as largely ineffectual cannon fodder.

As both sides braced themselves, moreover, it was the Imperials who found themselves outgunned, with only twenty-six artillery pieces to the enemy's fifty-six, and in the opening cannonades which lasted some two hours, the effects of this deficiency would prove crucial. For in spite of the obstruction of the marshy Lober river, the Swedes had succeeded in approaching the enemy in full battle formation, and purposely avoided reply to Tilly's guns – which had begun firing a little before midday at a distance of about 1km – until after his third salvo, by which time the advancing force had finally closed to around half that distance, making its subsequent response utterly deadly. Having stood firm against the fearful raking fire of their enemies, there now followed a Swedish counter-bombardment, which even Imperial accounts, including those of Tilly, Pappenheim and Count Ernesto Montecuccoli, described as 'ferocious, terrible, incessant' – 'a horrible incessant pounding'. 'Our guns answered theirs with three shots for one,' Gustavus later boasted, although the disparity may well have been almost double that, and throughout the proceeding storm, the toll was grievous. Colonel Baumgarten of the League cavalry was only one of many killed in the 'first Swedish salvo' – though, in his particular case, the killing shot had actually been fired from a Saxon gun – and as swathes of other officers and men fell like broken reeds under the onslaught of Gustavus's copper-cast 4-pounders, the threat of an early breakthrough increased.

Yet Tilly held firm. He had drawn up his troops on a slight rise running east to west on the relatively broad plain on which the battlefield stood, and his infantry were deployed in twelve large *tercios*, grouped in threes to a total distance of around a mile, with two further battalions posted on either flank to support the cavalry, around 4,000 of whom were placed on the left under Pappenheim who had the cream of the Imperial cuirassiers at his disposal. Each *tercio* comprised 1,500 men – probably fifty at the front and thirty deep, with the front five ranks able to fire at any one time – while the right of the Imperial formation was commanded by Count Ernst Egon of Fürstenberg, whose 7,000 troops had only just arrived and were still tired. Their morale, however, remained high, since, according to one captain, 'they had an invincible courage, believing they would be victorious', and Fürstenberg was able to take further consolation from the fact that 3,800 League cavalry were also under his command, along with 900 Croats. From Tilly's perspective, therefore, the secret was patience and watchfulness: to endure the carnage among his men for as long as necessary, waiting all the while for the first telltale signs of wavering in the enemy's progress, which would mark his signal to attack. If the Saxons, in particular, could be encouraged to falter, the day would still be his.

Three days earlier, in fact, Tilly had taken Leipzig and was fully prepared at that stage to avoid battle altogether, enjoying the opportunity to provision his army properly for the first occasion in months, while also appreciating his outnumbered soldiers' reluctance to abandon the comforts they had so recently acquired. But good sense was not, it seems, the guidelight for Pappenheim, his second-in-command, who had seen fit to transform a simple reconnaissance mission 4 miles north of Leipzig into an assault on Gustavus's camp and thereby commit the rest of the army to march to his aid. 'This fellow,' Tilly had complained at the time, 'will rob me of my honour and reputation, and the emperor of his lands and people.' Yet he had felt honour-bound to join his impulsive subordinate – and to watch now as Pappenheim's uncertain temper, frayed by the prolonged bombardment, mistook some movements of Gustavus's horse as an attempt at envelopment, and ordered his wing to advance at a brisk trot, 'with considerable impetus', taking Fürstenberg with him on the opposite wing. The time was 2 p.m. and whether the action had been taken under orders remains unclear. But Pappenheim's objective was apparent, and the 'moral force' of 3,800 heavy cavalry aimed at the enemy's own horse detachments, which had elected to fight at the halt, seemed irresistible.

Gustavus, meanwhile, had deliberately kept his own army separate from the raw Saxons under Arnim, who were deployed in a relatively deep formation east of the Leipzig–Düben road. Instead, the Swedes formed up to the west in a novel formation of two distinct lines, with Count Gustav Karlsson Horn – who was also second-in-command of the army – controlling the cavalry immediately next to the road, besides which lay seven infantry brigades, while the king himself and the rest of the cavalry were positioned on the extreme right opposite Pappenheim, though it was actually a general salvo from 2,450 Swedish troopers, stiffened by 860 musketeers, that thwarted the advancing enemy cavalry in its tracks. In fact, the psychological effect appears to have been out of all proportion to the actual impact, which amounted, perhaps, to no more than 150 hits. And neither was the brief cavalry engagement that followed especially significant in its own right. For as the Swedish cavalry advanced to 'bounce' the disordered Imperials, a few swords crossed and some pistols flashed, without any significant outcome until a second volley caused Pappenheim's force to disengage temporarily and slowly fall back from the barrier of steel and fire now awaiting them.

Seven more times, however, the Imperial cuirassiers charged forward, closing to within pistol range, in a vain attempt to envelop Gustavus, who prudently curled back his rightmost squadrons, consisting mainly of Finns, and moved the Rhinegrave cavalry regiment to extend their line further to the right. Coolly feeding in the squadrons of General Johan Baner's reserve at one and the same time, he thus blocked the enemy repeatedly, until by 4 p.m. Pappenheim's men were finally exhausted, disorganised, and loosely strung out along the entire length of the Swedish flank, creating the opening at last for a decisive counterstrike, which duly followed only fifteen minutes later, as Baner was ordered to attack the open left flank, and the Tott Cavalry Regiment, along with Uslar's 500 sabers, also struck in a flat-out charge, forcing the enemy to quit the field in disorder in the direction of Halle, some 24km away. As the Imperial cuirassiers crumpled, moreover, so Tilly's Holstein infantry, suddenly adrift in a sea of hostile cavalry, found themselves left to their fate within a circular 'crown' of beleaguered pikemen, pinning all hope on a desperate last stand and what seemed the slender possibility of better news from other sectors of the battlefield.

On the right, however, there had indeed been altogether more success for their Imperial comrades. For by 2.30, Fürstenberg had been grinding down the Saxons, sending Isolano's Croats to wheel around their flanks, and ordering Cronberg and Schonberg, 'the flower of the army', to bypass their gun line and strike at the main body of Saxon foot, which rapidly proceeded to disintegrate under the resulting pressure. Beyond the few men around the guns, indeed, who were still fighting and Arnim's 500 horse, the Saxon army had before long simply ceased to exist. For when they saw what was happening, the militia cavalry also panicked and fled, along with Duke John George himself, whose own guards swiftly joined the rout. As Gustavus put it subsequently:

> The Saxon cavalry and artillerymen stood bravely at first, but after the best of the gunners were shot, the rest began to abandon their cannons. The Saxon infantry did no better; they fled in whole companies, spreading the report that all was lost, terrifying our baggage train, who in turn ran as far as Duben … the elector, who had been in the rear, ran away with his whole life guard and didn't stop 'til he reached Eilenburg.

But Robert Monro was harsher still, particularly when noting how the Saxons had only slowed their flight to plunder the Swedish baggage, which he considered 'too good a recompense for Cullions that had left their duke, betrayed their country, and the good cause, whenas strangers were hazarding their lives for their freedom.'

In spite of Pappenheim's failure and the predicament of the Holstein infantry, therefore, there was still hope remaining. For at 2.30 also, Tilly had ordered his centre and reserve into action, anticipating that if Fürstenberg could yet be brought to bear on Gustavus's right, the Swedes themselves might falter. But the count had lost control of his wing as the Croats wandered off to plunder the Saxon baggage train, and others scattered to pursue what they wrongly considered the remnants of a vanquished enemy. In the resulting breathing space, moreover, the ever-dependable Horn found time to reinforce his own front and regroup along the road he was defending, moving it at right angles to the rest of the Swedish army, and thereby forcing Tilly, who was by then deprived of Pappenheim's cavalry, to swing east to face him. Unfazed by the Saxon collapse – meeting it, indeed, with all the vindicated satisfaction of the professional pessimist that he undoubtedly was – Horn was also aided by the time it took Tilly's *tercios* to regroup after the rout of Arnim's force, since it allowed him to summon reserves and thereby launch a furious attack of his own, with cavalry, musketeers and artillery all collaborating together in a remarkable display of the utmost proficiency that yielded extraordinary results. For incredibly enough, the central infantry units of the Swedish army were scarcely scathed as the *tercios* retreated and Gustavus wheeled in from the right after Pappenheim's collapse.

Lieutenant-Colonel Muschamp, a Scot commanding the Spens infantry regiment, reported pouring case shot from his three regimental guns into a final contingent of advancing Imperials, and holding his musket fire until they were 'within pistol range', whereupon his first three ranks discharged as one, before the next three moved forward and also volleyed. Thereafter the Scots 'fell pell mell' upon the enemy, in a crushing scrum of pikes and flailing musket butts, forcing them to fight for their lives as individuals while the artillery continued to fire, even after hand-to-hand slaughter had begun. And though an unnamed 'brave commander all in scarlet and gold lace' was, it seems, able to organise sufficient resistance to engage the Scots for 'over an hour', he too would ultimately fall and leave his men leaderless, which caused, we are told, 'their pikes to topple down, to tumble and fall cross one over another'. Exhausted, leaderless and bereft of all hope, the vanquished Imperials duly fled the field, leaving Muschamp's men to hunt them down avidly. 'We had pursuit of them,' the colonel reported, 'even until night parted us.'

Long before nightfall, however, the battle itself was indeed over in all sectors. By 5 p.m., in fact, Cronberg's was the sole remaining cavalry formation available to Tilly, who was wounded himself around that very time. Attacked by a Swedish officer as he tried in vain to reform his scattered troops, the Imperial commander-in-chief was shot in the arm and struck on the head with a sword before Duke Franz Albrecht Sax-Lauenberg shot the Swede with his pistol, and Cronberg appeared with 600 horses, to escort the stricken old man to safety at Halle. But while a wounded Pappenheim also made good his escape, later boasting that he was 'the last man to leave the field', the scale of the defeat could not be minimised. Tilly's veteran army, comprising troops that only one day earlier might well have claimed to be among the best in the world, had been mercilessly crushed. Some 7,600 were dead, 6,000 captured on the field, and another 3,000 taken at Leipzig when Baron Wangler surrendered the city to Gustavus Adolphus the next day. Thousands of others, meanwhile, were either cut down in the pursuit, died later of their wounds, or were murdered by the vengeful Saxon peasantry. Those more fortunate merely deserted: in most cases to the very enemy that had defeated them so comprehensively, taking not only all twenty-six of their cannon but 120 regimental and company standards as shining tokens of victory.

By contrast, the Swedes had lost 2,100 and the Saxons 3,000 in a battle that marked not only the dawn of a new era in the art of warfare, but, arguably, a watershed in European history itself. Hereafter, the *tercio* would become little more than a historical curiosity, as both sides acknowledged the triumph of a tactical revolution and resolved to fight 'Swedish-style', but so too, and far more importantly, would the dream of a definitive military victory unifying both Germany and the continent as a whole under Catholic-Habsburg domination. Indeed, though few may have realised it at the time, the very notion of Christendom itself had been dealt a mortal blow, as Gustavus exulted in the glory of victory. Already enjoying a glittering reputation, the King of Sweden was henceforth routinely represented as the new Joshua, while the English diplomat Sir Thomas Roe even grew his beard and moustache to imitate the Swedish ruler's style. The prisoners from Breitenfeld, Gustavus confidently asserted, would not only fill up his old regiments but form new ones, more formidable than ever. And as the duly vindicated instrument of God's hand, friend and foe alike would have to learn to bend the knee accordingly. For in the wake of his astonishing military success after the rout of the Saxons had placed all in jeopardy, he was now in a position to bully the princes of Germany, ride roughshod over neutrals, and adopt the kind of brusque intransigence and asperity of language towards allies that applied on occasion even to Richelieu. Already Gustavus had secured his kingdom's control of the Baltic for almost a century to come, and now he was planning not only the conquest of Franconia and Bavaria but even, perhaps, the surrender of Vienna itself – though the war that had made his name, as he would never live to learn, still had seventeen long years to run.

10

THE PLENITUDE OF POWER

That's what happens when one is too ambitious,
The Devil silently comes and trips him up,
No tree goes up to heaven,
The axe is already there, to fell it to the ground.

Contemporary soldiers' song.
(Tune: They are sent for storm and strife. Verse 8)

O n the morrow of Breitenfeld, Gustavus Adolphus had all Germany before him. The remnants of Tilly's vanquished army was in flight north-westward, and there was no other force in the vicinity capable of worthwhile resistance. Within logistical limits that had rarely been so generous, he could go where he would, and though he ruled out an advance on Vienna – wisely appreciating that it would achieve nothing without the destruction of the enemy's army – he soon set upon other objectives no less ambitious. The Duke of Saxony, on the one hand, was assigned the task of advancing up the Oder into Silesia with Arnim, while Gustavus himself would move towards the Rhine, rallying potential allies or coming to their aid if necessary, securing good quarters for his army, and driving a wedge between Tilly and his bases in Bavaria. By the third week in September, moreover, the Swedes were indeed safely ensconced in Thuringia, securing the vital communications centre of Erfurt on the 22nd, and deciding thereafter to 'infest' the rich bishoprics of Franconia, which had originally been targeted for the following year's campaign. In early October, the Upper Main was reached, and on 4 October Würzburg surrendered. Three days later, by another daring feat of arms which much impressed his contemporaries, Gustavus's troops stormed the episcopal fortress of Marienberg, making a vast haul of booty, including a rich store of books which was sent home to strengthen the meagre holdings of Uppsala's university.

Not all had been plain sailing, however, since the decision to advance in the direction of the Rhine had left Tilly to recover from his wounds and regroup his forces unmolested, so that by 25 October he had effected a junction with the army of Charles of Lorraine, and was actually endangering Ochsenfurt – only one day's march from Gustavus at Würzburg – at the head of some 40,000 men. But Tilly had orders to take no risks, and his threat to Ochsenfurt had in any case been no more than a feint as he withdrew to the Danube and winter quarters at Ingolstadt in preparation for the defence of Bavaria's northern borders. Pappenheim, too, was safely pre-occupied, holding the Weser, to protect against any westward advance across northern Germany. And with this in mind, Gustavus duly continued his unbroken progress, buoyed by the success of his tactics, the ever-increasing size of his armies and the vast new resources for recruitment and supply, which seemed to make anything possible. On 17 November, he duly entered Frankfurt, unopposed, assured, radiant with victory – a splendid figure in his scarlet 'Polish coat' astride a great Spanish charger. And by 20 December he had not only crossed the Rhine after a characteristically audacious personal reconnaisance, but achieved the surrender of the Spanish garrison in Mainz, where he kept Christmas in the knowledge that Arnim had entered Prague less than five weeks earlier in the company of Matthias von Thurn and a large number of Bohemian exiles, returning them to power eleven years after the Battle of White Mountain.

For the Habsburgs, of course, the entire military and political balance had now been transformed. Defeated in Zeeland and at Breitenfeld, outmaneouvred in northern Italy and with Thuringia, Franconia, Bohemia and the hitherto unspoiled lands of the wealthy ecclesiastical territories of the Rhineland all lost, they could only face the future with grim determination, and take some small consolation from the fact that it had been too late in the season for Gustavus to undertake the siege of Heidelberg as well. Upon hearing the news from Breitenfeld, Emperor Ferdinand had contemplated flight to Graz, or even Italy, while the Roman Catholic princes meeting in Frankfurt-on-Main to debate the Edict of Restitution dispersed in panic when the Bishop of Würzburg arrived as a fugitive in their midst. The myth of Catholic invincibility had, after all, been shaken to the core, and attempts by members of the Imperial Privy Council to explain the current turn of events were hardly reassuring. They did so by reference to 'the hidden hand of God, which was always at work and which undoubtedly had been provoked to inflict such a punishment by serious sins of all types committed by the undisciplined soldiery'. But the very real possibility that the defeats had been inflicted more by the superior generalship of a king at the height of his powers and the harrowing advantages enjoyed by Swedish cannon and Swedish cavalry remained inescapable.

And neither was the broader impact of Gustavus's occupation of the Rhineland lost upon Spain or, for that matter, the Dutch – who were quick to offer subsidies – and Richelieu too, who nevertheless remained in two minds about the situation. For in failing to accompany the Saxons into Bohemia, it was clear that Gustavus was acting wholly independently of French interests. Indeed, French troops had already been rushed into Alsace to protect it from the Swedes, though this in itself had been of advantage, since it established French power in an area previously dominated by Spain, and Spanish confidence had been further dented when the archbishop-electors of both Trier and Cologne turned in despair to Louis XIII rather than Philip IV for protection. Denying the Spaniards right of passage through their territories, they had also offered France the use of the fortresses of Ehrenbreitstein and Philippsburg once they had been cleared of Swedish and Spanish troops. And when Richelieu subsequently saw fit to strengthen French power in the Rhineland by a successful invasion of Lorraine, capturing the fortress of Vic on 31 December, the presence of the Swedish army made it impossible for Madrid to respond in kind.

In the meantime, as Gustavus found himself poised at the edge of the great Franco-Spanish struggle and an undeclared war in which each side still confined itself to acting as an auxiliary to the enemies of the other, the Swedes took stock of their position. As the king bided his time at Frankfurt, receiving embassies from George Rákóczy, the new ruler of Transylvania now that Bethlen Gábor was no more, as well as the Khan of the Crimean Tatars and their overlord, the Turkish sultan, he considered the opening of a second front against the Habsburgs. He also had the comfort of knowing that he now had 80,000 troops garrisoned in Mecklenburg, Hesse, Magdeburg, Franconia, across the Lower Saxon Circle and in the Rhineland, as well as the presence at his side of Axel Oxenstierna, who had at last disengaged himself from his governor-generalship in Prussia and joined him in the new year. Doubtless, his trusted minister's influence would help Gustavus quiet the fears of his councillors in Stockholm who were alarmed that any extension of his grip on the middle Rhine might finally put paid to peace with Spain, whose forces he had already attacked at Oppenheim and Mainz. And doubtless, too, the news that the king was planning to fund the recruitment of 120,000 more troops with contributions from wherever they were garrisoned would have been equally welcome tidings.

But for all the many attractive qualities which won him the loyalty of Oxenstierna and his subjects, and the shrewdness with which he interpreted the actions of others, Gustavus Adolphus remained a source of concern to those of more cautious temperament in the far-off north. As they fully appreciated, 'he had begun the work with God, and with God he would finish it', but his objective of reconstructing the Holy Roman Empire was no less vaguely formulated than his mission to safeguard Protestantism, and his ambitions had meanwhile grown apace. Already, the *assecuratio*, or safe base that he had sought for Sweden in northern Germany, was forgotten as he talked of forming a *corpus evangelicorum* within the Empire, or even of becoming Holy Roman Emperor himself. Yet if the Elbe were no safe boundary for Sweden, could he then contain himself within the Danube and the Rhine? And if success followed success could he also be relied upon to curb the arrogance with allies which was becoming increasingly manifest? None of Richelieu's envoys to Frankfurt could secure guarantees for any members of the Catholic League, save Trier, and the future of Bavaria looked uncertain. At the same time, Bernard of Saxe-Weimar, a soldier of fortune in Gustavus's employ, was rewarded with the bishoprics of Bamberg and Würzburg, while established princes like the king's brother-in-law, George William of Brandenburg, were treated with contempt. Indeed, when Frederick, the former Elector Palatine, for whose sake the Swedish king was ostensibly fighting, arrived at Frankfurt in February 1632 to be welcomed warmly as King of Bohemia, he was treated so obviously as a vassal that he declined his would-be benefactor's help. For over six months, in fact, he would dutifully accompany Gustavus on his marchings up and down Germany before receiving demands from his benefactor for absolute military control of the Palatinate and, worst of all, a further stipulation that he explicitly recognise how his lands were held by the grace of the Swedish crown alone.

No less provocative, however, was John George of Saxony's treatment, who soon found himself repeatedly denounced as a traitor no better than his son-in-law, George of Hesse-Darmstadt, who was casually and repeatedly dismissed as either a Saxon agent or Imperial spy. Perhaps it was small wonder in such circumstances that the duke's wife should have spoken for others too in describing the predicament facing all reluctant and subordinate allies of the Swedish ruler:

> It is hard [she complained] to hand over the best and most valuable places in our land to a foreign king on so new a friendship ... to bring down the emperor's heavy hand and displeasure upon us ... and to make enemies of the neighbours with whom we have lived at peace for countless years.

For, in spite of Gustavus's protestations that he had come as *'protector'* rather than *'proditor'*, i.e. betrayer, of Germany, even France was experiencing concerns.

In August 1630, Père Joseph had justified the expediency of an alliance with Sweden both accurately and succinctly:

> We must make use of these things [i.e. negotiations] as one uses poisons, which serve as an antidote if taken in small doses, but are fatal in excess.

But by the beginning of 1632, the cardinal too was beginning to wonder whether he had inadvertently swallowed too large a measure of Swedish goodwill, as the Treaty of Bärwalde signed in such hope only a year earlier seemed merely to have emancipated Gustavus from any need to consider his French ally at all. At Bärwalde, of course, Gustavus had agreed to respect Bavarian neutrality for so long as Duke Maximilian's behaviour complied with what might be expected from a neutral. Yet the events of the last twelve months had effectively disposed of any such fantasies, after Bavarian money, Bavarian troops and Bavaria's general had helped fight – and lose – the Battle of Breitenfeld. By March 1632, indeed, all thought of Bavarian neutrality was, in Oxenstierna's words, 'sunk', after an incriminating letter from Maximilian to the emperor was successfully intercepted, leaving Sweden's alliance with France still technically intact but drained of all substance, and French hopes of an independent 'third party' within the Empire finally dashed.

Plainly, with his entire German policy reduced to a fiasco, it was time for Richelieu to plan anew, and the same was no less true for the movers and shakers of policy in Madrid and Vienna. All the strategic considerations that had dominated Spain's policies for decades had, on the one hand, been rendered irrelevant by the destruction of her lines of communication to the Netherlands. But in this moment of crisis, Isabella, regent of the southern Netherlands, had detected one crumb of comfort. The Swedish occupation of the Rhineland, she wisely predicted, was sure to drive Maximilian of Bavaria into closer alliance with the emperor. What even she had not foreseen, however, was that Sweden's forward march would inject new life into another of Ferdinand's 'friendships'. For, after a judicious Imperial withdrawal at Arnim's advance upon Prague, none other than Albrecht Wenzel Eusebius von Wallenstein had been called to a meeting with Eggenberg only two days later, and within a month was once again the emperor's general on what appear to have been his own terms, though after sixteen months in the wilderness, he had nevertheless insisted that his appointment should last for only three months and for the specific purpose of reorganising the army over the winter.

From the very outset, indeed, he had been remarkably reluctant to return, even after the emperor had personally summoned him to Vienna in May, so that the situation could be discussed in person. As one English source, the *Swedish Intelligencer*, commented at the time, there was apparently:

> … a strange mixture of spirit in this Wallenstein; that being supposed as haughty and ambitious of Command as any man in the world; yet was he so farr foorth master of the greatness of his own desires, as that he could with as much moderation now refuse the Generalship as he had before resigned it: he would not have authority but with freedome, and his own Conditions.

Yet Wallenstein's hesitancy was born neither from petulance nor wounded pride. On the contrary, his health remained fragile, and while the military situation had changed out of all recognition for Emperor Ferdinand, the same political hostility persisted among those Catholic electors, as yet unaffected by the war. Ferdinand, too, was as penniless as ever, and Wallenstein's own resources close to breaking point after de Witte's bankruptcy. Though still loyal to the Imperial cause, the general seems to have felt, therefore, that, until Breitenfeld at least, Tilly was best placed to deal with the Swedish advance. Hitherto undefeated and at the head of a large, battle-hardened army, the old Belgian had in fact appeared a safe bet, but his defeat left Wallenstein with little personal choice, as most of Mecklenburg fell to the Swedes, further reducing his income, and the Saxon invasion of Bohemia brought with it attacks upon his Friedland properties by returning exiles.

For the generalissimo, therefore, the resumption of command was in many respects as much a return to the yoke as welcome return to the fold. Since his dismissal, he had lived in royal style upon his immense Bohemian estates, sometimes at his palace at Gitschin, but more usually in a vastly more sumptuous palace in Prague, specially designed for him by Italian architects. And as he set out from Znaim, about 50 miles north of Vienna, in December for his fateful meeting with Eggenberg, it was doubtless with heavy heart, while Tilly's relieved response to his discharge from Imperial command spoke, by contrast, for itself. When he had been handed what proved to be a poison chalice, there had been no alternative contender, and now the same was true for the very man whom he had replaced. The prospect of a limited term of service, furthermore, was never realistic, and by February Eggenberg was already telling Wallenstein plaintively that 'should Your Grace have decided irrevocably to resign after these three months it would be the death of me, as in that case I can clearly envisage our total ruin.' Within only six weeks, therefore, the general had duly travelled to Göllersdorf where the substance of his permanent appointment was settled in a relatively short time – complete with a guarantee of his right to Mecklenburg and the usual hollow assurances of regular and reliable payments, and Imperial support in the future. He was to hold his former powers, it seems, *in absolutissima forma*, and cover his costs in part from taxation in the Habsburg hereditary lands. But whether the second honeymoon would last, and whether he could indeed deliver victory with an army of low morale, which had been abruptly dismembered after his dismissal and some of whose units had only recently straggled back from the ultimately useless campaign in Italy, was far from certain. Whether he could prevail, moreover, against a living legend in the acutely limited time available to him made his prospects more doubtful still. For Gustavus would be in the field once more within the year at the head of a large, successful and buoyant army that had already swept all before it.

Nevertheless, by the end of April 1632 Wallenstein had indeed brought his troops up to about 65,000 in Friedland, as he chose to march into Bohemia with only half that number and Saxon resistance crumbled before him. Upon his approach to Prague, Arnim had evacuated the city and withdrawn in good order to Saxony, though there was no attempt to pursue him, and instead Wallenstein's army marched west to a rendezvous on 1 July with Maximilian, who now made every effort to court the man he loathed and distrusted with professions of personal friendship and declarations of undying loyalty to the Imperial cause, notwithstanding the role he had played at Regensburg or in earlier moves against the general, let alone his flirtations with Richelieu and attempts to desert the emperor by taking refuge in French-protected neutrality. Now, indeed, Maximilian studiously addressed Wallenstein as 'Duke of Mecklenburg' and not only loaned him 300,000 florins for provisions but earnestly listened to his military advice. And well he might. For in the preceding weeks the Bavarian army of twenty light-calibre guns and 22,000 men – most of whom were partially trained recruits and militia – had proved no match for the 38,000 troops and seventy-two guns of an invading Swedish army, which, at that very moment, was mercilessly pillaging his beloved duchy.

Perversely enough, it had been Maximilian and Tilly – restored to his former Catholic League command – who had not only opened hostilities in southern Germany in 1632 but enjoyed an early success at Bamberg on the evening of 9 March when Marshal Horn was taken by surprise. Breaking in at the Heiligengrab convent where a certain Sister Junius witnessed a Croat 'cut down a Swede on our field ... splitting his head from back to front leaving an ear hanging down', the struggle continued until midnight, at which point the Swedish rearguard abandoned the town. In the meantime, Tilly had placed two heavy guns in a beer garden, which killed Count Solms-Laubach, a veteran of White Mountain, with their first shot, before a second missile 'passed through a house and through two walls of the next where a child was sleeping in its crib, doing no damage beyond depositing some dust on the infant.' Thereafter in the struggle that followed Horn lost a third of his army, largely through surrender and desertion, before retiring to Schweinfurt.

But Tilly, at 73, was now a shadow of his former self, and proved unable to exploit his victory. Indeed, according to one eyewitness at the Bavarian head-quarters, Maximilian's commander-in-chief was not only 'wholly perplexed and cast down' but 'wholly irresolute in council'. He 'knows not how to save himself,' the description continues, 'abandons one proposal after another, decides nothing, sees only great difficulties and dangers – but has no idea how to over-come them.' And his mistaken decision to make a stand against Gustavus along the line of the River Lech near Ingolstadt was proof of the pudding. For while the position was a strong one, made stronger by the arrival from Bohemia of 5,000 reinforcements sent by Wallenstein, Tilly's foe was dangerously impetu-ous, constructing a bridge of boats, under cover of a smokescreen and artillery barrage, before forcing the river and storming the cliffs on the other side. In the process, Tilly was fatally wounded when his thigh was shattered by a 3-pounder almost immediately after his deputy, Aldringen, had been temporarily blinded by a glancing strike to the head from a falconet ball. And by sundown, around one hour later, the army's new commander, Duke Maximilian himself, was sum-moning his colonels to a hastily convened council of war on the battlefield, well aware that by conceding the Lech line, he would expose all Bavaria to destruc-tion. Yet he was outgunned, with the Swedes dug in at their bridgehead and both his flanks were threatened with enveloping cavalry. Reluctantly therefore, but wisely nonetheless, the duke directed his army to retire, sacrificing his duchy, but saving his troops in the process.

So well managed was the retreat, in fact, that the Swedes had not known of its occurrence until, at dawn on the 16th, they discovered that the main redoubt was empty. 'Had I been the Bavarian,' Gustavus declared, 'I would not have abandoned these works even if the ball had carried off my chin as well as my beard.' But it was not so much the loss of his beard as the imminent destruction of his army that had induced Maximilian to withdraw, and in the process he had extricated his troops without loss of man or gun. The duke's decision to regroup at Regensburg rather than attempt a defence of Munich was also a prudent one. For although Regensburg was not his own, without it there was no possibility of communication with Wallenstein in Bohemia. As such, his only alternative was to rescue his treasury and state papers from Munich before Gustavus entered it in triumph on 17 May – with the former Elector Palatine, Frederick V, at his side. Together they reviewed their troops, played tennis on the ducal courts, surveyed the ducal art collection, and plundered it as thoroughly as the Bavarians had plundered Heidelberg ten years earlier. Some 163,000 thalers were exacted and 119 artillery pieces that had been buried on Maximilian's orders – many of them formerly belonging to Frederick and his allies – were also dug up during Gustavus's ten-day stay. And as Catholic peasants prepared for a bitter guerrilla war against Swedish plundering that soon spread into Swabia, few were reassured by the king's decision to grit his teeth and attend a Catholic Mass.

'Your Grace would no longer recognise poor Bavaria,' Maximilian wrote soon afterwards to his brother, Ferdinand of Cologne; 'such cruelty has been unheard of in this war.' And it would be three full years before the duke could return to his capital. But while the duchy lay in ashes and word arrived in June that the Dutch had captured Venlo, Roermond, Straelen and Sittard in rapid succession, forcing the recall of a Spanish army defending the Palatinate, all was still not lost. Indeed, even the news that the Dutch had invested the great fortress of Maastricht, commanding all communications between Brussels and Pappenheim's force in Westphalia, could not obscure the all-important fact that Gustavus was unable to move down the Danube to Vienna while Wallenstein held Bohemia. In April 1631, just after the Swedes took Frankfurt-on-Oder, the Imperial councillor Questenberg was in despair: 'We cry "Help, Help," but there is nobody there!' By December, moreover, even the papacy was responding with threats and pleas of hardship when asked by the emperor for support:

> If peace is made with the Protestants [declared Maffeo Barberini, papal secretary of state] … His Holiness will withdraw his aid, the more so because, since the eruption of Mount Vesuvius, the collection of tithes has become more difficult.

But still there was hope with Wallenstein, as the King of Sweden made for Nuremberg, and the freshly-resurrected generalissimo set out to meet him.

Immediately after his victory at the Lech, Gustavus had successfully invaded Augsburg. But the last act of the dying Tilly had been to secure the fortresses of Ingolstadt and Regensburg, on the assumption that while these were retained, the Swedes could never hold Bavaria. On 27 April, in fact, Bavarian troops had overawed Regensburg's hostile citizens, and when Gustavus arrived at Ingolstadt two days later he found it impregnable. Even after the capture of Munich, moreover, the Swedish king remained concerned about the possibility of Saxony's defection to Wallenstein after his capture of Prague. So when Gustavus began digging in at Nuremberg on 28 June, to protect a prominent Protestant city that he could not afford to lose, it was not a moment too soon. For only ten days later Wallenstein took up a heavily fortified position – complete with

27,661 infantry, 12,118 cavalry, 1,000 dragoons and between 70 and 80 cannon – at Zirndorf, close to the medieval castle of Alte Veste. Lying just outside Nuremberg, the castle was an important priority for Gustavus, and since Swedish fortifications at Nuremberg itself deterred Wallenstein from direct attack, it also became a key objective for him likewise. Anxious to avoid Tilly's mistake at Werben, he would opt to follow a 'stomach strategy', avoiding a direct attack on Swedish entrenchments, while making his own camp – which stretched to a circumference of some 16km – effectively impregnable, after the felling of 13,000 trees and movement of some 64,000 cubic metres of earth.

In the meantime, though staging several unsuccessful assaults on Alte Veste, the Swedes found themselves effectively in deadlock, unable to abandon Nuremberg, but with only 18,000 troops and insurmountable supply problems as the city's 40,000 inhabitants were joined by 100,000 refugees. In fact 6,000 peasants had been conscripted to construct a huge ditch around the city and emplace 300 cannon from the city's arsenal. But all Gustavus could do now was stage raids and skirmishes, as he awaited the arrival of reinforcements, and the Imperials proceeded to burn all the mills outside his entrenchments, rapidly forcing his men onto half rations and spreading hunger throughout the locality. 'For three months we were besieged by our enemies; for four months we were eaten out by our friends,' lamented the Nuremberg patrician, Lukas Behaim, as he reflected ruefully on the year 1632. And the situation, it seems, was soon little better for Wallenstein as hotter weather arrived in August and the concentration of his troops with around 50,000 camp followers produced at least four tonnes of human excrement daily, in addition to the waste from cavalry and baggage horses. By mid-August, indeed, his army was no longer fully operational after the Swedes intercepted a supply convoy and found themselves free to receive a relief force from Oxenstierna comprising 24,000 men and 3,000 supply wagons.

Even now, however, the balance was not decisively tipped. For, at the end of the month, the Duke of Saxony saw fit to stir matters by invading Silesia and thereby precipitate an invasion of the south-western tip of his own duchy. With Wallenstein's own force at Zirndorf seriously compromised by disease and further depleted by the detachment of 10,000 men under Henrik Holk for the subjugation of Saxony, Gustavus was nevertheless forced to withdraw north-westwards from Nuremberg on 15 September, after a final assault on Zirndorf over three days cost him 1,000 dead and another 1,400 wounded. After the arrival of Oxenstierna's reinforcements on 27 August he had found himself, ironically enough, with the largest army he ever commanded – almost, indeed, an *embarras des richesses*, since the vast host, with its 175 guns, proved more awkward and unresponsive than the 20,000 or so men that had been his usual preference. But the high ground of Zirndorf and the strongpoint of Alte Veste, not to mention the role of abatis – the seventeenth-century equivalent of barbed wire made by felling and trimming trees to leave only sharpened branches pointing toward the enemy – had in any case proved too much even for him. And as Gustavus retired, losing 11,000 demoralised men to desertion in the process, the Imperials were already consuming Saxony, soon occupying Meissen and thereafter dispatching Croats in the direction of Dresden, with the message that John George would no longer need candles for his banquets, since the flames from burning Saxon villages would now be shedding light enough. On 1 November Leipzig itself fell, resulting in the court martial of its commandant by the furious duke, who then made the convicted man's widow pay for the trial.

From the perspective of Sweden's king, however, decisive action rather than spiteful recrimination remained the order of the day, since Wallenstein had not only vanquished his main ally, but was now endangering communications with his crucial Baltic bridgehead. Against Oxenstierna's explicit advice, therefore, Gustavus Adolphus raced north, covering 650km in seventeen days at the cost of 4,000 horses, to exploit what would amount to the most serious error of his enemy's professional career. For after holding his army at battle stations for two weeks, on 14 November Wallenstein carelessly concluded that the current campaign was over and gave orders for his troops to disperse into winter quarters. The protracted fighting at Nuremberg had convinced him, it seems, that the Swedish army was 'totally ruined', and upon the capture of Leipzig, he had duly declared that 'if the elector [of Saxony] is lost, the king [of Sweden] must be lost too'. Such was Wallenstein's confidence, indeed, that Gustavus Adolphus had already arrived in nearby Naumburg when Pappenheim was allowed to depart for Halle, leaving the Imperial general with only 19,000 troops at his disposal – almost precisely the same number as the Swedes. He had been duped, it seems, by Gustavus's ploy to fortify his own camp, which, as the Swedish correspondent Hallenus observed, 'was merely contrived to make the enemy feel secure in his quarters'. And now that self-same enemy would feel the full weight of his error.

On 7 November, as the concentration of Protestant forces reached completion at Erfurt, Gustavus had found a little time for his wife, though it was hardly an intimate moment. For as he dined with her in his chambers in the company of Duke Ernst of Weimar, there were constant interruptions from mail and intelligence reports. When he bade her farewell next morning, moreover, his army was already at full march, and the pace was such that the parting was hurried. But before the day was out, an advance party of about 100 men under Oberst Brandenstein had found the main bridge over the Saale poorly guarded and gone on to capture Naumburg only two hours before two Imperial regiments arrived too late to make a difference. And two days later, as Gustavus arrived with his main force, the response was rapturous – so rapturous, in fact, that it left him curiously uneasy, since the tightly packed crowds jostled to touch his clothes with the kind of ardour that bordered on religious enthusiasm. 'Everyone venerates me so, and treats me as some sort of God,' he confided to Dr Jacob Fabricius, his chaplain, before adding that 'the Lord will soon punish me for this.'

For the time being, however, there appeared no hint of either mishap or even inconvenience, let alone divine retribution, as Wallenstein proceeded to disperse his army, and news arrived of the ongoing Protestant push to the south, threatening the Archbishop of Cologne. Already, on 7 November, Horn had captured the key fortress of Benfeld south of Strasbourg, effectively closing the Rhine to the Spanish, and though Gustavus had initially found Wallenstein's army drawn up in full battle order at Weissenfels, complete with Pappenheim's corps, it was now melting before his eyes. So awesome had its initial appearance been, that the king was in two minds whether to contemplate battle at all. The Imperial cavalry particularly, which was superior to the Swedish both in numbers and quality, had troubled him. But the unseasonably cold nights and insufficient room for his troops in and around Weissenfels had finally persuaded Wallenstein to withdraw, since the road from Weissenfels to Naumburg was, in any case, narrow and hilly, making it hazardous to attack in battle order. And with this in mind, an Imperial staff conference at the *Zum Schützen* inn on the afternoon of 13 November accordingly concluded that there was no scope for a pre-emptive strike by either side.

By midnight on 15/16 November, however, Pappenheim was being awoken from his slumbers to receive an urgent summons to return with all haste, and only two hours later he was on his way with three cavalry regiments to another historic engagement – at Lützen, site of Wallenstein's new headquarters. The generalissimo's orders which still exist – soaked in Pappenheim's blood – left no doubt about the scale of his predicament:

> The enemy is marching towards us. Your honour shall drop everything, and route himself hereto with all troops and guns, to be with us early in the morning ... [The enemy] is already at the pass where yesterday the road was bad.

Nor was Wallenstein's anxiety in any way unfounded. For at 4 a.m. that morning, some three hours before dawn, the Swedish army had slinked into the wintry gloom in full battle order, carrying only essential supplies in no more than 100 wagons. Let down by Arnim who had refused to join him, Gustavus had nevertheless decided to make his move, and by late afternoon, after heavy skirmishing at the crossing-point of the Rippach stream, which had been pointed out by a local shepherd named Assmussen, the Swedes were finally tramping over open country towards Lützen itself. Already two enemy standards had been taken, and neither had the Imperial cause been helped by the late arrival of the Croats, whose commander, Count Isolano, had been delayed, 'because of his lust for Venus rather than Mars' as one chronicler put it, at the *Gasthof zum Rippach* inn.

One of the captured Croatian standards – painted on one side with the Imperial eagle and on the other with a cannonball marked 'Fortune' – had been seen by some as a good omen. But Gustavus, we are told, 'tooke no great content at it', and darkness was already falling, along with a heavy mist, when he reluctantly decided to make camp and abandon the hope of joining battle before the following morning. 'If only we had three more hours of daylight,' the king lamented to his officers. And as he surveyed the Imperial watch fires that could be clearly discerned from the Swedish lines, he knew full well the 'great effect' that his army might have had upon a disorganised enemy deprived of an extra night's breathing space. For Wallenstein, as General Holk observed, had determined 'not to retreat one foot', knowing that Pappenheim was on his way. With the armies separated by what Colonel Fleetwood, an officer serving with the Swedes, considered 'about an English myle', and Holk estimated as no more than four cannon shots, the waiting game would have to be played out in full, though neither side had much scope for reflection, as the Imperial forces were rearranged by candlelight in response to Wallenstein's signal, and the Swedes, having advanced without tents, slept in the open, 'every Regiment lying downe, in the same order they marched, with their armes by them'.

Yet with no tents to pack and because they had camped in battle order, the Swedes should at least have enjoyed the advantage of being able to march within minutes next morning, were it not for a dense fog that had descended during the night – 'as if foredooming how black a day it would be'. And since a pre-dawn start was consequently rendered impractical, the reveille seems to have been sounded only shortly before first light, about 7.30 a.m., followed by the usual sullen stirrings to wakefulness – made all the more baleful by the imminence of battle – and a morning service intended to alleviate the understandable misgivings of all present. In the gloomy time remaining before fighting commenced, Gustavus saw fit to deliver two rousing speeches of exhortation: the first to his Swedes and Finns, in which he promised his 'true valiant brethren' the 'mercy of God and honour before the world', while warning them, too, that, if defeated, 'your bones shall never come in Sweden again'; the second to his German troops – a brief address, mincing no words, which ran as follows:

You true and worthy Deutsch brethren, Officers and common soldiers! I exhort you all, and carry yourselves manfully and fight truely with me. Runne not away and I shall hazard my body and bloud with you for your best. If you stande with me, so I hope in God to obtaine victory, the profit whereof will redownd to you and your successors. And if otherwise you doe, so are you and your liberties lost.

Thereafter, with the morning mist beginning to lift, the king called his men to advance soon after 8 a.m. Gazing to heaven, he cried at the top of his voice: 'Jesus, Jesus, Jesus! Help me this day to fight for the glory of thy holy name!' And with that the march began – to the small town of Lützen, consisting of little more than a small moated castle and 300 primitively fashioned houses which had been constructed, about 20km south-west of Leipzig, around a toll station on the Frankfurt-Leipzig *Landstrasse*.

There, too, things were stirring, as those soldiers who could be spared from entrenchment work heard Mass and confessed their sins. Unlike his opponent, it was not Wallenstein's custom to deliver inspirational speeches – 'his stern countenance,' as Richelieu put it, 'being enough to remind his men of the punishments they might endure or the rich rewards awaiting them if they served well.' But he had focussed his thoughts with typical thoroughness and drawn up his battle line in a manner ideally suited for defence: deep, compact and allowing for transfer between units. According to Holk, the front line was of '5,000 on foot in five brigades; the middle of two brigades each of 1,000 and six companies of horse intermixed 2 by 2', while last, standing 'outcommanded' (i.e. made up of musketeers serving without pikemen) were arranged five companies of 500 men on foot, along with two squadrons of twelve companies of horse. Wallenstein, moreover, would be actively involved throughout. For contrary to Swedish propaganda, which suggested that he was confined to a litter as a result of his gout, the general was beside his horse on the left of the battlefield from the outset and ready to mount from the very moment that the Swedes engaged around 11 a.m., deployed in two lines, with cavalry on the flanks stiffened by detachments of musketeers.

As battle commenced, the best of Gustavus's infantry were in the first line, while the king himself commanded most of the Swedish and Finnish horse on the right, and Bernard of Saxe-Weimar led the 3,000 mainly German troopers on the left. Nor was it long before the Croats scattered at their advance, leaving Holk's musketeers to harry the attackers from the castle and the mud-walls of the gardens surrounding the town, before Wallenstein fired the town itself in fear of losing it and becoming outflanked. With characteristic efficiency, orders were issued that the townsfolk be locked in the castle cellars to prevent them from extinguishing the fires consuming their dwellings, and as a gentle breeze fanned the flames and blew straight into the advancing Swedes – causing, as their field-chancellery diary relates, 'such a thick fog that one could barely see another at four paces' – news arrived 'at about 12' that Pappenheim had arrived on the Imperial left wing, just as it was threatening to disintegrate. Already the proud bearer, it was said, of 100 battle scars, and plainly never one to worry about his personal safety, he would charge at once, at Wallenstein's command, 'with great fury', in an effort to restore order.

But the results did not match the bravado. For as Pappenheim's personal trumpeter, the 22-year-old Conrad Ehringer later related:

The [Count's] lifeguard company took great damage, and the Count himself was hit by a falconet round and three musket balls.

He had been laid low, in fact, by a contingent of the outcommanded musketeers and regimental guns accompanying Torsten Stålhandske's cavalry, and as Swedish horsemen milled about the stricken field marshal, Ehringer, his adjutant, finally rushed in to carry his master away. Seeing a regiment fleeing close by, Pappenheim still had sufficient resources to ask who they were, though upon learning that they were one of his own, he broke down tearfully, trying to wrench himself up to rejoin the fight, slapping his hands in frustration and shouting at them: 'Ach my brothers, may God have mercy on you! Will not one of you still fight loyally for the Emperor?' Still carrying Wallenstein's summons to the battlefield, he died in his trumpeter's arms before the coach carrying him to Leipzig had arrived at its destination.

Less than one hour later, however, the fighting at Lützen had claimed an even more illustrious victim, whose death altogether eclipsed Pappenheim's own. For as the battle disintegrated, amid the smoke and mayhem, into a series of isolated attacks by individual units, Gustavus Adolphus himself appears to have become lost as he rode out to rally his beleaguered infantry. 'What is the use of a king in a box?' he had once asked when urged to consider his personal safety on the field of battle. 'A general who keeps himself out of danger,' as he said on another occasion, 'can gain neither victories nor laurels.' But, as he now found out, a general of such sentiments is unlikely to stay a general for long. Nor is he likely, ultimately, to avoid the most constraining box of all. Already he was short of commanders. Stålhandske, with his Finns, was up to a kilometre away; Fredrick Stenbock, colonel of the Smålanders, with whom Gustavus now rode, had been shot in the foot; while the commander of the Östgöta cavalry, Lennart Nilsson

Bååt, had been fatally wounded by a bullet to the head. And in consequence, the king found himself compelled, both by circumstance and personal inclination, to lead the Smålanders forward through dense smoke into the havoc being wrought by the Imperial cavalry of Counts Johann Götz and Octavio Piccolomini.

Suddenly struck by a bullet, which also grazed the neck of his horse, Streiff, Gustavus was subsequently forced, however, to fall back with his entourage of six to eight persons – his left arm broken 'completely in two', just above the left elbow. Whereupon Piccolomini's horse cut clean through the Smålanders, and sent them, scurrying back for cover. Separated from his men, weakened and in shock from a grievous loss of blood, the king called to be taken out of the action and was being led back to the Swedish lines by the royal stablemaster, Von der Schulenberg, who had taken his reins, when a party of Götz's cuirassiers suddenly appeared from the mist to block his passage. One of them, moreover, rendered distinctive by his burnished steel armour and identified by some as Lieutenant Moritz von Falkenburg – a Catholic relation of the defender of Magdeburg – recognised Gustavus and exclaimed 'Here's the right bird!' before firing a pistol into his victim's back at such close quarters to Franz Albrecht of Lauenberg, who was accompanying the king, that the flash burned his face. Unable to support the wounded monarch in his saddle – a failure for which he was never forgiven – Franz Albrecht subsequently allowed him to slump to the ground, as the enemy closed in for the kill.

Even now, however, the drama was not quite done. First, Gustavus's body-guard, Anders Jönsson, tried to protect him before being cut down, and then the 18-year-old page Augustus Leubfeling turned to offer the king his own horse, only to be fatally wounded, at which point Gustavus took several rapier thrusts to his body. Unable to wear metal armour because of the pain resulting from the musket wound to the neck that he had received earlier in Poland, the king relied entirely for protection upon an elk-skin buffcoat made for him by an Englishman, which still attests to the ferocity of the deadly sword thrusts today, though the killing wound was inflicted by a pistol shot to the temple, delivered, it seems, in response to the approach of a body of Swedish horse. Before that time, an Imperial cuirassier had asked Gustavus his name. 'I was the King of Sweden,' he is said to have replied. But the civilities were short-lived, and when one of Piccolomini's men, a certain Innocentius Bucela, arrived on the scene shortly afterwards, the king's body, we are told, was 'still quivering' before being subjected to its ultimate indignity. For Piccolomini's soldiers purloined the famous buffcoat – which was handed back by the Austrian government after the First World War in gratitude for the work of the Swedish Red Cross – while Holk's trumpeter took one of the king's spurs, and another soldier pocketed the royal signet ring. Piccolomini himself, indeed, was only prevented from taking the actual corpse as a trophy by the appearance of another troop of Swedish horse, which forced him to retire and enable its retrieval.

Elsewhere, however, in that confused hour that saw the deaths of both Gustavus and Pappenheim, other nightmarish scenes were also unfolding, as the Swedes continued to press the attack, undeterred by rumours of their leader's death and further encouraged by the singing of psalms, organised by Fabricius, the royal chaplain. 'Sustain us by Thy mighty Word,' the Swedes sang, as Bernard of Saxe-Weimar, upon whom command had now fallen, determined to win the day. But the price was heavy. The famous Swedish Yellow Brigade, on the one hand, had been ordered 'to go boldly at the enemy and not take heed of their numbers, nor to fire any volleys until the Imperial musketeers had fired themselves.' But while the deadly 'Swedish salvo', fired at five to ten paces, had indeed worked to devastating effect on previous occasions, the attackers were presently faced with not one, but three Imperial brigades, all veterans, and as the Swedes continued their resolute approach, the Imperial quartermaster-general, Guilio Diodati, watched their slaughter in amazement:

> A great body with yellow casacks [coats] came up resolutely in formation and with pikes covering their musketeers. When attacked by our infantry, the body was completely overthrown, and it was a wonder to see in a moment the body reduced to a mound of corpses.

Count Brahe of Visingsborg was fatally wounded in the thigh, just above the knee, while the Scotsman Henry Lindsay of Bainshow 'was hurt with cannon, and musket twice', to be left lying for a while 'almost dead in the field'.

Moreover, the destruction of the other great infantry regiment of the Swedish army, the Blue Brigade, appears to have involved even greater slaughter still, at the hands of one of Tilly's oldest Walloon regiments, Comargo's, formed in 1619. Theodor Comargo himself had already been shot four times when his senior surviving officer, Hans von Münchhausen, laid a trap for the Swedes, who, as they advanced 'all clumped together', suddenly found themselves charged on both flanks at once, leaving 'over 2,000 enemy dead on the place'. Such, indeed, was the carnage that, of the fifteen enemy standards later presented to Wallenstein, ten were actually taken by Comargo's regiment alone – though for one Scotsman named Watts, the heroism of the Yellow and Blue Brigades, abided:

> These 2 brigades were the flower of the Army: old souldiers of 7 or 8 yeeres service (the most of them) and whom the king had there placed, for that he

most relied on them … their dead bodies now covered the same ground, which living they had defended. These were old beaten soldiers, indeed, but it was so long since they had beene last beaten, that they had by this time forgotten how to runne away.

And neither had their sacrifice been entirely in vain. For rather than pursue the enemy, the Imperials followed Wallenstein's orders merely to hold their ground. Smoke, after all, shrouded the battlefield, and few officers could see beyond their neighbouring formations. Furthermore, the Imperial centre had also taken heavy casualties and was under fire from the Swedish main battery. As such, caution seemed sensible, particularly since Pappenheim, unlike Gustavus who had disappeared in thick smoke, had fallen in full view of his regiments, causing morale to waver appreciably. When Bernard's troops threatened to turn the Imperial right, therefore, Hofkirchen refused a direct personal order from Wallenstein to attack, while several companies of Bönninghausen's regiment not only left the field along with their officers and standards, but, at around 2 p.m., encountered Pappenheim's infantry on the march from Halle, and told them that the battle was lost. Indeed, by that time scant few troops remained on the Imperial left to withstand any prospective attack from Stålhandske.

Notwithstanding the death of Gustavus, then, and the grievous Swedish losses in the centre, both sides were nearing exhaustion as the afternoon wore on. Confusion and rumour spread, and at one point members of the Swedish field chancellery, along with civilian observers and cavalry from the rear squadrons also began to stream back to Naumburg. The royal chaplain Fabricius, in fact, came across Swedish musketeers, horsemen and wounded officers making for the rear through the ever-thickening smog, and two fleeing members of the field chancellery who cried out to him: '*Fugiendum est*' ('It's a rout'). Replying also in Latin, he urged them to stand, 'otherwise by our flight we will provoke everyone to run'. And the Scotsman Watts witnessed similar scenes. 'The harder we shouted,' recalled George Fleetwood, a volunteer who had raised an English mercenary regiment originally stationed in Polish Prussia, 'the faster they began to run away, saying that the enemy was just behind them.' Yet a Croatian outflanking attack, involving at least 1,000 horses, and perhaps twice that, was nevertheless beaten back, while one of Germany's most experienced officers, Baron Dodo Knyphausen, kept a firm hand on the Swedish reserve line, convincing his troops that 'the king is only wounded' and allowing the fugitives from the front line to pass through the intervals in the second line to rally behind them.

By about 3 p.m., therefore, a relative calm of sorts had begun to descend on certain sectors of the battlefield as the two sides fell off from one another 'like two Duellers leaning on their swords to take breath againe,' as Watts put it. The artillery batteries continued to pound, but the musket salvoes were mostly gone and certain sectors of the battlefield even apparently abandoned. According to the *Spanish Relation*, indeed, many of Wallenstein's men believed the battle had been won, since so much of the Swedish line had disappeared from view, though the general himself was more cautious, sending forward his brother-in-law Adam Trčka and Piccolomini to 'take more exact notice of what was rumour'd'. And the caution was justified. For in the half-hour lull pertaining, Knyphausen had sensibly drawn the reserve lines out of artillery range, to reorder near their late-morning starting positions, while Bernard of Saxe-Weimar had successfully rallied his troops for a final do-or-die assault – seeing fit, in the process, to encourage a reluctant lieutenant-colonel of the Smålanders by a blow across the body with the flat of his sword.

The dismay of the troops at the summons to further sacrifice may well be imagined, of course, but their bravery was unbending, and Watts' account captures it poignantly:

When the word was given for a new Charge: 'alas Camarade' (said the poore souldiers one to another) 'must we fall on againe!' 'Come sayes tother' (embracing him) 'Courage; if we must, lets doe it bravely, and make a day of it'.

So when Trčka and Piccolomini returned, the news they bore was ominous, for in spite of the crushing toll on its troops' resources, 'the enemy in full Battell-ray was marching towards in as good order as the first'. Nor was the final Swedish assault to prove any less ferocious than what had gone before, as the volume of fire from their main field battery increased, and the musketeers now approached to barely five paces from the enemy before giving fire. No quarter was given or asked for when the fighting came to push of pike and skull-rending crunch of musket butt. No let-up of any kind occurred amid the terrific smoke and din. 'A fatal earnestness was seen on both sides,' observed a Saxon liaison officer by the name of Berlepsch.

Before long, Trčka had the heel torn from his boot by a cannonball, while Piccolomini, abuzz with ardour for the fray, was everywhere, now on his sixth horse, his clothing thick with blood from no less than five musket wounds. But his wounds were not unique, since nearly every senior officer among the Imperials was hit in one shape or fashion. Freiherr Rudolf von Colleredo, overall commander of the infantry, was grazed in the arm and head by musket balls, while Wallenstein's relative, Oberst Berthold von Waldstein, was wounded while 'standing with incredible heartiness at the head of his squadron, until eventually a musket ball hit him in the thigh'. Later his injury would fester and kill him – an even harsher fate, arguably, than that of another brigade commander, Friedrich Breuner, who was hit full in the face and killed outright. Even the generalissimo himself did not escape entirely, since a musket ball bruised his left leg without penetrating the skin, while in another incident a Hessian *rittmeister*, Bodo von Bodenhausen, managed to ride within four paces of him before loosing a pistol shot, which somehow missed.

Yet, for all the heroism and horror, by 5 p.m., with the November darkness fallen, the cannon fire and musket salvoes audible at one point from 20km away, had finally petered out entirely, leaving an eerie stillness over the field. Under pressure of the onslaught and at a cost of some 3,000 dead and wounded, including many officers, Wallenstein had finally retreated, abandoning his artillery, before reassembling only 'one half English mile away'. This time, however, there would be no counter-attack as he contemplated his return to Bohemia – with thirty-six Swedish standards and the knowledge that his enemies had lost double the amount of men, including, of course, their leader. Whether he had actually won, as he claimed, remains as debatable today as it was then. In many respects he had demonstrated far superior generalship, and if his objective had been the nullification of the Swedish threat, he had certainly gone some good way to achieving it, since from this time forward, though the war continued with all its familiar intensity, Oxenstierna's main priority was to extricate his country under the best possible terms.

But the bitterness with which Wallenstein punished the Imperial units that had fled in battle – executing seventeen men, including twelve officers, depriving Götz of his regiment, dishonourably discharging a further seven officers and placing prices on the heads of forty others in a way that appalled fellow commanders like Holk and Piccolomini – said more than anything, perhaps, about the battle's most telling outcome of all. For in Prague a joke was soon circulating that the so-called 'Blood Tribunal' had executed its victims for no more than fleeing 'just like the generalissimo'. Of those executed – a surprising number of whom refused the offices of a priest – most sympathy fell to Count Hillmair Staitz von Wobersnau, a handsome 19- or 20-year-old 'of great worth and of the highest blood'. He was originally intended to be executed fourth, but purposely kept back to the end in the hope that Wallenstein might listen to pleas for clemency, though by the time he finally mounted the scaffold, which was already slippery with blood, even the pleas of Piccolomini had been unavailing. 'I am not afraid to die, nor had I been so on the battlefield,' he declared amid the noise of the drum roll. 'I simply followed my colonel.'

Parallels with the executions of 1620 were, of course, palpable enough to the spectators in the old town square of Prague. And in the meantime the man responsible had not only abandoned the battlefield at Lützen, but his entire Saxon operation. Henceforth, with the respect of his army forfeit, he would avoid even the smallest risk – especially to himself. For by 8 p.m. on 16 November, the night of the battle, the Imperial army was already retreating to Leipzig, though most of its soldiers were still of the opinion that victory would have been certain with another day's fighting. As they moved into the night, therefore, 'without either sound of Trumpet or Drumme' for fear of alerting the Swedes, morale was at rock bottom and nowhere more so than among Pappenheim's corps. 'We marched,' wrote one, 'with our heads down like gypsies, some regiments with but 100 men in their colours.' And the English captain Sydnam Poyntz was another who left little doubt about the impact of Lützen upon Wallenstein' troops. For after dark on the day of the battle, he tells us,

> wee were scarcely laid down on the ground to rest and in dead sleep, but comes a command from the Generall to all Coronells and Sargeant Maiors to give in a note how strong every regiment was found to be.

The replies were not encouraging. Poyntz had only three officers left out of twelve, and in this regard, his unit was no more than typical. Yet still the biggest blow was not physical but psychological. For while Wallenstein might renew his army's numbers, he could not rebuild his reputation and, more importantly still, the will of his soldiers to fight, so long as he lived to command.

In Europe at large, meanwhile, news of the King of Sweden's death was met with incredulity. Wallenstein himself, indeed, was not convinced of its occurrence until 30 November, and even one month later at the court of Charles I in England, £200 was wagered on his continued survival. There the intervention of Sweden had so captured the popular imagination that Frederick of the Palatinate, who died from plague at Metz in the autumn of 1632, was mainly mourned as little more than 'the prince for whom Gustavus fell'. And when in the same year the grandson of Axel Oxenstierna and the nephew of Gustav Horn were awarded honorary degrees by the University of Oxford, the vice-chancellor's laureation compared their illustrious relatives to 'two thunderbolts of war … [who] to the terror of the house of Austria, have now for long been conspicuous in fighting for the hearth and home, the religion and indeed the liberty of the whole of Germany.' The fact, of course, that the King of Sweden's own death was quite literally an answer to the emperor's prayers was conveniently circumscribed in all quarters. For while Ferdinand – and Philip IV too – had ignored an earlier recommendation by a 'certain person' to assassinate Gustavus, on the grounds that such a deed was unworthy of a Christian and an emperor, he fully appreciated that outright defeat at Lützen, let alone his enemy's survival, was certain to have damaged the Imperial cause beyond all hope of recovery. Accordingly, in thanksgiving for the removal of his enemy, Ferdinand duly planned the erection of a monastery for the Spanish Benedictines near the Schottentor in Vienna. And when the city's military prefect complained that this might dangerously weaken the imperial capital's defences, Ferdinand duly assured him that the protection of Christ's mother, to whom the monastery was to be dedicated, would more than offset this.

If the Blessed Virgin truly were to reverse Imperial fortunes, however, it was clear that even she, as the emperor well knew, might have to enlist the aid of Spanish arms, though the Swedish campaign of 1631–32 had been no less disastrous for Madrid than for Germany's Catholics. For, during that time alone, the troops of Philip IV were driven from the Palatinate, those of her allies expelled from Alsace and the Spanish Road blocked. To cap all, the long-simmering southern Netherlands had also ignited after Hendrik van den Bergh was replaced as commander-in-chief in Brussels by the Spaniard Santa Cruz, causing the Count of Warfusée, President of the Council of Finance in Brussels, to travel to The Hague in the spring of 1632 to pledge the support of van den Bergh and other nobles to the struggle of their Dutch neighbours, in return for pensions and titles, guarantees of religious toleration, and the opportunity, should the south so wish, to amalgamate with France. The Siege of Maastricht had followed, and though van den Bergh's calls for a general rising proved unsuccessful after regent Isabella's reminder that the Habsburgs had more rewards in their gift than the republican oligarchs of The Hague, 'where a loutish and ill-mannered burgomaster can often lay down the law', Richelieu nevertheless invaded Lorraine, forcing Spain to dispatch Feria and thereby sanction fresh hostilities with France once the new campaigning season was underway.

In the event, Feria would be dead from plague, along with most of his army, in the Alpine foothills before the spring of 1633 arrived, and by December Isabella would be dead with him, to be replaced by the 24-year-old cardinal-infante Ferdinand, an able, if restless, prince who had chafed under the clerical role imposed upon him and eventually persuaded Olivares of his ability to breathe new life into the defence of Flanders. Yet all eyes remained on Germany and Sweden too, of course, where Queen Christina, a child of 6, had succeeded her father under the regency of Axel Oxenstierna, whom she later described thus:

He had studied much in his youth, and continued to do in the midst of business. His capacity and knowledge of the world's affairs and interests were very great; he knew the strong and weak points of every state in Europe ... He was ambitious but faithful and incorruptible, withal a little too slow and phlegmatic.

In a genius-crowded age, the new regent was in fact one of the ablest statesmen of his day, enjoying a reputation for silence and shrewdness that could indeed result in over-caution, but which had nevertheless served his country well, as he ruled it for two years during his master's absence. Nor would his wisdom fail him now – or over the coming twelve years for that matter – as he directed the armies of Sweden in Germany as well as affairs at home, providing a standard of probity and wisdom in government that was not bettered anywhere else in Europe, while devising in 1634 a 'Form of Government' specifying the composition and powers of each department in his administration that represents, in effect, one of the earliest known examples of a written constitution.

Staying at Frankfurt-on-Main when news of Gustavus's death reached him, Oxenstierna had moved swiftly to Dresden to maintain a watchful eye on John George, and it was from there too that he brought the emergency under control by arranging an almost seamless transfer of power, as the *Riksdag* technically entrusted the conduct of the regency to the *Råd*, or council of nobles. But since Oxenstierna was the dominant figure within that body, this alone gave him all the power he needed, placing him in full charge, at the age of 50, of the operations and supply of some 100,000 troops, as well as the cumbersome administrative machine that had been improvised in Germany in the wake of the flood of Swedish conquests. Everything, from the selection and dispatch of Rhenish wine for the court in Stockholm to the correct policy to be followed by the Swedish Mint, or the precise regalia to be placed on Gustavus's catafalque would now fall under the regent's ambit. And, unlike others, he would not hesitate when it came to the pursuit of Sweden's imperial destiny, convinced that the country's power in Germany was the basis for its domination of the Baltic, and resisting at every turn the growing concerns around him about the dangers of military overstretch. 'The branches spread outwards,' one councillor would warn before long, 'but the tree dies at the centre.' Yet if the remarkable gains in Germany could be consolidated – or so Oxenstierna believed – Sweden might both renew itself and achieve an ascendancy previously inconceivable.

All depended in the first instance upon the role of the Duke of Saxony who wished, in the wake of Lützen, to unite Germany's Protestants under his own leadership and negotiate a separate peace with the emperor. 'Should the war last longer the Empire will be utterly destroyed,' wrote his commander, Arnim. 'Our beloved Germany will fall a prey to foreigners and be a pitiable example to all the world.' And in the firm belief that Duke John George would be the key figure in any new negotiation, Cardinal Richelieu also lost no time in sending the Marquis of Feuquières to a poorly attended meeting of Protestant representatives at Dresden, while Oxenstierna busied himself in March 1633 with a meeting at Heilbronn involving the Franconian, Swabian, Upper Rhenish and Electoral Rhenish Circles, which was intended to establish within the Empire the nucleus of the *corpus evangelicorum* already envisaged by Gustavus. In an effort to keep him out of the clutches of the Duke of Saxony, George William of Brandenburg too was invited, and notwithstanding the latter's refusal to co-operate as a result of his objections to the occupation of Pomerania, the whole assembly otherwise chose to remain in alliance with Sweden, leaving the French with little choice but to embrace the new 'league', as its joint protector with the Swedes, and John George to remain on the sidelines – no more than a half-hearted and suspicious ally, caught for the time being between the devil and the deep blue sea, and mainly intent upon a further military campaign in Silesia for his own purposes.

Though Richelieu would certainly have preferred to work with Saxony, which was altogether more controllable than the Swedes, and Feuquières was soon scheming to undermine its operation, the League of Heilbronn was nevertheless a remarkable success for Oxenstierna who was awarded sole directorship of its activities as a result of what the members termed his 'God-given, exceptional qualities'. It was agreed that the fight would continue until three goals had been reached: first, 'until such time as the liberties of Germany, and a respect for the principles and constitution of the Holy Roman Empire, are once again firmly established'; second, until 'the restoration of the Protestant estates is secured, and a certain and just peace, in spirituals and temporals … is obtained and concluded'; and, third, 'until the crown of Sweden has been assured of an appropriate satisfaction'. Crucially too, at this time, France agreed not only to renew the Treaty of Bärwalde, but to continue paying subsidies directly to Sweden rather than the League, though money, from the outset, would remain the Achilles' heel of both the alliance in general and the Swedes in particular, since members' contributions guaranteed no more than 2.5 million thalers a year at a time when the actual cost of the army was a crippling 9.8 million.

Key to all, of course, was continued military success, and to this extent the activity – or otherwise – of the old enemy, Wallenstein, would be crucial. Throughout 1633, in fact, Bavaria remained under Swedish occupation and continued to be ravaged by Bernard of Saxe-Weimar, who had taken command of the army after Lützen and joined forces with Horn, the Swedish commander in Alsace. But in spite of appeals for action, Wallenstein remained curiously lethargic. At Maximilian's request, one of the generalissimo's lieutenants, Aldringen, was indeed sent to Bavaria, though with orders merely to keep the Swedes under surveillance and under no circumstances to hazard an engagement. Nor did Wallenstein make any effort to prevent Bernard from taking Regensburg, the vital link between Bavaria and Bohemia, which dismayed not only Maximilian but also Oñate, Spain's ambassador to the Empire, who was desperately trying to establish a safe route to the Netherlands for cardinal-infante Ferdinand and his army. More strangely still, when Oñate ordered the Duke of Feria to bring the advance guard down from Innsbruck into Bavaria, Wallenstein refused to let Aldringen go to his assistance. Indeed, only when Aldringen, baffled by his orders and resenting the ignominy of his inactivity, actually took matters into his own hands was support finally offered to Feria in September.

But while the two generals eventually relieved Breisach from Swedish attack – sparking a rebellion of almost 10,000 Upper Bavarian peasants in the process – Wallenstein's failures could be neither forgotten nor forgiven, even though Spanish access to Alsace and the Rhineland had ultimately been secured. The peasants of Bavaria, impoverished by the devastation of their land, bewildered by the apparent collapse of all authority, and influenced by refugees from Upper Austria who had fought in the similar rising of 1626, in fact were easily suppressed by Swedish, Imperial and Spanish commanders, who had no difficulty in discerning the danger to themselves, and cynically made common cause to crush them. Yet while Wallenstein could hardly be blamed for an episode whose origins lay in the very nature of the war itself, the mud thrown subsequently by his detractors continued to stick, as the emperor, above all, remained not only mystified by his orders to Aldringen, but suspicious of his correspondence with Arnim, John George and Richelieu, and outraged equally by the panoply of sovereignty that his leading general continued to maintain in Friedland. Proud, inscrutable and seemingly contemptuous, Wallenstein had been in negotiation, too, with Sweden and, equally worryingly, the Bohemian rebels, Thurn and Kinsky, who still hoped to expel the Habsburgs. If they succeeded, it was said, who else but Wallenstein would become Bohemia's king? And further substance was given to such rumours by the general's release of Thurn after his capture in Silesia. Richelieu too, through his ambassadors in Germany, was in touch with Kinsky who spoke in no uncertain terms of Wallenstein's willingness to desert the Habsburg cause.

Might not all this, therefore, reasonably explain Wallenstein's reluctance to act decisively in defence of Bavaria and Spanish interests? Thurn's release had, it is true, occurred in exchange for the valuable Silesian fortresses still held by the

Bohemian rebels, which were ostensibly of significant benefit to the emperor. But it was well known that Wallenstein had long harboured a romantic vision of a united, independent Bohemia, standing proudly as a bulwark against the Osmanli Turks, and it was suspected that this dream had now become nothing less than a dangerous obsession. Even in 1629, in the midst of enforcing the Edict of Restitution and sending troops to 's-Hertogenbosch and Mantua, he had written how 'it would be better to turn our arms against the Turks. With God's help our emperor would be able to place the crown of Constantinople on his head within three years.' But now Trčka was writing to Kinsky in Dresden that Wallenstein was ready 'to throw off the mask', and Feuquières, through Kinsky, was promising French support if Wallenstein did indeed seize the Bohemian crown. As shrewd a judge as Oxenstierna had in fact remained sceptical of such suggestions, though he had offered support at the end of June for any attempt upon the throne. And there were other reasons, too, for doubting the rumours. Certainly, Wallenstein's only credible statement on the subject – cited in a report from Johann Bubna, a long-standing Bohemian acquaintance serving as a Swedish major-general – alleges that he considered any attempt upon the throne to be gross villainy. And his own inherent caution – not to mention the fact that life as a puppet king of France or Sweden offered less, in some respects, than his current status – also suggests that his real priorities lay elsewhere.

Yet the general was by this time unquestionably weary of the war that had shaped his fortunes in the first place. 'When the various lands are laid in ashes,' he had reflected bitterly, 'we shall be compelled to make peace'. And with the prospect of kingship, an end to his labours on the battlefield, and the added spice of revenge for his dismissal in 1630, he still appeared, circumstantially at least, to have grounds enough for treason. Oñate was not the only one to consider him dangerously out of control, and the emperor's son, young Ferdinand of Hungary, was also urging Wallenstein's replacement by none other than himself. Nor was the general as invulnerable as he might, ostensibly, have seemed. For while his army was still a powerful force, it was held together increasingly only by its commanders, and Pappenheim's death had robbed it of the man most popular with the troops. Holk too, for that matter, had died from plague during a brief summer campaign in Saxony, and a debt of two million gulden on the emperor's behalf only added to the growing temptation to be rid of a man who was not only a dangerous liability but, from all accounts, less and less capable of the kind of energy that had hitherto made him so formidable. For by now Wallenstein's firm signature of 1623 had become little more than a crippled scrawl as the careworn 'man of destiny' found himself aging rapidly and suffering more than ever from gout and attacks of depression.

Accustomed for so long to the sound of gun and cannon, he could now no longer bear the jingling of spurs, the barking of dogs, the crowing of cocks or the jarring impact of loud voices. Shut off, too, from the wider world that threatened him, ailing and cantankerous, he had even ordered the hanging of a servant for waking him in his sleep. And if he could act with such vindictiveness towards the innocent, how, it was said, might he now react to those altogether greater 'inconveniences' in Vienna and elsewhere who disturbed his peace of mind much more troublingly still? Plainly, the time was ripe for action and accordingly, in August 1633, Emperor Ferdinand took the first tentative steps towards a remedy, when, under the guise of urging an assault upon the Swedes, Count Schlick was sent to sound out Wallenstein's commanders – and in particular Piccolomini and Gallas – as to whether they would obey their chief 'in the event of any change in his position which might arise for reasons of health or any other reason'. The results, moreover, were most encouraging, for, after Aldringen's defection in Bavaria, Piccolomini and Gallas proved more than amenable, the former even agreeing to keep the emperor informed of his supremo's activities – which, as events soon demonstrated, would prove the crucial tipping-point.

For during the winter Wallenstein not only realised that he could no longer trust his officers, but played directly into the hands of his enemies by forcing matters. The exaction of an oath of loyalty at Pilsen in January 1634 from the very commanders whom he had come to distrust so thoroughly was, of course, a pointless measure demonstrating only his desperation. And with his dismissal by the emperor thereafter inevitable, he found himself with no other option than to flee, carried in a litter and accompanied by no more than 1,300 men, to his fortress at Eger near the Saxon border, where he hoped, it seems, to join the enemy. The so-called 'Pilsen Revers', in which his few remaining loyal officers pledged their ongoing allegiance and swore never to separate from him, served merely, in the meantime, to confirm suspicions in Vienna, and when he appealed in vain for aid to Bernard of Weimar and to Arnim, his fate was effectively sealed. For on 24 January Ferdinand coolly signed and secretly dispatched a patent directed to Piccolomini, Gallas and Maximilian of Bavaria, ordering Wallenstein's seizure, dead or alive.

By then, the quarry had already informed Father Diego de Quiroga, a Spanish visitor, that 'he would gladly take the strongest poison in order to be free once and for all of the pains he had to endure, were it not that he had to fear hell and the devil.' But the actual details of the death awaiting him were neither so peaceful nor so dignified, as Piccolomini handed planning for the assassination over to Colonel Walter Butler, an Irish Catholic, who also enlisted the services of two Scotch Protestants – John Gordon, commander of the Eger garrison, and Gordon's friend, Major Walter Leslie – along with a further three Irishmen, another Scot, an Italian and a Spaniard. Realising that failure to dispatch Wallenstein would result in their own implication in his alleged crimes, the designated killers duly decided to separate the general from his remaining inner circle – which included Trčka, Kinsky and the commander of his bodyguard Captain Niemann – by inviting them to dinner and butchering each and every one before turning on Wallenstein himself. And the first part of the scheme did indeed, it seems, unfold with precisely the kind of flint-faced efficiency that might have been expected from such a group of hardened professionals. For, with the meal in full flow, a dozen dragoons duly burst in upon the victims crying 'Who is a good Imperialist?' before Kinsky was killed in his chair along with three others in attendance, as Gordon, Leslie and Butler leapt to their feet shouting 'Long live Ferdinand'.

Thereafter, with surprise still of the essence, the ringleaders rushed to the fine three-storey building on Eger's main square, which Gordon had used as his own quarters before offering it to Wallenstein upon his arrival three days earlier on 24 February. Two other accomplices, Major Robert Fitzgerald and Captain Walter Devereux were by now also present, and as the former secured the doors, so Devereux dashed upstairs, killing a page who had the misfortune to be in the way. Yet the inconvenience of breaking his sword in the process appears to have been minimal, since the murderer had gathered up a half-pike by the time he burst into the bedroom where Wallenstein had already removed his sword, boots and coat in preparation for bed. What each man said during the brief moment of hesitation that followed is unknown, although the most credible contemporary account suggests that the captain may well have shouted a short phrase of abuse as he prepared to the deliver the killer blow – perhaps, 'You evil, perjured, rebellious old scoundrel', as Gordon's report attests. In response, Wallenstein offered no more than the word 'Quarter' and an accompanying gesture of submission that constituted the traditional soldier's plea for mercy on the battlefield – which in this case went wholly unheeded, as his assailant ran him through with a single decisive thrust below the ribs and upwards into the chest, resulting in almost instantaneous death, which, under the circumstances, was no small mercy. As further soldiers crowded into room, one picked up the body and made to hurl it from the window, before Devereux, with a fleeting flash of decorum, forbade him. Whereupon the lifeless huddle was rolled up in a carpet, and dragged unceremoniously down the stairs to a waiting carriage, which took it to lie with the other victims of the night's carnage. 'Presently,' wrote Sydnam Poyntz:

[they] drew him out by the heels, his head knocking upon every stair, all bloody, and threw him into a coach and carried him to the castle where the rest lay naked together … and there he had the superior place of them, being the right hand file, which they could do not less, being so great a general.

Not long previous, the self-same bloody victim had been depicted by the painter Bartolomeo Bianco on the ceiling of his magnificent Prague palace as *triumphator*, standing indomitable in a chariot drawn at furious pace by the horses of the Sun. Contemporaries, moreover, had numbered his court at more than a thousand people, and marvelled at the splendour of his most impressive dwelling, designed by the Italian architects Spezza and Pieroni, which still stands today on the 'small side' of the Czech Republic's capital. Boasting stables for 300 horses, a riding school, loggias looking out on to magnificent gardens, a park with pleasant walks, exotic plants, and fountains and statues by Adriaen de Vries, the colour of its interior decoration was predominantly blue, which harmonised the fine leather, the gobelins and other tapestries with the silks and carpets from Italy, the Netherlands and the Ottoman Empire. No expense had been spared, no detail overlooked in what was originally intended as a splendid affirmation of its owner's rank and power, but had now become, from the very instant of his murder, an all-too-compelling reminder of something far more significant still: the fickleness of fortune and the price of ambition.

Within two weeks of his death and even before the thanksgiving service ordered by the emperor could be held, a profusion of gifts from Wallenstein's vast estates were lavishly distributed to the very men who had contrived his death. Matthias Gallas, it is reported, became the largest landowner in Bohemia for his trouble, while Leslie was promptly honoured and promoted, before becoming a count three years later, after his conversion to Catholicism. All three principals, in fact, were granted substantial properties from Wallenstein's lands, while Devereux and Fitzgerald received large bounties paid out in cash and property. Only Butler, it seems, felt truly hard done by, and wrote to Schlick complaining how everyone 'is giving the honour and thanks solely to Herr Leslie and Colonel Gordon, while he, who was in charge of the Friedland execution is forgotten, just as though he had done nothing.' Yet while the Irishman – and Piccolomini to a lesser extent – complained at their share of their spoils, few bemoaned the most important outcome of all. For the emperor was rid of his most onerous burden and his army free once more to prosecute the war anew under the leadership of his son, Ferdinand, King of Hungary, and the incorrigible drunkard Gallas, his Austrian chief lieutenant.

11

WAR WITHOUT LIMIT, WAR WITHOUT END

If it is a sign of singular prudence to have held down the forces opposed to your state for a period of ten years with the forces of your allies, by putting your hand in your pocket and not on your sword, then, when your allies can no longer exist without you, to engage in open warfare is a sign of courage and great wisdom.

Testament Politique du Cardinal Duc de Richelieu (1680)

Though Gustavus Adolphus had pre-deceased Wallenstein by all of fourteen months, it was not until 22 June, 1634 – more than half a year after the generalissimo's own wretched demise – that the King of Sweden was finally laid to rest. And by that time both his grieving wife and plans for Germany were showing serious signs of strain. In the aftermath of Lützen, the king's body had been taken first to Meuchen to be cleaned, and thence to Weissenfels where it was embalmed and dressed in a beautiful gold and silver woven garment before being taken in solemn procession to the port town of Wolgast. Not until the summer of 1633, however, was it finally brought over to Nyköping, accompanied by the royal widow, Maria Eleonora, the king's wounded warhorse, Streiff, his sword and armour, the so-called 'blood' and 'head' banners, and ceremonial flags from each of Sweden's counties and principalities. And by that time, the Dowager Queen was already exhibiting visible signs of breakdown, locking both herself and her 6-year-old daughter in a room with blackened windows, and ordering that her husband's coffin be kept open for the daily visits, which now became her only excursions. Ultimately, indeed, after Oxenstierna had finally succeeded in having the corpse interred in Riddarholm church in Stockholm, he was nevertheless forced to post guards all around after the despairing queen had tried to dig it up.

As the funeral ceremony had run its elaborate course, eight Imperial standards captured in battle, along with several trophy banners brought from Leipzig, featured particularly prominently as tokens affirming Sweden's newfound status as a continental superpower. But though the mists had parted long enough at Lützen to permit the King of Sweden's death to be avenged by the semblance of victory, they were continuing to thicken over both his own realm and Germany, too, even after Oxenstierna's skill had breathed life into the League of Heilbronn. Discipline within the Swedish army was suddenly declining, as demonstrated by its disorderly march through Franconia and the four-day sack of Landsberg on the Lech where 300 of the surrendering garrison were cut down, along with 154 inhabitants, including children. In April, moreover, the troops mutinied, demanding bonuses promised after both Breitenfeld and Lützen. Only the wholesale transfer of territories to officers like Gustavus's illegitimate son, Colonel Gustav Gustavsson, who received Osnabrück, eventually ensured the restoration of order. And this was not the end of Oxenstierna's troubles. For while the Imperial onslaught on Saxony had been halted and its duke tied to alliance with Sweden, there was little confidence in the permanence of either, or whether, above all, the unity of Germany's Protestants could continue without the former King of Sweden's inspirational leadership.

In the south, of course, princes and cities who feared the resurrection of Habsburg power and the implementation of the Edict of Restitution might still place their reliance on Swedish succour with some sincerity. But what prospect was there in the north – in those regions with which, after all, Sweden's interests were most directly concerned – of ensuring long-term commitment to a security system dominated by a foreign power? George William of Brandenburg continued to fret over Pomerania, and prior to his death Frederick V had been thrust aside and humiliated in the name of military necessity. The Duke of Saxony, meanwhile, was now free of his most formidable rival for the leadership of German Protestantism, and Sweden's other allies – Adolf Frederick of Mecklenburg, William of Weimar, Frederick Ulric of Wolfenbüttel, and the rest – had nearly all at one time or another been made to smart under Gustavus's impatience or contempt. How long, therefore, would they continue to fight, should a tolerable settlement be offered from without? Already in January 1633 George William of Brandenburg had sent envoys to Dresden, in an effort to persuade the Duke of Saxony to join him in a peace initiative, and shortly afterwards Landgrave George of Hesse-Darmstadt issued a similar invitation. Plainly, those German princes who had once been so near to drowning, now distrusted the direction of the life raft that had saved them, and with France angling for ever firmer control of the anti-Habsburg alliance, Sweden had even more reason to doubt the monopoly of leadership it had sought so ardently.

Nor were Oxenstierna's efforts to repair the divisions in the Protestant camp any more successful in early 1634. The meeting – which convened at Frankfurt to establish in precise terms which German lands Sweden was to retain after the war, and thereby entice Saxony, Brandenburg and the other territories of the north-east into membership of the Heilbronn League – began well enough, but foundered in April, all too predictably, over George William's ongoing insistence that the Swedes renounce their claim to Pomerania. Six months earlier, he had committed himself to no more than the Franco-Swedish alliance, and now, once again, he rejected membership of the League. By June, moreover, the members of the Lower Saxon Circle had agreed to support him, while John George of Saxony, affecting to be above such mundane matters, attempted to broaden support for peace talks begun by Imperial officials at Leitermitz with George of Hesse-Darmstadt, whose penchant for independent action had already undermined Sweden's grip on the north-west the previous year and resulted in the Battle of Hessisch-Oldendorf, at which Knyphausen narrowly defeated Imperial and Catholic League forces exploiting the lack of any centralised Protestant command in the area. Unless such divisions could be avoided in the future, as Oxenstierna well knew, the outcome might not be so fortunate next time. But in the summer of 1634, with two separate campaigns looming – one involving the Saxons under Arnim in Silesia, the other an assault on south-eastern Germany, staged by the Swedes and their Heilbronn allies – the deadlock in Protestant ranks was as pronounced as ever.

Superficially, at least, the lines were now more clearly drawn in Germany than for many years. On the one hand, there was the Heilbronn League, with all its limitations, in alliance with Sweden and France; on the other, two major Habsburg armies, led by Ferdinand of Hungary and the cardinal-infante Ferdinand, about to join forces in southern Germany. But it was not only the divisions within Protestant ranks that gave the advantage to the Habsburgs, since Oxenstierna and Richelieu also remained uneasy allies, as revealed by their correspondence over Philippsburg and other Rhineland fortresses captured by Swedish troops and claimed by the French. Nor was it proving any easier to control Bernard of Saxe-Weimar, whom Oxenstierna had reluctantly appointed commander-in-chief instead of his own son-in-law Horn. Demanding the fulfilment of a promise made by Gustavus Adolphus to create him Duke of Franconia, the ambitious general bristled troublesomely until his wish was granted – only to create further difficulties with the other German princes of the League.

At first the military campaigns of the summer went well. For although the Spanish Ferdinand marched through the Valtelline into the Tyrol, and his cousin, Ferdinand of Hungary, advanced up the Danube to meet him, Arnim's invasion of Bohemia soon took him to the very gates of Prague, while the army of the Heilbronn League not only took Landshut in Bavaria by storm but also succeeded in killing Maximilian's commander-in-chief, Aldringen. If Imperial forces could be sucked into the defence of Prague, or so Bernard of Saxe-Weimar hoped, by being made to follow him there, a decisive blow might well be dealt. But whether by luck or judgement, and notwithstanding the grave danger to the Bohemian capital, the emperor's son refused to take the bait, and as a result recaptured both Regensburg and Donauwörth, restoring contact between Bavaria and the Habsburg lands, and forcing Arnim's withdrawal from his now exposed position in Prague. Bernard too, whose own lines of communication lay up the Danube, now found himself forced to turn tail and follow in Ferdinand's wake, which lay in the direction of the Swedish garrison at Nördlingen – a strategic target threatening the Imperials' flank that would have to be destroyed at any cost.

As Ferdinand laid siege to the Protestant stronghold, bolstered by the arrival of his cousin, the cardinal-infante, and his 15,000 men from Spain and Spanish Italy on 2 September, Horn and Bernard arrived soon afterwards. But their troops were demoralised and tired from their fruitless campaign to the east, as well as outnumbered. And this was not their only predicament. For the two Ferdinands, appreciating their advantage, had prepared a heavily fortified camp in the hills south of the city, and though there was little chance of success, neither Bernard nor Horn dared avoid action of some kind, if the Heilbronn League were to stand any chance of survival at all. Their opponents were, of course, callow and untried, and this at least gave grounds for hope of a kind when battle commenced on 6 September between Habsburg armies numbering 33,000 and a Protestant force of only 25,000. Yet after seven hours of fighting, in which the Spaniards claimed to have withstood fifteen charges, some 12,000 Protestants lay dead on the field, with some 4,000 more, including Gustav Horn, captured. What boiled down to an endurance test between Spanish and Swedish infantry had finally been resolved when the Swedes eventually fell back and became entangled with Bernard's cavalry, turning a retreat into a rout, which Ferdinand of Hungary, aglow with his first flush of glory, encapsulated as follows:

The enemy scattered in such a way that ten are not found together. Horn is taken, and no one knows whether Weimar be dead or alive.

It was, in Olivares' opinion, 'the greatest victory of our time'. Nördlingen fell at once, and the remnants of the defeated army, under its leader Bernard, retreated into Alsace while Sweden reluctantly withdrew all her garrisons from south of the Main. Spain and Austria, moreover, had never been closer at this point. The two young Ferdinands in the excitement of their victory behaved like brothers, and their elders followed suit in October 1634 by drawing up the Compact of Ebersdorf, which pledged the emperor and the Roman Catholic German princes in his retinue to give full assistance to Philip IV, as Duke of Burgundy, in suppressing the Dutch revolt. And though the agreement did not carry the signature of Maximilian of Bavaria, or consider, for that matter, the possibility of French aid to the Dutch, it remained a long-awaited diplomatic triumph for Spain in particular, at the very time that Ferdinand of Hungary was proceeding to carry all before him in Württemberg, and the cardinal-infante, accompanied by Piccolomini, was marching swiftly through the Rhineland to bring his army to Brussels in November.

In the same month, Oxenstierna made no attempt to hide his despondency from Johan Baner, the only capable Swedish general left in Germany. 'I will struggle no longer,' he confided, 'but drift where the tide may take me … We are hated, envied, harassed.' At home there was open criticism of his policies by the regency council, prompting him to lament to his brother how 'such proceedings make me weary of my life', and November also witnessed the visit to Paris of delegates from the Heilbronn League, offering extensive concessions in return for a French declaration of war against Spain and the emperor. Even to Sweden's oldest ally, William of Hesse-Kassel, it had become clear that only Catholic France was now capable of saving the Protestant cause. 'The House of Austria,' he declared, 'wishes to subjugate all Germany, extirpating liberty and the reformed religion. So in this extremity we must look to France.' There was also, indeed, a recommendation from the landgrave that the King of France be elected emperor, since only this would truly guarantee the continuation of 'German liberties', though the biggest blow of all for Oxenstierna was still to come as the negotiations of Hesse-Darmstadt and Saxony with the Imperials, begun at Leitermitz and concluded in Pirna, finally produced an agreement.

For despite the resounding victory at Nördlingen, the emperor had at last acknowledged that the one major obstacle to peace within the Empire remained the Edict of Restitution, and that until it was rescinded Germany's Protestants could never be fully divorced from their alliance with Sweden. Furthermore, the growing influence of his son, whose interests were dynastic rather than imperial, had begun to convince him that perpetual war with northern Germany was hardly worth the effort, if it entailed, in the longer term, the sacrifice of the Habsburg 'hereditary lands'. Devoted almost exclusively to Austria, Bohemia and Hungary, where Roman Catholicism had been immeasurably strengthened since 1609, the young Ferdinand was convinced that now was the time for compromise, and as a result of his father's agreement, the so-called 'Preliminaries of Pirna' – the all-important prelude to a truce in the following February and subsequent peace treaty, which would ultimately serve as a model for future settlements involving other German Protestant rulers – was duly agreed with John George of Saxony in November 1634. Amnesty was offered to all save the family of the former Elector Palatine, the Bohemian exiles and those who remained obdurate in the future, while Lutherans were to retain all ecclesiastical territory in their possession in 1627. And as a result, the Edict of Restitution – suspended in theory for a period of forty years – was effectively ended, though Roman Catholics would indeed enjoy the benefit of the substantial recoveries they had made between 1618 and 1627, and Calvinism was to remain banned. At the same time, Maximilian of Bavaria's succession to the Palatinate was no longer to be questioned, a Saxon administrator was to be restored to Magdeburg, and Saxony's conquest of Lusatia confirmed.

Above all, John George promised to break off his alliances with foreign powers, making him, as Arnim warned, the enemy of Sweden and the ally of an emperor who was no less dangerous to Saxony's interests. Nor was it insignificant that a Protestant pamphleteer later claimed to have noted 371 changes detrimental to his faith between the original text of the 'Preliminaries of Pirna' and that of the final agreement eventually signed at Prague in May 1635. Yet the die had been cast and the ramifications for the Heilbronn League were undeniable, as its frightened and disorganised members met with Oxenstierna in Frankfurt to discuss their plight, only to disperse in haste as the cardinal-infante approached en route for Brussels. Now, it seemed, there were but two choices: surrender or seek succour elsewhere. For Richelieu, sensing his opportunity, was currently offering 12,000 troops and generous subsidies to all those continuing the struggle against the emperor. In return, there would have to be guarantees for the security of Roman Catholics within the Empire, a promise that no prince would follow Saxony's lead by negotiating a separate peace, and the cession to France of the fortresses of Schlettstadt and Benfeld, along with the bridgehead of Strasbourg, which would give her virtual control of Alsace – all of which were currently in Swedish control.

Even with these provisos, and in spite of Oxenstierna's best efforts, the resulting Treaty of Paris was too tempting an offer for the German princes to refuse, and by December Sweden had left the Heilbronn League, never to return. Though peace was still no option and the Swedish chancellor remained convinced that France could not manage without his assistance, the Swedes would nevertheless have to cut their cloth accordingly, as war with Denmark threatened and the expiry of the Truce of Altmark with Poland loomed. In April 1635, indeed, Oxenstierna would travel to Paris, demanding an outright declaration of war by France against both Spain and the emperor, though Richelieu still refused to commit and offered no more than the Treaty of Compiègne, which tactfully ignored the disputed matter of Alsace while guaranteeing the rights of Roman Catholics within the Empire without contesting the Swedish occupation of the bishoprics of Mainz and Worms. As a result, the dream of uncontested leadership in a German Protestant crusade was gone for good. Instead, Sweden would stick, like her competitors, to geopolitics and unadorned self-interest, as Europe slithered into a new more cynical stage of what had become – even in the language of contemporaries – its first 'great war'.

So wide-ranging now was the conflict, so complex the interaction of alliances, that even developments as far afield as Persia or Russia, let alone Turkey or Poland, might sway the course of events, though, for the moment at least, it was not so much the flap of a butterfly's wing in far-off places as the momentum of power politics closer to home that was shaping the course of events. In The Hague, for instance, Maurice of Nassau's successor, Frederick Henry, had now decided to join with the Calvinist ministers and directors of the West India Company to prosecute the war with renewed vigour. Long before the Habsburg victory at Nördlingen, peace negotiations were already foundering, and the enticements of Hercule de Charnacé, French negotiator of the treaties of Altmark and Bärwalde, no doubt played their part, too. If French support could be used to guarantee the supremacy of the House of Orange, while delivering the Netherlands from the renewed threat posed by the cardinal-infante, there was little that Frederick Henry might not render in return, and with this in mind, he duly offered to partition the southern Netherlands on the basis that 'the provinces in which the French tongue is generally spoken should be assigned to the crown of France'. Ultimately, moreover, since the projected frontier was to run in the west from Blankenberge on the coast north of Bruges to Rupelmonde, France would also be assigned a considerable portion of Dutch-speaking Flanders, as well as receiving guarantees for the rights of Roman Catholics throughout the provinces of the south that had remained loyal to Spain.

Unsurprisingly, of course, the proposals were strongly opposed not only by the Calvinist clergy but by moderates like Adrian Pauw, who sought the liberation rather than the conquest of the south and feared the consequences of having France as a neighbour. But Richelieu too disliked the offer, since, as he himself put it, 'it could happen soon afterwards that, lacking any barrier between ourselves and the Dutch, we may find ourselves entering upon the same war with them as they are presently engaged in with the Spaniards.' As reluctant as ever to challenge Spain outright, his preference still was for conflict by proxy, probing for weakness and exploiting the dilemmas of others who might be primed to fight on France's behalf. Louis XIII, after all, was no Gustavus Adolphus, and his government was both steeped in debt and lacking the reserve of trained soldiers necessary even for the sustained defence of the kingdom, let alone an outright assault on Spain. But the collapse of the Heilbronn League, the negotiations at Pirna, which threatened to pacify the Empire, and the arrival of the cardinal-infante demanded desperate measures, so that in February 1635 France and the United Provinces finally announced their formal alliance, whereby France would supply 30,000 men for the Dutch army – thus avoiding a direct declaration of war against Spain – and the southern Netherlands were given the choice of either rising as an independent state against Spanish rule or of submitting to conquest and partition.

For Sweden, it was another indication of the shifting balance of influence and the expansion of the war to a truly continental scale that defied her resources. But for France the arrangement was still essentially defensive in motive, and prompted primarily by her ongoing fears for the security of the Rhineland, since the compact of Ebersdorf between Spain and Austria, intended mainly for the defeat of the Dutch, was also an immediate threat to Alsace and Lorraine. When Spanish troops entered Trier in March 1635, therefore, and carried off the archbishop-elector to Germany as a prisoner, the time for hesitation was finally ended. For since 1631 the archbishop had placed himself under the protection of Louis XIII, and at an emergency meeting of the French royal council it was unanimously agreed that his arrest was a provocation that could only be avenged by war. Superbly placed now to disrupt Spanish lines of communication at the very moment when the enemy had been so well placed to deliver a final blow to her Dutch enemies, it was an opportunity that even the caution of Richelieu could no longer withstand. In 1632, he had written to an agent in Madrid that 'nowhere is Spain in a position to resist a concentrated power such as France over a long period, and in the final analysis the outcome of a general war must necessarily be calamitous to our Iberian neighbours.' But even the cardinal could not have imagined that Spain would inflict such a calamity on herself by tactlessness of the kind she had now exhibited. For no matter how poorly organised her national resources of wealth and population may have been in the spring of 1635, France could never ignore such a threat to her security or offense to her honour, and, in consequence, on 19 May 1635 a French herald was duly dispatched to Brussels bearing Louis XIII's formal declaration of war against his kingdom's old enemy.

Certainly, Richelieu's earlier caution about open confrontation was still borne out by numerous naked facts. For while in the past he had been able to employ as many as 50,000 troops to intervene as and when he chose in the conflicts of other states, now he needed three times that number merely to defend the long line of the French frontier, which at every point, from the Pyrenees to the Rhineland and the Netherlands, was vulnerable to invasion. It was an enterprise, in fact, for which France had only her famous Guards and the four great regiments of Picardy, Piedmont, Champagne and Navarre, which were the apple of Louis XIII's eye – carefully supervised by him even in such matters as the appointment of individual officers – but nevertheless wholly inadequate on their own for the forthcoming task. Indeed, as a measure of the government's desperation, even the feudal levies were initially summoned to the kingdom's defence, though the military obligations of the so-called *noblesse d l'épée* were largely defunct, and led Louis XIII to the following damning conclusion after commanding them in Lorraine:

> I regret to have to tell you that our nobles are unreliable. As soon as they are asked to exert themselves … all they are fit for is to help their king lose his honour. If one sends them no more than three hours' distance from here in the direction of Metz or Nancy, they begin to grumble and claim that they are being sent to perdition, and threaten to decamp.

Hencforth, therefore, it would become necessary to contract out recruitment to individual colonels, though this too presented difficulties, since their terms of employment made them very nearly autonomous.

And to compound Richelieu's problems, there was also the difficulty of finding reliable commanders, even after sufficient troops had been enlisted. The nobles Du Bec and St Léger, for example, would expose their inadequacies in their very first engagement and, out of a perverse sense of pride, choose exile among their country's enemies rather than face criticism at home. As such, the only two men of any real military talent available to the cardinal were Bernard of Saxe-Weimar, the German commander defeated at Nördlingen, and, ironically enough, the Duke of Rohan, the Huguenot and former rebel, who had been kicking his heels, since the Grace of Alais. 'I have the feeling,' Rohan had told his mother, 'that since the capture of La Rochelle and the waning of the religious wars in France, all theatres of war no longer concern me.' But now, it seems, he was energised once more by the prospect of glory and slaughter, and, in spite of his history, Richelieu was ready to call upon him – assuming, of course, that the troops under his command could actually be paid. For the royal council was already noting, with classic understatement, that 'by increasing His Majesty's forces, which are already very large, it will become difficult to pay them all for a while.'

In the event, French troops would be expected to live off the land on the wholly unrealistic assumption that 'they must not become completely undisciplined and disobedient'. And it was to Rohan's credit, in particular, that he achieved as much as he did under such circumstances. Welcomed by the Grisons in the Valtelline, who appreciated the tact displayed in sending a fellow Protestant, he was able in September to lead a rebellion against Spanish control, which had closed the valley by the end of the year, notwithstanding an injection of Habsburg troops from Milan and the Tyrol. But elsewhere Richelieu's plans rapidly foundered as the Italian states of Savoy, Venice and Tuscany failed him in Milan, and Bernard of Saxe-Weimar – whose hopes of creating an independent duchy of Franconia had ultimately been dashed at Nördlingen – failed to prevent the Spanish from consolidating their control of the Lower Palatinate. Promised territory in Alsace and given 4 million livres to maintain 12,000 men and 6,000 horse in the Rhineland, he had proved unable, too, to prevent a brief incursion into Lorraine by Gallas, who subsequently chose to settle down for the winter at Zabern with his army in control of the Vosges Gap.

In the Netherlands, by contrast, a French army did at least force its way across Luxembourg to join Frederick Henry near Maastricht, to create an allied force numbering 32,000 infantry and 9,000 cavalry, which succeeded in sacking Tirlemont and investing Louvain. But even here sickness struck the French camp and troops began to desert in large numbers for lack of pay, as Piccolomini approached with a relief force sent by the emperor, which crossed the Rhine at Mainz and duly cut French lines of communication with their home bases. Appreciating the subtleties of siege warfare in a way that his fellow French commanders plainly did not, Frederick Henry therefore chose not to pursue the siege when covered inadequately, and, amid loud complaints from his Gallic allies, duly used his own vessels to ship his men home in great humiliation, since the land route through Luxemburg was now barred. They had arrived in hope and left in tatters: ill-led, poorly paid and an altogether sorry contrast to the citizens of the so-called 'Obedient Provinces' in the south, whose morale had been transformed by the triumphant arrival of the cardinal-infante the previous year and his tactful demeanour as Philip IV's representative thereafter. Encouraged also by the incontrovertible evidence of Imperial support for their cause, furnished by Piccolomini's presence, they would soon be celebrating, too, his relief of Louvain and seizure of Schenkenschans at the junction of the Waal and the Rhine, which all but cut Maastricht off from the United Provinces.

Nor, in fact, were these the only Habsburg victories for Richelieu to brood upon as his own armies limped from one frustration to another. Ferdinand of Hungary, for example, occupied the whole right bank of the Rhine, and with his troops securely quartered in Württemberg, Swabia and Franconia, the Habsburg territories welcomed the rare luxury of having neither friend nor foe billeted upon them. Even more importantly, however, the negotiations initiated at Pirna with John George of Saxony had culminated in the Peace of Prague of May 1635, as a result of which the Saxon army, still occupying parts of Silesia, now became part of the Imperial host, along with the troops of Bavaria – albeit much to Maximilian's regret – as most Lutheran states hastened to abandon hostilities. After Nördlingen, both Saxony and Brandenburg had agreed a ceasefire with the emperor, and, aside from William of Hesse-Kassel, who would soon be driven out of his territory by George of Hesse-Darmstadt, there was a general desire to follow suit. Henceforth, indeed, the religious dimension of the conflict would be significantly scaled down, as the monopoly of Imperial policy by ultra-Catholics like the Jesuit Lamormaini came to an end, and the monolithic blocs that had divided Protestant rulers from their Catholic counterparts began to dissolve. If France, therefore, was now to thwart the Habsburg tide, she would have to face an Imperial army combining Catholics and Protestants, with only a handful of Calvinists still defiant and Maximilian of Bavaria also committed to the emperor's cause by reason of continued French and Swedish support for the former Elector Palatine's family, and the Peace of Prague's exclusion of them from its amnesty.

For Sweden, however, the prospects were even more daunting, since the Treaty of Compiègne, which promised French subsidies, had not been ratified, and the expiry of the Truce of Altmark now created the distinct possibility of hostility from Poland. In Stockholm the conduct of the war, not to mention the very rationale behind the conflict itself, was subject to increasing censure, while Oxenstierna, who had temporarily become more or less the prisoner of mutinous German officers in Magdeburg, was unable to return home to take charge of affairs. In his absence, moreover, the council of regency so bungled its negotiations with the Poles that its minimum terms were made public before a settlement had been reached, and only the full intervention of the French

eventually eased through the Truce of Stuhmsdorf, by which Sweden still had
to accept the loss of the Prussian ports, whose dues were currently producing
an income of more than 550,000 thalers a year. With hope of French aid now
abandoned and with such an additional loss of income into the bargain, Swedish
troops would have to live off the land in areas already substantially reduced by
Imperial victories and defections brought about by the Peace of Prague. And
with Baner's disorganised and mutinous army of 23,000 men being further
eroded by both Saxon and indeed Danish recruiting agents, any likelihood of
successfully safeguarding the line of communication between Stockholm and
Frankfurt, let alone defending Pomerania, was rapidly disappearing.

In August, at least, Baner and Oxenstierna had restored a measure of quiet
by making concessions to mutinous colonels who were threatening to defect
with entire regiments. But the general, in his turn, was hoping to create an
independent duchy for himself, and it was clear from his dispatches in October
that the scale of desertions to the Saxon army, in particular, was undermining
his ability to hold the line of the Elbe. Baner's concerns, indeed, were so serious
that by the end of the year 10,000 troops were released from the Polish frontier
to assist him – the first fruits of the Truce of Stuhmsdorf. But while morale was
improved after a successful series of skirmishes with the Saxons in the valley
of the Elbe, culminating in October 1636 with a major victory at Wittstock,
Sweden had been offered little more than a fragile lifeline, enabling Oxenstierna
to return to Stockholm to reassert his authority over the regency council as best
he might, and rescue Queen Christina from a mother who had been scheming
to marry her off to a Dane. Already, in April, even his brother had declared how
'it is intolerable to go on fighting in a war in which we have no interest', and
only if Baner was somehow to build on his success at Wittstock could Sweden
look forward to anything more than a punitive peace. A breakout from the
exhausted base in Pomerania and Mecklenburg, bringing fresh supply and new
possibilities for recruitment, must somehow be achieved if peace negotiations
were to offer any tangible benefit at all.

For this, however, the role of France would be crucial, though Oxenstierna's
ingenious policy to fight and negotiate while keeping the French on a string – to
which he committed the regency council in August 1636 – remained at best a
long shot, particularly when Richelieu was facing the worst crisis of his career as
Spain, Austria and Bavaria, in a rare combination of military might, bore down on
their quarry. The cardinal-infante and Piccolomini, reinforced by the Bavarian
cavalry under Johann von Werth, invaded Picardy, while Gallas and the exiled
Charles of Lorraine attacked through the Vosges Gap into eastern France. Aided
by widespread urban riots and peasant revolts against the cost of the war, which

affected nearly one quarter of the country between the Loire and the Garonne, the invaders had made good progress by July, overrunning the region between the Somme and the Oise, bypassing Amiens and taking Corbie, barely 50 miles from Paris in mid-August. Such was the danger, indeed, that when Werth's cavalry pressed on to Roye and Montdidier, his outriders were able to sweep through Pontoise and into the suburbs of Paris itself, forcing Richelieu, on the verge of a breakdown, to organise defences and reinforcements, while King Louis for once excelled himself by calming the frightened, rallying the dispirited, and riding out at the head of his troops to meet the enemy halfway at Senlis.

Most significant of all in saving the day, however, was the resistance offered by the village of Saint-Jean-de-Losne, which, against all odds, resisted Gallas so successfully that it was subsequently renamed Saint-Jean-Belle-Défense. Since Gallas could not take the village, his advance lost momentum, some of his men began to desert, and he himself became uneasy about the threat from Bernard of Saxe-Weimar, who was manoeuvring on his left flank. Though he had joined with Duke Charles to swell his army to some 40,000 troops, moreover, news of Baner's victory at Wittstock further weakened his resolve, and by autumn, bogged down by heavy rains and depleted by plague, both Gallas and his weary army were more than happy to withdraw, regardless of the fact that the cardinal-infante and Piccolomini now found themselves stranded to the north of Paris. For Werth their colleague, boldness seemed the best option and he urged a spirited dash into the capital. But the army was running short of supplies and men, and the risk was adjudged too great, in spite of the undoubted fact that the enemy lay prostrate. Had the planned invasion of Languedoc from Spain not been delayed until the following year, indeed, France's surrender might well have been assured, though any notion at the French court from this point forth that the kingdom was involved in anything other than a protracted struggle had certainly been exploded once and for all, as three key fortress commanders – Le Bec of La Capelle, St Léger of Le Câtelet and Soyecourt of Corbie – found themselves executed for cowardice in the invasion's aftermath.

In due course, only the failure of Austrian and Spanish Habsburgs to pursue unified objectives would bring about the withdrawal of their invading forces. Yet 1636 still constituted in many respects the high-water mark of Emperor Ferdinand II's entire reign, and it was only fitting, therefore, that in December an electoral Diet at Regensburg duly recognised his son, Ferdinand of Hungary, as King of the Romans. The 59-year-old emperor had, it is true, seemed stronger when the Edict of Restitution was in full force, but he had then been too dependent upon the unreliable strength of Wallenstein, and now his achievement was more solidly based. Throughout Bohemia and Austria, though not in Hungary, where the Osmanli threat compelled caution in dealing with the nobility, the administration had been centralised at the expense of local franchises and privileges, and the power of the Protestants reduced. Within the Empire, moreover, he now exercised authority greater than any other emperor for all of three centuries. Above all, no longer was there a Catholic League or an Evangelical Union to resist his policies or restrict his freedom of action. Instead, he was leader of a coalition of both faiths, bound to him by treaty against Sweden and France, and though he remained dependent – financially, militarily and politically – upon his Wittelsbach cousin and later son-in-law, Maximilian, in Munich, as well as Philip IV in Madrid, he had nevertheless navigated successfully between both, and remained free from domination. In doing so, furthermore, he had even been able, when possible, to avoid the rigours of repression for repression's sake. 'Non-Catholics,' he is once said to have confided to Lamormaini, 'consider me unfeeling in my prohibition of heresy. I do not hate them but love them; unless I loved them, free from any concern, I would leave them in their error.' Nor had he officially declared war on the French or they upon him. And now at the very zenith of his achievements, he had finally achieved his goal of securing the Imperial succession for his son – though only just in time. For by the occasion of that son's coronation on 30 December, he was already fatally ill.

Before the emperor's departure from Regensburg, his wife had planned a 'great masquerade' to lift his ailing spirits, but his health had caused its cancellation, and when he stopped at Straubing on the night of 25 January, he sent Lamormaini a brief note in his own hand requesting a dispensation from his usual hour of prayer while travelling, which was usually 4 a.m. By Sunday 8 February, however, he had returned to Vienna, and was not only able to venerate the shrine of Our Lady of Loreto in the Augustinerkirche, but to receive petitions, though the recovery lasted less than a week. For at around 11 p.m. the following Saturday, about two hours after retiring to bed after prayers, he awoke coughing and breathing with difficulty to bid his wife farewell and tell her that he would be dead the next day. Though he requested to hear Mass after confessing his sins to Lamormaini, his physician did not think he would last the service, and holy communion was brought to his bedside. Accordingly, at 9 a.m. on Sunday 15 February, in the company of his family and seven Jesuits, holding a blessed candle in his hand, the triumphant father finally expired, attaining what one anonymous manuscript – the *Relatio Obitus Ferdinandi* – described as the 'universal peace which he always desired but was never able to secure'.

And that failure to secure peace, in Germany above all, was now creating scenes of devastation and misery hitherto undreamed of, as armies large and small were beaten, but nothing checked the marauding instincts of common soldiers, garrison commanders and freebooters alike. Both William Crowne and the engraver Wenceslas Hollar accompanied Charles I's ambassadors to the Regensburg Diet of 1636, and though they passed through only one actual battle zone – at Ehrenbreitstein on the Rhine – the shocking destruction and poverty were apparent everywhere. Between Mainz and Frankfurt, they found the entire territory desolate, with the people of Mainz so weak from hunger that they could not even crawl to receive the alms that the travellers distributed, while at Nuremberg, the Earl of Arundel, one of the ambassadors, was able to purchase the fabulous Pirckheimer library, complete with manuscripts illustrated by Dürer and other masters, for only 350 thalers, since the owner was so short of money 'in consideration of the hard times and the difficulty of obtaining food'. Elsewhere, the English party came across one village which had been pillaged eighteen times in two years, even twice in a single day on one occasion, while their own approach, with eighteen horse-drawn wagons and cavalry escort, was mistaken in another place for an enemy attack and provoked panic defence measures.

In Linz, capital of Upper Austria, the travellers witnessed the execution of Martin Laimbauer, the leader of yet another peasant uprising, caused by conditions that had led to well-documented cases of cannibalism in the Rhineland the previous year. 'Men hunt men as beasts of prey, in the woods and on the way,' wrote Sir Thomas Roe, as both Catholic and Protestant armies cut swathes through once-thriving agricultural lands. In the three months following the great Habsburg victory at Nördlingen, according to the ministers of George of Hesse-Darmstadt, 30,000 horses, 100,000 cows and 600,000 sheep were lost, and damage worth 10 million thalers inflicted on the territory. But the Swedes, too, had taken no less a toll on occupied areas, as the city of Mainz lost perhaps 25 per cent of its dwellings, 40 per cent of its population and 60 per cent of its wealth. The duchy of Württemberg, occupied by Imperial and Bavarian forces after 1634, lost more than three-quarters of its population, while the demographic decline in several rural areas of Brandenburg – whether through war, famine or plague – exceeded 40 per cent. After Nördlingen, wrote Johann Valentin Andrea, supervisor of the Lutheran churches in Swabia, almost half of his communicants – including, as he noted, five intimate and thirty-three other friends, twenty relatives, and forty-one clerical colleagues – were subsequently killed by 'various misfortunes'. 'I have to weep for them,' he lamented, 'because I remain here so impotent and alone. Out of my whole life I am left with scarcely fifteen persons alive with whom I can claim some trace of friendship.'

But if 1635 had been dubbed by the chroniclers 'the year of great destruction' and 1636 had convinced Dr William Harvey – another of those accompanying the English embassy to Regensburg – that peace must surely be made 'on any condition, where there is no more means of making warr, or scarce of subsistence', the fighting still showed no signs of abatement. In the Valtelline, a successful revolt had been staged against French occupation, forcing the Duke of Rohan, who dared not face the rage of Richelieu, into the service of Bernard of Saxe-Weimar, while, in October 1638, the Dutch proceeded to seize Breda in an operation that became the talk of all Europe. By then, moreover, Baner had invaded Saxony, only for the Swedes to be surprised by Gallas at Torgau and driven back to Pomerania. But if Oxenstierna was at last convinced that Sweden could not fight on unaided, it only strengthened his resolve to elicit a new alliance with France, where by now Richelieu's misgivings about an open declaration of war upon the emperor had largely disappeared. In consequence, the Treaty of Hamburg of March 1638 breathed fresh and unexpected life into the Swedish war effort by guaranteeing an annual subsidy of 1 million livres to the Swedes in return for assurances that they abandon any claims to territory in the Rhineland. And though, for the first time, both sides set down their thoughts on the nature of a post-war settlement, the proposed restoration of the political, constitutional and religious conditions of 1618 reflected not only the futility of the war to date, but the unlikelihood of its resolution in the near future.

After the near disaster of 1636, furthermore, French military confidence had at last received a filip, which convinced both Richelieu and his allies that the stakes involved were worth the continued slaughter. For, encouraged by Gallas's absence in Saxony, Bernard of Saxe-Weimar took Rheinfelden, east of Basel, in February 1638, and from there advanced on Breisach, the most important link in the chain of Habsburg communications, capturing it, with French support, after a siege lasting from August to December. And though Bernard himself would succumb to smallpox in July 1639, leaving the army to his second-in-command, Hans Ludwig von Erlach, Richelieu was suitably buoyed by his most significant triumph for some time, since Imperial incursions into Alsace were now effectively barred. For four weeks, Breisach's garrison had gone without bread, surviving by chewing horse and cow hides, and upon its capture Bernard had been furious to discover that thirty of his own men, taken as prisoners of war, had starved to death. Three, indeed, had allegedly been eaten by the survivors. But France – or at least its cardinal – was re-energised, and in October 1639 came news that Erlach's troops were henceforth to be paid directly by the French and thereby obey orders from a French commander-in-chief.

By this time, too, the French army was becoming a more useful weapon of war in its own right. For while its administration was undergoing radical reform by two talented civilians, Abel Servien and Sublet de Noyers, the young commander

Henri Turenne was beginning to show his paces, after a small force had invaded Spain in 1638 to lay siege to the Basque port of Fuenterrabia. Though the siege was ultimately abandoned, a French naval squadron had defeated Spanish attempts to relieve the town, and there was the added consolation of a successful attack on Roussillon, a Pyrenean province lost to Spain in 1494. With growing French influence in Savoy, where Louis XIII's sister, Christine, was attempting to rule in the wake of her husband's death, Richelieu could therefore feel well satisfied with developments. He had ridden the storm of 1636 and three years later was witnessing the first significant fruits of his tenacity. For while his victories marked, at best, the end of the beginning rather than the beginning of the end, France was not only secure but holding the initiative. And there was the added consideration, above all, that if France was still incapable of delivering a killer blow in her own right, her enemy was nevertheless proceeding to bleed to death from its own internal wounds.

In spite of Spain's deficiencies, however, Olivares still hoped for divine deliverance and in 1639 prepared an armada of over seventy vessels, commanded by Antonio de Oquenda, to sail to Flanders in an operation that was as breathtaking as it was foolhardy. Recognising that the fall of Breisach and the French occupation of Savoy, Alsace and Lorraine made it impossible for him to reinforce the Spanish army in the southern Netherlands by any other means, he not only intended to transport reinforcements by ship but to destroy the hitherto invincible Dutch fleet, and thereafter join the Danes in an attack upon Älvsborg, Sweden's outlet on the North Sea. In this way, or so he believed, the United Provinces would be denied access through the Sound to the Baltic trade upon which their wealth depended. But the exceptional ability of Maarten Harpertszoon Tromp had not been accounted for, and when Oquenda arrived in the English Channel in September 1639, the Dutch admiral, though heavily outnumbered, succeeded in forcing his foe to seek the protection of English shore batteries covering the Downs roadstead between Dover and the North Foreland.

For several years, in fact, Charles I had used his supposed neutrality to connive in the movement of Spanish troops through English waters, and now, indeed, he was content to play host to the endangered armada in return for Spanish gold. But disputes over the North Sea fisheries had already strained Anglo-Dutch relations to the limit, and Tromp was given the green light for action. With no more than twenty ships to challenge the English guns and Spanish fleet of seventy, therefore, Dutch dockyards worked feverishly to convert merchant vessels into men-of war, and within three weeks Tromp's numbers had been trebled, in preparation for an engagement that began with the employment of fire-ships and ended with the destruction of most of Oquenda's fleet. Putting to sea in

panic and disarray, some ships ran aground, and those that survived the ensuing
'Battle of the Downs' were left to limp into Dunkirk a weakened and demoralised force. And though the Spanish navy would manage to convoy another 4,000
troops to Flanders until the fall of Dunkirk in 1646, the lesson was inescapable,
as losses by 1640 amounted to 100 warships, 12 admirals and 20,000 sailors, or
the equivalent of ten Trafalgars. Spain could not sustain such a rate of attrition,
and nor could she therefore hope to subdue the Dutch.

For quite apart from logistical, financial and strategic issues, the very
foundations of the Spanish homeland itself were presently endangered, as the
federal union over which Philip IV presided threatened to fall apart. Composed
of five kingdoms – Castile, Aragon, Navarre, Granada and Portugal – which
shared a common loyalty to one royal family but preserved their separate
constitutions, customs and liberties, Spain was always susceptible to fracture. But
now, under the agonising burden of a manifestly unwinnable war, what had once
seemed possible now seemed certain, as Catalonia, itself one of the three separate
kingdoms of Aragon, bridled under Madrid's dominance. Regarding Castile
as an allied but foreign power with whom it had neither economic links nor
historical associations, it had taken no part in Castilian enterprises in America,
nor for that matter in the Netherlands. On the contrary, as a Mediterranean
state, Catalonia resented its entanglement in Castile's wars, and balked at its
association with a kingdom crippled by overseas commitments and domestic
debts. Indeed, over a decade earlier, Catalonia had roundly rejected Olivares' call
for a Union of Arms, and in 1632 also rejected his appeal for financial aid. With
no sight of their ruler and neither honours, pensions nor employment from his
bounty, Catalans had in effect become 'entirely separate from the monarchy', as
Olivares put it, 'useless for service and in a state little befitting the dignity and
power of His Majesty.'

In 1636, Spain had not dared to invade France from Catalan soil, so uncertain
was the attitude of the inhabitants, and when the French besieged Fuenterrabia,
the Catalans refused to send help, as though Catalonia was not at war with
Madrid's arch-enemy. But by 1639, with the French invasion of Roussillon, such
indifference could no longer be tolerated, and the order went out to raise men
and money by force – with predictable consequences. 'The Catalans,' declared
the Marquis de los Vélez, the Spanish viceroy, 'are naturally fickle … Make them
understand that the welfare of the nation and the army must go beyond all laws
and privileges.' And by the spring of 1641, after the billeting of Spanish troops in
Catalonia throughout the previous winter, what Olivares swiftly came to inter-
pret as a second Dutch revolt was in full swing, aided by 3,000 French auxiliaries,
who on 26 January helped bring about the defeat of Los Vélez on Montjuic hill,

just outside the capital. Passing the point of no return, the rebels duly accepted Louis XIII as 'Count of Barcelona', and concentrated their fighting upon Lérida, which commanded the main road from Castile into the kingdom.

Two months earlier, meanwhile, rebellion had also broken out in Portugal, led by the Duke of Braganza, a claimant to the throne that had passed to the Habsburgs in 1580. Initially, at least, the Portuguese had contributed a relatively modest 1 million cruzados to the Spanish war effort after 1619, but Madrid's demand for treble that amount in 1634, followed by a further demand in June 1640 for 6,000 Portuguese troops to help crush the Catalans, proved a step too far. Storming the Lisbon palace of the vicereine, Margarita of Savoy, the rebels threw her principal adviser, Miguel de Vasconcellos, out of the window, leaving Braganza, spurred on by his indomitable wife, to proclaim himself John IV of Portugal in December. By the following June, a Portuguese army, improvised almost from scratch, had launched an offensive into Spain itself, and within a year Pope Urban had received King John's ambassador, implying recognition. By that time, too, the Duke of Medina Sidonia, a member of one of Spain's proud-est families and, like others of his class an inveterate hater of Olivares, had only just been thwarted in his plans to become master of an independent Andalusia.

Nor, as Spain imploded, was the news from abroad any more heartening. For in the Netherlands, the cardinal-infante, too, had begun to lose heart. He had saved Antwerp in 1638 and survived two attacks on Hulst in 1639, but could not fight successfully on two fronts at once and in 1640, notwithstanding the suc-cesses of his early career, lost Arras, the capital of Artois to the French. Though still barely 30 years of age, he was weary, indeed prematurely aged, by a barrage of endless and impossible demands to send aid to Castile while struggling to hold both the French and Dutch at bay, and reported in 1641 that:

> ... if the war with France is to continue we have not the means to take the offensive. The Spanish and Imperial armies are reduced to such a state that they can undertake nothing. The only solution is to establish supporters in France and use them to make the Paris government more amenable.

But it was a vain hope. The Dukes of Bouillon and Orléans, who were genuinely opposed to the war with Spain and who hated Richelieu's exercise of power, needed no prompting from Spain to promote a conspiracy in April 1641. For although the hated 'grey eminence', Père Joseph, had died three years earlier, the cardinal was continuing to surround the now ailing king with his own men, like the Neapolitan Jules Mazarin. Richelieu was, indeed, founding what amounted to a personal dynasty, making his relations marshals of France, generals of galleys, governors, dukes and peers, creating one of his nieces Duchess of Aiguillon and marrying another to the Duke of Enghien, rendering her a princess of the blood. He also owned fortresses at Brouage and Le Havre, and possessed both a company of infantry and another of gentlemen. Yet, for all this, no plot involving the invasion of the kingdom by a mercenary army in support of an attempt to persuade the king to switch to a pro-Spanish *dévot* policy was capable of success, and the planned revolt was duly defeated.

In 1641, too, the Count of Soissons – a member of the Bourbon family exiled for his part in a plot five years earlier – had led another conspiracy, defeating a royalist army in the process, before making the mistake of lifting his visor with a loaded pistol and accidentally pulling the trigger as he did so. 'If monsieur the count had not been killed, he would have been welcomed by half of Paris,' wrote one of the cardinal's own agents. But killed he was, and Richelieu duly spared. Indeed, the only crumb of comfort for Spain in 1641 was the first real evidence of dissension between Frederick Henry and the Dutch States-General, caused by doubts concerning his military performance and, more so still, his choice of a wife for his son. He had enjoyed no major triumph since the fall of Breda in 1637, and his decision to marry his son William to Mary, daughter of Charles I, had ramifications which led to a bitter dispute, as fears of Dutch involvement on the royalist side in the approaching English Civil War gathered pace. Reasserting their uncompromisingly Calvinist and republican principles, the regent class maintained that if any side were to be assisted, it should be the English Parliament, and even an eventual declaration of neutrality only papered over the cracks.

Yet in comparison to Spain's divisions, the tensions in The Hague remained minimal, and the death of the cardinal-infante in November 1641 merely provided one further fleeting footnote in the sorry tale of Spanish woes. He had been an excellent soldier but a poor statesman, and his demise served only to inaugurate a period of clumsy emergency measures, which terminated in effect only six years later, by which time a peace was looming that was no less catastrophic for the southern Netherlands than the war itself had been. Even the death of Richelieu himself, for that matter, in December 1642 and the demise of Louis XIII only a few months later, could not remedy Spain's own terminal ills or detract from her enemy's overall primacy. The French cardinal, worn out and depleted by his efforts, and weakened by the implacable hostility of his enemies, had fallen ill in November and died early the following month. Shortly before his death, moreover, he had inadvertently composed his effective epitaph when he told the king, who had come to visit him from his own sickbed, that 'in taking leave of Your Majesty I have the consolation of leaving your kingdom in the highest degree of glory and of reputation which it has ever had' – all of which was true. Roussillon and Perpignan, lost to Spain in 1494, had been recovered, Alsace and Lorraine were under French control, and French armies were carrying the war forward both in Flanders and in Spain itself under the command of men like Turenne and the young Duke of Enghien, who, at the age of only 22 – and in spite of his violent, morose and generally wayward nature – appeared to be sweeping all before him. Spain was in terminal crisis, France at a critical turning-point in her history.

If, moreover, it is the mark of a great statesman that his policies should survive him, particularly in a context of pressing difficulty, here too Richelieu was successful. For in March 1643, when Louis XIII's own tubercular lungs finally gave way, it was duly arranged that the king's 4-year-old successor should be placed under the regency of his mother, Anne of Austria, on the assumption that she and the Lieutenant-General of the kingdom, the Duke of Orléans, work in close co-operation with the cardinal's protégé, Mazarin. Fortunately, the deaths of Richelieu and Louis had not come until the moment of Spain's defeats, which made the prospect of intrigue with Madrid an altogether less attractive prospect for would-be conspirators. And by a judicious mix of guile, charm and exceptional acumen, the successor to Richelieu's seat was soon able to win not only the support of the so-called *noblesse de la robe* by a show of legality which appeared to place supreme constitutional authority in the hands of the Paris Parlement, but also the unswerving devotion of the queen herself, who became, some say, his lover. Created a cardinal at Richelieu's behest in 1641, Mazarin would even, indeed, become a Frenchman, converting his name from Giulio Mazarini and establishing firm roots in the kingdom to which he had arrived as papal nuncio only five years earlier. 'To a gentleman,' he had written, 'any country is a homeland', and he duly built a splendid town residence – which now houses the manuscript section of the French National Library – not far from the royal palace, ensuring, just as any loyal Frenchman and disciple of Richelieu was bound to do, that the new regent vigorously maintained the wars against both the King of Spain (her brother) and the emperor (her brother-in-law).

None of which is to deny, of course, the enormous cost, both human and financial, involved in maintaining the dead cardinal's legacy. 'If God exists,' commented Pope Urban VIII upon Richelieu's death, 'he will have to atone.' And while Mazarin might woo the queen and savour Spain's predicament, he too would have to ride a tide of popular unrest before France's many enemies abroad could be finally dispatched. Indeed, the price of military success was already so immoderately expensive that the victories were of less consequence than the measures taken to pay for them. For although the government had tried initially to fund its alliances and minor campaigns by creating more offices for sale within the administration, by 1636 it had been necessary not only to borrow massively, but to finance the new loans through what would eventually amount to a threefold increase in taxation – the most remarkable rate of increase in the entire history of the *ancien regime*. And as taxes mounted, so too did the arrears of payment, leading to the widespread confiscation of goods and chattels by collectors and the incidence of widespread revolts, principally in the south and west – and mainly in spring – throughout the war years. Even in 1636, the very year that Paris itself was threatened by Habsburg armies, Amiens and Rennes dissolved into disorder, along with rural areas of the south-west, as the so-called *croquants* wrought vengeance on the hated tax officials. In all, nearly one quarter of France was affected, between the Loire and Garonne, as crowds of peasants, sometimes numbering 60,000, gathered in strength to oppose the government in general and Richelieu in particular, who ultimately ended the rebellion with the slaughter of 14,000 people.

For the cardinal's successor, then, the way ahead presented no primrose path. On the contrary, Jules Mazarin would have to tread carefully and continually weigh the crippling difficulties of his enemy against the substantial obstacles that he himself faced. But at least he would not be locking horns with the most long-standing of Spain's champions, since the death of Richelieu was followed almost immediately by the fall of Olivares himself, who was made the scapegoat for Philip IV's abortive campaign against the Catalan rebels in the summer of 1642. Forced to abandon his assault when French troops reinforced Barcelona and advanced into Aragon, the king's humiliation, coupled to the frustrations of the preceding five years, finally forced him to order the minister's retirement in January 1643. For some time, in fact, the man who had scarcely left his monarch's side for thirty years had been displaying signs of mental instability – whisking away the poet Francisco de Quevedo from his lodgings one night, to become one of the 'disappeared' (*desaparecido*), after he had passed the king a satirical attack on the minister written on a napkin. And at Philip's personal command, the count-duke duly retired to his estates, never to meet his king again. But the blow, whether justified or not, remained a cruel one, and by July 1645 Olivares was indeed dead, relieved of the grief that had rendered him almost insane over the past two years, and free at last from the grandiose dream of a world-wide monarchy that had both driven and ruined his life.

With France exposed to the potential hazards of a regency, however, there was at least opportunity and good cause for a breathing-space in 1643, during which Spain could take stock, re-group and recover as best she might. For if the war could not be won, it might, perhaps, at least be lost with honour or even some semblance of victory, with minimum additional damage to the kingdom's social fabric. But Don Francisco de Melo, who had replaced the cardinal-infante as governor of the southern Netherlands, was anxious to make his mark and duly invaded France at the head of an army reinforced by the emperor, with the intention of breaking the line of fortresses guarding the head of the Oise valley by laying siege to Rocroi. It was a desperate resort and a reckless one at that, as events would soon prove, since he had not counted upon the arrival of a relief force under Enghien, which was only marginally smaller than his own and carelessly permitted to emerge unmolested from a narrow defile, where it engaged the enemy on open ground and triumphed after six hours of fighting. At one point, in fact, the French were no less exhausted than their enemy, but when 2,000 of De Melo's troops laid down their arms in return for guarantees of safe passage home across France, the crisis was overcome. De Melo escaped, losing his marshal's baton in the process, and though some 8,000 Spanish *tercios* held firm, it was utterly in vain. For, as their Walloon, German and Italian contingents deserted them, they too crumbled – and with them, once and for all, the legend of their invincibility.

'To tell the truth,' De Melo reflected sadly, 'we used to regard war here as a pastime; but the profession [of arms] is serious and it gains and loses empires.' For Don Luis de Haro, however, France's resounding victory was as incomprehensible as it was depressing. The nephew of Olivares, he had replaced his uncle in control of administration in Madrid, and on 17 November 1643, after a further cascade of French successes, expressed his concerns unequivocally:

> The defeat of Rocroi has given rise in all areas to the consequences we had always feared. It was a terrible outcome, and one for which most observers have failed to find any military or political cause. I must tell you that it is something that can only be recollected with great pain, because although the losses inflicted by God must be accepted, those which seem to stem from a human hand are always harder to bear.

Though the impact of the battle has sometimes been exaggerated, in so far as it had no immediate effect on Spain's control over the southern Netherlands, where she still maintained more than 77,000 troops in comparison to a Dutch total that had sunk to 60,000, its psychological impact and likely long-term significance were nevertheless indisputable at a time when the Spanish army's advance into Catalonia was grindingly slow, Portugal was consolidating itself as an independent state, and Philip IV's Italian possessions were also showing signs of unbearable strain. At a single stroke, in fact, Rocroi had now brought an abrupt end to all hope of launching another invasion of France from the Low Countries. Moreover, with Trier, Alsace and Lorraine in French hands, and with the Dutch in control of Limburg, the Channel and the North Sea, the Spanish government was now physically unable to send reinforcements to the Low Countries. The Spanish Road was blocked, and as the noose tightened, the southern Netherlands would ultimately prove unable to resist the progress of French and Dutch arms, after Gravelines fell in 1644, Hulst in 1645, and Dunkirk in 1646.

As Spain's miseries mounted, meanwhile, so the balance in her relations with Austria steadily altered, too. Having paid a respectable 426,000 florins to her Imperial cousin in 1640, she was no longer in a position to help significantly, delivering only 12,000 florins the following year and 60,000 as a loan in 1642. Nor was the early military success of Ferdinand III sustained. Aged only 29 at the time of his accession, he had grown up amid dynastic crisis and war, and had inherited his father's antipathy to heresy, though in a more moderate and pragmatic form, and along with Maximilian von Trauttmansdorff, his chief diplomat, was inclined to peace, should Sweden offer acceptable terms. But while the Habsburg homelands remained his priority and his main concern within the Empire was to uphold his constitutional prerogatives rather than impose religious uniformity, his difficulties remained considerable, even after his presence at Nördlingen had invested him with such a glittering start to his military career. Two of his three wives and six of his eleven children would die before him, compounding his naturally melancholic disposition, but it was the stresses, strains and frustrations of an Empire that could not be brought to peace, and a war that could not be won that by 1640 was doing most to undermine his health and sap his morale.

Late in 1638, after a year on the defensive in Pomerania, but now with Swedish reinforcements at his back and French subsidies in his pocket, Baner had driven the Imperials into Silesia again, and gone on, in April 1639, to defeat the Saxons at Chemnitz and threaten Prague. Though eventually forced to withdraw, the Swedes also mounted in 1640 a combined operation with their French allies, involving troops formerly led by Bernard of Saxe-Weimar, as well as contingents supplied by Brunswick and Hesse-Kassel. And it was in these ominous circumstances that in September 1640 Emperor Ferdinand III duly summoned to Regensburg the first full Imperial Diet to meet since 1603. His aim was to negotiate a general settlement on the best possible terms from the German princes before matters deteriorated any further. For while Sweden, too, was effectively on its knees, Baner's latest attack had suggested otherwise, and the emperor was faced with little choice – notwithstanding the fact that in

Stockholm, Oxenstierna's lugubrious brother, Gustav Gustavsson, was observing how 'the common man wishes himself dead'.

It was an indication of the changed circumstances of Imperial politics that the delegates at Regensburg readily accepted that Ferdinand's troops be stationed outside the city in case of attack by Baner – a defence measure which at any other Diet would have been loudly denounced as an act of intimidation. And it was a further fearful reminder of the Empire's current vulnerability that, as the Diet sat in enclave in January 1641, the sound of Swedish shelling was continual until the River Danube thawed and Baner was forced to withdraw for lack of supplies – firstly to Saxony and thence to Halberstadt, where he died in spring. Once again, Ferdinand had briefly revelled in his favoured role of military commander, organising Regensburg's defence as the Swedes lowered menacingly with only the frozen Danube between them and the city. But the Diet had not been summoned for the emperor to demonstrate his military prowess. Nor had it been called to end in anything other than peace. For, as events had finally demonstrated, a war without limit could not, after all, become a war without end, and everything now depended upon whether the victor of Nördlingen could turn his hand with equal skill to the subtler art of political negotiation.

12

THE CRISIS OF THE PEACE

They say that the terrible war is now over. But there is still no sign of a peace. Everywhere there is envy, hatred and greed: that's what the war has taught us … We live like animals, eating bark and grass. No one could have imagined that anything like this would happen to us. Many people say that there is no God. But we still believe that God has not abandoned us. We must stand together and help each other.

> Entry in a family Bible, from the Swabian village of
> Gerstetten, dated 17 January 1647

In the autumn of 1636, Pope Urban VIII had taken the first tentative steps towards the organisation of a general peace conference and, to that end, a papal legate arrived in Cologne that October to invite all interested powers. But nobody came. Neither France nor Spain trusted the Pope to be impartial, and the Protestants rejected papal mediation altogether, convening a largely fruitless conference of their own at Hamburg instead. Thereafter various soundings and overtures had been made, most notably between Swedes and Imperials, but they had invariably been washed away by mutual suspicion, irreconcilable objectives and the changing tides of war, which continued to deceive the protagonists into the vain belief that a decisive advantage might yet be gained. So when the Regensburg Diet opened with solemn ceremony in September 1640 in the hope of uniting the Empire and saving German liberty from the alien crowns of France and Sweden, there were few grounds for serious optimism. Over the year ahead, the three colleges of the assembly would, it is true, discuss with a new intensity the issues that kept their country at war. Indeed, no less than 185 formal sessions were held by the electors, and 153 by the other princes, along with another twenty-six joint meetings in all. But some rulers dared not attend, others refused on principle even to send delegates, and the emperor himself excluded the Protestant administrators of the dioceses affected by the Edict of Restitution, as well as those princes in arms against him. Even for those present, moreover, there were the inevitable delays for correspondence: two or three days for a letter from the princely court of Munich; between five and eight for dispatches from Mainz and Vienna; while from Königsberg, where the Elector of Brandenburg now resided, a message could take as long as three weeks in summer and five in winter.

At first, however, all went well from Emperor Ferdinand's point of view. Earlier that year he had met the electors at Nuremberg and agreed that the terms of the Peace of Prague would have to be modified if the Calvinists were to lay down their arms. He had also persuaded Maximilian of Bavaria that, if a permanent settlement were to be secured, some portion of the Palatinate might need to be relinquished. But though safe conducts were issued to Calvinists and even a representative of the former Elector Palatine's family was invited, the Regensburg Diet would ultimately fall foul of the ill-will of the young man who was imminently to take control of Brandenburg. Aged only 20, but a die-hard Calvinist who had been educated for a time at The Hague in the company of Frederick V's children, he had chosen to live outside Brandenburg until his recall in December 1640, as his father, George William, lay on his deathbed. And although he recognised the difficulties of governing and defending such a scattered and vulnerable patrimony as the one he was about to inherit, he nev-ertheless remained contemptuous of the predecessor who, in his view, had done so little to safeguard its interests. For Brandenburg was a battleground wasted by Imperials and Swedes, while Pomerania remained under Swedish occupa-tion, Cleves was dominated by the Dutch, and East Prussia had become a Polish fief. As a result, Frederick William, Brandenburg's new ruler, would deign to strike another path, denouncing in particular the Peace of Prague, which merely imposed on his people the burden of maintaining troops to serve an emperor who was unable to protect them from Swedish domination. And in doing so, he would wreck not only the emperor's hopes for the Regensburg Diet, but for controlling the entire peace agenda that was now slowly to unfold.

For when Frederick William succeeded in securing a truce with Sweden in July 1641, followed by a formal peace two months later, more and more repre-sentatives dared to question the emperor's appeal for a general renunciation of dealings with the French and Swedes, not to mention his request for a renewal of the taxes agreed by some Circle assemblies in 1638. Ultimately, he would succeed in his appeal for money, insofar as the electors and the cities conceded to his wishes, but thirty-one of the forty-six princes present at Regensburg nevertheless demurred, and when the war taxes he needed so badly were finally collected, compliance was poor. Plainly, the emperor's hopes for a united German front were as hollow as ever, and when he himself – independently of the Diet's deliberations – sent delegates to preliminary peace negotiations in Hamburg in December 1641, involving representatives of Sweden and France, the conclusion was inescapable: not only that war must end and peace be mutually agreed, but that the emperor and his subject princes must agree to differ as the process was played out – on the one hand at Münster, where matters relating to France would be hammered out, and also at Osnabrück for all matters pertaining to Sweden.

But if an end to hostilities was now the priority of all concerned, the date was still a far-off prospect, and in the meantime, as the rival parties continued to jostle for advantage, the war would persist with all its familiar intensity. After Baner's death, Karl Gustav Wrangel had briefly stepped into the breach, but with neither an inspiring commander nor pay, the Swedish army mutinied and threatened to join the so-called 'Bernardines' – the troops formerly led by Bernard of Saxe-Weimar. The result was a brief respite for the Imperials, though on 30 June 1641 Oxenstierna's envoys at Hamburg concluded a final alliance with France, to last until the peace, and Lennart Torstensson, one of Sweden's most successful generals, was sent to Germany to win the war. Elderly and rheumatic, with a reputation for savage discipline, Torstensson was nevertheless audacious and vastly experienced, and well suited to restoring discipline, as he withdrew the army east of the Elbe for a four-month period, gathered enough money to settle the mutiny, and bolstered his numbers with 7,000 Swedish conscripts who arrived at his camp on 25 November and subsequently formed the nucleus of a force that had been increasingly diluted by foreign recruits.

French subsidies, in fact, had been increased to 480,000 thalers that year, and Oxenstierna, too, had helped pack Torstensson's pockets with money gleaned from the sale of crown lands. Though the expedient was a dangerous one for the long-term financial health of its country, the Swedish government was intent, it seems, upon one final all-out effort, and, initially at least, the gamble seemed to pay off handsomely. For in the spring of 1642, the new commander-in-chief invaded Saxony, defeating the forces of John George at Schweidnitz, before advancing nearly 200 miles to the south-east in an astonishing campaign through Silesia and on into the heart of Moravia. His outriders would, indeed, press on to within 25 miles of Vienna before Piccolomini and the emperor's younger brother, Archduke Leopold Wilhelm, had even begun to organise the city's defences. Nor did a temporary retreat into Saxony after overstretching his lines of communication prevent Torstensson from ultimately achieving his most spectacular victory of all, when on 2 November he won a battle a little north of Breitenfeld, almost as complete as the triumph gained by Gustavus Adolphus at the same spot eleven years earlier. Some 5,000 Imperial troops were lost on the field, and a further 5,000 as prisoners, as well as forty-six field guns, and the archduke's treasury, chancery and supply train. Only one month later, moreover, Leipzig fell, resulting in the payment of an indemnity amounting to 400,000 thalers for immunity from Torstensson's men.

But the significance of the Second Battle of Breitenfeld reached far beyond Saxony and its capital, as terror among the emperor's allies in western Germany reached crisis point and Ferdinand found himself progressively abandoned by each and every one. Throughout Torstensson's campaign, the negotiations at Münster and Osnabrück in Westphalia had largely hung fire, and until the defeat of 2 November, Ferdinand remained convinced of an imminent split between both Sweden and Brandenburg, and Sweden and Denmark. Yet the French, too, were biding their time and remained confident that Torstensson would force the emperor to reduce his terms. And in the waiting game that followed, it was they rather than the emperor whose patience was duly rewarded, for in April and May matters reached a head as the electors of Mainz and Cologne invited Germany's princes to a conference at Frankfurt-on-Main at which the emperor fondly hoped to settle his disputes with all concerned, independently of France and Sweden. Maximilian of Bavaria, in particular, was horrified by the recent Swedish success and, as early as January 1640, had offered in secret talks at Einsiedeln to agree peace terms with Paris. But now both France and Sweden invited all German princes to join their ongoing discussions with the emperor in Westphalia, and in spite of Ferdinand's wishes, not only Maximilian but Frederick William of Brandenburg, too, accepted.

It was a key moment. By now the Bavarian army, led by Franz von Mercy and his cavalry commander Johann von Werth, was beginning to recover its reputation, and the emperor's need for its services in the wake of Breitenfeld made it virtually impossible for him to prevent Maximilian's defiance. Encouraged, too, by Mazarin's assurance that his rights in the Palatinate would not be questioned, the Duke of Bavaria was, indeed, effectively beyond the emperor's control, as was Frederick William of Brandenburg who fully appreciated the advantages he might enjoy over Ferdinand with the Swedes at Osnabrück. To all intents and purposes, the emperor was therefore a broken reed. Progressively abandoned by his German allies, the independent negotiating position he had hoped for, at the head of a united front, had evaporated before his eyes, and after almost a quarter-century of war, the deadlock in the struggle, which had prevailed since Lützen, appeared at last to be broken. For by the spring of 1643, Ferdinand had accepted that the Westphalian conferences at Münster and Osnabrück should be accorded the status of Diets, so that whatever they determined should become a law of the Empire and thus settle the Empire's internal issues in perpetuity.

There were still, of course, the wider theatres of war to be considered and the ongoing fluctuations of fighting to complicate even further the prospects for what was already a hugely intricate peace process. None therefore expected the joyful pealing of bells to be heard in anything like the near future. Spain, on the one hand, had been left so defenceless in Flanders after the defeat at Rocroi that Ferdinand was obliged to send Piccolomini to help, and, in the meantime, he himself depended increasingly upon Maximilian's revitalised Bavarian army to hold south-west Germany, where Mercy and Werth excelled themselves against the Bernardines. In the north, moreover, Christian of Denmark had recovered from his humiliation at the hands of Wallenstein and was now shaping to renew the struggle against Sweden, lured by the offer of Bremen and Hamburg from the Empire. Already, in 1635, he had attempted to exploit Baner's difficulties with mutinous troops, and four years later he had also planned with Olivares a joint attack on Älvsborg, which prompted Oxenstierna to quip how the King of Denmark had 'repeatedly tucked us under the chin to see if our teeth were still firm in our heads'. Now, however, Christian was probing again over the issue of the Sound dues from which Sweden was exempted, but not, or so he claimed, ships plying from Baltic ports under Swedish occupation or, for that matter, Dutch ships fraudulently sailing under a Swedish flag.

Plainly, Denmark would not rest until a reckoning had been made, and it was with this in mind that in the late autumn of 1644, Oxenstierna finally ordered Torstensson to abandon a campaign in Silesia to launch a surprise attack, which by January had left him master of the Danish mainland and poised to capture Copenhagen as soon as the Little and Great Belts froze over. Assisted by a Dutch fleet financed by Louis de Geer, the Dutch entrepreneur with a fortune invested in Swedish metallurgical industries, Sweden gained control of the Sound and captured the islands of Gotland and Osel, which commanded the shipping lanes into the eastern Baltic. And though the Little Belt eventually failed to freeze and unexpected resistance was encountered at Malmo, allowing Gallas to pursue and trap Torstensson in the Jutland peninsula, the Swedes nevertheless maintained their threat by achieving a naval victory off Fehmarn island on 23 October, which left Christian himself wounded, and by staging a further push on land, which led to a retreat by the Imperials across the Elbe. With Gallas blind drunk, two of his disillusioned subordinates tried to escape with 4,000 cavalry in November, but the attempt was unsuccessful, and the final blows followed swiftly as Bremen, Stade and Verden all fell in rapid succession early in 1645, by which time Danish power – just like Gallas who was dismissed on 24 January – was broken once and for all.

'It would be hard to find,' wrote the chronicler of Chemnitz, 'a similar example of an army brought to ruin in such a short time' after the retreating Imperial army, reduced from 18,000 to 1,000 men, had limped its way home to Bohemia through areas so devastated that most had died of starvation en route. But in Paris, too, the wheels of war were continuing to turn alongside talk of peace. After his early successes, Mazarin, indeed, was increasingly concerned by the tide of events, objecting to Sweden's attack on Denmark, on the grounds that it amounted to a misappropriation of French subsidies intended for the defeat of the emperor, and worrying above all that Maximilian of Bavaria had not ultimately been won from his alliance with the emperor. Nor was this the limit of the cardinal's worries. For in spite of its victories over Spain, the best of the French army was nevertheless succumbing to Mercy and Werth in the Black Forest, while a Spanish embassy had arrived at Münster, keen to be involved in the peace process. Since even the briefest of truces might allow Philip IV to assist his finances and restore some semblance of order to the Iberian peninsula before resuming the war with France, this last development was particularly unwelcome, and caused the Duke of Longueville, leader of the French delegation, to refuse to meet the Spanish ambassador in March 1644, on the grounds that his credentials credited Spain's monarchy with control of Navarre and Barcelona, both of which France claimed for Louis XIV.

Such issues of protocol would, indeed, delay the formal opening of the Westphalian conferences until December 1644, and guarantee the absence of any substantive progress throughout 1645. The Spaniards were determined that the emperor should not abandon their interests in the Rhineland, and to this extent they were prepared to quibble over every detail, relevant or otherwise, to resist French attempts to exclude them. Moreover, if this involved lengthening the misery of the war's innocent victims, then both they and their protagonists would feel little compunction at their unwillingness to expedite matters. For the procedural disputes that so dogged proceedings in Westphalia also reflected the ambivalence of objectives even within those countries represented at the conferences. Johan Salvius and Oxenstierna's son, for example, represented two opposing factions in the Swedish delegation, one anxious for compromise, the other keen to assert his country's power and to extract the maximum recompense for his country's costly intervention in Germany in the first place. Coarse, disagreeable and bellicose, Johan Oxenstierna was, in fact, the diametrical opposite of his father. But he was nevertheless head of the Swedish delegation, and directly responsible for the kind of in-fighting also witnessed among other parties at both Osnabrück and Münster. Amongst the Dutch, Johan de Knuyt of Zeeland and Adriaen Pauw of Holland advocated war and peace respectively, while, on more trivial grounds, the Duke of Longueville's assistants, the Count of Avaux and Abel Servien, were so jealous of each other that they could not agree on anything, and insisted upon reporting to Mazarin separately – a situation mirrored amongst the Spanish delegation, where the country's leading political thinker, Diego de Saavedra, resented his subordinate status to Count Peñaranda whose undistinguished career in financial administration was now compounded by an imperfect command of French and a debilitating preoccupation with the inclemency of the Westphalian weather.

It was hardly fertile ground for haste. But while diplomats squabbled and their governments continue to hedge for advantage throughout 1645, the killing continued. In February, Torstensson invaded Silesia, and was advancing rapidly across Bohemia with Imperial and Bavarian troops on his flank when he challenged and defeated them at Jankau. And the danger for Austria continued, as George Rákóczy of Transylvania, prompted by Swedish and French diplomacy, followed the example of his predecessor Bethlen Gábor and invaded Habsburg Hungary, to be acclaimed by the Protestant nobility. In response, Ferdinand rushed to Vienna to organise its defences, but was only saved ultimately by the garrison at Brno in Moravia, which held up Torstensson for five months and prevented the junction of the two invading armies. Bought off by the Treaty of Linz, which ceded extensive Habsburg lands and guaranteed full freedom of worship to Hungarian Protestants, Rákóczy duly abandoned the struggle, though the emperor's temporary relief was soon confounded by Turenne's invasion of the Upper Palatinate in spring. Even after Mercy's victory over the French at Bad Mergentheim, moreover, Enghien, assisted by Swedish reinforcements, was able to force his way through to the Danube and challenge the Bavarians at Allerheim, near Nördlingen in August. Both sides suffered heavy casualties and Mercy was killed instantly by a shot to the head as he entered the burning village where the battle was raging, though the eventual withdrawal of his troops did not prevent the emperor from continuing to hold the line of the Danube at Donauwörth.

Clearly, the process of peace-making would itself be bloody. For although, by now, several of the most intransigent figures in the conflict had been removed by death or disgrace, their successors were no less determined to exact the best possible return from the prodigal expenditure of human lives and resources. Losses, of course, may well have been exaggerated by some contemporary and later accounts, but the scepticism of those historians who wish to scale down one of the greatest demographic disasters in German history remains unwarranted.

Even ignoring those accounts of hanged offenders being torn from the gallows in Alsace to be eagerly devoured, or the confessions of those like the woman at Zweibrücken who admitted eating her own child, the impact of starvation, plague and general economic disruption makes harrowing reading. Already Germany had lost at least 25 per cent of its population, or some 6 million people, but much more likely 35 or even 40 per cent, and while areas like the north-west had hardly suffered, others experienced destruction of truly apocalyptic proportions. Mecklenburg and Pomerania, for example, suffered a decline in population of 60 per cent and Brandenburg a decline of 50 per cent. The Palatinate – to the left and right of the Rhine – Alsace and most of Württemberg, as well as the area between Ulm and Nördlingen, were also laid waste with losses of between 50 and 70 per cent. Nördlingen, indeed, did not regain its pre-war population level until the twentieth century, and while Magdeburg's recovery was comparatively rapid, other great cities like Heidelberg, Würzburg, Neustadt and Bayreuth all suffered lasting devastation.

In such places, industry declined for lack of producers, purchasers and trade; commerce largely hid its head; and once wealthy merchants begged and robbed for bread. Transport, too, was disrupted as roads were torn up with battle, made dangerous by brigands, or clogged with deserters and fugitives. Accordingly, in Stuttgart the birth rate fell by 48 per cent, in Nuremberg 36 per cent and in Augsburg 42 per cent, though Augsburg's population grew overall, largely as a result of the wholesale flight from marauding armies, whom their generals signally failed to restrain. Baner, on the one hand, freely admitted that he had not the slightest control over his men, and the sack of Kempten by the Imperials, and of Calw by the Bavarians suggest he was not alone. Both Bernard of Saxe-Weimar and Werth made it their business to burn everything they passed in hostile country, leaving Fürth, Eichstätt and Creussen as well as innumerable villages in ruins, while in Moravia, government officials and local landowners actually allied themselves with wandering marauders and shared the booty.

And while Bavaria in the meantime may have 'escaped' with demographic losses of between 30 and 40 per cent, and Saxony with less still – perhaps 20 per cent – the fact remained that even 'friendly' troops were capable of bringing devastation in their wake. Spanish troops passing through Munich, for example, had left a plague that in four months carried off 10,000 victims, and similar outbreaks in Frankfurt and Augsburg between 1632 and 1635 accounted for nearly 7,000 and 18,000 victims apiece. The great plague outbreak in Germany would last, indeed, until 1639, assisted in large part by the drain on local food supplies by passing armies, and in some cases by weather-damaged and blighted harvests. Nor, as an account from Prague, written in 1638, demonstrates, were such problems confined to the German portion of the Empire, for there too, it seems, an 'infectious epidemic of pestilence and other poisonous weaknesses', caused by 'hideous worms' in the seeds and roots of cereals, had 'started to rage mightily' – to the extent, we are told, 'that as well as the ecclesiastics, so also other secular persons have fled in great number out of the town into the surrounding villages where a not inconsiderable misery was to be observed.'

The same account tells also of dysentery among the Swedes, and the incidence of plague among the Transylvanian troops encamped just outside the city, though the Bohemian capital had at least been largely spared the worst excesses of the refugee problem that hit so many other places. Those who had fled from the south after Nördlingen died of plague, hunger and exhaustion in the refugee camp at Frankfurt or the overcrowded hospitals of Saxony. But 7,000 were expelled from the cantons of Zürich because there was neither food nor room for them, and at Hanau the gates were closed against their entry. At Strasbourg, we are told, they lay thick in the streets throughout the frosts of winter until the magistrates forcibly drove out the 30,000 that survived. And while there were tales of greater compassion elsewhere, the doers of good deeds were rarely equal to the task confronting them. After the incineration and desertion of Eichstätt, the Jesuits had rescued starving children and carried them off for education, but at Hagenau their efforts to feed the poor were frustrated when French troops raided their granary. And though William Crowne recorded at Rüdesheim how one of his party gave 'some relief to the poor which were almost starved as it appeared by the violence they used to get it from one another', he went on to note how at Bacharach 'the poor people are found dead with grass in their mouths'.

'From Coln hither [i.e. Frankfurt] all the towns, villages and castles be battered, pillaged and burnt,' Crowne recorded. At Neunkirchen, his party 'found one house burning when we came and not anybody in the village', before stumbling upon two bodies in the streets, one of which had been newly 'scraped out of the grave'. Later, at Elfkirchen, they 'dined with some reserved meat of our own, for there was not anything to be found'. And similar reports abounded elsewhere. Baner himself averred that there was not a grain of corn left for his men in Anhalt or Halle, and in Calw, a pastor claimed to have witnessed a woman gnawing on the flesh of a dead horse on which a hungry dog and some ravens were also feeding. Certainly, acorns, goats' skins and grass all became regular fare in Alsace, while cats, dogs and rats were routinely sold in the market at Wörms. And if reports that human hands and feet discovered half cooked in a gypsies' cauldron may remain questionable, there seems less doubt that in Fulda and Coburg and near the great refugee camp near Frankfurt, men and women went in genuine fear of being killed and eaten by those maddened with hunger.

How ironic, therefore, in the light of such accounts, that the wine harvest of 1634, which should have been excellent, was largely trampled down by fugitives and invaders after Nördlingen, and that the harvest of 1635, from Württemberg to Lorraine, would suffer a similar fate, leaving the worst famine for many years in its wake. Ten years into the war, the peasant Hartrich Sierk had offered up the following fervent prayer in his diary:

> God send that there may be an end at last; God send that there may be peace again. God in heaven send us peace.

Yet seven years later things were, arguably, worse than ever as the war continued to bring personal disaster to countless, mostly nameless, others like the wife of a certain Georg Rösch from the small village of Linden, who had been raped by a 'fat soldier' from east Finland and his friend, a 'white-haired young soldier'; or Dr Johann Morhard of Schwäbisch Hall, who had marked his 76th birthday in 1630 by contributing his pile of family silver to help save his city from Imperial occupation. Hans Heberle, the shoemaker of Neenstetten, would record thirty separate occasions when he fled with his family to safety in the city of Ulm, and his case was not unique. On the contrary, it reflected just one fragment of a human catastrophe that contemporaries commonly equated with the end of the world.

Even amid the agony, of course, everyday life continued. In the village of Virnesberg in Franconia, for instance, the wife of Hans Dobel attended a game-keeper's wedding amid skirmishing between Swedish and Imperial soldiers. And beneath the horror, there were acts of decency and civilised behaviour, too, like those recorded by Maria Anna Junius who had been placed in the Heiligengrab Convent outside Bamberg for her safety. Reflecting on the treatment of her convent by the Swedes, she commented:

> When one thinks of the danger we have been in … one will soon see how chivalrously we, as weak women, have survived these times. It is still wonderful to recount how the enemy themselves expressed their astonishment that we, as women, remained alone in this isolated house throughout this dangerous time … People said many bad things about us, but I can testify before God that not a single sister of our convent lost the slightest of her virginity. Though the Swedes visited us daily, they always behaved correctly and honourably towards us. Though they had appeared terrible towards us, as soon as they saw us and talked to us, they became tender like little lambs.

Yet those same Swedes had previously torched 'the entire Kaulberg district' after meeting resistance and 'ordered no one to be spared', while Junius's own father would later fall victim to one of the many witchcraft trials spawned by the mania of the times. And almost two-and-a-half decades into the conflict, as the suffering continued in manifold forms and diverse places, the peace process itself, which had finally become unavoidable, was now, too, dogged by crisis, as the French emissary at Münster refused to negotiate unless he was accorded the title *Altesse* – Highness – and the papal nuncio at Osnabrück refused to sit in the same room as Swedish 'heretics'.

It was just such intransigence, of course, that had caused the segregation of the peace talks between Münster – where France was treating with the Empire under the mediation of the papacy and Venice – and Osnabrück, 45km away, where no mediator at all was involved, since the smouldering enmity between Sweden and Denmark made it impossible for Christian of Denmark to assume the role that had originally been intended for him. And even after the eventual opening of the dual negotiations on 4 December 1644, which became collectively known as the Congress of Westphalia, the hair-splitting of lawyers and envoys, not to mention the sheer bureaucratic tangle entailed by the presence of 176 plenipotentiaries, representing 194 rulers (almost 150 of them German), threatened to undermine everything. The congress constituted by far the largest – as well as the longest-lived – peace conference held to that date, involving all the continental powers save England, Poland, Russia and Turkey, and would prove from the outset, arguably, one of the most persistently opportunistic too. 'In winter we negotiate, in summer we fight,' remarked one exasperated delegate. And while the fighting continued and the balance of forces continued to shift interminably, so progress achieved at one moment was apt to disappear the next, as Johan Adler Salvius made clear in his complaint to the Swedish council about the antics of the other parties:

> Their first rule of politics is that the security of all depends on the equilibrium of the individuals. When one begins to become more powerful ... the others place themselves through unions or alliances, into the opposite balance in order to maintain the equipoise.

For the Swedes, however, and the cause of peace in general, there was at least the consolation of an end to hostilities with Denmark. The young Queen Christina had come of age in 1644, a determined and intelligent ruler who acknowledged her country's impoverishment by warfare in regions as far afield as Jutland, Bavaria and Moravia, and who recognised too that until peace had been achieved she could not afford to dispense with Oxenstierna. 'I came into the world,' she once said, 'all armed with hair, my voice was strong and harsh,' which 'made the women think I was a boy.' And thereafter she had consciously cultivated her masculine image, scorning ornament, swearing manfully, taking to male dress and hunting wildly. But she was also conscientious, and gifted too with an exceptional mind. 'During a fever twenty-eight days long,' the Jesuit confessor to the Spanish ambassador would recall, 'she never neglected her state affairs', while the poet John Milton came to consider her 'fit to govern not only Europe but the world'. Pascal sent her his calculating machine with a letter proclaiming her queen in the realm of the mind as well as of government, and when Descartes tried to convince her that all animals are mechanisms, she quipped how she had never seen her watch give birth to babies. Plainly, she was a force to be reckoned with, and the Treaty of Brömsebro, concluded with Denmark in August 1645, was no mean testament to her influence.

By that time, in fact, Christian IV had no real bargaining power at his disposal save Christina's determination to end the fighting, though she was brought to modify her terms as a result of French and Dutch intervention, since the French desired a swift settlement so that the war in Germany could be renewed, and the Dutch feared that Sweden was already powerful enough in the Baltic to endanger their vital commercial interests. Ultimately, therefore, the treaty gave sole control of the Sound to no one, and Mazarin promised, too, that he would work to recover Bremen and Verden for Christian's son. Yet Sweden's acquisition of the provinces of Halland, Herjedelan and Jemteland would prove of lasting value, and this was not the limit of Christina's initial achievements, for with Brömsebro completed, she at once turned her energy to the deliberations underway at Osnabrück, and, in an effort to force the emperor's weakening hand, concluded a separate truce with John George of Saxony at Kötzschenbroda in September. With Brandenburg lost, Bavaria a prey to French inducements, Spain an empty vessel and now Saxony hopelessly adrift from the Imperial fold, the substantial advantages enjoyed by Ferdinand III in the year of his accession were little more than dust. And with Sweden too, as well as France, bent on peace, the inertia in Westphalia was surely bound to lift, at least in some measure.

Even in the Netherlands, moreover, notwithstanding Spain's agonies, the same stirrings were discernible. As captain-general and stadholder in five out of seven provinces, Frederick Henry had dominated the small standing committee of the States-General controlling foreign policy. But, as head of the House of Orange, he had also lived wholly at odds with the sober republicanism of Holland's regents, building grand palaces, maintaining an expensive court, framing royal marriages for his children and encouraging the attendance around him of the nobility of several countries. The French, indeed, no longer addressed him as Excellency but as Highness, a term properly reserved only for *Hun Hoogmogenden*, Their High Mightiness of the States-General, and it was even rumoured that with French support he might actually make Antwerp an independent principality for his own family. So it was no surprise that all manner of complaint had been directed against him, or that his capture of Sas van Gent in 1644 had nevertheless been compared unfavourably with the achievements of the French, who followed up their victory at Rocroi by storming across southern Flanders, taking Gravelines, Mardyck, Cassel, Ypres and Menin. The States-General had already balked at Frederick Henry's attempts to favour the royalist cause in the English Civil War, and when further pressure followed from him to support Denmark in its war against the Swedes, the breach attained a new intensity.

At the same time, there was increasing disenchantment among the Dutch with their French alliance, as Mazarin's troops advanced too successfully for comfort along the Flemish coast and Frederick Henry made little headway in the north, abandoning an attack on Ghent in 1645 as a result of what appeared to be French duplicity, while proving powerless to prevent the French capture of Dunkirk, whose privateers had for many years preyed upon Dutch shipping. Was not the legitimate pursuit of commercial profit rather than the military and political ambitions of the House of Orange therefore now the only valid priority? Already, in 1644 the directors of the Delft chamber of the West India Company had agreed that 'a merchant would do better honourably to increase his talent and send rich cargoes from Asia to the Netherlands instead of carrying out costly territorial conquests which are more suitable for crowned heads and mighty monarchs than for merchants greedy of gain'. And the implication was obvious, as were similar observations on the condition of France where, it was claimed, 'nothing is to be hoped for the common man', and ordinary people 'would be happy indeed if they could live under a republic in which the common man does not suffer too much from wars and may live quietly with his family in his own home.'

Allies of such a kind were clearly of dubious merit and, in spite of Frederick Henry's preferences and the Netherlands' existing treaty with France, the States-General had accordingly ordered Adriaen Pauw to join the discussions at Münster in an effort to secure peace with Spain. Upon his arrival, he found a town of some 10,000 inhabitants, swollen not only by the multitude of delegations but by the influx of beggars and whores, seeking rich pickings, as well as tradesmen and profiteers of various descriptions, since peace, like war, was good business. The representatives of the mighty states had come with typical pomp and circumstance past glaring poverty in town and countryside, and painters and engravers awaited them, to capture their images for posterity, along with clowns and English and Polish comedians who provided entertainment for their families, servants and scribes. The celebrated Dutch artist Gerard ter Borch had set up a studio especially for the purpose of painting the portraits of the leading participants and would make a good living from his appointed task over four fat years as the negotiations dragged on, irrespective of an early appeal by Alvise Contarini, the Venetian delegate, that agreement should be reached without delay, since the Turkish fleet had landed on Crete and necessitated a united assault against the 'arch-enemy'.

With even more good sense, Contarini pointed out, too, how a swift conclusion to proceedings would also dispose of the armies, which were becoming more and more restless and more and more of a burden with their demands, and their even more numerous camp followers. But the questions pending resolution – the internal affairs of the Empire, the status of Protestants, the tangle over ecclesiastical property, the 'satisfaction' of foreign powers, not to mention the settlement of the Eighty Years War between Spain and the Netherlands – could not be unravelled any more quickly, it seemed, were the Turks to be present in Münster itself. And the frustrations of the weary soldiery could in any case be expended by further fighting, for in 1646, with peace talks ongoing, a French army duly crossed the Spanish Netherlands to take Courtrai and Dunkirk, while a second occupied Elba and launched an attack on Naples, and a third, in the company of Swedish troops desperate for loot, invaded Bavaria to compel Maximilian to withdraw from the war. Bavaria, indeed, would be systematically plundered throughout the winter of 1646/47, as the Habsburgs scrambled together a field army of 40,000 men, which, without a pitched battle, was rapidly driven back towards Bohemia by General Wrangel, who thereafter led his forces back into Austria, invading the Vorarlberg, capturing Bregenz and plundering the surrounding area.

This, then, was the reality of the collective predicament confronting the would-be makers of peace in Westphalia. Forced by circumstance to make impossible choices, allies, on the one hand, frequently found themselves threatened more by each other than their common enemies. Maximilian of Bavaria was a perfect case in point. Fearing Spain's intentions in the Rhineland so intensely and faced with French and Swedish troops on the loose in his own duchy, he would urge Trauttmansdorff, the chief Imperial representative, to ignore the interests of Madrid and surrender with all speed to the demands of Paris and Stockholm. In the meantime, jurists quibbled over the precise definition of French sovereignty in the bishopric and city of Strasbourg, as well as six other free cities that retained their membership of the Imperial Diet. And when

Mazarin accepted the principle of a general settlement of German affairs, he did so only with the proviso that it excluded Spain and left her isolated in her war with France and the United Provinces, creating a whole new level of complexity to what was already one of the thorniest areas of negotiation. Nor was this all. For when the emperor finally ceded his rights and possessions in the Sundgau and Lower Alsace, he did so in the full knowledge that Lower Alsace did not formally belong to him in the first place.

At Osnabrück, the pace was no quicker, nor the tone any more conciliatory. Indeed, French demands seemed almost moderate in comparison to Sweden's opening bid for an indemnity of 12 million thalers, and control of Silesia, Pomerania and nearly every former bishopric in northern Germany. For while Queen Christina remained anxious to conclude the war, she was equally determined to honour her father's claims for 'security' and 'satisfaction', and declared in addition that the religious and political situation pertaining in 1618 should be restored. As early as 1638, in fact, the dour Glaswegian Presbyterian, Robert Baillie, had expressed puzzlement concerning Swedish war aims. 'For the Swedds,' he declared, 'I see not what their eirand is now in Germany, bot to shed Protestant blood.' Yet their objectives, as expressed now by their queen, had remained remarkably consistent. The only difference was the scale of these aims, as the strength of their enemies dissolved with even greater rapidity than their own. For by the summer of 1647 the Swedish troops' own envoy, Colonel Erskine, was putting forward a claim for no less than 30 million thalers, and the Swedish government's official representatives were proposing something far exceeding the intentions of the Heilbronn League of old: nothing less, indeed, than the 'atomising' of the Empire in order to create a permanent balance of power between the various creeds and princes.

In such circumstances, it would take no less than two years to settle the problem of Pomerania alone. Though no one could drive the Swedes from the duchy, Frederick William refused to abandon his claim to it entirely and demonstrated once again his ability to play a weak hand consummately well. For he not only won Dutch support for his interests in Cleves by marrying into the House of Orange, but went on to persuade Mazarin that Brandenburg should be made powerful enough to prevent any expansion of Imperial power into northern Germany. After these initial ploys, moreover, Sweden was won over by an offer of partition that left Frederick William in control of the eastern portion, despite its lack of ports, in return for compensation elsewhere – a plan heartily approved by the Dutch in particular, who were pleased to deprive Sweden of at least one stretch of the German coastline. Brandenburg's rights in Cleves, Mark and Ravensburg were all reluctantly confirmed by Trauttmansdorff, who also awarded its ruler the diocese of Halberstadt and Minden, the diocese of Cammin with the port of Colberg, which was adjacent to Pomerania, and the reversion of Magdeburg on the death of its existing administrator – all of which yielded far more territory than that yielded to Sweden and a much more significant strategic edge for the future, since it established a chain of links binding Brandenburg to the Rhineland territories.

For the Swedes, too, the resulting arrangement was, quite literally, thoroughly satisfactory. Indeed, with western Pomerania and its strategic ports now firmly in Sweden's grasp, 'satisfaction' appeared to have been achieved on a truly heroic scale, making security somewhat less of an issue, as Trauttmansdorff and his successor from 1647, Dr Isaac Volmar, nevertheless proved adept hands at playing off the French against their Swedish allies, and at mobilising a residual German patriotism against both. Yet the Imperial strategy was still shot through with obvious limitations, and the gains for Sweden proved hardly less considerable elsewhere. For once Brandenburg had been settled, Queen Christina's emissaries duly secured control of the mouths of the Oder, the Elbe and the Weser by the emperor's recognition of her occupation of the islands of Rügen, Usedom and Wollin, along with Stettin, Stralsund, Wismar, and the bishoprics of Bremen and Verden. Henceforth, Sweden would enjoy three seats in the Imperial Diet, though not the electoral title she had hoped for, and, in Bremen, a base from which to threaten Denmark further. She would achieve a 'satisfaction' for her army, too, amounting to up to 20 million thalers.

As negotiations ground to a halt once more in the winter of 1647/48, over Sweden's demands for an indemnity after her claims to Silesia had been refused, there were therefore solid grounds for content in Stockholm – so much so, in fact, that the Imperial ambassador remarked how the Swedes could not have asked for more, if the emperor were a prisoner in Stockholm itself. And, in the meantime, there had been momentous developments at Münster, too, where, to all Europe's surprise, peace had at last been finalised between Spain and the Netherlands. Already by the end of 1646 a treaty had been drafted which won the assent of all but the privateers of Zeeland and the strict Calvinists of Utrecht who could neither sanction a settlement with their old Spanish foe nor approve an alliance with France. But the death of Frederick Henry in March 1647 had marked an all-important breakthrough, since he alone had been the man capable of waging war in the field and of mobilising support for it in the States-General. The new prince, William II, by contrast, enjoyed nothing of his father's influence, and even a Spanish revival in Flanders at the eleventh hour, whereby Armentières, Commines and Lens all fell in 1647, could not allay Madrid's overriding fear of France, which, as the Count of Peñaranda made clear, continued to make a settlement with the Dutch imperative. For the latter, he believed, would prove 'more scrupulous and reliable than the French in carrying out the undertaking and commitment to peace' and 'their power can never be so formidable to His Majesty as that of the French'. Above all, however, there was the added consideration that the Dutch themselves would in the longer term provide an invaluable check against France, since, as Peñaranda put it:

> If we cede territory to the French in the Low Countries we give them the arms and means to make themselves masters of all seventeen provinces ... but if we cede territory to the Dutch in the Netherlands, we make them formidable to the French.

It was an irrefutable case, and one which carried Philip IV with it so unreservedly that one Portuguese observer commented how the King of Spain was now so committed to a settlement that he was prepared 'to give in on every point' and 'if necessary would crucify Christ again to achieve it'. In the event – as rebellion flared in Sicily and Naples, plague claimed half a million victims in Andalucia, Valencia and parts of Castile, and Spain once more accepted its bankruptcy by suspending interest payments – Philip offered terms in January 1648 more favourable to the Dutch than any offered or sought at the time of the Twelve Years Truce almost forty years earlier. For not only did the Treaty of Münster acknowledge the United Provinces as an independent sovereign state, Spain's earlier insistence on freedom of public worship for Catholics was now abandoned, and a series of further sacrifices conceded. Hereafter, the Scheldt was to remain closed, thereby guaranteeing the economic subordination of Antwerp to Amsterdam, and Dutch conquests in Flanders and Brabant, including Maastricht and 's-Hertogenbosch, were confirmed, while Dutch overseas conquests also received formal recognition, along with the right to trade freely in both the East and the West Indies.

So it was small wonder, perhaps, that news of the treaty was greeted with such enthusiasm in The Hague or that the date of its formal ratification by the States-General, in June, should have been selected so symbolically. For, as the Portuguese ambassador was able to report:

> The peace was proclaimed here ... at ten o'clock on the morning of the fifth of this month, that day and hour being chosen because on that day and at that time eighty years ago the counts of Egmont and Hoorn had been executed by the Duke of Alba in Brussels, and the States wished their freedom to begin at the same time as these two gentlemen had died in defence thereof.

French attempts to derail the peace from without, by creating what one Spanish negotiator termed 'an artificial labyrinth, constructed in such a way that those who allow themselves to be led into it can never find the exit', had been unavailing, as had similar ploys by Zeeland from within. And all that Spain had received in return was the recognition of their own sovereignty over the southern Netherlands, and the end of the Franco-Dutch alliance.

But the latter at least could not have come at a more critical juncture for Mazarin who had still been gambling upon winning the war before France's own domestic problems had reached crisis. In the very month, indeed, that the Treaty of Münster was sealed between Spain and the Netherlands, the cardinal encouraged young Louis XIV to force the Parlement of Paris to accept the new taxes needed for another military campaign. But there was unprecedented opposition on the grounds that the king was still a minor, and by May the various courts in Paris had issued an *arrêt d'union*, or declaration of solidarity, and refused to authorise any new financial measures. Without guarantees of repayment, the government's bankers, too, became restive, and in spite of what seemed to be a clear military and diplomatic advantage abroad, Mazarin therefore found the carpet pulled from beneath him in France itself, as the opposition of the law courts and a spreading tax strike forced him to instruct his negotiators at Münster to make peace in Germany on the best possible terms. 'Shedding tears of blood', he informed Abel Servien on 14 August how the collapse at home had occurred at a time when 'our affairs have never been in a more prosperous state'. 'It is almost a miracle,' he reflected, that 'amid so many obstacles' France had nevertheless seized and maintained the initiative. But it was also clear to him at this point that 'we should not place all our trust in the miracle continuing for long', and that it was therefore time 'to make peace at the earliest possible opportunity.'

Even now, however, the guns continued to rumble. For although the blueprint of an agreement between France and Spain had been drawn up as early as January 1646, the improvement in Spain's position after the conclusion of peace with the Netherlands, as well as the subsequent suppression of revolts in both Sicily and Naples, had made Philip IV declare that he was no longer prepared to accept Mazarin's 'exorbitant conditions'. The result was an abortive invasion of France, which ended in a crushing Spanish defeat at Lens in the very month that Mazarin was shedding his 'tears of blood' at not being able to prosecute the war to a victorious end. It was certainly a development that made the pill of peace even more difficult for the cardinal to swallow, especially when French and Swedish troops had defeated the Bavarians at Zusmarshausen in May and systematically devastated the duchy for a second year running. But, with triumph in sight, his government remained virtually bankrupt, and while he agonised at the fact that the emperor would now escape 'the total ruin which, considering the lamentable situation to which his fortunes had been reduced, was imminent and almost ineluctable', one further incident confirmed his predicament.

For the Swedes, too, had been busy making war while talking peace, and by July were besieging Prague. In Bohemia, however, the mood of the people had changed, and it was now perhaps the most exquisite irony of all that in the city of the famous 'defenestration', no longer Protestant and rebellious, the emperor himself had come to represent security and the best hope of peace after the horror of the Swedish invasions since 1639. When the Swedes therefore captured the Hradčany – including the very room in which the defenestration had occurred thirty years earlier – and occupied the Kleinseite opposite the citadel of Prague, it was the citizens themselves who rallied against the enemy at the gates, holding on throughout the summer while praying for news of the peace settlement which was still pending in Westphalia, until, as one Brandenburg delegate put it, 'Spain and France had finished their game'. For three long months, indeed, the people of Prague would have to withstand the onslaught, following the Swedish general Königsmarck's decision to loose his troops for three days after their initial success, murdering 200 inhabitants, plundering the vast treasures of Bohemia's clergy and aristocracy, and carrying off what remained of Rudolf II's famous art collection, while other Swedish detachments under Wittenberg and Carl Gustav also headed for the honeypot.

But Prague's resistance was not in vain. For as Swedish guns continued to fire across the Vlatva, and students and citizens struggled to block the Charles Bridge in an effort to prevent an enemy incursion into the New Town, word of peace arrived on 5 November. The final assault, indeed, had been conducted in the knowledge that an end to hostilities was imminent, and in the hope that one last burst of plunder could be achieved before that time. But the preliminary agreement signed between the Swedes and the emperor in August had ultimately borne fruit as exhaustion took its final toll, and both France and Sweden, mutually acknowledged that neither could be relied upon to support the other any longer. Like a pair of flagging marathon runners who had propped each other up throughout the final stages of the race, they could go no further, and at last this realisation had triggered the end. For five more days the Swedes continued their assaults on Prague, but the whole rationale that had driven the conflict in the first place was by now an irrelevance, and talks were already underway to demarcate the areas that both sides would occupy until demobilisation had been completed.

On 23 October, Mazarin had lamented the arrival of peace, which he blamed, with a notable disregard for his own decisions reaching back over several months, upon the inconstancy of his Swedish allies:

> It would perhaps have been more advantageous for the conclusion of a univer-
> sal peace [he informed Servien] had the war in the Empire continued a little
> longer, rather than hastening the settlement of matters as we did – assuming
> that it had been in our power to proceed more slowly in this matter without
> being abandoned by the Swedes, who manifested a passionate desire to settle.

But next day, amid ceaseless bell-ringing and countless services of thanksgiving,
and as burning beacons lit the hills along the River Main and poets wrote of
swallows nesting in soldiers' helmets, the French did indeed commit themselves
to the abandonment of hostilities. Though Pope Innocent X refused to do so,
lodging a formal protest at the terms, and condemning the resulting settlement
as 'null, void, invalid, iniquitous, unjust, damnable, reprobate, inane, empty of
meaning and effect for all time', neither Mazarin nor his countrymen could
afford such recalcitrance. For the Bohemian scholar Comenius too, there was
dismay at the outcome. 'They have sacrificed us at the treaties of Osnabrück,'
he wrote, adjuring his fellow Protestants 'by the wounds of Christ' that 'you do
not forsake us who are persecuted for the sake of Christ.' But, as Mazarin well
knew, the war had been concluded 'more out of exhaustion', as one anonymous
observer put it, 'than from a sense of right behaviour', and, under such circumstances, there was never any more genuine prospect for fair play than for the
kind of lasting 'universal peace' touted so earnestly by the cardinal and others.

Along with the Treaty of Brömsebro and the earlier Treaty of Münster
between Spain and the United Provinces, the two treaties of Münster and
Osnabrück, agreed to in October 1648 and finally ratified by the respective governments in February 1649, certainly encompassed the issues underlying nearly
every international crisis that had occurred in the first half of the seventeenth
century. Indeed, what became known under its umbrella designation as the
Peace of Westphalia constituted, in effect, a summary of the history of European
conflict since the death of Philip II. But its very scope encapsulated not only
its achievements, which were undeniable, but also its limitations. For while
the old controversies which combined territorial and religious interests were
forever settled and Gustavus Adolphus became, in effect, the last great European
monarch to equate religion with power politics, the way was merely opened
for a new type of international aggrandisement as the prospect of Habsburg
hegemony vanished once and for all, only to be replaced in due course by the
ambition of Louis XIV and the alternative prospect of domination by France.
Hereafter, the impotence of both the Holy Roman Emperor and Imperial Diet
would ensure that as the Habsburgs became preoccupied with their hereditary
possessions in the east, so Germany would remain mostly weak and disunited,

with the sole exception of those few territories, like Brandenburg, capable of establishing forceful and coherent states in their own right. And Germany's weakness was, of course, France's strength.

In the shorter term, moreover, peace would prove patchy, and the disbandment of armies a long and cumbersome process, since many of the delegates at Münster and Osnabrück, weary from their labours in pursuit of a political settlement, were soon transferring nevertheless to Nuremberg, where a new conference assembled to supervise, among other post-war practicalities, the payment of the 200,000 soldiers still mobilised. Yet no agreement on a phased withdrawal was reached for a further eighteen months, and even after that, Brandenburg and Neuburg engaged in minor hostilities – dubbed the 'Düsseldorf cow-war' – over Jülich-Cleves, while Sweden and Brandenburg did not finally partition Pomerania until 1653. Outside Germany, furthermore, fighting between France and Spain would continue until the French project of stopping the 'progress' of Spain finally ended with the Treaty of the Pyrenees in 1659. Thereafter, wars for dynastic, commercial or colonial ends would be fought with no less ardour, and though the disregarded protests of the Pope regarding the Peace of Westphalia confirmed the end of the papacy as international power – a development that had actually been in progress since at least the death of Sixtus V in 1590 – newcomers like the United Provinces and eventually Brandenburg Prussia would not be long in taking their place as challengers to the status quo. Sweden, too, would complicate the politics of north-east Europe by its domination of the Baltic over the next fifty years.

Certainly, the drafting of the Peace of Westphalia, whether consciously or otherwise, was extremely ambiguous in places, and never more so, perhaps, than in certain provisions relating to France. The French, in fact, were confirmed in their possession of Metz, Toul and Verdun, which they had held since 1552, and were also granted Breisach, and the right to station garrisons in Philippsburg, beyond the Rhine, and Pinerolo in northern Italy. Territorially insignificant, these nevertheless gave them gateways into Germany and the plain of Lombardy. More importantly still, however, in addition to the Sundgau and full sovereignty (*supremum dominium*) in Alsace, France was also granted 'provincial prefecture' over ten Imperial towns in Alsace, including Münster itself, which were to retain the privileges that they enjoyed in relation to the Empire, *ita tamen*, i.e. provided that this should not detract from the 'full sovereignty' already conceded. And here, of course, lay a rub of truly momentous consequence. For in following a concession with a crucial reservation and thereafter stipulating that nothing in the reservation was to detract from the scope of the concession, the peacemakers at Westphalia had merely spawned a further crisis of even greater proportions and far more destructive potential in centuries to come, as the armaments available to seventeenth-century rulers became dwarfed by those of 1870 and 1914.

Within the Empire, at least, there was arguably more success, though once again a largely equitable and tolerant settlement would prove conducive neither to German unity nor the long-term harmony of the continent as a whole. Maximilian of Bavaria, whose ambitions had been instrumental to the outbreak and early dynamics of the war, was in fact rewarded for the wholesale decimation of his duchy with the Upper Palatinate and the electoral status that came with it, though an eighth electorate was created for Frederick V's heir, Charles Louis, the current Elector Palatine. Duke John George of Saxony was satisfied, too, by receipt of Lusatia, while certain lesser princes like the dukes of Brunswick and Mecklenburg and the landgrave of Hesse-Kassel either recovered their old lands or acquired new ones. But with regard to the constitution of the Empire – the question that, in conjunction with religion, had fuelled the conflict throughout – any progress was tempered by undesirable long-term side effects and a residing sense that, in many essentials, things had moved in circles rather than forward. For while the independence of Germany's princes was guaranteed, so too was the impotence of the emperor and the Imperial Diet, and therefore any prospect of effective central administration. And while 'the Emperor' henceforth became little more than a misleading name for the ruler of Austria, so 'the Empire' was on its way to becoming an equally meaningless designation for an atomised area of central Europe consisting, in effect, of 337 independent states – 152 under lay rulers, 123 under spiritual ones, along with 62 Imperial cities.

At Westphalia, to all intents and purposes, the separate states of the Holy Roman Empire were recognised as sovereign members of the Imperial Diet, free to control their own affairs independently of each other and of the emperor – an arrangement which included their right to make alliances among themselves or with foreign countries, provided that these were not directed against the emperor or his interests. At the same time, the principle of *cuius regio, eius religio* was reaffirmed, but construed to relate only to public life, so that private worship was permitted, and Calvinism, too, was accorded the same protection as Lutheranism under the Augsburg Settlement of 1555. Furthermore, any change of religion by the ruler was not to affect his subjects, while the Edict of Restitution, first modified in 1635, was finally abandoned, so that, with the exception of Austria and Bavaria, ecclesiastical lands were to remain in the hands of those who held them in 1624. Religious minorities, too, were to be granted five years' grace in which to move to another state if they wished, while in matters of religion, there were now to be no majority decisions taken by the Imperial Diet. Instead both sides were to meet separately to prepare their cases on the understanding that disputes were to be settled by compromise.

Plainly, these religious provisions of the peace embodied a striking contrast in attitudes to those of 1618, though one contemporary wit could not forbear to comment how, in Bohemia at least, which was now part of the Austrian dominions and therefore once more Catholic, 'the men who were thrown out of the window triumphed in the end'. The principle of co-existence had prevailed between, if not within, states, and toleration among princes would indeed mean that the Thirty Years War became the last religious conflict of its kind in Europe. But the circular movement of events in Bohemia was also mirrored more broadly within the Empire, where the situation in 1648 was remarkably similar to that pertaining in 1618. The Catholic powers, on the one hand, had hoped in vain to recover the land secularised since 1559, while the emperor had unsuccessfully sought to revive Imperial authority, and the Swedes to control the destinies of German Protestants. Instead, the Empire remained, as it had been at the time of the Augsburg Settlement and would continue to be until its final dissolution under Napoleon in 1806, an untidy collection of autonomous states, some Catholic, some Protestant. Ironically, if the fighting had stopped in 1621, 1629, or even in 1635, there might have been many significant changes to record, but its wearisome promulgation had finally brought Germany back to its starting point, to perpetuate for more than two further centuries the political fragmentation of old.

Yet if the Empire had not yet transformed itself, neither had it stayed the same, and along with continuity came significant individual differences of emphasis and direction. The Palatinate, for example, was never again to be the hub of international Calvinist politics, while Saxony was to all intents and purposes a spent force. At the same time, the Habsburgs' failure to defeat the oligarchic, federalist and centrifugal forces ranged against them within the Empire had effectively assured the future for nation states and, indeed, the men of commerce who funded them. It was no coincidence in this respect that Mazarin secured the creation of a separate estate within the Imperial Diet for the Free Cities, 'since it is principally they who have the money, the lands and the munitions of war'. And though the great days of those particular cities were in fact passed, the more general principle remained true, as the success of the United Provinces had demonstrated already and would continue to do. Now, as the Austrian House of Habsburg looked east to restore its reputation on the Eastern March against the Osmanli Turks and to satisfy its dynastic ambitions by liberating Hungary and creating a Danubian monarchy, the princes of Germany would be free to assume the dominant role on the shoulders of those very merchants, traders, bankers and businessmen who, more than two centuries later, would ultimately supersede them.

For, in spite of the grievous damage caused by thirty years of warfare, the potential for recovery remained considerable. Over the next decade and a half – until the mid-1660s when the Holy Roman Empire became engaged once more in long, expensive wars against the Turks and French – the economic revival of much of central Europe was in fact marked, as fields were reclaimed, good harvests ensued, damaged wooden buildings were swiftly reconstructed, the number of marriages increased rapidly, births outnumbered deaths, and old patterns of trade and production resumed. The engravings of the Frenchman, Jacques Callot, *Les Grandes Misères de la Guerre* (1633), and the descriptions in *Simplicissimus the Vagabond*, written by Johann Jacob Christoffel von Grimmelshausen more than a decade after the war was finished, have etched the horrors of the war into the popular imagination until this very day – and not without good reason. For although their purpose was satirical, their fictions were based in no small measure upon a broader canvas of undeniable fact. But when the central character in Grimmelshausen's tale reached Switzerland after witnessing the carnage in his homeland, it seemed to him:

> … as strange as if I had been in Brazil or China. I saw how the people did trade and traffic in peace, how the stalls were full of cattle and the farmyards crowded with fowls, geese and ducks, the roads were used in safety by travellers, and the inns were full of people making merry. There was no fear of an enemy, no dread of plundering, and no terror of losing goods and life and limb …

And when those last three scourges were finally removed in Germany too, there were soon the seeds of hope that a similar state of harmony and well-being might yet pertain.

Much would depend in the short term, of course, upon the speed and success with which the hitherto contending armies might be demobilised, and this did not prove easy, since the delegates gathered at Nuremberg in April 1649 to arrange payment of the now redundant armies were rightly fearful that dislocated soldiers might yet refuse to disband, simply because they could envisage no way of life other than that of warfare – especially at a point when the ambition or disgruntlement of a commander or government might still trigger conflict at any time. Spain, after all, was aggrieved by her exclusion from the settlement of Imperial affairs and might feel justified in renewing the war in the Rhineland, while Prince Karl Gustav, Queen Christina's heir presumptive, continued to harbour military ambitions that had been thwarted by the peace. Similarly, when the 500 Imperial troops still stationed in Lindau were ordered to march out in August 1649, a mutiny resulted which lasted two months, while elsewhere, in Alsace, the French army too was restless, so that when political turmoil in Paris resulting from the so-called *Fronde* of January 1649 disrupted the flow of funds, even an experienced commander like Hans Ludwig von Erlach, who had been in French service for almost a decade, could not prevent his men from running amok.

In the event, the bankrupt condition of Spain and the desire of Mazarin, Christina and Ferdinand III to apply themselves to domestic problems ensured the execution of the treaties, though Mazarin himself was declared an outlaw by the Parlement of Paris at one point early in 1649, and it would not be until 1653 that he had thwarted all attempts to oust him. If, therefore, the arrival of peace had been a matter of necessity, so too was its preservation, and when negotiations at Nuremberg finally concluded in June 1651, the risk of a major conflagration – in the short-term, at least – was limited. Late in 1648, three months' severance pay had been granted to the troops raised by the German Catholic princes, and in January 1649 Imperial garrisons were duly withdrawn from Bavaria. Almost eighteen months later, moreover, on 26 June 1650, amid firework displays and general rejoicing, the Swedish and Imperial delegates signed an agreement for the phased withdrawal on prearranged days of all troops from the areas of Germany not ceded to France, Sweden or the emperor.

Not all, of course, were convinced by the departures. Like Grimmelshausen's 'Mother Courage', many of those who fought in the war did indeed have no wish to leave the ranks. For them, the talks at Westphalia and Nuremberg were just that, and in any case only the transition from one chapter to another, rather than the end of the tale. Certainly, the cynics were numerous. As the poet Johann Vogel wrote:

Something you never believed in
Has come to pass. What?
Will the camel pass through the Needle's Eye
Now that peace has returned to Germany?

And if Vogel's observation exhibited a clear hint of scepticism, others were more forthright still. 'Peace is uncertain, wickedness more certain,' wrote Friedrich von Logau. 'There are many evil-doers and few real penitents.' Nor was it any coincidence that a certain Latin maxim became the watchword of many. *Mars gravior sub pace latet* – under peace a worse war is often waiting – warned those who believed they had witnessed not so much a crisis concluded as a crisis postponed, particularly when the threat from princes and generals was not the only burden for common people to bear. In an *Eclogue or Conversation between Two Herdsmen about War and Peace*, written shortly after the Peace of Westphalia, one of the fictitious characters expresses a broader concern:

> You poor fool, you've been tricked;
> As if the soldier has not stripped you entirely,
> There comes the bailiff from the castle, the scribe and the tax official,
> They take hair and head and bring new torments.

Yet for a while at least, hope rather than suspicion generally held sway, and who, after all their suffering, could honestly blame the citizens of Ulm and the neighbouring villages for taking solace from the prayer written specially to be said in every pulpit on 22 August 1650?

> We thank you, Dear Lord, that you have given us peace after years of turmoil and war, and that you have granted our pleas. We thank you for pulling us like a brand out of the fire, allowing us to rescue our life almost as if it were itself war booty … Oh Lord, you have indeed treated us with mercy that our city and lands, which had previously been full of fear and horror, are now full of joy and happiness. We beseech you, who has saved us from the sword, mercifully to let our corn grow again, that we may multiply and prosper once more … Oh God, the lover of peace, grant us henceforth permanent peace and leave our boundaries and houses in calm and peace that the voice of the war messenger shall not frighten us and the man of war touch us not.

Even the generals, it seems, were prepared to embrace the general enthusiasm, after a fashion. For only a little earlier, on 22 June 1650, another celebration had taken place in Nuremberg to commemorate the successful activities of the commissioners who had organised the 'satisfaction' and demobilisation of the soldiers. Appropriately enough, the city's children – whose delight in war games had actually become a cause of increasing concern among their parents – featured prominently, and 1,500 of them, all boys, rode on hobbyhorses in a noisy throng through the streets. Their destination, moreover, was the grand residence of none other than Lieutenant-General Octavio Piccolomini, who was soon to become a prince of the Empire for services rendered, and personally commission a cycle of twenty-one vast battle paintings from the Dutch artist Peter Snayers, to commemorate his illustrious career as a commander of Spanish and Imperial troops. Seizing the opportunity to exploit the children's high spirits, he responded in suitably generous fashion, having minted silver 'peace pennies', bearing a hobbyhorse rider on one side and the Imperial eagle on the other, which he duly distributed to his jubilant admirers.

But the grandest celebration of all had been reserved for the 'Peace Banquet' held in honour of Piccolomini himself and his other, newly-redundant, colleagues. Twelve chefs supplied the tables in Nuremberg's splendid Town Hall with 150 meals of six courses each, not to mention the mountains of cakes and confectionery that had been specially prepared for the generals in attendance. The fifth course, we are told, consisted of garden fruits, some of which were served on dishes, while others hung from little green trees concealing incense in their foliage. Nor was this all. For in the corner-galleries of the great hall where the banquet took place, four choirs intoned a solemn *Te Deum*, along with psalms and hymns of thanksgiving in what one observer described as an 'artistic and delightful manner', as the warrior-diners found themselves treated to further moral uplift by two centrepieces embellished with ingenious figures and slogans. One, an *Arcus Triumphalis Concordiae* with innumerable inscriptions, was intended to symbolise the residing unity of the three monarchs of Germany, France and Sweden, while the other was decorated with an eagle – the heraldic beast of the emperor – sitting peacefully in its nest; a cockerel – the symbol of France – crowing from its perch on a helmet; and a lion recumbent on a shield and sword. Outside, for the curious and hungry people in the streets, large quantities of bread had also been distributed, along with meat from two oxen, specially roasted on spits, and large quantities of wine, flowing, appropriately enough, from the snarling jaws of a wood and cardboard lion, holding a broken sword in its right paw and a palm-branch in its left.

All, indeed, was harmony and goodwill, splendour and largesse: wholly fitting, in every exquisite detail, to mark a continent's deliverance from the crisis that had come so close to consuming it. But even such an evening, it seems, would not have been complete without one final gesture – and one final twist. For at a late hour the diners decided that they should play soldiers once again, and, to the accompaniment of much noise and merriment, formed ranks behind Piccolomini as their 'captain', who duly led them in a rowdy torchlit march up to the city's castle. On their arrival, cannons and muskets were fired, and on the way back, their spirits bolstered by the fine wine and rich food they had taken with such relish, each of the individuals involved drank yet another toast before proffering his resignation from military service – though only, we are told, 'as a jest'.

ACKNOWLEDGEMENTS

No author is an island, and least of all this one. Accordingly, my sincere thanks are due to those individuals, living or otherwise, who either taught me my subject more than four decades ago or assisted my own teaching of it thereafter. They include Helmut Koenigsberger, Claus-Peter Clasen, Herbert Langer, Josef Polišenský, Michael Roberts and David Maland, as well as J. P. Cooper, R. J. W. Evans and S.H. Steinberg. I am indebted, too, to Geoffrey Parker and Peter H. Wilson, along with Tryntje Helfferich, Robert Bireley, Charles W. Ingrao, Ronald G. Asch and Geoff Mortimer. As always, the patience and encouragement of Mark Beynon, Alex Waite and the rest of the team at The History Press has been unstinting.

Last but never least, there is Barbara my wife, not to mention Genevieve, Winifred and Humphrey, without whom life would be altogether less complicated but not nearly so fulfilling.

To all concerned, I raise my glass at journey's end.

INDEX

Alais, Grace of (1629) 144, 185, 212, 273
Albert, Archduke, Governor of South Netherlands 28, 83, 93, 101, 120, 123, 125, 126, 127
Aldringen, Johann von 162, 191, 242, 259, 261, 267
Altmark, Truce of (1629) 197, 203, 270, 274
Alte Veste 244, 245
Amsterdam, Bank of 121–22, 123
Anne of Austria 284
Arnim, Hans George von 180, 181, 214, 228, 231, 232, 233, 235, 236, 239, 241, 246, 258, 259, 261, 266, 267, 269
Augsburg, Religious Peace of (1555) 28, 29, 31, 32, 34–37, 43, 46, 57, 58, 166, 176, 191, 194, 195, 310, 311
Austria
    historical background 42
    Lower 16, 42, 46, 88, 90, 100, 161
    Upper 16, 32, 42, 46, 68, 88, 90, 105, 115, 157, 161, 171–72, 177, 182, 259, 278
    peasant rebellions 16, 171–72
    Protestantism 30–31, 46
    regional divisions and administration 42

Baden-Durlach, Margrave of 59, 130, 132, 133, 215
Baillie, Robert 303
Baner, Johan 231, 232, 268, 275, 276, 279, 287, 288, 291, 293, 296, 297
Bärwalde, Treaty of (1631) 213, 216, 218, 239, 258, 270
Bedmar, Marquis and Cardinal of 127
Bergh, Hendrik van den 188, 189, 256
Bernard of Saxe-Weimar 227, 238, 248, 251, 252, 253, 258, 259, 261, 266, 267, 268, 272, 273, 276, 279, 287, 291, 296
Bethlen Gábor 88, 90, 93, 94, 98–99, 100, 108, 132, 133, 139, 142, 148, 157, 165, 167, 168, 169, 170, 171, 172, 237, 295
Bouillon, Duke of 61, 134, 282
Breitenfeld
    first battle of (1631) 228–34
    second battle of (1642) 292

Brömsebro, Treaty of (1645) 300, 308
Brussels, Conference of (1626) 165
Bucquoy, Charles 83, 87, 88, 94, 100, 105, 106, 107, 108, 113, 132, 139
Butler, Colonel Walter 261, 262, 263

Callot, Jacques 155, 312
Calvinism 11, 13, 14, 25–26, 27, 30, 34, 36, 44, 48, 49, 52, 58, 60, 61, 62, 66, 67, 68, 71, 78, 91, 92, 94, 95, 97, 99, 102, 103, 113, 114, 121, 122, 124, 127, 137, 161, 171, 174, 189, 191, 194, 204, 214, 217, 269, 270, 271, 274, 283, 290, 304, 310, 311
Camerarius, Ludwig 61, 80, 92, 97, 111, 141
Canisius, Peter 23, 24
Carleton, Sir Dudley 91, 92, 94, 104, 116,
Catholic League 60, 68, 69, 71, 72, 100, 102, 103, 104, 105, 115, 140, 141, 151, 165, 166, 175, 177, 181, 182, 189, 196, 204, 213, 214, 215, 220, 238, 241, 266, 277
Charles I, King of England 131, 142, 147, 165, 174, 216, 255, 278, 280, 283
Charles IX, King of Sweden 91, 203, 205
Charles V, Holy Roman Emperor 29–30, 31, 49
Charles, Duke of Lorraine 236, 275, 276
Charles Emmanuel, Duke of Savoy 88, 146, 147, 159, 181, 186, 190, 191
Chemnitz, Bogislav Philipp 202, 207
Cherasco, Treaty of (1631) 226
Christian I, Elector of Saxony 48
Christian II, Elector of Saxony 19, 68
Christian IV, King of Denmark 27, 68, 111, 112, 116, 141, 142, 148, 149, 150, 151, 156, 165, 166, 167, 168, 171, 172, 175, 179, 180, 187, 189–90, 196, 202, 293, 299, 300
Christian of Anhalt 52, 59, 60, 61, 62, 68, 70, 73, 74, 80, 87, 88, 90, 106, 165, 219
Christian of Brunswick 130, 133, 134, 141, 142, 165, 167
Christian Wilhelm of Brandenburg 217, 218
Christina, Queen of Sweden 256, 275, 299–300, 303, 304, 312, 313

Cœuvres, Marquis 145, 146, 160
Collegium Germanicum 47
Comenius, Jan 63, 64, 308
Compiègne, Treaty of
    (1624) 145
    (1635) 270, 274
Contzen, Adam 27, 191, 192, 216
Córdoba, Gonsalez de 128, 133, 141, 182, 186, 189
Coryat, Thomas 16, 17
Croats 11, 152, 154, 220, 229, 230, 232–33, 241,
    245, 247, 248, 252

Dampierre, Henri Duval 88, 100
Declaratio Ferdinandea 36, 46
Defenestration of Prague (1618) 81–82, 191
Dessau Bridge 167, 219
Dunkirk, privateers of 141, 301

East India Company (Dutch) 75, 121, 123
Ebersdorf, Compact of (1634) 268, 271
Edict of Restitution (1629) 191–92, 198, 200–1, 214,
    218, 228, 236, 260, 265, 268–69, 276, 290, 310
Ehrenbreitstein, Fortress of 104, 237, 278
Elizabeth, daughter of James I 68, 89, 94, 106, 115, 130
Enghien, Duke of 283, 284, 286, 295
Ernest of Bavaria 35
Evangelical Union see Protestant Union

Fadinger, Stefan 171–72
Falkenberg, Dietrich von 218, 219, 220
Ferdinand I, Emperor 29, 30, 31, 35–36, 42
Ferdinand II, Emperor 43, 44, 45, 59, 73, 74, 77, 78,
    79, 80, 81, 82, 83, 86, 87, 88, 90, 92, 93, 96, 98,
    99, 100, 102, 105, 106, 109, 112–16, 132, 138,
    139, 140, 142, 151, 157, 166, 170, 172, 176, 177,
    181, 182, 187, 189, 190, 191, 192, 193, 194, 195,
    198, 200–1, 202, 203, 207, 208, 214, 215, 216,
    217, 226, 236, 239, 240, 255–56, 261, 276–77
Ferdinand III, Emperor 157, 260, 263, 266, 267–68,
    269, 274, 287, 288, 290, 292–93, 295, 300, 313
Ferdinand, Cardinal-Infante of Spain 256, 259, 266,
    267, 268, 283
Feria, Duke of 103, 117, 132, 147, 256, 259
Feuquières, Marquis of 258, 260
Fontainebleau, Treaty of (1631) 216
France
    domestic politics, 144, 184–85, 190, 211–12,
    284, 306, 313
    financial problems, 285, 306
    military capability, 272–73, 279–80
Frederick II, King of Denmark 30
Frederick III, Elector Palatine 30, 36, 48, 60
Frederick IV, Elector Palatine 52, 60, 61, 71,
Frederick V, Elector Palatine 55, 61, 62, 68, 73, 87–89,
    91–98, 100, 102, 105–12, 114–16, 131, 133–35,
    141–2, 145, 150, 176, 216, 238, 242, 255, 265
Frederick Henry, Prince of Orange 151, 174, 182,

188, 270, 273, 283, 300, 301, 304
Frederick William, Elector of Brandenburg 290,
    292, 303
Fronde 313
Fuenterrabia, Siege of 280, 281
'Fuentes Fort' 76

Gallas, Matthias 261, 263, 273, 275–76, 279, 293–94
Gaston, Duke of Orléans 211, 212, 282, 284
George William, Elector of Brandenburg 102, 214,
    217, 226, 238, 258, 265, 266, 290
Germany
    demographic and economic impact of war
    12–13, 277–78, 295–98
    pre-war condition
    administration, 14–15
    culture and society, 18–19, 21–2
    economy, 15–21
    military ethos, 65–66
    peasantry 16–17
    population 20
    religion, 23–30, 34–36, 41, 46, 47–8
    universities, 22–23
Gondomar, Count of 101–2, 117, 131
Gravelines 287, 301
Grey Leagues, see Grisons
Grimmelshausen, Hans Jakob Christoffel 312, 313
Grisons 76, 103, 104, 132, 160, 164–65, 273
Grotius, Hugo 124, 125, 202
Guericke, Otto von 12, 220, 221, 222
Gustavus Adolphus, King of Sweden 94, 100,
    140–41, 148–51, 164, 179, 181, 194, 196, 197,
    199, 201–2, 204–8, 210, 212–19, 225–39,
    241–52, 255, 256, 258, 264–66, 308

Hagendorf, Peter 11
Hague, alliance of The (1625) 165
Halberstadt, 59, 130, 141, 150, 152, 156, 157, 167,
    176, 195, 217, 288, 304
Hamburg, Treaty of (1638) 279
Hanseatic League 21, 100, 157, 165, 166, 172, 178,
    179, 180, 187, 195, 203, 218
Heberle, Hans 12–13, 129, 298
Heilbronn, League of (1633) 258, 265–71, 303
's-Hertogenbosch 183, 188, 260, 305
Heyn, Piet 187–88
Hoënegg, Hoë von 26
Holk, Henrik 244, 247, 248, 250, 254, 260
Holstein 111, 149, 175, 176, 190, 232
Holy Roman Empire
    administration 13–15
    composition 13, 42
    constitution 31–4
    demographic and economic impact of war
    12–13, 277–78, 295–98
    economy, pre-war 16–18, 20, 21, 162
    historical background 42, 52

military ethos 65–66
population 20
post-war status 310–12
relationship with Spain 73, 74, 75, 99–100,
    religion 23–30, 34–36, 41, 45–8,
Horn, Gustav 231, 233, 241, 242, 246, 255, 258, 266–67
Hradčany, Palace of 38–41, 45, 81, 94, 307
Huguenots 26, 60, 88, 105, 116, 144, 146, 159, 160,
    164, 166, 174, 182, 185, 212, 272

Isabella of Austria 27, 123, 128, 145–47, 172, 176,
    178, 239, 256

James I, King of England 27, 62, 68, 70, 71, 89, 102,
    112, 115, 116, 131, 134, 147, 148, 150
Jägerndorf, Margrave of 90, 108, 133
Jenatsch, Jorg 103
John Sigismund of Brandenburg 48, 52, 68, 71, 92–3
John George, Elector of Saxony 17, 26, 52, 77, 92,
    93, 102, 103, 106, 114, 194, 214, 215, 227, 228,
    232, 238, 245, 257, 258, 259, 266, 269, 274, 291,
    300, 310
John William, Duke of Jülich 67–69
Joseph, Père 143, 198, 201, 216, 239, 282
Jülich-Cleves crises 67–72

Kepler, Johannes 25, 41, 64, 136
Klesl, Cardinal 44, 45, 54, 72–73, 77, 80
Königsberg, Treaty of (1627) 214

Lamormaini, William 192–95, 200, 274, 277
La Rochelle 101, 160, 166, 174, 175, 182, 183, 184,
    185, 186, 191, 272
Leipzig, Conference of (1631) 214–15, 226, 228
Leopold, Archduke, Bishop of Passau and Strasbourg
    55, 69, 70
Leopold Wilhelm of Austria, 217, 218, 291
Lerma, Duke of 83, 85, 117–18
Lesdiguières, Duke of 146
Letter of Majesty 54, 55, 77, 78, 81, 95, 114, 172
Liechtenstein, Prince Gudacker of 112, 113
Linz, Treaty of (1645) 295
Lobkowitz, Polyxena 81, 82
Lobkowitz, Zdenek 54, 77, 78, 80, 104
Lorraine, Charles, Duke of 236, 275
Louis XIII, King of France 27, 103, 116, 126,
    142–43, 160, 164, 181, 185, 198, 211, 212, 237,
    271, 272, 276, 280, 282, 283, 284
Louis XIV, King of France 294, 306, 308
Lübeck, Treaty of (1629) 187, 189, 190, 191
Lutheranism 11, 14, 23–30, 34–36, 46–48, 51, 52,
    56, 57, 59, 60, 67, 68, 72, 78, 81, 95, 97, 102,
    114, 149, 161, 171, 173, 194, 195, 203, 214, 217,
    220, 269, 274, 278, 310

Magdeburg, Sack of 12, 217–26
Mansfeld, Ernst von 74, 88, 90, 91, 105, 108, 111,
    129, 130, 133, 134, 139, 142, 147, 148, 151, 153,
    157, 164, 165, 167–70
Martinitz, Jaroslav von 54, 81, 82, 113
Matanzas Bay 188
Matthias, Emperor 42–45, 54, 55, 72, 73, 74, 77, 79,
    80, 82, 83, 87, 88, 89, 99, 138
Maurice of Nassau, 27, 61, 70, 104, 121–26, 131,
    142, 145–47, 151, 204, 229, 270
Maximilian, Duke of Bavaria 27, 49–52, 57–60, 71,
    72, 73, 87, 92, 93, 98, 100, 103–9, 111, 115, 116,
    117, 131, 134, 135, 141, 148, 157, 161, 166, 170,
    172, 176, 177, 192, 194, 195, 200, 215, 216, 218,
    226, 227, 239, 241, 242, 243, 259, 261, 267, 268,
    269, 274, 277, 290, 292, 293, 294, 302, 310
Mazarin, Cardinal 282, 284, 285, 292, 294, 295, 300,
    301, 303, 306, 307–8, 311, 313
Mercy, Franz von 292–95
Merian, Matthäus 15, 16
Milan, Articles of (1622) 132
Monro, Robert 180, 184, 229, 232
Münster, Treaty of (1648) 291–95, 299, 301–6, 308, 309

Nevers, Duke of 181, 182, 186, 190, 201, 226
Nikolsburg, Treaty of (1622) 133
Nördlingen
    first battle of (1634) 267–68, 274, 278
    second battle of (1645) 295

Oldenbarnevelt, Jan van 122, 123, 124–25, 150, 174
Olivares, Gaspare de Guzman 118–19, 120, 126,
    131, 158, 159, 164, 165, 173, 174, 178, 181, 182,
    186–89, 197, 256, 268, 280–82, 285, 293
Oñate, Count of 75, 77, 83, 99, 100, 101, 117, 259, 260
Oquenda, Antonio de 280
Osmanli Turks 260, 277, 311
Osnabrück, Treaty of (1648) 291, 292–93, 299, 303, 308
Overbury, Sir Thomas 15
Oxenstierna, Axel 162, 197, 201–3, 206, 207,
    237, 239, 244, 245, 254, 256–58, 260, 264–66,
    268–70, 274, 275, 279, 291, 293
Oxenstierna, Johan 294

Papacy 60, 63, 73, 87, 90, 111, 243, 299, 309
Pappenheim, Gottfried 172, 176, 218–22, 229,
    230–33, 236, 243, 245–47, 249, 252, 255, 260
Pareus, David 26, 27
Paris, Treaty of (1634) 270
Pauw, Adriaen 271, 295, 301
Philip II, King of Spain 29, 39, 44, 83, 85, 308
Philip III, King of Spain 27, 60, 74, 84, 85, 89, 93,
    99, 100, 101, 116, 119, 126
Philip IV, King of Spain 118, 120, 134, 145, 146,
    172, 176, 181, 187, 195, 237, 255, 256, 268, 277,
    281, 285, 286, 294, 305, 306
Piccolomini, Octavio 246, 247, 250, 251, 258, 260,
    265, 270, 272, 273, 288, 290, 311, 312
Pirna, Preliminaries of (1634) 269

Poyntz, Sydnam 255, 262–3
Prague, Peace of (1635) 269, 274, 275, 290
Protestant Union 59, 61, 62, 68, 69, 70–74, 78, 89,
    91, 101–4, 114, 115, 116, 128, 130, 131
Pyrenees, Treaty of (1659) 309

Rákóczy, George 237, 295
Regensburg, Diets of 58, 72, 198–200, 207, 216,
    241, 276–78, 287, 288, 289, 290–91
Regensburg, Treaty of (1630) 201, 212
Reservatum Ecclesiasticum 35, 36, 72
Richelieu, Cardinal 38, 142–45, 147, 157, 160, 165,
    174, 184–85, 186, 190, 197, 198, 211–12, 214,
    215, 216, 226, 234, 237–39, 241, 248, 256, 258,
    259, 264, 266, 269–76, 279, 280 282–85
Rohan, Benjamin de, Duke of Soubise 160, 185,
    272–73, 279
Rosicrucianism 63, 89, 91
Rudolf II, Emperor 18, 38–47, 52–55, 58, 68–70,
    76, 78, 80, 307

St Clemente, Count of 165
Savoy 73, 74, 75, 83, 87, 89, 146, 158, 165, 181, 186,
    190, 191, 273, 280
Savoy, Duke of, see Charles Emmanuel
Schlick, Count von 77, 88, 91, 176, 261, 264
Schroderus, Johann 203
Scultetus, Abraham 94, 171
Sigismund III, King of Poland 93, 100, 140, 166,
    175, 180, 196, 197, 203
Slavata, Vilém 54, 81, 82 113
Sound, the 149, 150, 179, 196, 280
Spain
    crisis and decline 84–85, 99–100, 128, 172–74
    domestic politics 85, 117–19
    finances 84–5, 123, 172–74
    revolts of Catalonia and Portugal 281–82
Spanish Road 101, 104, 117, 165, 256, 287
Speier 128, 129, 130
Spinola, Ambrogio 73, 89, 101, 103, 104, 115, 116,
    123 128, 141, 145, 146, 151, 158, 166, 174, 182,
    187, 188, 189, 197, 198
Stuhmsdorf, Truce of (1635) 275
Sweden
    army 204–5, 265
    domestic politics 257, 275
    economy and finances 164, 196, 202–4, 213, 258
    historical development 203

    relations with Denmark, 149, 150, 179, 182, 202,
        203, 293, 299
    relations with Poland, 140, 166, 173, 175, 179, 197

Taxis, Gerhard von 152, 157
Thurn, Count Heinrich Matthias von 77, 78, 80, 82,
    86–89, 90, 94, 95, 106, 108, 138, 236, 259
Tilly, Count Jean 105, 107, 133, 134, 138, 141,
    148, 151, 154–58, 160, 165, 167, 168, 169, 170,
    175–77, 189, 194, 200, 216–17, 218, 219, 220,
    222, 224–33, 235, 236, 240–44
Torstensson, Lennart 291, 292, 293, 295

Trauttmansdorff, Maximilian von 302, 303–4
Tromp, Maarten 280
Tschernembl, Georg Erasmus von 32, 66, 89, 106
Tserclaes, mme de 125–26, 142
Turenne, Vicomte de 11, 280, 284, 295
Twelve Years Truce 28, 68, 71, 74, 75, 89, 92, 117, 305
Tyrol 17, 31, 42, 74, 76, 83, 101, 162, 267, 273

Ulm, Treaty of (1620) 103, 105
Uzkok War 74–75, 87

Venne, Adriaen van de 27
Vosges Gap 273, 275

Wallenstein, Albert of, Duke of Friedland (1625) and
    Mecklenburg (1628) 136–40, 151–58, 160, 163,
    165, 166, 167, 168, 169–71, 172, 175–82, 186–90,
    193–95, 198–201, 207, 208, 214, 216–18, 227,
    239–49, 251, 252, 254, 255, 258–63, 276, 293
Werth, Johann von 275, 276, 292–94, 296
West India Company (Dutch) 121, 127, 158, 188,
    270, 301
White Mountain, 107–8, 110–12, 130, 133, 236
William, duke of Jülich-Cleves, 67
William II, Prince of Orange 121, 122
Witte, Hans de 113, 151, 154, 163, 198, 199–200, 240
Wolfgang Wilhelm of Neuburg 68, 71
Wrangel, Karl Gustav 11, 162, 291, 302

Xanten, Treaty of (1614) 71

Zeiler, Martin 15, 16
Žerotin, Karl 80, 89, 138
Zuñiga, Balthasar de 83, 117, 118, 119, 120, 126–27